The Next Generation of Responsible Investing

Advances in Business Ethics Research

A Journal of Business Ethics Book Series

Series Editors

Deborah C. Poff

Alex C. Michalos

For further volumes:
http://www.springer.com/series/8805

Tessa Hebb
Editor

The Next Generation of Responsible Investing

Springer

Editor
Tessa Hebb
Carleton University
DT 2104
1125 Colonel By Drive
Ottawa Ontario
Canada K1S 5B6
thebb@attglobal.net

ISBN 978-94-007-2347-4 e-ISBN 978-94-007-2348-1
DOI 10.1007/978-94-007-2348-1
Springer Dordrecht Heidelberg London New York

Library of Congress Control Number: 2011938237

Printed on acid-free paper

Springer is part of Springer Science+Business Media (www.springer.com)

Acknowledgements

As editor of this volume I would like to thank all the contributors who provided such excellent chapters enabling us to gain a deeper understanding of how responsible investing is growing and evolving over time.

This volume is primarily drawn from a set of academic papers presented at two annual conferences if the Principles for Responsible Investing (PRI) Academic Network. The first conference was held in Ottawa, Canada in the fall or 2009 and the second was held in Copenhagen, Denmark in the spring of 2010. I would like to thank the organizers of these two conferences for their support. Most particularly the PRI secretariat and Christina Gehring, as well as the hosts of these two conferences Carleton University, Ottawa Canada and Copenhagen Business School and the Danish Government for their support.

Several of the chapters have been published as earlier journal articles and appear here courtesy of these journals. I would like to acknowledge and thank the *Journal of Business Ethics* that produced a special issue on "The Next Generation of Responsible Investing" Vol. 92 Sup 1, in which the Woods, Urwin chapter "Putting Sustainable Investing into Practice: A governance framework for pension funds" and the Gifford chapter "Effective Shareholder Engagement: The factors that contribute to shareholder salience" first appeared. I would also like to thank the *Journal of Sustainable Finance and Investment* for the inclusion of Ben Richardson's article "From Fiduciary Duties to Fiduciary Relationships for Socially Responsible Investment" that appeared in its inaugural volume 1 1. Additionally I would like to thank the *Osgood Hall Law Journal*, where the Waitzer, Jaswal chapter "The Good Corporate Citizen" was first published in 2009, Vol. 47. Finally I would like to acknowledge the *Financial Analysts Journal,* where the Bauer, Braun chapter "Misdeeds Matter: Long-Term Stock Price Performance after the Filing of Class-Action Lawsuits" was first published in Vol. 66 6. Tom Croft drew on from his recently published book *Up from Wall Street: the Responsible Investment Alternative* for his chapter, "Targeted Responsible Investing".

I would like to thank Carleton University and Social Sciences and Humanities Research Council for support of my work on responsible investing. This support has enabled me to explore responsible investing working with partners and colleagues both in Canada and around the world on a topic of considerable interest and importance. I would particularly like to thank my team at Carleton, Genevieve Harrison and research assistants Urszula Adamik, Michelle Guevara, and Heather Wood who assisted me in organizing the volume.

A thank you goes to Neil Olivier, Springer Publishing who assisted in the production of this volume and whose gentle encouragement kept me on track. I would also like to thank the two anonymous peer reviewers who provided insight into ways to improve the volume.

I would like to thank my colleague and mentor Professor Gordon Clark, University of Oxford for his role in encouraging this research not only with me but with other contributors to this volume. His insights continue to be a guiding force in our work.

Finally I would like to thank my family and especially my husband Bill for his support. Without such support none of this would be possible.

Ontario, Canada Tessa Hebb

Contents

Contributors

Rupert Allen Industry Canada, Ottawa, ON, Canada K1A 0H5, Rupert.Allen@ic.gc.ca

Rob Bauer ECCE, 6211 LM Maastricht, The Netherlands, r.bauer@maastrichtuniversity.nl

Robin Braun ECCE, 6211 LM Maastricht, The Netherlands, robin.braun@db.com

Tom Croft Steelvalley Authority, Swissvale, PA 15218, USA, t.w.croft@steelvalley.org

James Gifford PRI, EC2A 3DR London, UK, james.gifford@unpri.org

Heather Hachigian Carleton University, Ottawa, ON, Canada K1S 5B6, hhachigian@gmail.com

Tessa Hebb Carleton University, Ottawa, ON, Canada K1S 5B6, thebb@attglobal.net

Johnny Jaswal Osgoode Hall Law School, Toronto, ON, Canada M5V 3Y9, johnny.jaswell@gmail.com

Cary Krosinsky Trucost, New York, NY 10167, USA, cary.krosinsky@trucost.com

Caitlin McElroy School of Geography and the Environment, Oxford University, OX1 3QY Oxford, UK, caitlin.a.mcelroy@gmail.com

Michael Musuraca Queen's College, Flushing, NY 11367, USA, mmusuraca@gmail.com

Benjamin J. Richardson Faculty of Law, University of British Columbia, Vancouver, BC, Canada V6T 1Z1, richardson@law.ubc.ca

Nick Robins HSBC Climate Change Centre of Excellence, New York, NY 10167, USA, nick.robins@hsbc.com

Roger Urwin Towers Watson, RH2 9PQ Reigate, Surrey, UK, roger.urwin@eu.watsonwyatt.com

Stephen Viederman New York, NY 10028, USA, s.viederman@gmail.com

Edward J. Waitzer Stikeman Elliott, Toronto, ON, Canada M5L 1B9, EWaitzer@stikeman.com

Claire Woods School of Geography, Oxford University, OX2 6JE Oxford, UK, claire.woods@ouce.ox.ac.uk

About the Editor

Tessa Hebb is the Director of the Carleton Centre for Community Innovation, Carleton University, Canada. She is also an Adjunct Professor with the School of Public Policy and Administration, Department of Geography and the Sprott School of Business, Carleton University. Her research focuses on Responsible Investment and Impact Investment is funded by the Social Sciences and Humanities Research Council, Government of Canada. The Carleton Centre for Community Innovation is a leading knowledge producer on Responsible Investment tools and instruments. Tessa Hebb obtained her doctorate in Economic Geography from University of Oxford specializing in pension fund corporate engagement.

About the Authors

Rupert Allen is a natural resource economist at the Federal Government of Canada where he focuses on issues related to manufacturing and sustainability. Rupert has also worked as a stakeholder development consultant for various government departments and private companies. Prior to his work in the public sector Rupert worked for museums, galleries and biennials in the UK, Italy and Brazil. Rupert has an MA in Art Criticism and Philosophy from the University of Essex and a BA in Architectural History from Carleton University.

Rob Bauer is Professor of Finance (*chair: Institutional Investments*) at Maastricht University, School of Business and Economics in the Netherlands. In addition, Rob is managing director of an investment consulting firm in which he advises pension funds and institutional asset managers on pension and investments related subjects. His present academic research focus is on pension funds, mutual funds, behavioural finance, socially responsible investments (SRI) and corporate governance. His academic work has been published in various professional and academic (international) research journals. Rob is a Board Member of the International Centre for Pension Fund Management (ICPM) at the Rotman School of Management in Toronto, director of the Netspar-UM SBE Academy and director of the European Centre for Corporate Engagement (ECCE) at Maastricht University. Rob is also a senior researcher of Netspar. Moreover, he teaches at various executive courses.

Robin Braun is a PhD candidate in finance at Maastricht University School of Business and Economics, the Netherlands, and has also been affiliated with the European Centre for Corporate Engagement (ECCE). He performed parts of his research while attending New York University, Stern School of Business, as a visiting scholar. He was also a teaching assistant for several courses covering the whole spectrum of corporate finance. His work has been presented at various universities and international conferences and has also been published or is forthcoming in international refereed academic journals. Robin is also currently working for DWS Investments GmnH in Frankfurt, Germany.

Tom Croft is an authority on innovative jobs policies and responsible capital strategies to revitalize the economy, and author of Up from Wall Street: The Responsible Investment Alternative (Cosimo, 2009). Tom is also the Managing Director of

Heartland Capital Strategies (HCS), a responsible pension investment network in the U.S. and Canada which commissioned Working Capital: the Power of Labor's Pensions (Cornell University Press, 2001). Tom has been responsible for numerous other books, book chapters, reports and articles. In his other day job, Croft is the Executive Director of the Steel Valley Authority (SVA). You can reach Tom by emailing him at t.w.croft@steelvalley.org, or visiting www.heartlandnetwork.org.

James Gifford is Executive Director of the PRI and has been guiding the initiative since its inception in November 2003. He has a PhD from the Faculty of Economics and Business at the University of Sydney on the effectiveness of shareholder engagement in improving corporate environmental, social and corporate governance performance. He was a member of the Global Reporting Initiative Working Group on environmental indicators for the finance sector. He has a background in IT and environmental protection. James has degrees in Commerce and Law from the University of Queensland, and a Master's of Environment Management from the University of New South Wales. He was named in 2010 by the World Economic Forum as one of the 200 Young Global Leaders.

Heather Hachigian is currently a Doctoral candidate at the School of Geography and the Environment, University of Oxford. She worked as a research assistant over the past 2 years at the Carleton Centre for Community Innovation on the Responsible Investing Initiative. She has contributed to several research papers and publications related to a broad range of topics related to responsible investing, focusing on the Canadian landscape. She has a BA Combined Honours in Economics and Political Science from McMaster University and a Master's of Arts in Public Policy and Administration from Carleton University with a specialization in International Development.

Johnny Jaswal completed his JD/MBA at Osgoode Hall Law School and the Schulich School of Business. Johnny completed his articles at a top tier law firm in Toronto and also holds a BEng in Electrical Engineering.

Cary Krosinsky is Co-Editor/Author of Sustainable Investing: the Art of Long Term Performance (Earthscan, 2008) and lead editor of a related book for Wiley due later in 2011. He is Senior Vice President in North America for Trucost, and has served as an advisor to the Newsweek Green Rankings in 2009–10. He teaches at Columbia University, as well as an MBA class at the University of Maryland's Smith School of Business, regarding Sustainability & Investing. He was a member in 2005 of the 70 person Expert Group that helped oversee and create the United Nations Principles for Responsible Investment (PRI).

Caitlin McElroy is a Dphil candidate at the University of Oxford's School of Geography and the Environment. BA, University of Pennsylvania. MSc (distinction), Oxford University. Current Clarendon Scholar. Her research career has focused on the mining industry and has addressed historical, governance, investment and development issues. Of particular interest is the relationship between corporate social responsibility and private sector involvement in development. Her doctoral work is investigating this through studies of corporate foundations in the mining industry. She has recently conducted empirical research in Namibia and Chile.

Michael Musuraca worked for District Council 37, AFSCME, AFL-CIO for over 20 years, and served as the union's Designated Trustee to the New York City Retirement System for over 13 years. Michael was also a founding board member of the UN Principles for Responsible Investment. For the last 2 years, Michael has worked as Managing Director at Blue Wolf Capital Partners, a private equity firm practicing responsible investment. Michael is currently working as a consultant and a Lecturer at Queens College, City University of New York. He serves on the boards of Verite, Sustainalytics, and the Shareowners Education Network

Benjamin J. Richardson holds the Canada Research Chair in Environmental Law & Sustainability, at the University of British Columbia. Previously, he was a Professor at Osgoode Hall Law School of York University (2003–10) and earlier a Senior Lecturer at the law faculties of the University of Manchester and University of Auckland. Prior to working in academia, Professor Richardson was a policy advisor to the NSW National Parks and Wildlife Service in Australia, and a legal consultant to the IUCN (International Union for Conservation of Nature) in Nepal and Kenya. Among his professional responsibilities, Professor Richardson is an elected member of the Governing Board of the IUCN Academy of Environmental Law, and co-chairs the SRI Research Cluster of the Canadian Business Ethics Research Network.

Nick Robins has 20+ years experience in the policy, business and investment dimensions of sustainable development. He currently heads HSBC's Climate Change Centre of Excellence, and writes in a personal capacity. Prior to this, he was head of SRI funds at Henderson Global Investors, where he launched the world's first climate audit of an investment fund and designed the multi-thematic Industries of the Future sustainability fund. He is author of The Corporation that Changed the World: How the East India Company Shaped the Modern Multinational 92006) and co-editor of Sustainable Investing: the art of long-term performance (with Cary Krosinsky, 2008).

Roger Urwin Roger assumed the new post of Global Head of Investment Content in July 2008 after acting as the Global Head of the Watson Wyatt investment practice from 1995 to 2008. Roger joined Watson Wyatt in 1989 to start the firm's investment consulting practice and under his leadership the practice grew to a global team of 500. His prior career involved heading the Mercer investment practice and leading the business development and quantitative investment functions at Gartmore Investment Management. Roger's current role includes work for some of Towers Watson's major investment clients both in the UK and internationally. He is also involved with the Watson Wyatt thought leadership group (Thinking Ahead Group). He is the author of a number of papers on asset allocation policy, manager selection and governance. He is on the Board of the CFA Institute and an Advisory Director to MSCI Inc. Roger has a degree in Mathematics from Oxford University and a Masters in Applied Statistics also from Oxford. He qualified as a Fellow of the Institute of Actuaries in 1983.

Stephen Viederman "My vocation is sustainability, leaving options open for me and all grandkids. I am now focusing on overcoming institutional investor inertia to acceptance of sustainable investment because the future matters."

Edward J. Waitzer is a professor and the Jarislowsky Dimma Mooney Chair in Corporate Governance and is Director of the Hennick Centre for Business and Law at Osgoode Hall Law School and the Schulich School of Business at York University. He was Chair of Stikeman Elliott LLP from 1999 to 2006 and remains a senior partner whose practice focuses on complex business transactions. He also advises on a range of public policy and governance matters. He served (1993–1996) as Chair of the Ontario Securities Commission (and of the Technical Committee of the International Organization of Securities Commissions) and (until 1981) as Vice-President of The Toronto Stock Exchange. He has written and spoken extensively on a variety of legal and public policy issues and serves or has served as director of a number of corporations, foundations, community organizations, editorial boards and advisory groups. Earned his LL.B. (1976) and LL.M. (1981) from the Faculty of Law, University of Toronto. Called to the Ontario (1978) and the New York (1985) Bars.

Claire Woods is in the final stages of her DPhil (PhD) as a Clarendon Scholar at the University of Oxford. Her thesis explores the legal framework around sustainable investing, including the structure imposed by fiduciary duty in theory and practice, the role of governance and the challenges involved in navigating the conflict between short and long term interests. Her other research interests include climate change law and the concept of intergenerational equity. She has published articles and book chapters on sustainable investing and pension fund fiduciary duty, and is a contributing author to the 2009 UNEP FI report on fiduciary duty. Prior to coming to Oxford, Claire worked in the mergers team at the Australian Competition and Consumer Commission. Claire has been admitted by the Supreme Court of Victoria as an Australian Lawyer.

Abbreviations

AGM	Annual general meeting
CEO	Chief executive officer
ESG	Environmental, social and corporate governance
NGO	Non-governmental organisation
OECD	Organisation for Economic Cooperation and Development
PRI	Principles for Responsible Investment
SRI	Socially responsible investment
ESG	Environmental, social and governance
RI	Responsible investment
SI	Sustainable investing
SRI	Socially responsible investment
UN PRI	United Nations Principles for Responsible Investment

Chapter 1
Introduction – The Next Generation of Responsible Investing

Tessa Hebb

In order to ensure the stability of our global economies, the financial market crash of 2008 points to the critical need for greater oversight of today's financial markets. In the aftermath of the financial crisis institutional investors are increasingly realizing that while much of this oversight will occur through government regulation, increasingly large institutional investors are being called upon to provide this type of active engagement and ownership in our capital markets.

The result is not the institutional investor "socialism" envisioned by Peter Drucker (1976), but rather a reconfigured capitalism crafted by these enormous financial pools. Many institutional investors are using their influence to engage and in some cases aggressively challenge the management of corporations in order to improve the environmental, social and governance (ESG) standards of the firms in which they invest (Bogle, 2005; Clark & Hebb, 2004; Davis, Lukomnik, & Pitt-Watson, 2006; Hebb, 2008; Monks, 2001; PRI Initiative, 2007). Such activity, known as responsible investment (RI), seeks long-term shareholder value for future beneficiaries.

In light of recent financial and environmental crisis, such long-term investment policies are seen as essential to ensuring the health and growth of our economies going forward (Lydenberg, 2009; Hawley & Williams, 2000). This volume explores responsible investing post the financial crisis. It asks whether responsible investors, bringing environmental, social and governance factors into their investment decision-making could have better predicted the onset of the financial crisis and protected their assets from the worst of the market downturn.

Responsible investing has always had a broad mandate. Put simply, it is a long-term sustainable investment strategy that values environmental, social and governance factors in investment decision-making. To date much of that activity has taken place in the public equities portfolios of investors concerned with the long-term risks that ESG considerations might pose. Increasingly there is an interest in

T. Hebb (✉)
Carleton University, Ottawa, ON, Canada K1S 5B6
e-mail: thebb@attglobal.net

T. Hebb (ed.), *The Next Generation of Responsible Investing*,
Advances in Business Ethics Research 1, DOI 10.1007/978-94-007-2348-1_1,

extending responsible investing to other asset classes including real estate, private equity, infrastructure, and fixed income. Responsible investing in these alternative assets includes both developed and emerging markets. There is a new willingness to target these asset classes in order to generate desired positive environmental, social and governance outcomes from investment in addition to long term stable financial returns.

In these asset classes responsible investing often takes on a proactive form, with investors seeking out investment opportunities that offer both strong financial performance and positive ancillary benefits. Such environmental, social and governance impacts are not only valued in and of themselves, but are also seen as ways to generate out-performance (also known as alpha in the investment industry) and reduce risk in investment portfolios.

Given that today's institutional investors are increasingly concerned with long-term share value, it has been determined that raised environmental, social, and governance standards of firms can increase share value and lower risk over time (Bauer, Koedijk, & Otten, 2005; Gompers, Ishii, & Metrick, 2003; Kok, 2008). As a result institutional investors including banks, insurance companies, mutual funds, pension funds, foundations and endowments are developing responsible investing policies that look for ways to have a positive impact on society as a whole, while simultaneously reducing risk in the investment portfolio and adding to long-term returns (Hebb, 2008).

In the aftermath of the financial-crisis, responsible investors are increasingly concerned about risk in their portfolios. This marks another profound shift in thinking about responsible investment. In its early days, savvy investors realized that factoring environmental, social and governance factors in their investments could provide a source of out-performance in their stock portfolio. Increasingly these investors see ESG factors as sources of risk in the portfolio. Witness the BP oil spill in the Gulf of Mexico through the summer of 2010. During the course of that spill (with its estimated costs of $40 billion) shareholders lost over 50% of their value. A year later BP shares remain 25% below their value before the spill. Again, with catastrophic losses (loss of lives, environmental destruction, and financial costs) as a direct result of a variety of low environmental standards, responsible investors are asking how they should protect themselves from such risks in the future.

We are just beginning to understand that the shift to responsible investment requires deep changes at the institutional and policy level in order to move beyond simply advocating change to actual change in institutional behaviour. This volume explores that shift in greater detail. It builds on a variety of disciplines in order to gain deeper understanding of the topic. These disciplines include finance, management, law, public policy, and economic geography. It also draws on the experience of practitioners to gain a deeper understanding of the development of responsible investing. The volume is intended to provide a conceptual framework for understanding the evolution of responsible investing as the field matures and grows.

This volume examines the impact of the financial crisis on responsible investing. Were funds that engaged in responsible investing better able to protect themselves from risk as the financial crisis unfolded? Did the consideration of ESG factors in investment selection insulate these funds from the impact of the crisis? What have we learned from this experience and how will we integrate sustainable investing practices going forward? These questions are explored in Chapters 2–4.

The conceptual underpinnings of responsible investing are deepened through both a legal and practical exploration of the role of trustees (Chapter 5). This chapter questions whether a new relationship is required between pension fund trustees and their beneficiaries in order to advance responsible investing within the funds themselves. The conceptual framework that underpins the logic of responsible investing requires an understanding of the salience of these stakeholders in engaging companies with weak ESG standards (Chapters 6 and 7). The authors of these two chapters ask what elements within the funds make them effective in their engagement with companies. They draw on stakeholder theories of power, legitimacy and urgency.

The final four chapters of the volume investigate a variety of approaches to responsible investing. Beginning with the "G" in ESG, Chapters 8 and 9 examine responsible investors' ability to raise the corporate governance standards of firms in which they invest. This question is addressed through two very different approaches. The first is through a legal understanding of the role outside agents play in ensuring that companies behave as "good corporate citizens". The second is through standard finance methods providing a quantitative exploration of the impact of engagement on the corporate governance standards of firms.

The final two chapters address the environmental and social aspects of ESG. Chapter 10 looks at direct targeted investments that produce both a financial return and a positive ancillary benefit for communities such as urban revitalization, brown field redevelopment, and affordable housing. The volume concludes with a chapter on responsible investing in the extractive sector around the world. Much of this work is carried out in emerging markets with weak regulatory regimes. Here the role responsible investors' play in developing countries is explored.

As suggested in this period following the financial crisis, and with a growing awareness of sustainability issues, mainstream investors are increasingly taking on responsible investing practices (Hoepner & McMillan, 2009, SIO, 2008, PRI Initiative, 2009). The old mindset of RI as divergent and to some extent adversarial to company and shareholder goals (Friedman, 1970) is eroding (Donaldson & Preston, 1995; Jones & Wood, 1995; Freeman, 1999). Responsible investing is being seen as a means of driving shareholder profit rather than a performance laggard (Porter & Kramer, 2002; SAM, 2009). This fundamental change in mindset is being brought about by the reinforcement of the RI business case that seeks to develop and bind the notions of financial performance with environmental, social and governance indicators. The business case contends that it is not simply a matter of ethics but rather that financial gains, management of risk and corporate responsibility converge in the long run (Hill, Ainscough, Shank, & Manullang, 2007; Louche & Lydenberg, 2006). The RI advantage is one of anticipating and mitigating long-term risks, through raised environmental, social and governance (ESG) standards, not simply moral and ethical considerations (Scholtens, 2010; UNEP FI, 2008).

The theoretical underpinnings of responsible investment address problems associated with Efficient Markets Hypothesis (Fama, 1970; Samuelson, 1965) and Modern Portfolio Theory (Markowitz, 1959) with their assumptions of a rational market. There is increased criticism of this theory in light of the financial crisis of 2008/2009 (Bogle, 2008; Fox, 2009; Taleb, 2009) with behavioural finance (Lo, 2005; Shleifer, 2000; Shiller, 2005) coming to the fore. Rather than an efficient market, information asymmetry in the financial market is the norm (Akerlof, 1970; Stiglitz, 1976). Responsible investing builds on this theoretical framework, recognizing that ESG factors are a source of information asymmetry in financial markets.

Traditionally ESG factors have been viewed as externalities of the firm and therefore not considered in its value (Hebb, 2008; Kiernan, 2009; UNEP FI, 2008). Yet taking ESG into consideration can reduce risk for investors and add value over time (Gompers et al., 2003; Porter & Van der Linde, 1995). This understanding is known as "the business case" for responsible investing. Building on the critique of efficient markets, the "universal owners hypothesis" (Hawley & Williams, 2000) goes on to suggest that because large institutional owners own the whole market, what may be negative externalities for one company in the portfolio are direct and often costly impacts on another holding. As a result today's institutional investors must be concerned about the ESG standards of the firms they hold.

The second major theoretical underpinning for responsible investing is the principal-agent problem (Jensen & Meckling, 1976; Fama & Jensen, 1983; Shleifer & Vishny, 1996). The struggle for corporate control between owners and managers has a long history in legal, financial and economic literature (Berle & Means, 1932; Roe, 1994). Responsible investing represents a shift away from firm managers and toward owners of corporations. It encourages owners to provide active and engaged oversight of today's corporations (Monks, 2001; Davis et al., 2006, US Gov. Senate, 2010). Increasingly such oversight is seen as critical to the health of our financial market. (Gillan & Starks, 1998; Useem, 1996). As corporate decision-making is delegated from shareholders to top managers, problems arise when the interests between managers and shareholders do not coincide. This happens when the basic opportunistic behavior of individuals means they would rather make choices that maximize their own benefit over that of others (Eisenhardt, 1989; Luft, 1997).

Responsible investing is a growing phenomenon among institutional investors. In 2005, a small group of institutional investors, under the auspices of the UN Environment Programme and the UN Global Compact, developed a set of six principles for responsible investing. By 2011, global signatories to the Principles for Responsible Investment (PRI) totalled $25 trillion of assets under management. Signatories commit to taking ESG factors into consideration in their investment decision-making and integrating this approach throughout their organizations, with their external money managers and within the industry as a whole. While there have been increased numbers of signatories from North America, Africa, South America and Austral-Asia, by far the largest body of new signatories has come to PRI from Europe.

A sub-group of the PRI is the PRI Academic Network. This network from around the world provides on-going academic research that underpins responsible investing and deepens our understanding of this phenomenon. This volume builds on a set of papers presented at two PRI Academic Network Conferences. The first held in Ottawa in 2009, the second in Copenhagen in 2010. Roughly half the collection has appeared in previously published academic journals. All have undergone a thorough peer review. This body of work adds substantially to our knowledge and understanding of responsible investing.

The volume is laid out in the following manner. In the first section of the book, authors Robins, Krosinsky and Viederman; Woods and Urwin; and Musuraca interrogate responsible investing and its implication in light of the financial crisis of 2008 and 2009. With pension funds around the world losing upwards of a quarter of their value during this period, the implications for responsible investors raises serious questions. Should responsible investment have been able to predict such outcomes and protected investors from the worst of the financial crisis? What should responsible investors do differently now that could insulate them and the financial market generally, from such risk going forward?

In Chapter 2 Robins, Krosinsky and Viederman, use the term sustainable investing to describe responsible investing in a larger context. Robbins et al suggest that investors who utilize environmental, social and governance in long-term investment decision-making are able to anticipate positive trends or "predictable surprises" ahead of the market that help to ensure shareowner value over time. Drawing on the work of John Maynard Keynes (1952, 1978), these authors propose two hypotheses—the "reasonable person hypothesis", and the "resilient markets hypothesis" as key underpinnings of responsible investment. These hypotheses replace the ideals of efficiency and rationality as a more durable basis for investment success.

Similarly, Woods and Urwin (Chapter 3) build on the theme of sustainable investing and offer advice for the practical implementation of such policies to Anglo-American pension funds. Woods and Urwin believe that sustainable investment decision-making must be based on the pension plans mission and investment beliefs. This chapter presents the relevant Anglo-American legal framework and outlines how pension funds adopting sustainable investing practices should approach their fiduciary obligations. The chapter concludes with an examination of the regulatory framework necessary for pension funds to take on sustainable investment as a key part of their investment strategy.

In contrast to the previous two chapters, Michael Musuraca provides an examination of this topic from the perspective of the pension fund trustee on whom responsible investing decisions ultimately fall. As a trustee of the New York City Employees Retirement System through the period of the financial crisis, Musuraca reflects on the implications of the financial crisis for pension funds and the fiduciaries responsible for the stewardship of theses funds. Musuraca takes as a starting point for his commentary the current funding crisis of many of today's pension funds with the losses that resulted from the financial crisis combined with the failure of many governmental plan sponsors to make the required employer contributions to the funds in the past (particularly when the market was performing well) and an increase in benefit levels for some plan participants. The result has been a questioning of the sustainability of the traditional governmental defined benefit pension plan many U.S. states and localities. Musuraca explores the implications of these three trends on today's pension system and the role responsible investing has to play in pension fund sustainability both now and in the future.

The next section of the book looks more deeply at the conceptual underpinning of responsible investing, exploring the implications of responsible investing for trustees and fund managers. Richardson (Chapter 5) explores the nature of the fiduciary relationship and the role of the plan beneficiaries in responsible investment. His chapter considers potential legal reforms that better reflect the interests of plan beneficiaries. The chapter suggests there are legal and practical obstacles to this approach. The chapter details the various legal "duties" of trustees that inhibit taking the will of plan beneficiaries more directly into account. Richardson concludes by suggesting some potential legal reforms to strengthen reliance on the will of beneficiaries as a means of responsible investing.

The next generation in responsible investing reflects a shift from passive monitoring of companies environmental, social and governance standards, to active and engaged dialogue between pension plan trustees and managers and officials of companies in these plans' investment portfolios. Increasingly such corporate engagement is suggested as the preferred mechanism to implement responsible investing. Chapters 6 and 7 explore the effectiveness of corporate engagement as a tool for responsible investing.

James Gifford applies a model of stakeholder salience to the shareholder context, analysing the attributes of power, legitimacy and urgency, to determine the factors that are likely to enhance shareholder salience through engagement. He finds that a strong business case and the values of the managers of investee companies are likely to be the most important contributors to shareholder salience. In Chapter 7, Hebb, Hachigian and Allen build on Gifford's work, further exploring the attributes of corporate engagement that lead to successful outcomes in raising companies' ESG standards. Like Gifford, Hebb et al draw on three case studies of engagements between institutional investors and companies in Canada over the past 5 years in order to examine the outcomes of engagement from the perspectives of the investor.

The second half of the volume investigates responsible investing approaches through a variety of asset classes. Chapters 8 and 9 examine issues of corporate governance in publicly held companies, taking into account the implications for activist shareholders seeking to improve such standards and by extension lower risk and raise share value over time.

Legal scholar Edward J. Waitzer of Osgoode Hall Law School considers the use of various legal instruments to advance a more expansive, but focused, view of directors' duties and discretion – one which focuses on the longer term rather than short term interests of the corporation. Waitzer draws on two Canadian cases in which the Court took a broad view of the purpose of the corporation but failed to provide clear logic or operational guidance as to consequential directorial responsibilities such a broad purpose entails. Waitzer finds that as a result "the Court may have afforded directors increased deference (assuming they comply with prescribed procedural steps) without a clearly stated legal rationale." He outlines various legal theories that courts might consider and elaborate on. He concludes the chapter with an examination of complementary legislative and shareholder-initiated reforms.

Rob Bauer and Robin Braun (Chapter 9) extend our understanding of the impact shareholder-led initiatives can have on corporations and their long-term value. This quantitative chapter tests the claim that responsible investing can and does have a positive impact on long-term share value. Bauer and Braun find that consistent with theory, shareholder activism leads to a general transformation in company characteristics and risk exposures. They also find that generally negative short- and long-term performance effects differed substantially between two different types of activist approaches.

The next two chapters move away from responsible investing in large public equity markets to increased investor engagement in both private equity and emerging markets. Both have implications for responsible investing going forward. Tom Croft (Chapter 10) examines the relatively new phenomena of targeted investing, that is increasingly seen as a key aspect of a responsible investment portfolio. He finds that institutional investors are exploring "alternative investments" that put capital to work creating long-term, sustainable wealth for workers, communities and shareholders. In contrast with the last decade when many global investment managers invested in short-term speculative investments such as sub-prime mortgages, value destroying hedge funds, and derivatives and credit swap schemes, these new private equity investments are designed to both achieve market-rates of return and positive impacts for communities. These new alternative private equity investments are found in such areas as affordable and green housing, clean energy, urban revitalization, and sustainable forestry.

The volume closes with a look at responsible investing in emerging markets, particularly in the extractive sector that dominates investment in so many of the world's developing countries. In Chapter 11 Caitlin McElroy investigates the relationship between the increasing importance and prevalence of corporate social investment and the direct impact of responsible investing initiatives in the multinational mining sector. She deconstructs the corporate foundations established by the extractive sector to improve conditions in mining affected communities, to deeper understand the distinction between corporate social responsibility (CSR), based on a set of normative values, and responsible investing initiatives that stem from the empirical "business case" for improved corporate standards.

Responsible investing is based on two key propositions. The first is that because of their need to pay out liabilities over a long period of time, institutional investors (particularly pension funds) must have a long-term investment horizon. The second is that environmental, social, and governance factors have a direct impact on both risk and financial return in investment. As a result ESG factors must be taken into consideration in investment decision-making. Events such as the financial crisis of 2008–2009, and the environmental crisis in the Gulf of Mexico in 2010 have served to reinforce these tenets. In the past it was assumed that if an investor was unhappy with a company they held in their portfolio they simply sold the company and moved on. This is known as the Wall Street Walk. But with institutional investors so large and with so much invested in stock market indexes it has become virtually impossible for large institutional owners to exit many of their positions. As the financial crisis and events in the Gulf Coast have demonstrated it turns out, "if you can't sell, you have to care (Monks, 2001)."

Chapter 2
After the Credit Crisis – The Future of Sustainable Investing

Cary Krosinsky, Nick Robins, and Stephen Viederman

2.1 Winning the Battle, But Losing the War?

Sustainable investing is an investment discipline that explicitly considers future social and environmental trends in financial decision making, in order to provide the best risk-adjusted and opportunity-directed returns for investors. By anticipating these trends ahead of the market, sustainable investing seeks to identify "predictable surprises" that can help ensure shareowner value over the long-term.

In our book, Sustainable Investing: The Art of Long-Term Performance (Krosinsky & Robins, 2008), we showed how this burgeoning investment philosophy had become a powerful force, consistently outperforming conventional strategies in global equity markets and attracting ever-increasing funds under management. We had started the book as credit markets crunched, and finished it in July 2008 as once famous names in the investment world, such as Bear Stearns, buckled under the strain. We concluded that sustainable investing had now completed its apprenticeship, arguing that the challenge ahead lay not in becoming more like the "mainstream" but in replacing it. Then came the collapse of Lehman Brothers and with it the end of the short era of financialization, which had driven the global economy since the late 1970s. As if waking from a drug, the world has realized that markets are neither perfect nor efficient, that investors are not always rational or far-sighted, nor fully considering all relevant risk factors and opportunities, and that decisive public intervention is an essential prerequisite for capital markets.

One of the enduringly positive aspects of the financial landscape over the past 12 months has been the continued rise of sustainable investing. We are wary of semantic battles and definitional boundary disputes between socially responsible investing, responsible investment and sustainable investing. For us, we believe one of the key distinguishing features of sustainable investing is its forward-looking,

C. Krosinsky (✉)
Trucost, New York, NY 10167, USA
e-mail: cary.krosinsky@trucost.com

T. Hebb (ed.), *The Next Generation of Responsible Investing*,
Advances in Business Ethics Research 1, DOI 10.1007/978-94-007-2348-1_2,

prospective methodology which we argue will systematically add value over time. Our hypothesis rests on two assumptions:

The first is that the best way of generating returns in the twenty-first century, both risk-adjusted and opportunity-directed, is to acknowledge long-term economic, social and environmental realities and integrate these into investment and ownership decision-making ("the reasonable investor hypothesis").

The second is that capital markets themselves need to be recast to confront the risks of financial collapse posed by long-term economic, social and environmental realities ("the market resilience hypothesis").

If the first assumption above speaks the language of financial value at the micro-level, the second refers to the imperative of structural reform at the macro-dimension. Sustainable investing thus provides an agenda for action for purely financially motivated investors eager to mitigate risk and benefit from upside opportunities, as well as for governments seeking long-run economic development and civil society organizations aiming to achieve social and environmental progress.

One year on, we have reviewed the investment performance of the sustainable fund universe on a global basis, and found once again, that the class has outperformed conventional peer strategies, up through the first half of 2009. For us, this result comes as no surprise.

Sustainable investors start from the premise that today's markets are deeply flawed, failing to reflect long-term social, economic and environmental value in asset prices. As a result, they can achieve a significant information advantage by analyzing these values and integrating them both into asset selection decisions, as well as through the exercising of ownership rights – in effect anticipating underlying changes in the economy long before the mainstream.

The tragic reality, however, is that this relative outperformance cannot hide an absolute loss for sustainable investors over the course of 2008. The structural failings in financial markets simply overwhelmed the fund-level advantages secured by sustainable investors. Reflecting on the current crisis, we believe that the credit crunch is just one manifestation of a much deeper crisis of unsustainability in the global economy encompassing severe imbalances in demographics, geopolitics, natural resource use, pollution, labor and human rights, as well as wealth distribution. Unless sustainable investors rise to the challenge of market reform so that asset prices tell the truth and owners become fully accountable, then they risk winning the micro battle, but losing the macro war. With the prospect of runaway climate change, this is not a war we would wish to lose. To avoid this, the failed financial theories that underpinned the market practice that resulted in the current crisis need to be discarded in favor of a new synthesis that brings together the best insights of behavioral finance with the socio-ecological perspectives of sustainable investment.

This chapter takes up where Sustainable Investing left off, updating the performance analysis of sustainable investment funds, extending our scope to examine the systemic failings of today's financial markets, and highlighting some necessary avenues for reform to upgrade sustainability from a simple question of investor taste to one of fundamental market integrity.

But first we turn back to the last century and investigate the evolving strategies of that grandfather of behavioral and long-term investing, John Maynard Keynes, whose turbulent experience as a market practitioner contributed powerfully to his prescriptions for the reform of capitalism in the Great Depression.

2.2 How to Lose a Fortune (Three Times) and Save the World

No decent analysis of the current crisis can escape a few choice references to Keynes, a man for all crashes. In most cases, the focus is on Keynes' recommendations for macro-economic intervention to deal with the persistence of boom and bust in modern capitalism. He has thus become the unwitting grandfather of economic stimulus plans across the world – and by extension, the promotion of a "green recovery". Far fewer examine how his experience as an active investor over many decades informed his broader beliefs about economic management. According to Keynes' biographer, Robert Skidelsky, Keynes was "a spectacularly successful investor", even though he suffered three major setbacks in 1920–1, 1928–9 and 1937–8 (Skidelsky, 2004). But he was an investor who fundamentally changed his strategy for generating returns, an epistemological break that was crucial for his role as theoretician and policy maker. From his own investment ups and downs, Keynes appreciated that to first understand and then improve capitalism, it is important to start with capital, in other words the behavior of investors.

For Keynes, familiarity with real world investors bred something close to contempt. In the Treatise on Money, he concluded that investors "do not possess even the rudiments of what is required for a valid judgment and are the prey of hopes and fears easily aroused by transient events and as easily dispersed". In this, he was in tune with Adam Smith's own less than complimentary comments about merchants. Like Smith, Keynes recognized the necessary utility of the market economy to drive human development. But over time, experience taught him that the "invisible hand" would often miss the catch, potentially losing the game.

Immediately following the First World War, Keynes and his investment partner, Foxy Falk, started to play the money markets, forming a syndicate to take long and short positions in a basket of international currencies. At the time, he was described by Gaspard Farrer of Barings as "a man who is governed largely by pure reason and thinks others are governed in like manner and he is apt to omit to human equation" – a surprising conclusion given Keynes' subsequent emphasis on the power of "animal spirits" (Kynaston, 2000). For all this, by February 1920, he had generated book profits of £18,525 on an investment of £200,000. In March, he went long dollars, buying £150,000. He was still on a high in April when he wrote that "win or lose, this high stake gambling amuses me". By May, however, he was ruined, losing all his capital, and with massive debts outstanding. But for an emergency loan of £5,000 from Sir Ernest Cassel, Keynes would have been bankrupt. Yet by 1922, Keynes had paid off his debts, generating some £25–30,000 for himself. Later in the decade, he turned to the commodity markets, boosting his assets to £44,000 in 1927. But he was caught out again, missing the mounting imbalances in the markets as the decade closed, and by the end of 1929, his own wealth had slumped along with the global economy to just £7,815. Worst of all, he even had to put up for sale two of his treasured impressionist paintings by Matisse and Seurat. From the raw experience of these two profound investment failures, Keynes made an about turn and adopted the policy of "faithfulness", investing in a few favored shares and sticking to them through thick and thin. A decade spent trying to "beat the market had convinced him that this was the only rational response to uncertainty". (Skidelsky, 2004).

Buying into Wall Street in 1932, his capital had grown twenty-three times by 1936, the year of the publication of his masterpiece, The General Theory of Employment, Interest and Money. In his celebrated Chapter 12 of the General Theory, Keynes looked deep into the mind of the investor, and found a fundamental tension between alternative investment strategies: the first, a momentum-driven approach to beat the market in an endlessly reflexive beauty contest ("speculation"), and the second, a value-led quest for long-term yield ("enterprise"). It was the predominance of the first approach that resulted in the eternal instability of capitalism, which Keynes was quite clear rested "on the bad faith of investors". From bitter experience, he recognized that "it is the longterm investor, he who most promotes the public interest, who will in practice come in for the most criticism wherever investment funds are managed by committees or boards or banks" (Keynes, 1978).

Indeed, the following year, however, Keynes was once again left exposed by a turn in the markets, losing two-thirds of his own money. This time, his General Theory at least provided the justification for his policy of "hanging on for a rise" to the range of institutions he advised: King's College, Cambridge as well as the Provincial Insurance company, and the National Mutual. In a combative mood, Keynes defended his policy to Francis Curzon, chair of the National Mutual. "I feel no shame", he wrote "at being found still owning a share when the bottom of the market comes. I do not think it is the business of a serious investor to cut and run on a falling market. ... I would go much further than that. I should say that it is from time to time the duty of a serious investor to accept the depreciation of his holdings with equanimity and without reproaching himself. Any other policy is anti-social, destructive of confidence and incompatible with the working of the economic system. An investor is aiming or should be aiming primarily at long period results and should be solely judged by these." Curzon and the rest of the board were unconvinced, however, and Keynes resigned in October 1938. By the end of the year, his own net assets had fallen from a high of £506,222 at end of 1936 to just £181,244 by the end of 1938. Yet, at the time of his death in 1946 – and following the ravages of the Second World War – Keynes position had recovered to £479,529.

Keynes' struggles to develop a successful investment strategy for his own money had profound implications for his macro-economic analysis, and still have a deep resonance today. We should certainly not deify an economist who lived and worked in another age – but we should also not be resistant to learning lessons from the past, particularly when we have taken a half century detour away from his insights. As Peter Bernstein has ably shown, the "capital ideas" that have dominated investment theory and practice in recent decades have owed little to Keynes, resting on the utopian assumption that "investors have no difficulty in making optimal choices in the bewildering jumble of facts, rumors, discontinuities, vagueness, and black uncertainty that makes up the real world" (Bernstein, 2007). Amid the wreckage that these ideas have generated, Keynes provides some footholds for the next phase of making "capital ideas" sustainable. In particular, Keynes highlighted:

- first, that human emotions – his famed "animal spirits" – have a profound impact on the actions of investors and thereby market movements, making him one of the first exponents of behavioral finance;
- second, that investment and speculation are radically different, and that investors like government policymakers – should aim for long run returns, and fight the "mania for liquidity"; and
- third, that investment has a social as well as a private purpose, which he eloquently described as focused on defeating "the dark forces of time and ignorance that envelop our future."

2.3 Sustainable Investing Practices and Performance – An Update

The first funds with a sustainable investing strategy were launched in the late 1980s. Over the past 20 years, sustainable investing has grown from small beginnings to becoming a powerful force in investment markets. One of the core themes it shares with Keynes' approach is a focus on long-term, real world drivers of value.

Back in the 1930s, Keynes observed that it was the long-term investor that "should be eccentric, unconventional and rash in the eyes of average opinion", and so it has often been with sustainable investing. Keynes added that "if he is successful, that will only confirm the general belief in his rashness; and if in the short run he is unsuccessful, which is very likely, he will not receive much mercy."

John Kenneth Galbraith echoed some of the same thoughts: "Only after the speculative collapse does the truth emerge. What was thought to be unusual acuity turns out to be only a fortuitous and unfortunate association with assets. Over the long years of history, the result of those who have been misjudged (including invariably, by themselves) has been opprobrium followed by personal disgrace or a retreat into the deeper folds of obscurity, or in modern times, at least moderately uncomfortable confinement" (Galbraith, 1990).

In our book, we originally highlighted the practices and outperformance of sustainable investing vs. both mainstream as well as purely negative strategies, for the 1-, 3- and 5-years leading up to the end of 2007. However, by the time our book was published in November 2008, deep market declines had been underway, extending into 2009.

It was therefore quite heartening to discover upon further examination of the performance of the funds studied in the book, that sustainable investing strategies had been outperforming both ethical and mainstream strategies leading up to the end of 2008, as well as in the first half of 2009. This further extends our previous finding that sustainable investing has already been a winning strategy. Even with the hard times of 2008 factored in, long-term returns have been best served by the application of a sustainable investment philosophy.

In 2008, on average, sustainable investing held its own (–39.3%) with some funds faring better than others, while slightly underperforming negative strategies (–36.3%) and the S&P 500 (–37.0%) but outperforming the MSCI World (–42%). Of course, specific 2008 performance was universally poor, but it is useful to note that sustainable investing on average did not do worse than any other equity strategy.

Through the first half of 2009, as markets fell further and then recovered, sustainable investing was easily the out performer, returning on average 7.63%, with some of the worst performing sustainability minded funds of 2008 bouncing back. Negatively screened funds delivered 6.75%, both of which were better than the S&P 500's 4.97% and MSCI World's 4.76% respectively. In both cases, that represents flat index returns so these results would be even better vs. actual investable versions of these indices.

The outperformance of sustainable investing also emerged when extending the study to what is now 6-years leading up to the end of 2008, adding 1 year to the previous study, with sustainable investing returning on average 9.5%, as well as the 5-years leading to end 2008, when the S&P 500, for example, returned a negative 2.19%. One other performance related metric that we would like to reiterate is that between portfolio turnover and fund performance. Our book highlighted the fact that across all 11 strands of socially responsible investing, those funds which had the lowest turnover (those funds which in effect traded least often), performed best, and those which traded most frequently, performed worst of all. A graphic to this effect, with additional granularity, illustrates this quite clearly (see Fig. 2.1).

A range of other studies published in 2009 have further correlated & confirmed these findings. In terms of sustainable investing, for example, SAM's "Alpha from Sustainability" report concluded that there was "a positive correlation between Corporate Sustainability and financial performance measured by stock returns, and

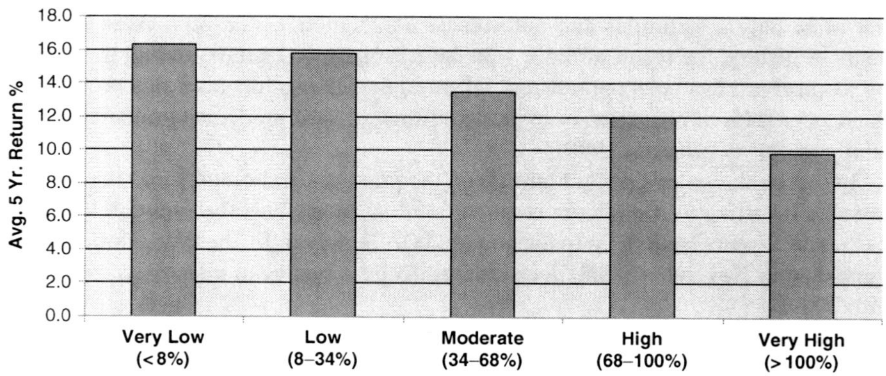

Fig. 2.1 Krosinsky, April–May 2008
Source: Krosinsky

that the investment strategy based on SAM's Corporate Sustainability data delivered positive information ratios in bull and bear markets, highlighting its effectiveness as an all-weather approach" (SAM, 2009).

And so, as the evidence mounts that sustainable investing offers the best chance of outperformance in the modern age, the question becomes what barriers remain to incorporation within mainstream investment practice, and what strategies could be considered towards encouraging maximum adaptation.

2.4 Where the Dog is Buried – Explaining the Crisis of Financial Unsustainability

The world is awash with interpretations of the current crisis and prescriptions for change. Many of these explanations and proposals are not new – suggesting a remarkable ability on the part of the financial establishment to ignore warnings and resist essential reform. From the equity market mania of the 1990s, we learned of the follies of "irrational exuberance" (Shiller, 2000) and the persistence of "infectious greed" (Partnoy, 2004) leading to a veritable "battle for the soul of capitalism" (Bogle, 2005) requiring investors to develop out a "Wall Street self-defense manual" (Blodget, 2007). With many of these problems unresolved – indeed exacerbated – the current crisis has led us to experience the profound shocks "when markets collide" (El-Erian, 2008), painfully relearn the importance of Keynes' "animal spirits" (Akerlof & Shiller, 2009), suffer the consequences of "chasing alpha" (Augar, 2009) through the pursuit of "fool's gold" (Tett, 2009a) and recognize the fundamental importance of "rethinking capital" (Chapple, 2009).

From these insights and our own analysis as markets practitioners, we identify the key flaws in conventional financial markets – and the elements for a more sustainable financial system. The task ahead is to create a new synthesis combining the best of behavioral finance – with its significant empirical strengths in revealing the human dimension of investment – with a macro theory of sustainable investment to inform both market design as well as investment practice.

2.4.1 The End of Neo-Classical Finance

The credit crunch probably spells the death-knell for the dominant neo-classical approach to investment theory. Indeed, it is difficult now to find a good word said about the core beliefs that have dominated investment practice for the past three decades, most notably the Efficient Market Hypothesis (EMH) on which rests Modern Portfolio Theory (MPT). For leading behavioral financial analyst, James Montier, "EMH is the financial equivalent of Monty Python's dead parrot. No matter how much you point out that it is dead, the believers simply state that it is just resting" (Montier, 2009).

EMH assumes that rational actors act in a self-regarding way so that market prices reflect all available information and tend towards equilibrium. The reality is of an electronic herd grazing across global assets creating one bubble after another with benefits narrowly distributed and costs widely shared.

The artificiality of the hypothesis rests on at least two fundamental flaws: First, human beings do not fit the abstract model of rationality. This does not mean that we are necessarily irrational or stupid. The human brain simply does not operate in the way the model suggests. For the EMH to be true, "every single one of us would have to know and understand everything, completely, and at once", according to Daniel Kahneman, a pioneer in behavioral finance [emphasis in the original] (quoted in Bernstein, 2007). Leading economist John Kay goes further and describes EMH as "illuminating but not true" (Kay, 2009). A more empirically based theory of finance would acknowledge modern psychological and neurobiological understandings which highlight the importance of emotional drivers that "motivate us, help us to think and make life meaningful", indeed which act as "core drivers of our capacity to act" (Tuckett, 2009). Moreover, markets are driven by hard to quantify but very real factors such as confidence, fairness and corruption, all of which create systemic risks poorly understood by conventional investors. Our ability to act rationally is also bounded or constrained by a series of systematic biases such as framing, group think and herding, which when compounded with market flaws help explain the persistence of manias.

Second, markets aren't perfect – indeed are fundamentally unstable, as first Keynes and then Hyman Minsky identified decades ago (Minsky, 1992). Markets suffer from profound asymmetries of information and conflicts of interest, which in many ways have been exacerbated by the process of consolidation and conglomeration in financial markets over the past 50 years. According to Richard Thaler, "we have now had three enormous price distortions in recent memory. They led to misallocations of resources measured in the trillions, and in the latest bubble, a global meltdown. If asset prices could be relied upon to be always "right" then these bubbles would not occur" (Thaler, 2009). New insights in market dynamics are being gained from analyzing out of equilibrium natural systems such as earthquake prone areas which are subject to abrupt upheavals. Starting from the assumption of market fallibility seems to yield more fruitful avenues of enquiry than presuming perfection.

It has taken a crash of monumental proportions to reveal the flimsiness of this theoretical framework. Part of the problem has been, as John Kenneth Galbraith observed almost two decades ago, that "markets are theologically sacrosanct.... Some blame [for bubbles] can be placed on the more spectacular or felonious speculators, but not on the recently enchanted (and now disenchanted) participants. The least important questions are ones most emphasized.... Accepted in reputable market orthodoxy ... is the inherent perfection of the market" (Galbraith, 1990).

The current crisis has certainly shaken the faith of investment practitioners in efficient markets and the "rational man" – and one hopes permanently. According to a poll conducted by the UK Chartered Financial Analyst (CFA) group of its members, two-thirds no longer believe that market prices reflect all available information, and 77% of respondents "strongly" or "very strongly" disagreed that investors behave rationally (Tett, 2009b). Looking back, this myth of market perfection is a perfect example of what Keynes described as "conventional judgment". In the process, many market practitioners became "rational fools" in Amartya Sen's damning phrase, overemphasizing what could be modeled and quantified even if this diverged dangerously from reality; many market regulators also became foolish abdicating their proper role to the equilibrium of the markets.

EMH is not a victimless theory – it has severely disabled the investment profession and prevented structural reforms that would have controlled asset bubbles: under EMH, bubbles can't occur and so countervailing regulation is unnecessary. This conventional wisdom has served to slow the adoption of sustainable investment practices in spite of the growing empirical evidence of success. The assertion that the "price is always right" allowed many to claim without fear of denial that if environmental, social or governance factors are material then they are already in the price, and therefore no further analysis or investigation is required. Furthermore, the "no free lunch" aspect to EMH – that it is difficult, if not impossible, to "beat the market" – has led to a proliferation of backward-looking index tracking and benchmarking hugging strategies that profoundly limit the willingness and ability of fund managers to deviate from accepted asset allocation strategies. Again, Keynes had it right when he noted that "worldly wisdom teaches that it is better for reputation to fail conventionally than to succeed unconventionally". Index funds can certainly offer good value for money to investors, but in return they disengage from the process of price discovery, and as a result, argues Steven Lydenberg, makes the market more speculative, amplifying pricing irrationalities. A new generation of forward-looking sustainable investing indices – such as SAM's DJSI – can counter these downside impacts.

2.4.2 *Blinded to Social Realities*

By over-emphasizing the quantifiable monetary dimensions of investment performance, conventional theory has blinded practitioners to a suite of social, economic and ecological realities. For Financial Times writer Gillian Tett, "the finance world's lack of interest in wider social matters cuts to the very heart of what has gone wrong." (Tett, 2009a) Prevailing financial theories have not just caused immense damage, but also blunted reform, she adds: "elites maintain their power not simply by garnering wealth but by dominating mainstream ideologies both in terms of what is said, and also what is not discussed. Social 'silences' serve to maintain power structures in ways that participants often barely understand, let alone plan".

Behavioral economists George Akerlof and Robert Shiller highlight, for example, the importance of "fairness" as a motivation for action that can "override the effects of rational economic calculation" (Akerlof & Shiller, 2009). Behavioral economics shows that the "most beneficial trade may occur between mutually supportive and trusting individuals" (Lunn, 2009). If behavioral finance offers a theoretical framework for appreciating the human dimension, sustainable investment provides the tools, analyzing the importance of understanding supply chain quality, employee engagement, community relations and consumer satisfaction as drivers of investment returns: tracking the "invisible handshake" as well as the "invisible hand". For the mainstream, this blinkered vision has had real consequences: the credit crunch arose directly out of the provision of inappropriate banking products to low income ("subprime") consumers who lacked both the financial knowledge to understand and the financial depth to weather economic shocks. Sustainable research analysts, such as those at Innovest and The Corporate Library, by contrast, were among the few that were alert to the criticality of irresponsible lending. Even with these signals, many sustainable investors were insufficiently assertive to protect their portfolios from exposure to the banking sector, often for the same benchmark hugging mentality that afflicts conventional management.

2.4.3 A Failure of Governance

Akerlof and Shiller also highlight the darker side of human psychology – the eternal tendency towards bad faith, corruption and fraud. The traditional guard against those entrusted with other people's money – whether corporate executives, pension fund directors as well as managers of mutual funds – has been good governance. And for Keith Ambachtsheer "the fundamental cause of the crisis is a widespread failure of financial sector governance mechanisms in both governments and the private sector" which have "manifested themselves in undisciplined and value-destroying risk-taking, fuelled by inappropriate, poorly conceived compensation schemes" (Ambachtsheer, 2009). Back in 1949, Benjamin Graham described stockholders as "a complete washout" (Graham, 1949). Sixty years on, things have not got much better with a vacuum in ownership resulting in failures right along the investment chain, resulting in: a significant shift in value added from savers to the fund management and investment industries; collusion between institutional investors and corporate executives to entrench excess remuneration packages that fail to drive performance and defy "fairness"; and uncritical acceptance of flawed investment theories and performance management strategies that have accentuated trading over ownership, exacerbating market risk in the process.

Certainly, the basic architecture of "shareowner democracy" remains primitive. In the UK, for example, "shareholders are not, in the eyes of the law, part owners of the company." And the question remains whether if shareholders became full owners that they would actually exercise these rights and obligations in a responsible manner.

2.4.4 Ill-Prepared for Structural Change

Neither the economy nor investment stands still. From a strategic perspective, sustainable investment is a response to three long-run disruptions: technological, geopolitical and ecological. The first is the continuing ramifications of the information technology revolution that began in the 1970s. According to Carlota Perez, technological revolutions and financial markets are closely interlinked, following a recurrent sequence of irruption, frenzy, rethinking, synergy and maturity. The dot.com crash in 2000 marked the end of the frenzy phase of the IT revolution, when financial markets became inebriated with the growth potential of the "new economy". The frenzy phase is also a time when financial capital takes off on its own, "a time of extremely unbalanced prosperity and of polarization on all fronts", creating a permissive atmosphere for ethical softening and outright illegality (Perez, 2002). Following the crash, Perez argues that economies have potential for expanding the new technology across the economy through a process of re-regulation that brings the spread of positive externalities.

In the investment sphere, the full investment implications of the information technology revolution have yet to be fully understood or confronted. One immediate impact has been the way in which the combination of market deregulation and greatly enhanced computing power has driven down the costs of trading – with the inevitable, but perhaps unintended, consequence of increased trading boosting transaction costs and depressing the incentive to evaluate consequences of long-term factors. Stock market turnover has increased in the US, for example, from 25% in 1986 to 150% in 2004 (Bogle, 2005). Processing power has also provided the bedrock of much financial innovation over recent decades which has progressed without the requisite "technology assessment" to assess and manage systemic risk – belatedly realizing that "not all innovation is socially useful" (Turner, 2009).

In the case of innovation, sustainability thinking has much to teach financial markets, not least in the application of the "precautionary principle" to risk management. Furthermore, sustainable investors have appreciated that the continuing roll-out of the "knowledge economy" enabled by information technology has placed a new premium on the quality of human resources. Labeled by the mainstream as "intangibles" (and thereby of limited relevance to investors focusing on the "numbers"), sustainable investors regard them as tangible and fundamental drivers of value in areas such as employee engagement and intellectual capital.

Intersecting with this technological revolution is the wider geopolitical transformation generated by the spectacular rise of emerging markets. For Mohammed El-Erian, cochair of PIMCO, "the present turmoil is neither the beginning nor the end of the transformation", but a regime change that will impact four key variables that impact investment strategies: growth, trade, price formation and capital flows (El-Erian, 2008). From this perspective, the credit crunch can be seen to flow from the structural rise of emerging markets, generating excess capital that could not be accommodated through traditional market adjustments (such as exchange rate appreciation and/or a refocusing of growth from export-led to domestic-driven development strategies). This provided the capital for a surge in cheap finance for speculative activity in developed economy housing markets, notably in the US and the UK – against all the predictions of economic theory. El-Erian highlights the difficulty of distinguishing long-term signals from the noise of the markets, with conventional investors often labeling the conundrums they face as "aberrations" and "anomalies" which they trust that the market's tendency to "mean reversion" will eventually eliminate.

Sustainable investors have generally focused on the downside ethical and operational risks implied by globalization, focusing on human rights management. A few have sought out new investment opportunities that have opened up by providing access to essential goods and services to those at the "base of the pyramid", notably microfinance. But, by and large, sustainable investors in Europe and North America have been as immune to the investment disruptions flowing from the "emerging market century" as the investment mainstream (IFC, 2009). As with other sources of innovation in a global world, the drive for sustainable investing in emerging markets is no longer coming from the developed world, with Brazil in particular demonstrating considerable momentum among asset owners, asset managers and equity markets (IFC, 2009).

What El-Erian and Perez have in common is their appreciation that structural change forces the redundancy of existing institutional structures that have been established to manage the challenges of a previous era. For El-Erian "structural transformations have enabled – and will continue to do so – new activities that cannot as yet be supported. As a result, it will be inevitable that there will be a series of collisions between the world of yesterday and that of tomorrow" (El-Erian, 2008). Nowhere is this threat of collision greatest than in the conflict between routine investment practice and the planet's social and environmental realities.

2.4.5 The Missing Planet Problem

In a refreshing way, the world of finance is shedding the obsolete mechanistic metaphors that have driven neo-classical economics in favor of new insights from biology. Thus, Andrew Haldane, executive director for financial stability at the Bank of England, argues that the financial system has "shown itself to be neither self-regulating nor self-repairing. Like the rainforests, when faced with a big shock, the financial system has at times risked becoming non-renewable" (Haldane, 2009). Michael Mainelli and Bob Giffords have also revealed the damaging implications for system resilience of declining diversity in financial markets brought about through the process of "deluded demutualization" and the "rising monoculture of reckless self-interest" (Mainelli & Giffords, 2009). But when it comes to the ecological resource base that underpins all wealth generation, there is a yawning gulf. Strong synergies undoubtedly exist between new behavioral finance and the social and governance dimensions of sustainable investing. But in the case of the environment, there is a "missing planet problem".

One obvious example of this is the way in which the world of finance appears to exempt itself from nature. Warren Buffett observes, "In nature, every action has consequences, a phenomenon called the butterfly effect" (Buffett, 2009). His own investing, however, does not appear to consider the risks and opportunities of social and environmental issues (Piller, 2007). The same is true of his billion-dollar donor peers Bill Gates, George Soros, Gordon Moore, Eli Broad and Michael Dell. They leave these allegedly non-financial issues for their philanthropy. This separation of vocation and avocation appears all too common and is reflected in the boardrooms and finance committees of many institutional investors. This "bounded awareness" encompasses "a variety of psychological processes, all of which lead to the same error: a failure to see, seek, use, or share important and relevant information that is easily seen, sought, used or shared" (Chugh & Bazerman, 2007). It reflects a closed mind to new ideas – and also to "predictable surprises" (Bazerman, 2006). As the term implies, these are events, such as climate risk, or the onset of the housing bubble, which could have been foreseen (and in these cases were) well before their onset was felt. Predictable surprises are different from "black swans" where the probably of a particular event occurring is low, and is not expected.

Asset prices in financial markets still fail to "tell the social and ecological truth". Climate change, for example, is recognized as the world's "greatest market failure" (Stern, 2006) – and is as much a failure of capital markets as a failure to adequately price the external costs created by greenhouse gas emissions. The shift to a low carbon economy is no longer a matter of uncertainty that investors can ignore, or a risk that can be managed away, but a reality that is already and will increasingly determine asset values. Yet, standard financial analysis of fundamental value using "discounted cash flow" models still largely fails to appreciate this: we knew that all terminal values are wrong in the context of climate change, but not how wrong. We know that emissions of greenhouse gases need to peak and decline to prevent severe disruptions to the global economy and financial markets, yet fossil fuel reserves are still valued as assets in corporate balance sheets. We have seen how entire financial markets can be disrupted by failures in systemic risk management in core sectors such as banking, but have yet to explore how markets could be equally destabilized by the mismanagement of climate risk.

Sustainable investors have, of course, been at the forefront of action to recognize the importance of "natural capital" in capital market transactions driving up allocations towards sustainable energy five-fold in the past 5 years, and increasingly holding corporations to account for their climate performance. With the Copenhagen climate conference on the horizon, deeper thinking is required to make capital markets "fit for purpose" for the decades ahead. One urgent issue is to work through the implications of the waning trust in efficient markets for policy tools such as carbon trading. If investors are not as rational and markets not as perfect as once thought, then reliance on a fluctuating carbon price as the primary driver of the transition to a low carbon economy looks increasingly unwise. Some observers have gone so far as to predict that a future involving robust global carbon markets and related arbitrage and leverage, could well lead to a repeat of inefficient markets and a "subprime carbon" crisis (Chan, 2009).

Targeted action in terms of capital markets reform is also required in terms of listing rules, stress testing and risk assessment, so that investors are made mindful of the climate liabilities attached to their assets. In a complementary fashion, new institutions and new investment options will be required to drive the long-term transformation in energy and natural resource management. These include the need for "green reconstruction banks" to crowd in capital for the long-term infrastructure underpinning the climate economy, as well as "green bonds" to finance the expansion.

Beyond the problem of pollution as symbolized by climate change lies the system-wide financial implications of accelerating resource depletion. If a failure to appreciate the value of "fairness" underpinned the irresponsible banking practices that resulted in the subprime crisis and excess liquidity generated by global imbalances provided the fuel, then the oil price shock of 2007–8 provided the trigger for collapse. This chain of causation suggests that a more profound investigation of the implication of "peak oil" and "peak water" is required, with the impacts felt far away from the obvious sectors, assets or regions.

2.5 Rewarding Reason and Resilience: The Future of Sustainable Investing

Sophisticated it may have been, but the short era of financialization rested on an incomplete picture of human action and market purpose. In place of the ideals of efficiency and rationality, a more durable basis for investment success could be constructed from the theoretical insights of behavioral finance and the practical lessons of sustainable investment. Tentatively, this could be based on two revised hypotheses.

The first is the "reasonable person hypothesis" which extends the narrow self-regarding, all-knowing archetype of neo-classical theory to encompass the full range of human motivations based on the ability of people to have "sound judgment", reconnecting investment theory with the fiduciary duty of prudence. While a "rational man" may not be able to appreciate the importance of fairness, integrity or environmental health, these factors can be quickly understood by the "reasonable person" on the basis of evidence and argument.

The second is the "resilient markets hypothesis" which, again, looks beyond the normative ideal of "efficient markets" to acknowledge the inherent tendency to both instability and unsustainability, requiring rules, incentives, skills and behaviors that aggregate towards the ability of markets to prevent and withstand shocks. This starting point enables investment practice and regulation to derive further benefit from the ongoing shift in scientific metaphor from mechanics to ecology.

For us, there is now an urgent need to develop strategies of research and market reform that can make sustainable investing the norm. We are heartened by the growing awareness of the need for a transformational shift towards sustainable investing after the credit crunch. As part of its recognition of the need for a fundamental "reset" in the global economy, the world's largest corporation, General Electric (GE), has recently underscored the importance of sustainable investment. "Financial services will never return to its previous level as a proportion of the global economy – and never should", GE writes in its latest Corporate Citizenship report. "Financial markets remain crucial as the circulatory system for commerce, but they must be reset to enable long-term sustainable performance in the real economy. This means less leveraged finance, a fundamental re-pricing of risk, the ability to account for externalities like greenhouse gas emissions, and a realignment of executive responsibility and compensation with longterm performance" (Singer, 2009).

But we are also well aware of a financial culture that exhibits a continuing failure or desire to see the new reality, a willful blindness (Kiernan, 2009). Preconceptions about ethical and sustainable investing have converged in a prevalent myth of underperformance. In addition, the alleged absence of multi-year data sets on the use of sustainability factors has become another excuse for inaction (Yegnasubramanian, 2008). There is a sad irony in this as the market was brought down in 2008 by, among other things, financial instruments that seem to have been developed by the minute and with no track record and with no shortage of buyers and traders.

We should also be aware that language plays a powerful role, especially in institutional settings. "Social", "ethical", "responsible", and in some places even "sustainable", are all seen as suspect by the mainstream. Positive screening of "good companies" or negative screening of "bad companies", done every day on Wall Street for financial reasons somehow becomes suspicious when financially tangible social and environmental factors are used. Furthermore, outdated interpretations of fiduciary duty that place an undue burden of proof on investments that exhibit social and environmental parameters are often a limiting factor. The lawyers are asked, "can we . . .?" rather than "how can we . . .?", and the answer is all too often "no!" Maximizing return gives precedence to short-term thinking rather than long-term investing The latest legal insights that challenge this "conventional wisdom" have yet to impact the bedrock of investment opinion (Viederman, 2008; UNEP, 2009).

The UNEP report recommends that investors should ask their managers to include social; environmental and governance issues in financial-decision making. But given institutional cultures, there is no discussion of how to move the institution to make that request. This is the continuing dilemma.

The culture of finance within organizations also tends to replicate what they know, rather than what is needed for change. The internal incentive systems are not calibrated for environmental, social and governance issues. Board dynamics are crucial, but boards often have set patterns, providing too little time for real discussion of new issues and new ideas, for which there is no strong perception of need. (Clark, 2008) Consultants are more often than not gatekeepers for the old school of investing.

Relationships are where the value driver is perceived to be, rightly or wrongly, and fear of jeopardizing these is all too often the overriding motivation, so changing nothing is perceived as the best way of preservation. There are very few institutional consultants well versed in sustainable investing. If asked, many claim competencies that they do not actually possess – and some with a reasonable degree of competency do not offer it unless asked.

2.5.1 Designing Breakthrough Strategies

Investment managers and nonprofit organizations have produced shelves of documents, and attended conferences designed to encourage aspects of social and responsible investing. They are in varying degrees good "how-to" manuals and events. Dissemination, however, is not the same as utilization, and little attention seems to be paid to the myriad of problems in the culture of institutions that often inhibit taking the first steps.

Researchers have addressed parts of the proverbial elephant, but the whole remains unexamined. Only a few papers that we are aware of examine impediments to adoption of sustainable investing. In short, attention has been more focused on tactics, rather than strategies that address systemic institutional change.(Viederman, 2004; Jurvale & Lewis, 2008).

By definition, the decision-making system in any institution is multi-layered. A strategy is a plan of action, not a piece of paper, that sees the whole for all its complexity and links various activities by appropriate actors constructed around an analysis of the ecology of the social and political culture and power dynamics of the institution.

A strategy will seek to influence the behavior of the key decision-makers, both directly as well as through key influencers. This will require an understanding of the cultural and psychological barriers faced by the players. An analysis of the power dynamics within an institution is essential. For example, in US foundations, the finance committee, and particularly the chair are the locus of attention.

From our perspective, key elements for the design of a breakthrough strategy for sustainable investing will include:

- revamping business and financial education to take account of the failings of prevailing theoretical approaches and undertaking a fundamental reassessment of the structure of finance, and a redefinition of risk
- drawing lessons from the regulation of other sectors (such as pharmaceuticals and water) to help ensure that financial innovation delivers social value
- changing investor rights (e.g. those related to voting and dividends) to reinforce the responsibilities of ownership linking the remuneration of investment professionals and corporate executives, not just to long-term performance, but to the imperatives of fairness and ecology
- encouraging long-termism, for example, through changes in the taxation of trading and capital gains, and incentive systems that reward related performance and not risk
- building on the behavioral insights surrounding "choice architecture" and "choice editing" to help make sustainable and responsible investing the "default option"
- learning from previous technological revolutions to better understand the ongoing disruptions created by emerging markets and the shift to a low carbon economy
- undertaking institutional changes to the structure of capital markets to reflect environmental and natural resource values
- redeploying the significant subsidies for savings and investment to deliver public goods in financial markets
- bringing a broader array of research approaches to bear on investment practice and sustainability
- deepening investor collaboration – such as the Investor Network on Climate Risk – to encompass questions of market design. (Thamotheram & Wildsmith, 2007; Guyatt, 2008)

- organizing consultations between investors and regulators to redefine fiduciary duty for the new age of sustainable investing
- raising the skills and awareness of consultants so that they become part of the solution rather than part of the problem

We don't pretend to have all the answers, but rather would like to issue a call to further dialogue on what additional steps our readers see as necessary for this transformation to be realized, and we welcome comments accordingly via the UN PRI Academic Network. It is time for all investors and asset owners to fully examine and seize this opportunity for change. Writing in the Financial Times, the eminent author and columnist Martin Wolf observed "Already the panic of the autumn of 2008 is fading. The period within which the lessons can be learned and changes made is closing. Yet without radical changes, another crisis is certain. It may not even be long delayed." His concern was inadequate attention to the reform of the banking system, but we share a similar concern about investment practice more generally.

The time for action is now. For this task, we can take inspiration once again from Keynes. Writing in 1929 in the face of academic and political obstinacy to change following the Great Crash, he wrote that:

> There is no reason why we should not feel ourselves to be bold, to be open, to experiment, to take action, to try the possibilities of things. And over against us, standing in the way, there is nothing but a few old gentlemen tightly buttoned up in their frock coats, who only need to be treated with a little friendly disrespect and bowled over like ninepins. Quite likely they will enjoy it themselves (Keynes, 1952).

Chapter 3
Putting Sustainable Investing into Practice: A Governance Framework for Pension Funds

Claire Woods and Roger Urwin

3.1 Introduction

The recent global financial crisis has given Anglo-American pension funds cause to consider the suitability of their investment strategy and the adequacy of their governance techniques. While the crisis can provide no certain solutions as to how pension funds should invest, it does reveal shortcomings in some current approaches to investment. Most notably, it underlines the danger of becoming beholden to herd culture in which prudence is judged by reference to convention (that is, what other investors do) (Woods, 2011). The crisis also reveals that a constant focus on short-term performance may distract attention from large, latent longer-term risks and hazards, to pension funds' detriment (Waitzer, 2009). Time will tell how far-reaching is the consequences of the financial crisis for pension funds.

In the fallout of the crisis, many pension funds have focused any strategic efforts, understandably, on the question of how to meet their obligations to beneficiaries under conditions of dwindling funds (see for example Clary, 2009; Walsh, 2010). Some, however, have used the time to consider a more fundamental shift in the way they meet their obligations to beneficiaries (see generally Anson, 2008; Senior, 2009; but contrast Burr, 2009). For those pension funds that have chosen to rethink their investment strategies, one approach has been to consider including an aspect of "sustainability" in their investment strategy, whether it be in the form of longer-term investment focus (Exley, 2009), a move toward the integration of environmental, social and governance criteria within mainstream funds, the creation of specialised funds with green themes such as clean water or renewable energy (Senior, 2009), or some combination of these. This diversity of approaches underlines the flexibility of sustainability as a concept.

This chapter is a republished article that first appeared in Journal of Business Ethics in 2010.

C. Woods (✉)
School of Geography, Oxford University, OX2 6JE Oxford, UK
e-mail: claire.woods@ouce.ox.ac.uk

T. Hebb (ed.), *The Next Generation of Responsible Investing*,
Advances in Business Ethics Research 1, DOI 10.1007/978-94-007-2348-1_3,

Beyond the world of investment, the concept of sustainability is now applied widely with varying significance to everything from power generation to agricultural production (compare Basiago, 1995 with Brown, 1987). For clarity's sake, this chapter adopts the definition of sustainability derived from the World Commission that sustainable development "is development that meets the needs of the present without compromising the ability of future generations to meet their own needs" (World Commission on Environment and Development, 1987). This definition, while vague, captures a key idea: that growth should occur while ensuring a certain level of economic, social and environmental security for future generations – that is, a degree of intergenerational equity.[1] In this broader context of growing social awareness of, but not necessarily understanding of, the idea of sustainability, investors are more than ever in need of guidance about what sustainability might entail in investment practice.

The growing consciousness within the business and investment worlds of the idea of sustainability (McKinsey & Co, 2010) occurs in the context of the historical backdrop of investment practices related to the notion of socially responsible investment (SRI). Many changes have occurred across the broad field of SRI over the past 30 years (see Richardson, 2009). The field has grown beyond the negative-screening approach of many early ethical to encompass a broader range of investment strategies (Hawley, 1995; Sparkes & Cowton, 2004). Most important, perhaps, is a movement (championed by the United Nations Principles for Responsible Investment (UN PRI)) toward integration of environmental, social and governance (ESG) issues into mainstream investment analysis and decision-making (Wheelan, 2008). In contrast to an ethically-oriented investment approach, UN PRI defines responsible investment (RI) as "the integration of ESG criteria into mainstream investment decision-making and ownership practices",[2] and underlines the business-case justifications for its adoption (Richardson, 2009). The incorporation of sustainability into investment strategies may be seen to be strengthening and adding to the RI movement through its focus on intergenerational equity and the long-term.

This chapter presents a framework for Anglo-American pension funds who wish to invest more sustainably, but who are unsure of the practical requirements of such a change. The framework focuses on the adjustments that should be made to the fund's strategy and governance in order to achieve a broader (ESG-inclusive) and longer-term approach to investing. Acknowledging that the needs of every pension fund are different, our framework is structured as a spectrum, allowing for more or less extensive change to investment strategy and governance. The chapter proceeds with a brief review of SRI and more recent RI literature, in the context of growing

[1] Intergenerational equity may be defined as a principle of distributive justice (Frischmann, 2005) requiring some level of equality between members of different generations. See also Edith Brown Weiss (1984). In the context of pension fund investment, we see intergenerational equity as requiring some level of equality between members of a fund that have different expected retirement dates.

[2] Available at: http://www.unpri.org/.

public awareness of the concept of sustainability (Section 3.2). It then examines the literature on pension fund governance, arguing the need for more detailed practical guidance for funds moving toward sustainable investing (Section 3.3). Our framework is then presented as a practical means for Anglo-American pension funds to go about implementing a sustainable investing approach (ESG-inclusive, and long-term focussed) through the adaptation of its investment strategy and governance practices (particularly through the formulation and articulation of clear investment mission and strong investment beliefs) (Section 3.4). Finally, Section 3.5 outlines the Anglo-American legal background, first examining how fiduciary duty might affect pension funds who adopt the framework we present, and then looking briefly at potential regulatory enablers of sustainable investing.

3.2 Literature Review of SRI Field: SRI, RI and Sustainable Investing

In this section, we look first at the multiple meanings that the terms SRI and RI have accrued over time, and, referring to Gallie's notion of essentially contested concepts (1956), argue that SRI is a confused and confusing term that connotes financial motivations for some and ethical motivations for others. We then suggest that the successful growth of membership of the UN PRI may have led to a degree of standardisation across understandings in this area, particularly with respect to RI. Finally, we note the wide public awareness of the concept of sustainability, and suggest that some pension funds rethinking their approach to investment following the global financial crisis are attracted to the flexible concept of sustainable investing. We argue that such investors will benefit from the clarity and concreteness provided by our framework.

3.2.1 SRI – A Radically Confused Concept?

Spreading far from its roots in negative screening of certain investments (such as tobacco or firearms) by church-based investors (Schueth, 2003), the term SRI has become something of an "umbrella concept" (Sethi, 2005) for a range of different ethically, socially and/or environmentally oriented investment practices (Hawley, 1995; Sparkes & Cowton, 2004; Schueth, 2003; Richardson, 2009). Many authors have described a definitional ambiguity surrounding the term SRI (O'Rourke, 2003; Sethi, 2005; Viederman, 2004; compare Sandberg & Juravle, 2009), with some seeing the ambiguity as detrimental to the success of SRI movement (Sethi, 2005; Viederman, 2004; Sparkes, 2002), and others seeing it as necessary to retain nuances (see Sandberg & Juravle, 2009).

Sandberg and Juravle (2009) argue that while there are "terminological" ambiguities associated with the concept of SRI – different authors use the terms "socially responsible investment", "social investment", "responsible investment", and "ethical investment" (p. 521) – all of these terms mean more or less the same thing, their "main characteristic" being "the integration of certain non-financial concerns in the investment process" (p. 519).[3] Similarly, Sandberg and Juravle's content analysis of the websites of 101 UN PRI signatories finds that investors use these various terms to describe the same thing: the "integration of ESG criteria into mainstream investment decision-making and ownership practices".[4] Not all scholars agree that there is a consensus definition of SRI centred on the UN PRI's Principles. For example, Richardson argues for the grounding of SRI within an ethical context, stating that current SRI practice has "problematically disavowed [its] ethical posture" (2009). Richardson's argument suggests that the business-case justification for SRI, when divorced of ethical grounding, may act as a double-edged sword: for example, "[w]ithout demonstrated financial advantage, a [business-case SRI] investment analysis may advocate delaying or halting measures that mitigate pollution" (2009). Thornton, writing in a different context, also acknowledges a fundamental difference between financially and ethically motivated SRI (2008).

At this point it is worth asking whether the term SRI is an "essentially contested concept", or whether it is merely "radically confused" (see Gallie, 1956). Gallie argues that there are certain concepts (for example "democracy" and "social justice"), "which are essentially contested, concepts the proper use of which inevitably involves endless disputes about their proper uses on the part of their users" (p. 169). An essentially contested concept should be distinguished from a "thoroughly confusing term which cloak[s] the possibly perfectly consistent use of two or more concepts" which may simply be defined separately (p. 175). Why does the distinction matter? Essentially contested concepts will never have unanimous definition amongst users, and are able to develop and flourish through continuous contestation. A confused term, by contrast, may be divided into its correct parts through careful analysis; these parts may then be separated so that they can each be the subject of meaningful discussion in the future.

In Gallie's view, the competing interpretations of an essentially contested concept are "derived by a process of imitation and adaptation from an exemplar" which all holders of competing views recognize as their source of the concept. Yet, due to the complex nature of the concept, "it is natural that different features in it should be differently weighted by different appraisers, and hence that [competing views] should have come to hold their very different conceptions" of the concept (p. 176).

[3] Sandberg and Juravle (2009) suggest several explanations for the heterogeneity found within the SRI terminology, including regional or cultural forces, differing influences from stakeholders, and most interestingly, market pressures: "there is a commercial need for SRI fund managers and rating agencies to attain a strong identity in order to differentiate themselves from the rest of the 'flock' and to attract investors" (p. 526) see also (O'Rourke, 2003).

[4] Sandberg and Juravle's (2009) analysis shows that 43% of investors refer to these same activities as "socially responsible investment", 10% as "sustainable investment", 9% as "responsible investment" (p. 523). We note, however, that the study focused on UN PRI signatories, whose understandings of these terms are no doubt moulded by the framing of the UN PRI's Principles.

By contrast, the multiple meanings associated with a confusing term cannot be derived from a single exemplar, as they actually represent a number of different and distinguishable concepts.

Even a perfunctory application of Gallie's test indicates, in our view, that business case RI and ethics-based ethical investing cannot be said to have derived from the same exemplar: the two appear to have contradictory cores, with the former having at its heart improved financial return for beneficiaries through the exploitation of ESG-related market inefficiencies, and the latter focusing on the promotion of ethically sound corporate behaviour through techniques such as negative screening and engaged ownership. If we accept that SRI is one of Gallie's "radically confused" terms, then different species of SRI (for example, RI and ethical investing) would perhaps be more successfully advanced once distinguished from one another, so that their separate goals may be pursued with greater transparency and clarity of aim. It is with this distinction between RI and ethical investment in mind that we pitch our framework in Section 3.4 solely to pension funds pursuing an RI-like sustainable investing strategy.

3.2.2 UN PRI – Standardising Understandings of RI?

The SRI definitional debate aside, it could be argued that a level standardization of some of the RI terminology is occurring through the UN PRI movement. The 719[5] signatories to the PRI commit to six Principles of Responsible Investment (the Principles),[6] whose central focus is the integration of ESG criteria into mainstream investment decision-making and ownership practices. The UN PRI movement, with its financially-oriented justifications, has made RI more palatable to pension funds and other institutional investors who were traditionally cautious about the concept of ethical investment, whether due to an aversion to screening's reduced investment universe (Langbein & Posner, 1980), concerns (justified or not) about fiduciary duty (discussed more in Section 3.5) (see Richardson, 2008; UNEP FI, 2005, 2009; Woods, 2011), or a general sense that ethics should not drive investment decision-making (compare Friedman, 1970).

---

[5] As of 4 April 2010 there are 719 signatories to the UN PRI.

[6] Signatories to the UN PRI commit to the following (see : http://www.unpri.org/principles/)

1. We will incorporate ESG issues into investment analysis and decision-making processes.
2. We will be active owners and incorporate ESG issues into our ownership policies and practices.
3. We will seek appropriate disclosure on ESG issues by the entities in which we invest.
4. We will promote acceptance and implementation of the Principles within the investment industry.
5. We will work together to enhance our effectiveness in implementing the Principles.
6. We will each report on our activities and progress towards implementing the Principles.

If the Principles are to go forward as a quasi-standard in RI, their strengths and weaknesses should be subject to scrutiny by the academic community. In our view, whilst the Principles rightly make clear the importance of ESG integration and active ownership, they do not adequately address the issues of short-termism and intergenerational equity in investment. These issues need to be addressed particularly for Anglo-American pension funds, with large funding obligations going into the future. For that reason, our framework makes specific reference to the strategic and governance changes that should be implemented in order to foster longer-term investment.

3.2.3 Sustainability – Emphasising the Long-Term and Intergenerational Equity

The increasing prominence in recent years of the terms "sustainable" and "sustainability" in the public arena (Vos, 2007) adds another layer of complexity to how pension funds approach RI. This greater prominence of the term may be related to increasing public awareness of intergenerational problems due to factors such as ageing populations in many Western countries, resource constraints, and long-term environmental impacts from climate change. Moreover, there appears to be an increased general acknowledgement of the interplay between environmental risk and economic performance: the US Securities and Exchange Commission, for example, recently released interpretive guidelines about whether and when listed companies should disclose climate change risk (including risk from the impact of legislation and regulation, international accords, indirect consequences of regulation or business trends, or physical impacts of climate change) (see Broder, 2010). That said, an increasing public awareness of the concept of sustainability does not amount to an understanding of it.

Sustainability is another term that is subject to deep definitional ambiguity (Basiago, 1995; Brown, 1987; IUCN, 2006; Ratner, 2004; van Marrewijk, 2003; Vos, 2007).[7] Beyond providing the World Commission's (1987) definition as a starting point (see Introduction), we do not look further into the competing definitions of sustainability here – for it is the malleability of the term that interests us. Industry experience has shown us that pension funds that consider moving toward some form of RI may value the term "sustainable investing" both for its flexibility and for its distinction from the connotations of ethical investment.

The notion of sustainability, on a larger scale, has much to add to pension fund investment. It is arguable that it has different ontological foundations to that of responsibility: while responsibility implies duty, sustainability implies ensuring that the *conditions* for responsibility remain intact – that a level of intergenerational

[7] Sustainability is another term that could be subjected to Gallie's test for essentially contested concepts. While this is beyond the scope of this chapter, other authors have looked at this question: see for example (Jacobs, 2006; Connelly, 2007).

equity is fostered. Ensuring sustainability in its wider social sense implies constraining actions, including investing, to ensure the workability of the economic system as a whole. This is a consideration for governments. However, in our view, the scope of the term is such that pension funds adopting a sustainable investing approach may flounder without practical knowledge about the changes to investment strategy and governance that should accompany any successful implementation of a sustainable investing strategy. Our framework is intended to provide guidance to this class of investor. In order to underline the importance of long-term investing and intergenerational equity for pension funds, and to distinguish itself from the connotations of ethical investment, which we see as generally undesirable from a fiduciary's perspective, our framework is designed for pension funds adopting what we term a "sustainable investing" approach. In our view, a sustainable investing approach requires RI's ESG inclusiveness and active ownership, but also emphasises the importance of long-term, intergenerational awareness.

3.3 Anglo-American Pension Fund Governance

The investment industry relies on certain assumptions about how markets work – that markets are relatively efficient, that regulation by the market (rather than governments) is effective, that financial innovation is necessarily beneficial (De Graaf & Williams, 2009). Following the advent of 2008s global financial crisis, some of these assumptions are being questioned not only by left-leaning economists (see for example Stiglitz, 2004), but also by their former champions (for example Greenspan, 2008) see De Graaf and Williams (2009). In this regard, pension funds are subject to the same fundamental uncertainties as the investment industry as a whole (Clark & Urwin, 2008a, 2008b, 2008c; Hess, 2005). Under conditions of risk and uncertainty (Knight, 1921), pension fund governance processes help to bring some structure to investment practice (Merton & Bodie, 2005). Ambachtsheer and Clark have written extensively on pension funds governance (Ambachtsheer, 1997, 2007; Ambachtsheer, Capelle, & Lum, 2007; Clark, 2007, 2008; Clark & Urwin, 2008a, 2010).

Pension fund governance can be described as "the oversight, accountability, transparency, and decision-making norms underpinning the operations and investments of a pension plan" (Monk, 2009). Anglo-American pension fund governance is framed by legal requirements, both under the common law of trust and under statute (Richardson, 2007a, 2007b; Woods, 2011). Under these laws, pension fund trustees owe certain duties to the beneficiaries of the funds that they manage (see Section 3.5 below). Pension fund trustees and their advisors use a number of techniques in order to ensure that they meet their legal obligations to beneficiaries. Clark and Urwin (2008) conducted research into pension fund governance in order to discover what constitutes best-practice.

Here we begin our discussion by revisiting Clark and Urwin's (2008a) framework for pension fund governance. In doing so, we focus particularly on two core elements of their framework: investment mission and investment beliefs. This sets the scene for Section 3.4, in which we present our framework for sustainable investing, describing changes both to investment strategy and pension fund governance designed to aid Anglo-American pension funds pursuing a strategy of sustainable investing.

Clark and Urwin (2008a) present a pension fund governance framework based on their observations of best-practice amongst a range of institutional investors (including both public and private Anglo-American pension funds) who demonstrate exemplary governance practices. In examining a range of pension fund governance processes, Clark and Urwin distil twelve "best-practice factors" (p. 13). Noting that not all institutional investors have the resources to implement these governance principles to the same extent, they designate six of the twelve as "core" factors. They view the other six principles as only relevant to resource-rich organisations comprising of an executive team in addition to board of trustees and investment committee. As our framework builds on that of Clark and Urwin (2008a), we reproduce their core best-practice factors in Table 3.1.

Of Clark and Urwin's six core best-practice factors, we emphasise the two that we see as most integral to our framework for sustainable investing governance: mission clarity and strong beliefs (highlighted in Table 3.1). In our experience, moreover, whilst the use of the terms "investment belief" and "mission" is widespread within the investment industry, these terms may be unclear to those with less practical familiarity with the industry. For that reason, it is worth discussing the terms in some detail here. While we do not discuss Clark and Urwin's other core governance factors in detail in this section, we view them as important and make reference to them in Section 3.4.

3.3.1 Mission Clarity

Trustees must have a clear understanding of what they are required to do on behalf on beneficiaries. Trustees' aims in dealing with trust funds on behalf of beneficiaries may be described as an "investment mission". Investment mission is rarely

Table 3.1 Clark and Urwin (2008a): Core best-practice governance factors for pension funds

1. Mission clarity	Clarity of the mission and the commitment of stakeholders to the mission statement
2. Effective focusing of time	Resourcing each element in the investment process with an appropriate budget considering impact and required capabilities
3. Leadership	Leadership, being evident at the board/investment committee level, with the key role being the investment committee Chairman
4. Strong beliefs	Strong investment beliefs commanding fund-wide support that align with goals and inform all investment decision-making
5. Risk budget framework	Frame the investment process by reference to a risk budget aligned to goals and incorporates an accurate view of alpha and beta
6. Fit-for-purpose manager line-up	The effective use of external managers, governed by clear mandates, aligned to goals, selected on fit-for-purpose criteria

defined in academic articles. Instead, authors tend to provide assertions about the characteristics an investment mission should have. It should be "clear" (Clark & Urwin, 2008) and should be communicated to relevant stakeholders (see for example Clark & Monk, 2008). Clark and Urwin (2008a, p. 9) argue that a clear mission and "the commitment of stakeholders to the mission statement" is a core factor in pension fund governance. An investment mission *statement* articulates the mission of the trustees: it is a statement that defines the goals of trustees and their agents in investing trust funds on behalf of beneficiaries.

Academic work on corporate mission statements provides some insight that may be applied to pension fund mission statements. Whilst corporate mission statements tend to have a broader focus than pension fund investment missions (they often refer amongst other things to customers, employees, products or services, markets, public image, and growth (David, 1989)), studies nonetheless emphasise the role of mission statements in providing clarity of aims (Williams, 2008), and in communicating them (see Bartkus, 2000). In our experience, it is useful for pension fund trustees to articulate their mission with respect to specific factors as well as specifying an overall mission statement. As such, pension funds might have, for example, a financial mission statement, a long-term mission statement, and an ownership mission statement in addition to their overarching investment mission statement.

Many pension funds (both public and private) create a written a statement of their investment policy[8] (US) or principles (UK), whose aims may be used to inform trustees' understanding of their mission, and therefore an investment mission statement. In the UK, the *Occupational Pension Schemes (Investment) Regulations 2005* require all pension funds to create a written statement of investment principles.[9] While neither private nor public US pension funds are required by law to produce a written statement of investment policy, it is considered best-practice to do so (Martin, 2009). Moreover, the US Department of Labor has released interpretive guidelines endorsing the use of such statements.[10] These statements of investment policy and principles are more extensive than mission statements. For example, UK statements of investment principles must contain a statement of the fund's policies in relation a number of factors, including "the kinds of investments to be held", "risks, including the way risks are to be measured and managed" and "the extent (if at all) to which social, environmental or ethical considerations are taken into account in the selection, retention and realisation of investments."[11] In our view, as most

[8] The US Department of Labor defines "statement of investment policy" as "a written statement that provides the fiduciaries who are responsible for plan investments with guidelines or general instructions concerning various types or categories of investment management decisions." See Interpretive bulletin relating to written statements of investment policy, including proxy voting policy or guidelines: 29 CFR 2509.94-2(1).

[9] *Occupational Pension Schemes (Investment) Regulations 2005* (UK): cl. 3(b).

[10] The Department of Labor states that "a statement of investment policy designed to further the purposes of the plan and its funding policy is consistent with the fiduciary obligations set forth in ERISA section 404(a)(1)(A) and (B)": see 29 CFR 2509.94-2(1).

[11] *Occupational Pension Schemes (Investment) Regulations 2005* (UK): Cl. 3(b).

trustees will have prepared these statements already, they may provide a convenient starting point for articulating, and then evaluating, an appropriately considered and clear mission statement.

3.3.2 Investment Beliefs

Our experience has shown that while the concept of investment beliefs is widely used within the pension fund industry, it has been subjected to little academic scrutiny. Koedjik and Slager (2007, 2009) have addressed the subject in some detail; Ambachtsheer (2007) and Clark and Urwin (2008a, 2010) have also made reference to the concept as part of their broader work on pension fund governance. The term "investment belief" itself is widely used without being widely defined. We have found the definitions that do exist to be perfunctory in most cases. Koedjik and Slager treat investment beliefs in more detail than most authors, and define investment belief as "a statement about human behaviour in the financial marketplace" (p. 13). Gray (2009) defines investment beliefs as "assertions about critical aspects of investing regarding the drivers of return generation, the multi-dimensional nature of risk, the dynamic scenario-dependent trade-offs between the two, and expectations about outcomes, and others' expectations." As both of these authors note, investment beliefs are not always articulated; in our view, the terms "statement" and "assertion" do not adequately acknowledge the fact that many beliefs are in fact implicit. Therefore, we prefer to define investment beliefs as the conjectures (see Popper, 1963) and working assumptions about the investment world (including the economy, the workings of the financial system, and social, environmental and other risks) that underlie and inform investment decision-making.

Despite the scarcity of detailed definitions, there seems to be a level of agreement in the literature, both implicit and explicit, that strong, sound investment beliefs are beneficial to pension fund governance. According to Koedjik and Slager (2007), beliefs are important because they improve stakeholder governance by reducing conflict of interest. In other words, when investment beliefs are out in the open, pension fund trustees, their advisors, asset managers and beneficiaries have a common understanding about the working assumptions underlying the pension funds' investment practices; there is a meeting of minds. The transparency achieved allows any of the stakeholders to question first whether a stated investment belief is sound, and second whether a particular investment practice or decision is consistent with the stated investment beliefs. Moreover, clearly stated investment beliefs may help pension funds to design investment strategies that are appropriate for the needs of their beneficiaries (Gray, 2009; Koedijk & Slager, 2009).

In order to make the discussion less abstract, it is worth providing some hypothetical examples of investment beliefs, and evaluating them. Here we provide a range of the sorts of beliefs drawn from our experience that pension fund trustees typically advance in the context of RI:

1. RI has produced better performance than conventional investing.
2. RI has produced worse performance than conventional investing.

3. RI is likely to produce performance as least as good as conventional investing because it uses additional information that influences price and value.
4. RI is likely to produce lower performance than conventional investing because it acts as a constraint on choice.
5. There is no firm evidence that RI will perform as well as conventional investing.
6. There is no firm evidence that RI will perform any worse than conventional investing.
7. Extra-financial factors including ESG factors influence returns and risk over extended time periods.
8. The active use of ownership rights through company engagement can enhance the value of an investment if deployed appropriately.

Statements like (1) and (2) are not definitive. Performance is always contextual to a particular set of conditions or particular period, so the statement may be true and false. In any case, the inductive step that links past and future performance is relatively weak. Qualitative arguments like (3) or (4) have greater merit but they may prove difficult to advance with high conviction. RI approaches vary widely and the belief that RI works may be difficult to advance as a generality. This leads many fiduciaries to favour a null form of belief like (5) or (6). The beliefs in (7) and (8) correspond to a more constructive approach. Our framework is designed to provide a structure from which trustees can articulate more concrete beliefs such as the latter two.

Writing in the *Financial Times*, Skypala notes that "there is a danger [in acknowledging investment beliefs] that the realisation of how much [of investment practice] is based on beliefs rather than facts may reveal how little certainty there can be about investment outcomes" (Skypala, 2009). In our view, this danger is a reality in that uncertainty and potential ambiguity are endemic to the investment world. That said, a distinction should be drawn between the largely subjective investment beliefs of naïve investors, and the beliefs of investment experts that are trialled and reformed through a recursive process in practice. We view lack of transparency as a much greater danger: even if a pension fund does not make beliefs explicit, they exist (Gray, 2009; Koedijk & Slager, 2007). Pension fund investment practices rely on conjectures and working assumptions about the world in which investing occurs. In our view, the articulation of investment beliefs allows for them to be tested, and for investment practices to be altered as necessary.

3.4 Sustainable Investing Framework

In this section we put forward our sustainable investing framework for Anglo-American pension funds. We base our conception of sustainable investing around the notion of RI as designed by UN PRI, modified by an additional emphasis on long-term investing and intergenerational equity. Our sustainable investing framework is therefore designed for pension funds that take into account ESG issues and practice active ownership, but also to emphasise long-term risk control and value creation, and to ensure that their investment strategy and governance are appropriate to sustainable investing aims. We look first at investment strategy for sustainable investing, and then turn to pension fund governance for sustainable investing. In doing so, we outline conventional pension fund investment strategies and governance practices in order to provide a point of comparison.

3.4.1 Investment Strategies for Pension Fund Sustainable Investing

In our experience, conventional pension fund investment strategies usually fail to bring ESG issues sufficiently into account in making investment decisions and specify investment targets that are relatively short-term. We refer to this conventional strategy as Strategy A. This sort of strategy has significant limitations, as it does not align sufficiently with the long-term investment principles to which pension funds are suited (Sethi, 2005). Furthermore, delegation to asset managers of too much responsibility for exercising their ownership interests and duties and reliance on short-term performance benchmarks creates a risk of thoughtless adherence to herd investing (see Johnson & Jan de Graaf, 2009).

In order for a pension fund to take up a sustainable investing approach, a number of adjustments to investment strategy are required. First, investment strategies could integrate ESG issues into investment decision-making and analysis (Sethi, 2005; Sandberg & Juravle, 2009; UNEP FI, 2009). Second, trustees could provide more specific instructions to asset managers with respect to (a) ESG integration; and (b) engagement with investee companies. Third, performance benchmarks and the associated investment focus for activities could be based on longer-term horizons, with more emphasis on absolute returns. We refer to this sustainable investing strategy as Strategy B.

In addition to these measures, some pension funds may wish to make targeted investments in sustainably-themed products, such as clean technology ventures (we will refer to these as "environmentally targeted investments"). This sort of investment should be distinguished from community investment, where the aim is to create benefits for communities (see Schueth, 2003) – the focus for pension funds here must remain on creating return for beneficiaries as part of risk-adjusted portfolio (see Section 3.5). Furthermore, any such environmentally targeted investments must be in line with investment beliefs (discussed more below). This area is likely to involve allocations outside quoted equities and bonds in areas like venture capital, private equity, real estate and infrastructure. The typical pension fund employs external managers to cover these areas; the fund's responsibilities hinge on being able to select these managers successfully, draw up appropriate mandates governing their actions and targets and apply effective oversight. We refer to this type of extended sustainable investing strategy as Strategy C. Environmentally targeted investments are unlikely to be appropriate for all pension funds; as with any investment, an environmentally targeted one must be considered in light of a fund's own risk budget (see Clark & Monk, 2008). Table 3.2 summarises these strategies.

Table 3.2 Comparison of conventional and sustainable investing (SI) pension fund investment strategies

Conventional investment strategy (Strategy A)	• Performance benchmark and therefore investment focus based on short-term time horizons High degree of delegation of ownership interests to managers
SI strategy (Strategy B)	• ESG issues integrated into investment decision-making and analysis including active ownership • Managers given specific instructions with respect to ESG integration and the exercise of ownership interests Performance benchmarks and therefore investment focus based on longer-term time horizons
SI extended strategy with targeted investments in sustainable areas (Strategy C)	• Strategy B components, plus: Investment in environmentally targeted investment, such as clean technology ventures and other sustainable themes

3.4.2 Pension Fund Governance for Sustainable Investing

The most detailed analyses of pension fund governance have dealt with how pension funds can best meet their financial obligations to beneficiaries (see for example Ambachtsheer, 2007; Clark & Urwin, 2010; Monk, 2009). Very little of this literature deals specifically with governance with respect to sustainable investing or, more generally, in the context of the requirements of a more sustainable economy. What has been written about Anglo-American pension fund governance with respect to sustainability has been reasonably high-level (see for example Sethi, 2005). As our framework aims to aid pension funds with the practical implementation of a sustainable investing process, we provide a more detailed outline of governance for sustainable investing. As foreshadowed in Section 3.3 above, we look first at mission clarity for sustainable investing, then at investment beliefs for sustainable investing. Finally, we address Clark and Urwin's (2008a) remaining core pension fund governance factors.

As we note in Section 3.3 above, mission clarity is one of Clark and Urwin's core best-practice governance factors for pension funds; it is essential that pension funds adopting a sustainable investing approach ensure that they adjust their mission appropriately. An example of a conventional pension fund investment mission (Mission 1) might be to invest trust funds with appropriate risk in order to meet future liabilities to beneficiaries at an appropriate cost. In our experience, the conventional mission, Mission 1, exists in the vast majority of pension funds. A sustainable investing mission (Mission 2) would focus on continued value creation as in Mission 1, but it would also aim to manage risk more effectively through integrating ESG into investment decision-making (in order to evaluate the value of potential investments more accurately) (Wheelan, 2008) and through active ownership actions with investee companies over ESG issues where relevant. Furthermore, a sustainable investing mission would include dedication to long-term planning and intergenerational equity.

An extended sustainable investing mission (Mission 3) would allow for a more significant level of commitment to sustainability goals, but this would rarely be appropriate for pension funds because of its extra-financial reach (discussed more below). Investors adopting an extended sustainable investing mission as described here would have the value creation and ESG integration/active ownership/long-term planning aims described in Mission 1 and Mission 2 respectively, and they would also aim to achieve certain extra-financial goals (for example, the creation of a national fund for education, or the production of cleaner energy through investment in renewable energy technology), such goals overlapping with the financial goals. The focus for funds wishing to adopt Mission 3 would remain on the creation of "value" for beneficiaries, but the "value" might be more social or environmental than strictly financial. In adopting Mission 3, funds would have to make clear the balance between their financial and extra-financial aims.

It is important to emphasise that Mission 3 is an example of a specialised mission that will *rarely be consistent with pension fund fiduciary duty*, because it is likely to involve a conscious compromise on a portion of financial return in exchange for an extra-financial reward. Under Anglo-American law (both statute and case law), fiduciary duty requires trustees to manage trust funds in the best interests of beneficiaries, which generally means in their best financial interests[12] (Woods, 2011; on pension fund fiduciary duty, see Section 3.5 below). Only where all beneficiaries of a pension fund agreed to such a mission would it be in keeping with fiduciary duty (Thornton, 2008; see UNEP FI, 2005).

An extended sustainable investing mission like Mission 3 is therefore more likely to be an appropriate for a sovereign wealth fund that may have national environmental or social goals to incorporate in its investment mission, or an endowment fund that aims to marry a financial purpose with some wider social agenda. While an extended sustainable investing mission like Mission 3 will rarely be suitable for pension funds, it is nonetheless worth noting for completeness' sake that such mission could exist, and that it would lead to a significantly different investment outcome. A spectrum of investment missions: a conventional mission (Mission 1); a sustainable investing mission (Mission 2); and an extended sustainable investing mission (Mission 3) are canvassed in Table 3.3.

As emphasised in Section 3.3 above, best-practice pension fund governance requires both clarity of mission and effective communication of mission. Therefore, a pension fund sustainable investing mission should be communicated through a clear mission statement. In addition to the overall sustainable investing mission statement, it may be useful for trustees to articulate their mission with respect to specific areas of governance under sustainable investing as well. Examples of possible mission statements for pension funds adopting a sustainable investing mission are shown in Table 3.4.

---

[12] The notion of what constitutes a beneficiary's "best interests" is deeply problematised. Part V of this chapter goes into the issue in more detail, but the interested reader should look further afield: see for example (Johnson & Jan de Graaf, 2009; Langbein, 2005; Richardson, 2007a, 2007b, 2008; UNEP FI, 2005; Woods, 2011).

Table 3.3 Conventional investment mission compared to sustainable investing (SI) missions

Conventional investment mission (Mission 1)	Invest trust funds with appropriate risk in order to meet future liabilities to beneficiaries at an efficient cost
SI mission (Mission 2)	• As for Mission 1, plus: • Avoid various risks associated with investment ownership by integrating ESG and active ownership into analysis and decision-making • Promote intergenerational equity within fund by focusing resources and planning on the longer-term
Extended SI mission (Mission 3) NB: Mission 3 will rarely be consistent with pension fund fiduciary duty	• As for Missions 1 and 2, plus: • Achieve certain extra-financial goals, with respect to environmental or social issues (recognising that these might conflict with the financial goals)

Table 3.4 Sample sustainable investing (SI) mission statements

Type of mission	Sample mission statement wording	Value created if mission is implemented successfully
Financial mission (for all Missions)	Create value for beneficiaries at appropriate levels of risk through investment practices and decisions	Net financial returns in excess of liabilities allowing for risk
ESG mission (for Missions 2 and 3)	Manage certain extra-financial risks by integrating ESG assessment into investment practices and decisions	Net financial returns from risk mitigation; non-financial returns
Ownership mission (for Missions 2 and 3)	Manage ownership risks through exercising voting and/or engagement with investee companies on ESG and long-term issues	Net financial returns from risk mitigation; non-financial returns
Long-term mission (for Missions 2 and 3)	Create value by exploiting the long-term endowment of the fund while avoiding the inefficiencies in short-term behaviours	Net financial returns over long-term allowing for risks and costs
Intergenerational equity mission (for Missions 2 and 3)	Ensure value is sustained for current and future generations of beneficiaries by investment practices and decisions that focus on planning ahead	Net financial returns to successive generations of beneficiaries
Extra-financial mission (for Mission 3 only)	Create extra-financial value for beneficiaries (and other stakeholders) by investing in ESG-related opportunities	Non-financial returns to explicit wider missions

In Section 3.3, we define investment beliefs as the conjectures and working assumptions about the investment world (including the economy, the financial system, and social, environmental and other risks) that underlie and inform investment practices and decisions. We argue, as others have (Ambachtsheer, 1997, 2007; Ambachtsheer, Capelle, Lum, 2007; Clark & Urwin, 2008, 2010; Clark & Monk,

2008; Gray, 2009; Koedijk & Slager, 2007, 2009), that strong investment beliefs are vital to best-practice pension fund governance. In order for pension funds to successfully adapt their governance practices to the requirements of sustainable investing, we suggest that it is essential that they re-examine their investment beliefs.

Why is a re-examination of investment beliefs necessary in order for pension funds to pursue sustainable investing? Articulating investment beliefs aids investors in making sensible decisions about investment strategy. If a pension fund is considering moving from a conventional investment mission a sustainable investing mission, then the trustees of that fund are likely to have altered their beliefs about the value of sustainable investing. For example, a pension fund that becomes interested in sustainable investing is likely to hold an investment belief that ESG issues influence financial returns and risk over the long-term, and should form part of all investment analysis and decision-making. If the pension fund in question did not hold this belief, then adopting an investment strategy in which ESG issues are included in investment analysis and decision-making would be inappropriate. In order to ensure that a sustainable investing strategy is appropriate for beneficiaries, trustees of pension funds considering sustainable investing should therefore a) articulate their investment beliefs; and b) assess whether these are compatible with a sustainable investing strategy. Once investment beliefs that support the introduction of a sustainable investing strategy have been acknowledged and articulated, pension fund stakeholders (including beneficiaries and asset managers) are able to see the trustees' justification for a sustainable investing strategy.

Having underlined the importance of ensuring that investment beliefs fit sustainable investing goals, we note that institutional change is rarely easy (see Ambachtsheer, 2007; Clark & Urwin, 2010). In Ambachtsheer's (2007) view, pension funds are too often chained to investment beliefs that are no longer appropriate: "the beliefs of many funds continue to be based on historical rules of thumb" that are ill suited to the current environment. The acknowledgement of new investment beliefs is no different from other types of institutional change in this respect, as it means accepting that one's underlying assumptions about the workings of the investment world have changed. Nonetheless, the acknowledgement and expression of appropriate beliefs is a necessary precursor to the successful implementation of sustainable investing practices. Examples of investment beliefs that might support a sustainable investing strategy are set out in Table 3.5.

Finally, there are four best-practice governance practices in addition to mission clarity and strong investment beliefs (outlined by Clark & Urwin, 2008a – see Table 3.1) that may be adapted in order to pension funds to pursue a strategy of sustainable investing successfully. First, *effective focusing of time*: trustees should map out the resources needed to implement a sustainable investing strategy, including parts of the implementation process that will be delegated to asset managers. Second, *leadership*: trustees should provide strong leadership to mediate varying opinion about the value of a sustainable investing strategy. Where applicable, the pension fund's Investment Committee Chairman should play the main leadership role. After the sustainable investing strategy has been introduced, the Chairman should continue to mould consensus (see Clark & Urwin, 2008a). Third, *risk budget framework*: trustees should attempt, as far a possible, to place quantifiable risk

Table 3.5 Examples of investment beliefs supporting sustainable investing

Source of risk/return	Related investment belief
ESG issues	ESG issues influence financial returns and risk over the long-term, and should form a part of all investment analysis and decision-making
Active ownership	The execution of ownership rights can influence performance and risk over time
Engaged ownership	The active use of engagement with investee companies can enhance the financial performance of an investment over time
Contracts with asset managers	Contracts and fees for asset managers can be designed to align their long-term interests with those of the fund
Oversight of delegated investment responsibilities	Appropriate oversight of asset managers' integration of ESG issues into investment analysis and decision-making can improve its effectiveness
Environmental change	Longer term risks of climate change and resource degradation can be offset by investment in environmental opportunities and clean technology

parameters on risk related to ESG issues. Fourth, *fit-for-purpose manager line-up*: it is essential that asset managers have appropriate capability for implementing a sustainable investing strategy, including understanding how to integrate ESG issues into investment analysis and decision-making, and how to lengthen the investing time horizon where relevant.

We have argued that in order for pension funds to implement sustainable investing effectively, they should make certain adjustments to their investment strategies, including the integration of ESG issues into investment analysis and decision-making and engagement with companies where necessary, and the emphasis of longer-term investment time horizons (see Table 3.2). In addition, pension funds implementing sustainable investing should ensure that their governance practices align with their sustainable investing strategy. Building upon Clark and Urwin's 2008a study of best-practice pension fund governance (see Table 3.1), we have argued that pension funds implementing sustainable investing should articulate both a clear sustainable investing investment mission (see Tables 3.3 and 3.4) and strong investment beliefs with respect to the soundness of sustainable investing as an investment approach (see Table 3.5). Finally, we note that best-practice pension fund governance indicates that effective focusing of time, leadership, risk budget framework and appropriate management should all be adjusted to meet the needs of sustainable investing.

3.5 Legal Context: Barriers To and Enablers of Sustainable Investing

Anglo-American pension funds planning to engage in sustainable investing should not overlook their fiduciary requirements. We have examined these issues in detail elsewhere (see Woods, 2011). We argue further that debate surrounding fiduciary duty with respect to sustainable investing, and more generally SRI and RI, should move beyond references to the 1984 UK case of *Cowan v Scargill*[13] and the early US work of Langbein and Posner (1980), upon which many industry discussions on the subject appear to be built. We find the preliminary work of Johnson and Jan de Graaf (2009) with respect to the oft-forgotten duty of impartiality useful in this regard. Our fiduciary focus here is practical – we emphasise the importance for pension funds of documenting prudence and loyalty. The framework we have presented is designed to help pension fund trustees to do so, and therefore to protect themselves (and their beneficiaries) against potential breaches of fiduciary duty. We then turn to the law's constructive capacity, and suggest a number of potential regulatory enablers of sustainable investing for future discussion and research.

3.5.1 Fiduciary Duty and Sustainable Investing: The Need to Document Prudence and Loyalty

Many authors have addressed the issue of whether various forms of SRI and RI are consistent with fiduciary duty (Langbein & Posner, 1980; Richardson, 2007a, 2007b, 2008; UNEP FI, 2009; UNEP FI, 2005; Martin, 2009; Langbein, 2005; Weinrib, 1975; Woods, 2011). It is beyond the scope of this chapter to examine all of their arguments in depth. It suffices to say that the issue of whether SRI and RI are compatible with fiduciary duty centre on two element of fiduciary duty as it applies in the context of US[14] and UK[15] pension funds: the duties of loyalty and of prudence. Putting aside the minor variations in formulation between sources of law,[16] the duty of loyalty requires trustees to act in the best interests of the beneficiaries. The duty of prudence requires trustees to exercise prudence, or skill, care

[13] Cowan v. Scargill Ch. 270 [1985] (UK).

[14] In the US, the duty of loyalty is contained in *Uniform Prudent Investor Act* (*"UPIA"*) at s. 5 for public pension funds in almost all states); and in *Employee Retirement Income Security Act 1974* (*"ERISA"*) at 29 USC § 1104(a) for private pension funds. The duty of prudence may be found in *UPIA* at s. 2(a) for public pension funds; and in *ERISA* at 29 USC § 1104(a)(B). In US case law, the classic statement of the duty of prudence is: a trustee must "observe how men of prudence, discretion and intelligence manage their own affairs, not in regard to speculation, but in regard to the permanent disposition of their funds": Harvard College v. Amory (1830) 26 Mass. (9 Pick.) at 461.

[15] In the UK, the duty of loyalty may be found in *Occupational Pension Schemes (Investment) Regulations 2005*, which provide that the trustee's foremost duty to beneficiaries is to act in their "best interests", except in the case of a conflict of interest, when they must act "in the sole interest of members and beneficiaries": cl. 4(2). The duty of prudence requires the trustee to manage the trust in the same manner as an ordinary prudent man of business would conduct his own affairs: Speight v. Gaunt 9 App Cas 1 (1883) (HL) at 19 (judgement of Lord Blackburn) (approving 22 ChD 727 at 739–740, CA, per Jessel MR); Re Whiteley, Whiteley v. Learoyd (1886) 33 ChD 347 (CA) at 355 (Lindley LJ). Under the UK Trustee Act 2000, all trustees are required to "exercise such care and skill as is reasonable in the circumstances", having regard to "any special knowledge or experience that he has or holds himself out as having" s. 1(1)(a).

[16] See notes 12 and 13 above.

and diligence, in managing trust funds for beneficiaries. Under both US and UK law, prudent management of trust funds today means managing trust funds in accordance with modern portfolio theory (see Woods, 2011).

Following a spate of ethically-driven SRI in the late 1970s and 1980s (mainly consisting of divestment from companies in Apartheid Africa, (Richardson, 2008)) critics argued that trustees were using SRI to further their own moral or political purposes, rather than to promote the financial interests of beneficiaries, and in doing so narrowed their funds' investment universe in what amounted to a violation of both the duties of loyalty and prudence (see for example Langbein & Posner, 1980; compare Thornton, 2008). These views were backed up by judicial decisions in both the US and the UK.[17] However, the form that SRI took in the early cases such as these differs markedly from the form of RI or sustainable investing around which we have designed our strategy and governance framework.

Nonetheless, the persistent lack of clarity in this area, combined with a tendency for courts and commentators to equate prudence with adherence to the status quo (Woods, 2011), continues to dissuade trustees from adopting investment strategies (such as Strategy B) that break with convention (Strategy A) (see Table 3.2) (Johnson & Jan de Graaf, 2009). In this climate of legal anxiety, it is all the more important for pension funds trustees to protect themselves (and the beneficiaries of their funds) with good governance. Where pension fund trustees can document the steps they have taken to arrive at the decision to implement an RI or sustainable investing strategy, and where those steps are based on sound investment beliefs, they should be able to demonstrate that their decisions were in the best interests of beneficiaries. In this context, our framework provides trustees with a transparent structure, which, if executed properly, should establish that any such strategy is based on strong beliefs about the advantages it will provide to beneficiaries. It is difficult to see how a well articulated RI or sustainable investing approach demonstrably based on sound investment beliefs in and designed in the best interests of beneficiaries can be said to violate either the duty of loyalty or of prudence (see UNEP FI, 2005).

In our view, the debate over whether RI or sustainable investing (in the form presented in this chapter) violates the duties of loyalty and prudence has become somewhat stale. Until a new case on point is heard or relevant legislation is enacted, little can be gained from continuous rehashing of these old issues (compare Woods, 2011). That said, Johnson and Jan de Graaf's (2009) recent article questioning whether pension fund trustees are adequately addressing another aspect of their fiduciary duty, the duty of impartiality, does bring some fresh thought to the area. The duty of impartiality requires trustees to "make diligent and good-faith efforts to identify, respect, and balance the various beneficial interests when carrying out the trustees' fiduciary responsibilities in managing, protecting, and distributing the

[17] See e.g. Cowan v. Scargill Ch. 270 [1985] (UK); Univ. of Oregon v. Oregon Inv. Council 82 Or. App. 145 (1987), 728 P.2d 30 (US).

trust estate".[18] While it is a long-standing duty in trust law, courts and scholars "have generally left the nature and implications of the duty vaguely defined and little explained" (Halbach, 1992).

Johnson and Jan de Graaf argue that pension fund trustees who are overly short-term oriented may breach their fiduciary duty by, in essence, favouring older beneficiaries over younger ones:

> Excessive focus on short-term investment horizons, use of short-term benchmarks and evaluation of portfolio managers based on short-term results, as well as a lack of attention to the risks associated with potential long-term value destruction ... should ring fiduciary alarms for pension funds that are managing assets to meet liabilities over several generations (Johnson & Jan de Graaf, 2009).

It is difficult to know where to limit Johnson and Jan de Graaf's argument. In the context of pension funds, which often have thousands of beneficiaries at any one time, a narrow interpretation of the duty of impartiality could place unreasonable burdens on trustees. However, it is an argument worth developing further, and may provide extra support for the value to be derived from long-term investing strategies.

3.5.2 Potential Regulatory Enablers of Sustainable Investing

Fiduciary duty is chiefly seen as a preventer of harm; regulation may also act as an enabler of constructive behaviour. Here we suggest that leaders in both the US and the UK could consider a number of potential regulatory enablers of sustainable investing. Our suggestions here are not detailed, and do not presume to answer the questions they will raise, but instead to outline some discussion points for future research:

- The introduction of "safe harbour" principles: this approach could create incentives for sustainable investing by preventing litigation against fiduciaries with respect to practices covered by safe harbour clauses (where fiduciaries have followed due process and acted in good faith). The safe harbour clauses could be designed to protect from litigation fiduciaries that choose to adapt an RI or sustainable investing approach as described in this chapter. Safe harbour principles have been used to provide trustees with a degree of certainty of compliance with their fiduciary obligations with respect to defined contribution default plans in the US under ERISA (Shaw & Hagigi, 1988).
- The introduction of a "comply or explain" process with respect to sustainable investing: under this approach, legislators would encourage pension funds to think of sustainable investment as a norm, by requiring them to either comply and adopt aspects of sustainable investment ("comply") or provide a written explanation detailing why they have chosen not to comply and for what

[18] Restatement of Trusts (Third), comments to § 79(1).

time period ("explain"). This approach portrays sustainable investing as legislatively sanctioned, while allowing an alternative line of action to be pursued subject to explanation. Similar legislation has been effective in raising governance standards in the UK with respect to corporate governance (see *Combined Code on Corporate Governance 2003* (UK)) and pension investment governance ("Myners Principles", see Myners, 2001), and has already appeared to a limited extent for UK pension funds with respect to ESG issues. Under the *Pensions Act 1995*, pension funds must produce a written statement of investment principles ("SIP").[19] The SIP must cover "the extent (if at all) to which social, environmental or ethical considerations are taken into account in the selection, retention and realisation of investments".[20] This regulation stops short of being a comply or explain approach because it merely requires pension funds to state whether they take social, environmental and ethical considerations into account, but not why they choose not to do so. This approach, while accommodating very limited response by many funds, is still productive in that it is sufficiently flexible to allow pension funds to adjust their strategies at their own pace, while gradually contributing to a change in expectations about sustainable investment (compare Thaler, 2008).

- Government funding for a permanent academy for training with respect to RI or sustainable investing: this has occurred in Australia, with the creation of the Responsible Investment Association of Australasia in 2007 (previously known as the Ethical Investment Association).
- Government support for and engaged oversight of collaborative responsible investing activity: the UN PRI Clearinghouse arrangement is an early example of appropriate support for such activity.

3.6 Conclusions

This chapter has presented a governance framework intended to provide Anglo-American pension funds with practical guidance for the successful implementation of sustainable investing. We have focused on the changes that pension funds adopting sustainable investing could make to their investment strategies and governance (in particular with respect to investment mission and investment beliefs). We have discussed how our framework is positioned with respect to fiduciary duty, arguing that it offers pension funds a structure that will help them to demonstrate their compliance with the fiduciary requirements of prudence, loyalty and impartiality. Finally, we note that regulation, while often proscriptive, may also act as an enabler

[19] See *Pensions Act* (1995) (UK) ss. 35–36.

[20] *Occupational Pension Schemes (Investment) Regulations* 2005 (UK) cl. 3(b)(vi). Similarly, it must cover the fund's "policy (if any) in relation to the exercise of the rights (including voting rights) attaching to the investments": cl 3(c).

of constructive behaviour – to this end we have recommended several potential regulatory enablers of sustainable investing for future discussion.

We have acknowledged the extensive terminological debate in this area. It is our hope that wide-spread, successful implementation of sustainable investing or RI would put an end to the need for such debate. That is to say, if over time ESG-inclusive, intergenerationally equitable investing can be shown to be effective and desirable, at some point its goals will become internalised into pension fund investment beliefs systems. At this point, terminology would change: the terms sustainable investing and RI could drop from the lexicon, and the actions they describe would become merely "investment". Behavioural norms have been shown to have a deep influence on the development of legal understandings (see for example Posner, 2000). Thus, in this situation of changing norms with respect to investment a parallel development might be expected of law. If sustainable investing were to become increasingly conventional, it is arguable that trust law would treat it increasingly as a prudent manner of investing (see Woods, 2011), obviating the need for inquiry into whether sustainable investing (as opposed to mainstream investment) met with fiduciary standards.

Beyond the practical focus of this chapter, there is a wider story to tell. In today's changing economic conditions, a question arises about how pension fund investing should evolve to deal with emerging intergenerational problems associated with environmental and social risk and uncertainty. The US Securities and Exchange Commission's release of interpretive guidance about whether and when public companies should disclose climate change risk demonstrates, at the very least, an acknowledgment of the potential of climate change risk. Beyond climate change, other issues are changing the world economy. Ageing populations are expected to put increasing burdens on the pension fund industry (Disney, 2000). The developing economies of countries such as Brazil, China, India, Indonesia and South Africa are now increasingly influential. The scale of the US's debt to China seems to suggest if not the start of a new economic order, than at least the potential of a new economic order (see Epstein, 2010).

Under these circumstances, it is not inconceivable that pension fund governance may need to be rethought in the future. The pension fund, after all, is one of the few institutions that has a truly intergenerational role – arguably more so than governments, whose mandates often go no further into the future than the date of the next election. As the demands of the economy change, the role of pension funds in ensuring a level of intergenerational equity between members may become increasingly significant, perhaps through a renewed interpretation of the duty of impartiality. For the time being, however, our framework provides a practical way for pension funds to implement a sustainable investing strategy that not only includes ESG and ownership considerations, but also provides for a focus on the long-term, allowing funds to prepare themselves for the economic and legal challenges of the future.

Chapter 4
Avoiding the Next Financial Crisis, or Notes of a Former, Flawed Fiduciary

Michael Musuraca

4.1 Introduction

I served as a designated trustee on the board of the New York City Employees Retirement System (NYCERS) for over 13 years, from 1996 to 2009. NYCERS is a defined benefit pension plan covering over 300,000 active and retired members who work for the City of New York and its covered organizations. My frame of reference, then, for a discussion of how fiduciaries can act to avoid the next financial crisis is based on the experience of the U.S. public pension fund world over that period. As U.S. public pension plans have plan assets in excess of $2 trillion, and are major players in the all of the world's financial markets, such funds serve as a good proxy to explore both the role that institutional investors played in the global financial crisis and suggestions for how to avoid another one.

The plan assets of the public pension funds represent, it need be noted, the deferred wages of people who work in state and local governments, and the goal of fiduciaries on the pension plan board is to protect and grow fund assets so as to insure the promised payment of those deferred wages to fund participants in retirement without causing undue stress on the plan sponsor (in my case the City of New York and its covered organizations) or the current or future generations of workers and taxpayers.

4.2 U.S. Public Pension Plans in 2010

The fiscal health of U.S. public pension plans has become front page news in the nation's newspapers for all the wrong reasons. Investment losses resulting from the global financial crisis have eroded their funding base and placed great pressure on plan sponsors in state and local governments to raise pension contributions in order

M. Musuraca (✉)
Queen's College, Flushing, NY 11367, USA
e-mail: mmusuraca@gmail.com

T. Hebb (ed.), *The Next Generation of Responsible Investing*,
Advances in Business Ethics Research 1, DOI 10.1007/978-94-007-2348-1_4,

to offset investment losses, at the same time that tax revenues to fund other governmental purposes have plummeted due to the financial crisis. When combined with the failure of many governmental plan sponsors to fully make required employer contributions in previous years, and an increase in benefit levels for some plan participants, the sustainability of the traditional governmental defined benefit pension plan is now being called into question in a great number of U.S. states and localities.

Analysts at Standard and Poor's, for example, noted in a recent report that the need for state and local governments to raise pension contributions before a "meaningful [economic] recovery has taken hold" is causing "many states [to] re-think core services, programs, and benefit levels – including pensions." Simply put, if there were ever reason for pension fund fiduciaries and those concerned with retirement security for working people and the building of a more sustainable economy to stop and re-examine some of the major assumptions that have guided investment decisions over the past two decades, that time is now.

4.3 From Bubble to Bubble, or Getting to 2010

I joined the NYCERS Board in 1996 as the fund was experiencing a period of phenomenal investment returns. Indeed the fund's annual investment returns over the second half of the decade beat the fund's assumed rate of return two to three times over. The fund's investment performance also allowed for employer pension contributions to be lowered and for benefit levels to be increased. The prodigious investment returns of the late 1990s actually marked the end of a long run of good fortune for NYCERS and other institutional investors that began in the 1980s.

In addition to allowing for pension benefits to be increased and for plan sponsor contributions to be decreased (or, in some cases, temporarily eliminated through contribution holidays in certain states) the long run of excellent returns also reinforced the faith that the efficient workings of the market would, over the long-haul, generate more than adequate resources to meet plan liabilities. This faith was misplaced on two levels. The first is that many trustees and plan sponsors underplayed the importance that the annual required payments from plan sponsors were to the long-term fiscal health of the pension funds. Just as important, the notion that the efficient market would continue to work wonders missed the fact that even during the market boom of 1980–2000, there had been a number of crisis moments, as Jeff Madrick nicely summarized in a recent book review.

There was also one financial crisis after another, often leading to a recession or slow growth and often requiring federal bailout... [T]he Mexican crisis of 1982; the stock market crash of 1987; the savings-and-loan and junk bond failures of late 1989 and 1990; another Mexican catastrophe and hedge fund failures in 1994; the Asian financial crisis of 1997 and the collapse of Long-Term Capital Management in 1998; and the bursting stock market bubble of 2000–2001.

The periodic crisis moments, each of which necessitated some level of intervention by national or international bodies, did little to undermine the idea that properly diversifying the assets of the pension plans alone would work to insure that plan liabilities were met, but they should have. This is not an admonition to fiduciaries that they should forsake their attempts to properly diversify investment holdings, but that fiduciaries need to account for far more than what is included in the typical risk/return modelling of standard efficient markets analysis to accomplish their goals. This theme will be fully discussed following a brief recap of NYCERS' investment experience over my tenure representing municipal workers on the board.

In 1996, NYCERS' equity portfolio was invested primarily in U.S. equities, with an additional allocation to the mature economies in the international arena, and a customized fixed-income portfolio. The domestic equity allocation was heavily invested in domestic index funds, and was the key driver in the outsized investment returns of the mid to late 1990s. The logic of investing in domestic equities primarily through domestic index funds was, at the time, compelling. Index funds, like the Russell 3000 or the S & P 500, allow for a large institutional investor to gain access to a broad range of stocks cheaply and efficiently. This not only allows the institutional investor to implement, in part, the dictum from modern portfolio theory that the investor should seek to diversify their holdings, but was also premised, in the U.S. context, on the notion that all the necessary information regarding any company in the index was widely available in the public domain. This being the case, it was further assumed that the market price as reflected in the index reflected the actual value of the companies based on that information. Hence, there was little reason for institutional investors to pay active managers a premium fee for trying to "beat the market", when the market price already incorporated what the investor needed to know about any given company.

Moreover, NYCERS was (and is) an activist investor that long promoted improvements in corporate governance as a key component in helping to insure that the companies it invested in would generate the long-term returns that NYCERS needed to pay pension benefits in retirement to members of the fund. NYCERS, for instance, was one of the founders of the Council of Institutional (CII) in 1985, the largest organization of institutional investors dedicated to improving corporate governance in the U.S. In addition, NYCERS consistently engaged corporations on various ways, including board director independence, the procedures for establishing levels of executive compensation, and majority voting for directors, that a company could utilize to improve its governance in direct dialogue, often times with other like-minded investors, as well as through the shareholder resolution process. NYCERS also urged governmental regulatory authorities, especially the Securities and Exchange Commission, to live up to its mandate to be an effective regulator of the nation's financial markets by being the investor's advocate.

NYCERS focused its activism on other than financial issues as well, like the impact that climate change and labour standards had on the long-term return potential of any individual company, by requiring, for example, companies to disclose and report to shareholders on such risks and, in certain cases, demanding that companies change their behaviour by adopting codes of conduct over labour standards in their supply chain and verifying improvements through independent means. In short, the NYCERS Board, like many other institutional investors, acted in some ways like a model fiduciary, seeking to implement an investment program similar to those of other pension funds that generated the necessary risk adjusted rate of return in a prudent and efficient manner after consulting with a range of investment professionals to meet its long-term liabilities. Moreover, NYCERS actively sought to protect its assets by promoting an agenda to improve corporate governance and insure that companies were seeking to address issues of societal concern that might have an impact on long-term performance. This activism, however, rarely directly affected how NYCERS invested the assets of the fund, leaving the fund, like others, exposed to a range of risks.

The reality of how exposed NYCERS and other institutional investors were to the risks associated with their investment decisions became abundantly clear in 2000, even though NYCERS and other investors had been acting in a prudent manner consistent with fiduciary standards of conduct. Led by the collapse of Enron and the bursting of the dot.com bubble what became clear to NYCERS and other institutional investors was that in markets, like the U.S. for example, important information about individual companies was not known. Even worse, in many instances, the NYCERS Board had to accept that the investors' safety net, including companies' boards of directors, governmental regulatory agencies, ratings firms, investment managers and analysts and the accounting and legal professions, failed miserably in their tasks in helping investors fully assess the risks in their investment portfolio.

The crisis of confidence that followed the wave of corporate scandals and the bursting of the dot.com bubble was profound, as was the devastation wrecked on pension fund returns and state and local government budgets, which constituted the first "Perfect Storm" of the 21st Century for institutional investors. After experiencing an era of extremely high returns, institutional investors faced a severe plunge in asset values that caused great strains on the funds' governmental sponsors, and led many institutional investors to reassess their place in the capital markets. To reassess, in other words, what level of risk the assets of their funds were actually exposed to.

The reassessment stirred many institutional investors to play a more activist role in the capital markets, and, in the U.S., many institutional investors were key actors pressuring the U.S. Congress to pass the Sarbanes-Oxley Act to improve corporate accounting, as well as in efforts to force companies to improve disclosure about extra-financial risks to their long-term performance through collective efforts with other institutional via organizations like CERES around climate change, and in 2006, the Principles for Responsible Investment (PRI) around a fuller range of environmental, social, and governance (ESG) issues.

As important as the increased activism was, NYCERS, like many other funds, also began to re-think their reliance on domestic equity in their investment strategy, and to seek out investments in other asset classes that would mitigate the risks attendant with an overreliance on domestic equities and fixed-income products. In doing so, NYCERS and other institutional investors were again acting prudently in utilizing the tools of modern portfolio theory, to diversify their holdings into new markets, like emerging and frontier markets, and employing a range of alternative investments strategies, like private equity, hedge funds, and real estate, in an attempt to minimize risk for an expected level of return.

As the recession lifted in 2003 and confidence returned to the capital markets, investment returns for institutional investors began to rise as well, averaging in the mid-teens from 2003 to 2007 for U.S. public pension plans. Indeed, it seemed that the "Perfect Storm" was passing, and that U.S. public pension plans were beginning to recover from the depths of the recession that greeted the new century. Such optimism, however, was short-lived as the global financial crisis began to hit in 2007, and pension plan returns once again plummeted in 2008 and 2009, resulting in the current debate whether or not the traditional U.S. public pension plans are sustainable in the long-run.

4.4 Fiduciaries and the Global Financial Crisis

The question of who is responsible for the carnage resulting from the global economic order as a result of the financial crisis is an important one. Indeed, in the U.S. it had become fertile ground for a partisan debate within the ranks of the Congressional Financial Crisis Inquiry Commission, with Democrats blaming risk-taking on Wall Street and Republicans focusing on Fannie Mae and Freddie Mac.

I have my own favourite list of culprits responsible for the global financial crisis, including the de-regulatory mania of the Bush Administration, or its record of class warfare conducted, in large part, through the tax code. I could also mention the failures of that great oracle and former Federal Reserve Chairman Alan Greenspan, whose devotion to the unregulated free market, and his failure to turn off the credit faucet after opening it full throttle, sometime in late 2001, ushered in an era of cheap credit that led to a great number of citizens and financial institutions drowning in a sea of toxic assets. Or, finally, I could point to the unbridled greed and corruption of many in the financial industry, especially the perverse compensation system they created that led market players to place short-term gains ahead of long-term value creation. While laying the blame at the various door steps mentioned above would certainly tell a large part of the story, it would not necessarily get to a set of lessons that trustees and other plan fiduciaries need to learn from the collapse of the world's financial markets in 2007.

In short, the stewards of other people's money, especially the fiduciaries responsible for the deferred wages of working people, need to fundamentally re-evaluate the role of the funds they oversee in the global economy; what such a re-evaluation will mean for how we understand fiduciary duty; and how such a re-evaluation might influence investment policies in the decades ahead. The ability of fiduciaries to accomplish these tasks will not, by themselves, avoid another market collapse. A robust and well-funded governmental regulatory regime on the national and international levels is equally vital. Yet, as Donald MacDonald, chair of the PRI noted in early 2009, "As clients and part-owners of the financial institutions at the core of this crisis, institutional investors should accept some shared responsibility for the behaviours that led to the crisis. In response, and to protect our investments in the long-term, institutional investors need to greatly improve our due diligence within the investment chain, and to practice and incentivize much smarter risk management." The issues that MacDonald addresses and others inform remainder of this essay.

If institutional investors are to change their behaviour to better protect the funds, a starting point is an examination of the role that pension funds and other institutional investors play in the global economy. As Keith Johnson and Frank Jan de Graaf noted early in 2009, fiduciaries and policy makers have not adjusted for the

> ...growth of pension funds into huge pools of capital and the correspondingly expanded influence that pension fund practices now have on the larger economy. For example in the United States, institutional investor ownership of Fortune 1000 companies has increased to 76 percent of outstanding equity. With retirement savings making up the largest block of these holdings, pension funds are central to the health of the financial system and are a primary source of capital. In some countries, the aggregate value of pension fund assets even exceeds the Gross Domestic Product...

As pension funds and other large institutional investors are important sources of capital for the global economy, it also follows that the performance of the global economy is of primary importance to the financial health of the institutional investors. Certainly, it has become all too evident that among the greatest victims of the global financial crisis have been institutional investors, like the U.S. public pension plans.

From my experience what Johnson and de Graaf note as the "symbiotic nature of this relationship between pension funds and corporations...that neither can succeed without [the] success of the other" is rarely scrutinized by pension plan fiduciaries. Take, for instance, the isolated actions made by hundreds of pension funds to shift assets from public equities into private equity, hedge funds, real estate, and other alternative investments over the past two decades (especially after the market collapse in 2000). This is what James Hawley portrays as the "search for alpha" that transformed such investment funds from relatively marginal players in the world's financial markets into major players that changed landscape of the investment universe, an unintended outcome that resulted, in great measure, because of a short-term need of pension funds and other institutional investors to find sources of return, albeit at a projected lower risk, to meet the assumed rate of return projections. In essence, pension fund fiduciaries did not take away from the market collapse of 2000 the need to re-examine whether or not their assumptions about how to properly finance long-term liabilities were valid, but also did not ask what, if any, impact their investment decisions might have on the larger economy.

What I and thousands of pension fund trustees were thinking about as we made the decision to allocate 5%, 10% or more of pension fund assets into alternative investments was that we were, in fact, simply following the dictates of fiduciary conduct that we seek prudent ways to improve the projected risk/return profile of the funds by diversifying into uncorrelated asset classes. Implicit in these actions was the belief that prudent diversification strategies would lead to higher future investment returns that would generate needed returns to fund liabilities and alleviate the need for plan sponsors to raise contribution levels. In doing so, fiduciaries were acting much like Charles Prince, the former Citibank CEO and Chairman, who as late as July 2007 was quoted in the Financial Times dismissing fears about the impact of the sub-prime mortgage crisis in the United States by stating, "When the music stops, in terms of liquidity, things will be complicated. But as long as the music is playing, you've got to get up and dance. We're [Citibank] still dancing." While it was undoubtedly easier for Prince to walk off into the sunset carrying the proceeds of a generous severance package as things became more "complicated," the same cannot be said for many of the institutional investors that are still reeling from the impact of the global financial crisis.

Moreover, what neither fiduciaries nor our advisors noted was that given the tremendous growth pension fund assets, the "search for alpha" in the aggregate contributed to the exponential growth in the importance of alternative investments (replete with high fees, little to no regulatory oversight, inadequate transparency, and high levels of leverage and illiquidity), all of which helped contributed to greater market volatility and a new set of risks to the pension funds and the financial system. While private equity and hedge funds did not cause the financial meltdown, neither did they manage to save the pension funds from the impact of the meltdown. Moreover, the time and attention devoted to establishing such programs took trustees away from a more thorough analysis of the risks in other areas of their portfolios.

Trustees often neglect the role that their isolated decisions have on the investment industry and the larger economy because of the customary wisdom about fiduciary duty, which, in simple terms, directs trustees to act like other trustees in setting investment policy and making investment decisions. This tends to not only reinforce a herding behaviour amongst trustees and their funds (evident in the rush into alternative investments), but one that centres attention on short-term investment returns. The emphasis on short-term returns has been cited by the CFA Institute Center for Financial Market Integrity, among others, for "...destroying long-term value, decreasing market efficiency, reducing investment returns, and impeding efforts to strengthen corporate governance".

The emphasis on short-term results also calls into question whether or not trustees are adequately addressing the need to both generate current income for retirees and long-term value creation for active members – an essential part of their fiduciary duty that is often overlooked. This is most evident in the failure of fiduciaries, when setting their asset allocations and investment strategies, to confront questions about the long-term sustainability of the larger economy, whose performance is crucial to the long-term fiscal health of the pension fund. As Cary Krosinsky, Nick Robins, and Stephen Viederman note in a chapter included in this volume, Keynes differentiated between investors and speculators when he devised an investment strategy for himself. In doing so, Keynes held that real investors sought long-term returns versus the speculative mania of the short-term investor. Moreover, in Keynes' view, such long-term investment actually had a social purpose. While pension fund fiduciaries typically discuss the need to meet the long-term liabilities of their funds (i.e. the payment of monthly pension check to plan members long into the future for a pension plan), a fuller discussion about how long-term trends in the economy might undermine their efforts to meet those liabilities, or the social purpose of the investments are rarely discussed when trying to ascertain their funds' quarterly performance or its ability to meet the annual assumed rate of returns on investments. Failing to address the impact of long-term economic trends and the social impact of investment decisions, it seems to me, undermine the ability of pension fund fiduciaries to meet their stated goals.

Take, for instance, another aspect of Keynes' work that is more often associated with his body of work: how much the average worker earns and how secure he/she is in the labor market and its importance to the functioning of the economy. In the U.S. (and elsewhere in the mature economies to greater or lesser degrees) there has been steady erosion in the real wages of the median worker and a corresponding increase in the level of income inequality in the last 30 years. One of the principal reasons why workers became addicted to credit in the U.S. is that their wages no longer allowed for the maintenance of their lifestyle (this is true even after, in two-income households, both adults moved into full-time employment). Hence, the availability of cheap credit allowed, for a time, the maintenance of a lifestyle that most U.S. citizens simply could not afford. This is the definition of unsustainable, which became clear to all of us as credits markets froze 2 years ago, and, in the U.S and other nations, the residential housing market collapsed. Yet, I cannot recall an extensive discussion of growing wage inequality and what risks it might present for pension fund investments during the many asset allocation debates that took place over my 13 years on the NYCERS Board.

In many ways a discussion about the importance of income inequality on the long-term performance of fund investments would have been ruled out of bounds by many in my pension fund and others, because it would have violated the fiduciary's duty of loyalty solely to the members of his/her own pension fund by forcing what many would view as a social issue onto the agenda of the pension board, and challenged the notion that the fund should only be interested in seeking the highest risk adjusted rate of return. Yet, the growth in income inequality over the past 30 years has had an impact on the sustainability of pension funds in the U.S. and other mature economies, and should have been carefully examined by fiduciaries. Moreover, as the global economy begins to recover from the worst of the global financial crisis, high levels of unemployment and income inequality bring into question, according to the International Monetary Fund (IMF) and the International Labour Organization (ILO), how vibrant the recovery will be and how long lasting. Hence, both issues should be key concerns for any prudent fiduciary, and not because the issues are moral ones, but because both get to the heart of what it means for a fiduciary, as Johnson and de Graff argue, to try and balance the needs of retirees and active members of the pension fund.

The growth in income inequality, however, is not the only issue that posed risks to pension fund assets that had a hard time penetrating board room discussions over investment policy in the years I served on the NYCERS Board. Indeed, the entire range of issues generally lumped under the rubric of environmental, social, and governance issues (ESG), like the risks posed by climate change, occupational safety and health standards, the adequacy of governmental regulatory actions (or inactions), and the composition and independence of company boards have most often been dealt with by pension funds and other institutional investors as being in the purview of proxy or policy committees of the board, and not as a central part of the investment decision making process. As with the growth in income inequality, one of the lasting impacts of the global financial crisis should be that a fiduciary must fully take into account the broadest range of ESG issues in actually setting investment policies and strategies in their efforts to avoid another market failure. This has, in fact, become one of the central goals of the PRI, and will be of increasing importance in the years ahead as pension funds and other institutional investors dig out of the depths of the global financial crisis.

4.5 Improving Fund Governance

It is one thing to say that fiduciaries will need to incorporate a much broader understanding of the factors that will yield the long-term value creation necessary from investments to meet their liabilities (whether those liabilities are pension payments, or to fulfil the mandates of sovereign funds, endowments and foundations), and another to set the conditions to make it possible. Over the last few years there has been an increasing amount of research on the significance of fund governance and investment success by Keith Ambachtsheer, Gordon Clark and Roger Urwin among others. Among the fundamental tenets of this research is that how fiduciaries are chosen and trained; whether or not the mission of the fund is clearly articulated; how responsibilities between board members and staff and divided; and whether or not staff are adequately trained and compensated are all areas for fiduciaries and policy makers to pay much closer attention to.

Another crucial arena for governance reform is in the relationship between fiduciaries and those that they hire in the investment management community. The sordid details regarding the pay-to-play corruption scandal at the New York State Common Retirement System and other U.S. public pension plans speak to the need for all trustees and staff to establish and adhere to a set of ethical guidelines in the selection of investment managers, consultants, and other service providers. Yet simply establishing and adhering to a set of guidelines in the selection process is not enough. Fiduciaries need to begin fully exerting the power and accepting the responsibilities that come with investing other people's money as a way of both meeting the long-term liabilities of the funds they represent and better aligning the funds with the interests of the larger society. Accomplishing this task will not be simple. Attempts, for instance, to change the way investment managers are paid, so that the interests of the fund and the investment managers are truly aligned will be difficult to fashion and implement. Moreover, insuring that a fuller assessment of ESG issues is made part and parcel of the investment decision making process will bring with it the need to provide plan fiduciaries and the people they hire the tools they need to adequately perform such tasks.

I have been particularly impressed with the work that Claire Woods and Roger Urwin have developed in this area. Their insistence that pension funds seeking to adopt a sustainable investment strategy clearly define their mission statement and investment beliefs seems to me to be the right prerequisite for enabling trustees to both ascertain how they might construct a sustainable investment strategy. Just as important, adopting a mission statement and set of investment belief will also force trustees to fulfil their responsibility to document their adherence to the fiduciary code of conduct that demands both prudent deliberation and loyalty to fund members.

Indeed, I would argue that forcing trustees, whether or not they seek to adopt a sustainable investment strategy, to clearly articulate their mission statement and set of investment beliefs has not been taken seriously enough over time by plan trustees, but has been lost in the myopic pursuit of the highest risk adjusted investment returns possible. Forcing fiduciaries to first focus on their mission and how they propose to carry out their mission is one of vital changes that should come out of an examination of how fiduciaries can try and avoid getting caught in another global financial collapse. Whether or not such an examination leads to the incorporation of some or all of the positions I have advocated throughout this essay may well be less important than the need for fiduciaries to explain themselves to fund members and the larger society. I also agree with Wood and Urwin when they argue that government, through its regulatory role, should establish basic and standardized principles of fund governance that will force trustee boards to articulate why they have adopted particular investment policies and strategies. Government could also establish a set of guidelines for the selection of trustees and mandate on-going fiduciary training. This is not an argument for the creation of professional trustees. I firmly believe that, especially in pension plans, worker representation on the boards of trustees is vital, but recognize as well that trustees need to dedicate a good deal of time and attention to properly overseeing their funds, and need be trained in more than basic financial and actuarial practices to carry out their charge.

The focus on the mission of the institutional investor and the role that its investment policy and strategy plays in the larger economy and society are, I would argue, a way of moving institutional investors to work towards meeting the goals articulated in the preamble of the PRI. As a participant in the process of constructing the principles back in 2005, I can attest to how difficult it was to get a consensus around the preamble that simply said:

As institutional investors, we have a duty to act in the best long-term interests or our beneficiaries. In this fiduciary role, we believe that environmental, social, and corporate governance (ESG) issues can affect the performance of investment portfolios (to varying degrees across companies, sectors, regions, asset classes, and through time). We also recognize that applying these Principles may better align investors with broader objectives of society. There, where consistent with our fiduciary duties, we commit to the following.

The preamble, to my mind, centres the discussion about fiduciary behaviour on the need to act in members' long-term interest, but also clearly acknowledges the interdependence on the larger society as well that I believe has been sorely missing in recent years. Moreover, each of the six principles commits members to be active in trying to insure that this interdependence is central to how investments are made, and to report to their members and the larger community on their progress. Now, none of this is to suggest that the PRI, or any other such organization, is the key to insuring that another global financial crisis is avoided. Yet, it is my fervent belief that the PRI offers fiduciaries a place to collaborate on how to better align the long-term interests of fund members and the larger society, which is clearly a first step that fiduciaries can take to avoid another financial crisis.

Chapter 5
From Fiduciary Duties to Fiduciary Relationships for SRI: Responding to the Will of Beneficiaries

Benjamin J. Richardson

5.1 A Neglected Aspect of Fiduciary Finance

There has been a long-standing debate regarding the legality of SRI (Langbein & Posner, 1980), which in recent years has focused on the "financial materiality" of environmental, social and governance (ESG) issues to investment performance as a legal justification for SRI (Gay & Klaassen, 2005; Richardson, 2007a; Martin 2009). However, little attention has been given to whether financial institutions subject to fiduciary duties do, and should, engage in SRI if it fulfills the will of their beneficiaries. The Freshfields Report (UNEP FI, 2005) briefly acknowledged this issue, but did not explore its full legal and practical ramifications. This chapter elucidates the scope for giving effect to the will of beneficiaries under current fiduciary law and, considers how that law could be adjusted to realize the will of beneficiaries in a more participatory fiduciary relationship.

A "fiduciary" is a person holding the character of a trustee, being charged to act primarily for another's benefit with regard to specific property or affairs. Among the various types of relationships that the law has characterized as having a fiduciary character are those that exist in investment institutions between those who manage the assets and the beneficiaries or members who contribute capital. At common law and in legislation, therefore, investment decision-makers may be impressed with fiduciary status and, consequently, owe specific obligations to beneficiaries. These include a duty to act with loyalty for the benefit of the beneficiaries and a duty to act reasonably and prudently.

It should be noted that some commentators suggest that these duties should be described as elements of trust law rather than fiduciary law. Flannigan, for example, contends that the function of fiduciary law, based on its traditional jurisprudence,

This chapter is a republished article that first appeared in the inaugural edition of the Journal of Sustainable Finance and Investment in 2011.

B.J. Richardson (✉)
Faculty of Law, University of British Columbia, Vancouver, BC, Canada V6T 1Z1
e-mail: richardson@law.ubc.ca

T. Hebb (ed.), *The Next Generation of Responsible Investing*,
Advances in Business Ethics Research 1, DOI 10.1007/978-94-007-2348-1_5,

is merely to control opportunism and self-interested behaviour in those situations in which "an actor has access to the assets of another for a defined or limited purpose" (Flannigan, 2004, 281). Thus, the fiduciary accountability of trustees should be regarded as functionally distinct from other specific legal duties in trust law, such as to invest prudently. To commingle trust law (or other sources of legal duties) with fiduciary law might thus be problematic given that, as Flannigan believes, "there are different triggers for liability . . . and different remedial consequences" (Flannigan, 2009, 425). Nonetheless, apart from the fact that many scholars ignore or gloss over this distinction (Birks, 2002; Hudson, 2007), whether we label the duties of institutional investors as part of fiduciary law or trust law, the underlying norms regarding how fund managers or trustees must act with regard to beneficiaries remain.

That the law may allow SRI to fulfill the wishes of the beneficiaries is a complex issue. Where investors act for themselves, there is of course no legal obstacle to SRI since a fiduciary relationship does not exist. But where such a relationship governs investment decisions, if the beneficiaries are unanimous in their views about SRI, trustees may and perhaps even should take those views into account as part of their consideration of the beneficiaries' "best interests." However, some SRI issues involve deeply contested moral dilemmas for which there is no established ethical custom, or there are at least significant differences of opinion regarding how to address the issue and at what cost.

By focusing on the will of beneficiaries, in this chapter I wish to broaden the SRI debate beyond current analyses of fiduciary duties to consider the broader context of the fiduciary *relationship* between trustees and beneficiaries. In attempting to illuminate the current state of the law, and how it should be reformed to improve the voice of beneficiaries in SRI, the following legal and practical questions are addressed in this chapter. Firstly, while it is widely agreed that trustees must act in the "best interests" of beneficiaries, how are those interests to be deciphered and can beneficiaries instruct trustees on how they should act? Secondly, because a financial institution, such as a pension fund, typically has many beneficiaries, may a trustee act when there is an absence of unanimity among them regarding the desirability of SRI? Thirdly, to what extent may evidence of social customs, as expressed for example in international treaties or national legislation, be a proxy for the will of beneficiaries upon which trustees could act? Similarly, may the interests of third parties such as local communities or other organizations be lawfully taken into consideration by trustees looking for a wider social mandate? Fourthly, without a consensus of opinion among beneficiaries or established social customs, to what extent may trustees rely on consultation processes or even having beneficiaries' representatives appointed to governing boards as a basis for engaging in SRI? Finally, what potential legal reforms could help strengthen the fiduciary relationship as a basis for financially prudent and democratically-based SRI decisions?

In addressing these questions, this chapter focuses on common law jurisdictions, such as the United Kingdom and United States, where the concept of fiduciary duties originated and is most well established. Some functionally equivalent fiduciary norms exist in civil law systems as a result of financial markets legislation.

The chapter is structured as follows. Section 5.2 examines the legal relationship between trustees and beneficiaries, including both how trustees' duty to treat different beneficiaries even-handedly and the traditionally passive role of beneficiaries has hindered beneficiaries from exerting a voice for SRI. Having analysed the basic legal obstacles, Section 5.3 examines some practical challenges to ascertaining the will of beneficiaries as a means of SRI. It considers the impact of a lack of unanimity among beneficiaries, whether fiduciaries can rely on widely-held social customs and consideration of third parties' interests as a proxy for the will of beneficiaries, and the scope of statutory reforms to democratise fund governance. Section 5.4 canvasses some potential legal reforms to strengthen reliance on the will of beneficiaries as a means of SRI. Section 5.5 summarises the chapter's principal findings. The normative rationale for SRI is not explored in this chapter. My other publications discussed such issues (Richardson, 2008, 2009), which do not need to be repeated here for the purposes of this chapter.

5.2 The Trustee-Beneficiary Legal Relationship

5.2.1 The Passive Beneficiary

The legal relationship between trustees and beneficiaries is governed by several duties that serve to ensure that trustees do not act contrary to the interests of the beneficiaries. The idea that there is a *relationship* between the parties has been obscured because traditionally trust law cast beneficiaries into a *passive* role. They are entitled to be informed about the administration of the trust assets, but they traditionally have not enjoyed unqualified rights to be consulted or to instruct trustees on how they should undertake their responsibilities in the absence of legislative provisions. Consequently, the potentiality of basing SRI decisions on the will of the beneficiaries has been legally obscured and hindered.

Rather than treating beneficiaries as self-governing and responsible owners of assets, the trust provides a legal fiction whereby ownership and control become separated, with the owners (beneficiaries) assuming a subservient role while control is vested in trustees to act on their behalf (Watt, 2006). Trustees, unlike an agent who is subject to control of his or her principal, are not legally obliged to consult with beneficiaries. They only need to act in their "best interests," yet they need not inquire what those best interests are. The beneficiaries' active rights reside mainly in their legal remedies for breaches of trust, but which require time-consuming and expensive litigation to secure.

This legal arrangement, which largely silences beneficiaries, has become the basic framework governing the relationship between investors and financial institutions in many countries. Historically, trusts arose in England primarily to protect family wealth and to provide for the wife and children, who were socially constructed as passive and dependent. Modern investment law transplanted these arrangements for the private trust into a very different context. The transplantation has ostensibly been successful because of the widespread assumption that investment management is a complex, specialist activity that few lay persons could competently undertake. It would require considerable input of their time and resources, which presumably few would wish to devote. Because of the common practice of trustees to delegate fund management to external providers, beneficiaries can become even further removed from ultimate decision-making. Thus, the fiduciary relationship has become cemented in the governance of financial institutions, such as pension funds, on the basis that investment decision-making is best left to full-time professionals.

Even in financial institutions whose legal architecture draws heavily on other legal norms including contract law, as for mutual funds, the notion that investors are expected to be largely passive has become well-entrenched as a matter of law and business practice. In the retail market, mutual funds operate on the assumption that most investors are not interested in getting involved in investment decisions because they are too busy or unqualified (Llewellyn, 2004, 10). While mutual fund investors on paper enjoy some rights—for example under the United States' *Investment Company Act* major decisions, such as a change to the fund's investment strategy, must obtain investors' approval—in practice, the label "mutual" is largely nominal in the governance of mutual funds (Bogle, 2005, 178–179).

As some financial institutions are constituted as actual corporations, for example banks and life insurance companies, shareholders may be considered among their approximate equivalent "beneficiaries."[1] Shareholders acquire relatively more voice in corporate affairs than analogous beneficiaries under a trust arrangement. They have rights to attend and vote at meetings, and file resolutions, in order to sway corporate policy (Nolan, 2006). However, various factors blunt shareholders' voice, especially when they are small, numerous, and dispersed. Legislation also commonly restricts the form and content of shareholder resolutions, while corporate management retains much control of the proxy voting process. And corporations' boards of directors, whom management tends to appoint in practice, can be ineffectual watchdogs for shareholders (Eaton, 1991). Some commentators, however, hail the rise of powerful institutional investors as majority shareholders as an answer to these problems (Black, 1992, 873–888).

Credit unions, in theory, are the most democratically-governed financial institutions (Arness & Howcroft, 2001). Organised as co-operatives, they are owned by those who use them, not by investors who only wish to make a profit from them. Voting in credit unions is based on a one-member, one-vote (regardless of financial stake), giving each a notionally equal voice in the management of their credit union. Further, the law typically allows any member to submit any issue for discussion of a meeting of credit union members, and they may participate in the management of credit unions (e.g., serving voluntarily on the governing board or

[1] Depositors, in the case of banks, and insurance policy-holders, in the case of insurers, are other parties who in certain circumstances might resemble "beneficiaries" in a fiduciary relationship.

advisory committees). But legal restrictions and market barriers have hindered the growth of credit unions, and they remain a relatively minor actor in the financial markets.

In many of these financial institutions policies to promote SRI may be found. These policies are not ordinarily derived from participatory processes involving lay investors. Rather, they are mostly based on the decisions of trustees, investment advisers and other financial experts. Yet, many financial trustees and managers appreciate the value of open, democratic decision-making, because they rely on such opportunities for undertaking corporate engagement, filing shareholder resolutions and other actions to exert a voice on behalf of their investors in the companies they hold (Hebb, 2008; Kanzer, 2009).

While the aim of this chapter is not to canvass the extensive, long-standing debates about the virtues or limitations of democratic decision-making, more participatory governance of financial institutions could provide another basis for SRI. The democratic process is one of the world's most influential and cherished ideals, providing the basis for people reaching collective decisions and effecting change. Democratic decision-making on social and environmental issues has been rationalized from both process and substantive perspectives (Spyke, 1999, 269–270). The latter reflects arguments that people's participation improves the substantive quality of decision-making. The former is based on claims that it bolsters the public accountability and legitimacy of those decisions. A particular value of participation for SRI is that it may help ground it in a process of ethical deliberation.

The seminal Freshfields Report on the legal framework for fiduciary finance, prepared by the London law firm on behalf of the United Nations Environment Programme Finance Initiative (UNEPFI), suggests that beneficiaries' wishes could underpin SRI decisions. It explains (Freshfields Bruckhaus Deringer, 2005, 12):

> [A] decision-maker may integrate ESG considerations into an investment decision to give effect to the views of the beneficiaries in relation to matters beyond financial return. Courts in the UK have recognised that trusts such as charities are entitled to exclude investments that conflict with their values and that the concept of beneficiaries' "best interests" under a general pension trust may extend beyond their financial interests to include their "views on moral and social matters." In a similar way, US law permits investments to be excluded where the beneficiaries so consent.

Despite this optimism, and to the dissatisfaction of some commentators (Sandberg, 2010), the Freshfields Report does not explain how it reaches such a conclusion or how, as a practical matter, beneficiaries would consent to SRI. While the duty of loyalty requires a trustee "to administer the trust solely in the interest of beneficiaries" (Serota & Brodie, 1995, 25), it does not necessarily require trustees to consult with or take advice from beneficiaries. Further, even if trustees can lawfully respond to the will of beneficiaries, the practicality of ascertaining what their will is, especially if they are not unanimous in their opinions, must be resolved.

5.2.2 Following Beneficiaries' Instructions

In analyzing the legal ramifications of this aspect of the Freshfields Report, it is important to consider whether trustees must follow the instructions of the beneficiaries. In other words, does the law allow beneficiaries to instruct trustees to adopt a policy for SRI or any other investment approach?

Trust law has recognised that beneficiaries may instruct trustees in some circumstances. The principle was established in 1841 in the English case of *Saunders v Vautier*.[2] It ruled that the sole beneficiary of a trust, if of the requisite legal capacity in terms of age and mental fitness, could request trustees to transfer property held by the trust to him, despite the trust deed envisioning transfer to occur only later in time. In such circumstances, fiduciary law is giving effect to the idea of the beneficiary as the absolute owner, which the trust is restraining. The principle has been recognised in subsequent English case law, and is illustrated in *Butt v Kelson*.[3] Here the trustees, who owned certain shares in the name of the trust, were held by the court to be obliged to vote in a shareholders' meeting as instructed by the beneficiaries. The principles established by these courts have been recognised in other jurisdictions, such as Australia.[4]

Such judicial precedents, however, do not mean that beneficiaries in *any* trust can issue *any* instructions. Most likely, they could issue instructions if the trust in question is a small, intimate arrangement, such as a private family trust, where all the beneficiaries are adults with full legal capacity, and if they strongly and unanimously take a particular view about a specific investment. In *Cowan v Scargill*, an English case involving a legal challenge to an SRI policy of the trade union trustees of the mineworkers' pension scheme, Robert Megarry V-C gave one example:

> Thus if the only actual or potential beneficiaries of a trust are all adults with very strict views on moral and social matters, condemning all forms of alcohol, tobacco and popular entertainment, as well as armaments, I can well understand that it might not be for the "benefit" of such beneficiaries to know that they are obtaining rather larger financial returns.[5]

Not only, as Megarry cautioned, are such cases likely to be rare, there is other case law and arguments that suggest limitations to beneficiaries' capacity to control trustees.[6] The United States Supreme Court in *Shelton v King*[7] long ago disavowed the idea that beneficiaries could alter the intent of testators or settlers (i.e., those who established the initial trust) by issuing instructions to the contrary. In Canada, the Ontario Law Reform Commission (1984, 74) has observed in its study of the law of trusts that "[t]o allow beneficiaries to direct the ongoing administration of the

---

[2] (1841) 4 Beav. 115, 49 E.R. 282, aff'd Cr. & Ph. 240, 41 E.R. 482.

[3] [1952] Ch. 197, [1952] 1 All E.R. 167 (C.A.).

[4] *See CPT Custodian Property Ltd. v. Commissioner of State Revenue; Commissioner of State Revenue v Karingal 2 Holdings Pty Ltd,* [2005] H.C.A. 53.

[5] [1985] Ch. 270, 288.

[6] See, e.g., *Re Brockbank* [1948] Ch. 206, [1948] 1 All E.R. 287.

[7] 229 US 90 (1913).

trust confuses the role of trustee and beneficiary and is inconsistent with the trust concept. If the creator of a trust wishes the beneficiary to be actively involved in the administration of the trust, such person may always be appointed as trustee."

A further seminal consideration that militates against trustees acting without qualification on beneficiaries' instructions is that they have a duty to act prudently, which includes taking independent professional advice. To act blindly on beneficiaries' instructions without careful consideration of the wisdom of those instructions could cause legal problems. In the British case of *Martin v. City of Edinburgh District Council*, which involved a challenge to the legality of a policy of the District Council to divest from South African assets, Lord Murray stressed that: "It is their duty to obtain and take into consideration professional advice on whether proposed investment switches are in the interests of the beneficiaries ...."[8]

Importantly, if beneficiaries can instruct trustees, and thereby acquire significant powers of control over investment decisions, trustees could be considered the beneficiaries' agents. Consequently, beneficiaries might be liable as principals to third parties for any losses, such as in tort or contract law. The extent to which common law jurisprudence recognises an agency relationship in a trust where beneficiaries exert control, has been contested by legal scholars (Flannigan, 2006a, 2006b; Cullity, 1985–86). The willingness of United States courts to permit actions against beneficiaries has largely been based on the principle of subrogation, such as in relation to contracts made for their benefit (Cullity, 1985–86, 48). In Canada, beneficiary investors incurred liability in *Trident Holdings Ltd. v. Danand Investments Ltd*,[9] which concerned a bare trust in which the trustees lacked discretionary powers and were considered effectively to be in an agency relationship with the beneficiaries. While beneficiaries' risk of liability may be considered slight in investment funds because the trust instrument is commonly drafted to exclude the default duty of beneficiaries to indemnify trustees for any losses, or because a limited liability corporate structure may shield the ultimate investors, these and other safeguards are not always effective (Flannigan, 2006a, 276).

5.2.3 Treating Beneficiaries Even-Handedly

Another complication with the notion that beneficiaries can instruct trustees arises where the trust has several beneficiaries (Moffat, Bean, & Dewar, 2005, 59). What if they are not unanimous in their views on how the trust should be administered or its assets invested? This issue brings to the fore the distinctive legal duty to act *impartially* towards beneficiaries.

Essentially, this duty requires a trustee to treat different beneficiaries equitably. In another case disputing the legality of SRI, *Harries and others v. Church Commissioners for England*, Donald Nicholls V-C ruled that: "trustees should not

[8] 1988 S.L.T. 329, 332.

[9] (1988) 49 D.L.R. (4th) 1, 64 O.R. (2d) 65, 25 O.A.C. 378 (C.A.).

make investment decisions on the basis of preferring one view of whether on moral grounds an investment conflicts with the objects of the charity over another. This is so even when one view is more widely supported than the other."[10] Consequently, if a trustee adopted a policy of SRI to please some beneficiaries, and incurs a financial loss, a breach of this duty to the non-SRI beneficiaries could occur (Dobris, 2008, 761).

The duty of impartiality is subject to modification in the governing trust instrument. As the authoritative United States' *Uniform Trust Code* states, the trustee must treat the beneficiaries equally "*in light of the purposes and terms of the trust.*"[11] Otherwise, trustees must treat beneficiaries even-handedly. The American Law Institute's third *Restatement of Law, Trusts* (2003, s. 79.1) explains: "In what might be called the 'substantive' aspects of impartiality ... trustees [must] make diligent and good-faith efforts to identify, respect, and balance the various beneficial interests when carrying out the trustees' fiduciary responsibilities." However, it would surely be rare for a trust instrument to specify that trustees could give precedence to the ethical values of one group of beneficiaries over another group to whom they are otherwise equally accountable.

One situation, however, where an SRI policy could be acceptable in the absence of a consensus of opinion is where there are several classes of beneficiaries spanning different generations. American case law recognises that the duty of impartiality can include an intergenerational equity dimension, behoving trustees to consider the long-term consequences of their investment decisions. In *Withers v. Teachers' Retirement System*, the Federal District Court held that the New York City pension fund must "manage the fund so as to enable it to meet its obligations not only to current retirees, but also to those scheduled to retire in the future."[12] Conceivably, on this basis therefore, trustees could justify SRI that focused on long-term, sustainable investment as a way to ensure that investments could meet the needs of future beneficiaries even if this approach reduced financial returns for current retirees of the pension plan.

In recognition of the potentially divergent opinions among beneficiaries regarding SRI, as well as how beneficiaries are assuming greater financial risk under defined contribution pension plans, some governments have enacted legislation that allows beneficiaries to choose the investment portfolio that best matches their ethical and financial preferences. Australia's *Superannuation Legislation Amendment (Choice of Superannuation Funds) Act* of 2004 gives employees the right to choose to some extent the investment portfolio into which their compulsory superannuation contributions are paid. In the United States, the vast majority of private sector defined contribution pension plans also offer a large number of investment options, pursuant to the section 401(k) retirement savings plans established for workers covered by the *Employment Retirement Income Security Act* of 1974. In

[10] [1992] 1 W.L.R. 1241, 1247.

[11] (2000), s. 803.

[12] 447 F. Supp. 1248 (S.D.N.Y. 1978), 1257–58.

both jurisdictions, SRI funds may be included among the portfolio options offered to employees.

While it can thus be seen that trustees are not ordinarily obliged to heed the views of the beneficiaries, they must still act in their best interests. To act loyally not only requires being able to demonstrate that a fiduciary decision serves the "interests" of the beneficiaries; it may also permit trustees to take active steps to ascertain their views, especially where considerable discretionary judgment is involved in the exercise of trust powers. The practical challenges of doing so are canvassed in the next section.

5.3 Ascertaining the Will of Beneficiaries

5.3.1 Finding Unanimity

In light of the foregoing analysis, a trustee could probably only give effect to any overt desire among beneficiaries for SRI where there is unanimity among them. According to the Freshfields Report (UNEP FI, 2005, 12), "a decision maker who chooses to exclude an investment or category of investments on this basis will need to be able to point to a consensus amongst the beneficiaries in support of the exclusion." But how likely is such a situation?

A cursory analysis suggests the likelihood of beneficiaries of a particular fund holding similar views on the desirability of SRI would be far-fetched. Disagreements over social values are rife in modern society (Zimmerman, 1994). Disputes often arise over the environmental consequences of economic developments, which human rights deserve respect, and a host of other ethical issues. There is little doubt that investors have similarly diverse values. Legal commentators sceptical of the legality of SRI have observed that "[w]hat is considered to be 'ethical' in investment terms is inherently subjective, imprecise and continually changing with altered societal perspectives" (Thornton, 2008, 419). It is thus not surprising that an advisory committee of the Ontario Teachers' Pension Plan Board (2005, 18) spoke of the following challenges to SRI:

> The committee does not recommend any attempt to put definitive screens, either positive or negative, in place. We feel that any attempt to satisfy some particular part of the membership by being definitive about the kinds of investments to be prohibited would simply lead some other part of the membership to feel disadvantaged, or worse, disenfranchised in the decision making process. At worst, screens could lead to litigation on the part of those who feel that the risk accepted or returns realized had negatively affected their pension promise.

Unanimity on ethical issues can be difficult to establish even within groups ostensibly sharing the same fundamental beliefs, such as among religious investors. In *Harries and others v. Church Commissioners for England*, the court observed that "different minds within the Church of England, applying the highest moral standards, will reach different conclusions" as to the merits of a particular investment.[13] Accordingly, the Church Commissioners were vindicated in their decision not to prefer one ethical view to another "beyond the point at which they would incur a risk of significant financial detriment."[14]

If beneficiaries do not presently share agreement on what is "ethical" or "socially responsible," could they do so through education and dialogue? We might view this as a hopelessly naive aspiration, given the likelihood of investors' apathy or the risk of relentless squabbling among the few active participants. Yet, theories of ethical and democratic deliberation suggest that social values can evolve among participants through appropriately structured forums for reasoned discussion (Pateman, 1970; Barber, 1984). Process-oriented legal scholarship and deliberative democratic models emphasise the potential of participatory and transparent decision-making procedures for engineering changes in social values and practices (Gutmann & Thompson, 2002; Richardson & Razzaque, 2006). The SRI community itself has promoted more consultative processes as a means of education and consensus-building, as is evident for example in the Global Reporting Initiative's multi-stakeholder consultation process and the UNEPFI's working groups and round-tables. If ethical deliberation is to be harnessed as a means of developing beneficiaries' will on SRI, legal changes are likely necessary to enhance their participation rights in investment decision-making (as discussed later in this chapter).

Academic research that has scrutinised the psychological and socio-economic characteristics of individual social investors and their opinions on various ethical matters, suggests that ethical deliberation must bridge some significant differences of opinion. Some empirical studies suggest that many such investors are unwilling to be altruistic if they would incur a financial loss (Rosen, Sandler, & Shani, 1991; McLachlan & Gardner, 2004; Lewis & Webley, 1994; Nilsson, 2009). Self-styled ethical investors also may hold investments in regular funds, confirming the inclination for financial returns (Lewis & Mackenzie, 2000). Conversely, some surveys suggest that most social investors support SRI causes even if they under-perform the market (Williams, 2007; Beal, Goyen, & Phillips, 2005). Research has also found differences among social investors concerning which SRI issues they care about the most; one study identified military equipment, tobacco and gambling as common concerns (Anand & Cowton, 1993), while another concluded that environmental protection and labour relations were more salient (Rosen et al., 1991). Current research thus suggests that social investors have fairly diverse values; presumably, the heterogeneity of values among "regular" investors is even greater.

Another variable that likely influences attainment of unanimity among investors is the type of financial institution they belong to. Most of the research discussed above has canvassed social investors belonging to dedicated SRI funds, where one would expect to find a relatively high convergence of opinion. In the mutual fund sector, investors can shop for an investment product tailored to their own values

[13] [1992] 1 W.L.R. 1241, 1251.

[14] Ibid.

without the need for agreement with their peers. SRI funds typically do not design their investment policies on the basis of any formal voting among members, and most do not promote their participation in investment decision-making (Cowton, 1999, 64). In an occupational pension fund, whose members come from a specific organisation or distinct locality, there might be less divergence of opinion among beneficiaries than in a life insurance company whose policy-holders or shareholders are typically drawn from a wide cross-section of society. Disagreement on SRI issues would presumably be greatest in a national fund, such as the Canada Pension Plan, whose beneficiaries would comprise most of the country's adult population.

A further consideration is what exactly are beneficiaries expected to agree on? The simplest choice would be whether to boycott a specific company or country (one historical example is the divestment campaign against South Africa's former apartheid regime). But it would be more difficult to ascertain the will of beneficiaries on an assortment of fluctuating social and environmental issues, such as climate change, labour standards and human rights. There would simply be too many issues to survey, as well as the challenge of integrating beneficiaries' views into a coherent SRI policy. Furthermore, even if beneficiaries could agree on the substantive ethical issues, such as to protect animal welfare or reduce carbon emissions, they could still disagree on the extent to which financial returns should be sacrificed to avoid unethical conduct.

Alternatively, ascertaining beneficiaries' views on the general *principles* to guide SRI decisions might be feasible. The aim would be to reach agreement on the norms governing *how* decisions should be made, rather than any tedious case-by-case consideration of the social and environmental ramifications of individual proposed investments. This approach could be undertaken, to illustrate, by requiring that any company proposed for an investment portfolio have an unblemished record of compliance with environmental regulations, be certified under a rigorous performance standard (e.g., ISO 14001)[15] or be a member of a credible SRI stock market index (e.g., Dow Jones Sustainability Indexes).[16] Through this approach, therefore, trustees would follow agreed decision-making principles as a framework for taking ESG issues into account.

5.3.2 *Following Social Customs*

Another approach to act on the will of beneficiaries is to consider the values of the society they belong to. The Freshfields Report (UNEP FI, 2005, 96) suggests that trustees could rely on well-established social customs as, in effect, a proxy for the values of the beneficiaries:

---

[15] The International Organization for Standardization, at http://www.iso14000-iso14001-environmental-management.com.

[16] See http://www.sustainability-index.com.

> There will be a class of investments that could reasonably be assumed offensive to the average beneficiary such that they could lawfully be excluded from an investment portfolio without all the beneficiaries' express consent. That class of investments will not be fixed and a conservative approach is advisable, but the types of investment that might fall into that class include investments that are linked to clear breaches of widely recognised norms, such as international conventions on human rights, labour conditions, tackling corruption and environmental protection.

One reason why such social customs could be considered a *proxy* for the value of beneficiaries is, as Gifford (2004, 141) explains, that "given the ubiquity of pension fund membership, especially in the developed world, it can also be argued that the interests of members of funds are broadly consistent with those of the society in which the members live." But whether trustees could rely on such social customs only when it is impractical to ascertain the views of the beneficiaries is unclear from the Freshfields Report. Quite possibly, trustees could not base an SRI policy on such social conventions if the views of beneficiaries on such issues had been explicitly conveyed to the contrary.

Interestingly, the successor report by UNEP FI (2009, 26) retreats somewhat from the Freshfields' position on the salience of social customs. It states:

> [A] pension fund in its Statement of Investment Principles ... may amplify its requirements for monitoring and assessment of ESG considerations. This may be achieved by using examples of a few international law treaties or conventions and/or voluntary guidelines or principles *which the investment industry accepts widely as relevant and having a material effect on investment value* (my emphasis).

Thus, even if a social custom reflects a very widely-held value, this UNEPFI report suggests it would still need to have financial significance to the investment portfolio before trustees could take it into account. However, other legal commentators make no mention of a financial salience criterion; Scott and Fratcher (1988, s. 227.17) explains that trustees "may consider such matters as pollution, race discrimination, fair employment and consumer responsibility" when making investment decisions.

There are numerous international treaties governing issues of interest to social investors, including environmental protection (at least 500 such treaties and other international instruments),[17] human rights (some 300 instruments),[18] and labour standards (nearly 200 treaties).[19] Some are widely ratified and thus putatively reflect a near-consensus of international opinion. They include the 1992 *Convention on Biological Diversity* (adopted by approximately 190 states) and the 1966 *Convention on the Elimination of All Forms of Racial Discrimination* (adopted by nearly 175

---

[17] The Ecolex project sponsored by several United Nations identifies at least 520 international environmental treaties: http://www.ecolex.org.

[18] Consider the list complied by the UN High Commissioner for Human Rights: http://www2.ohchr.org/english/law.

[19] International Labour Organization, ILOLEX: Database of International Labour Standards: http://www.ilo.org/ilolex/english/convdisp1.htm.

states). Some institutional investors rely on such treaties as a benchmark for consideration of ESG issues. The Ethical Investment Research Service (EIRIS) in Britain offers a service for fund managers called "Convention Watch," whereby it scrutinises companies for their compliance with various international treaties and other global instruments.[20] The Guardians of the New Zealand Superannuation Fund (2007, 5), whose governing legislation requires in section 58(2)(c) that their investments "avoid prejudice to New Zealand's reputation as a responsible member of the world community," relies on compliance with the *UN Global Compact* and international treaties to assess corporations.

However, relying on international treaties or other evidence of social mores to legitimate fiduciary finance faces difficulties. First, while certain social norms, as embodied in international treaties or national laws, reflect to a large extent democratically-determined decisions, invariably not everyone agrees with them. For instance, some environmental laws involve ethical trade-offs between nature conservation and poverty alleviation (Peritore, 1999). Second, many environmental standards and human rights are too vague to provide concrete guidance. To illustrate, the *Convention on Biological Diversity* states in article 10 that: "Each Contracting Party shall, as far as possible and as appropriate: ... encourage cooperation between its governmental authorities and its private sector in developing methods for sustainable use of biological resources." This and other clauses in this treaty may be interpreted in various ways to justify divergent actions. The drawback, therefore, with such open-ended standards is that fund managers or trustees may make decisions contrary to the expectations of many others.

5.3.3 Third Party Stakeholders

Closely related to the previous discussion of whether the fiduciary relationship can be informed by established social customs as a proxy for the will of beneficiaries, we must ask whether trustees could also take into account the views of third party stakeholders, such as community groups, as both an indicator of such social mores and as a means of fulfilling a socially responsible agenda. It is a controversial issue, and one seemingly directly at odds with the essence of a fiduciary relationship tethered to a trustee's exclusive loyalty to the beneficiaries. The principal objection to any dilution of this exclusivity is that it would unduly complicate decision-making and foster agency problems. Marcoux (2005, 4) explains that "the nature of the fiduciary relationship is such that it is impossible for one to act as a fiduciary for multiple parties where the interests of those parties are (or are likely to be) in conflict." If fiduciaries must also serve other constituencies, their decisions might degenerate into an arbitrary balancing of competing interests or could cloak self-interested choices by trustees emboldened by greater discretionary power.

[20] See http://www.eiris.org.

Yet, even if this objection is plausible, already the fiduciary duty to act in the best interest of beneficiaries has been interpreted by courts and regulators in some jurisdictions as at least not prohibiting decisions that provide collateral benefits to others (e.g., to a local community or another organisation). In the United States, the *Employee Retirement Income Security Act* (ERISA) has been interpreted by the federal Department of Labor as "not preclud[ing] consideration of collateral benefits, such as those offered by a 'socially-responsible' fund" (Doyle, 1998). In *Donovan* v. *Walton*, the court observed that "ERISA . . . simply does not prohibit a party other than a plan's participants and beneficiaries from benefiting in some measure from a prudent transaction with the plan."[21] A further consideration is that conceivably the "best interests" of beneficiaries could include explicitly taking the welfare of third parties into account, especially if the governing trust instrument states such intentions.

In the related area of corporate governance, courts and legislators have gradually broadened directors' fiduciary responsibilities and powers to permit some consideration of outside interests, such as those of employees, consumers, creditors, and other parties with whom the corporation has contractual or other relationships that may affect its financial success. This represents a departure from the traditional legal doctrine that directors' owe fiduciary duties exclusively to the company or the firm and its shareholders. The trend began when courts approved of directors making charitable donations with company assets (Adams & Knutsen, 1995). In 2004 the Supreme Court of Canada ruled in *Peoples Department Stores v Wise* that directors may consider factors beyond the short-term maximization of the value of the company, such as "consumers, governments and the environment."[22] Likewise, the United Kingdom's *Companies Act* of 2006, which Williams and Conley (2007, 354) salute as "close to a stakeholder model of director's duties," permits by section 172(1) company directors to consider community and environmental impacts among issues relevant to promoting their company's financial success. Another approach, found in the United States, is the so-called "constituency statute," authorizing directors to consider the effects of their decisions on specific categories of stakeholders, such as employees, suppliers, customers, and local communities (Bainbridge, 1992). A limitation of all of these models is that third parties cannot normally *oblige* company directors to take their interests into account. There is a material difference between being able to consider the welfare of other parties and *owing a duty* to them. Thus, outside stakeholders without legal remedies risk having their interests ignored.

While we should be careful about analogizing how fiduciary duties apply in corporate governance to all financial institutions, given that corporations are generally embedded in a much wider and more complex array of legal and business relationships, the analogy is pertinent for some reasons. Firstly, some financiers have a corporate personality, such as banks, and are immersed in similarly complex social

---

[21] *Donovan* v. *Walton*, 609 F. Supp. 1221 (D.C. Fla. 1985), 1245.

[22] [2004] 3 S.C.R. 461, 2004 S.C.C. 68, para. 42.

relationships that may engender fiduciary-like responsibilities. Secondly, environmental and community groups are helping to illuminate the connections between finance and its social effects, thus creating legal and financial risks for investors who are perceived to profit from environmental degradation or human rights violations (Waygood, 2006). Some experts thus suggest there is an emerging fiduciary duty to consider the financial risks associated with climate change (Mercer Investment Consulting, 2005) and treatment of human rights (Williams & Conley, 2005, 76–77). Thirdly, legislation may sometimes impose specific obligations on financiers to consider the interests of third parties. One example is the United States' *Community Reinvestment Act* of 1977, which obliges commercial banks to improve access to affordable banking services to the local communities in which they are chartered.

In conclusion, the fiduciary relationship is increasingly viewed by some regulators and investors as not simply a bilateral relationship between financial trustees and beneficiaries. Rather, it may also encompass third parties potentially affected by their investment decisions. While we have yet to reach a situation where third parties have legally enforceable claims, at least trustees are beginning to have a legal mandate to take their interests into account.

5.3.4 Consultation with and Representation of Beneficiaries

Democratizing the governance of funds can provide a means by which the will of beneficiaries can be expressed. This approach can be rationalised from an SRI perspective on the basis that if we expect financial entities to be more accountable for the social and environmental consequences of their investments, then the ultimate owners of capital should have more voice in the determination of those investments. By providing for representation of beneficiaries in fund governance, it might no longer be necessary for trustees to find a consensus among beneficiaries in order to take ESG issues into account. Rather, through beneficiaries' representatives such issues would be considered and ultimately decided by the governing board. In an ordinary trust, the trustees cannot make decisions unless they are unanimous, but legislation commonly allows trustees to make decisions by a majority vote.

Being a representative of beneficiaries however does not under fiduciary law allow a trustee to consider him or herself an *agent* of the beneficiaries, acting only on instructions given. In *Cowan v Scargill*, the court held that trustees who could be considered as having been appointed in a representative capacity would violate their duties if, instead of applying their minds independently to a fiduciary issue which was before them, they merely followed a policy decision of the body (in this case the National Union of Mineworkers) which they might be regarded as representing.[23] Robert Megarry V-C rejected the suggestion that the defendants' impugned investment policy could be justified because it was consistent with the majority views of a

[23] [1985] Ch. 270, 293.

representative body of beneficiaries as expressed by their investment policy adopted by their union at their annual conference.

Several jurisdictions have legislated for employees' representation on pension fund boards. It has proven controversial in some cases, leading to claims that investment decision-making has become more "politicised," creating conflict rather than consensus (Hess, 2005; Taylor, 1986). In addition, Canadian researchers Weststar and Verma (2007) have observed that "labor trustees ... face many challenges acquiring the skills, knowledge and networks to assist them in becoming active and integrated participants on the pension board." Among the statutory reforms, in Britain, amendments to the *Pensions Act* in 2004 prescribed that "at least one-third" of the trustees must be "member-nominated" (section 241(1)(a)) and the government may enact regulations to raise this number to one-half member-nominated trustees (section 243(1)). Australia's *Superannuation Industry (Supervision) (SIS) Act* of 1993 mandates 50 percent member representation on trustee boards of funds that have at least five members (section 89). Likewise, South African's *Pension Funds Act*, 1956, as amended, mandates at least 50 percent member representation on trustee boards (section 7A). Representation of employees in the governing boards of pension funds also occurs in several continental European countries, including Denmark, Switzerland and the Netherlands (Stewart & Yermo, 2008).

Financial trustees may also be subjected to a statutory duty to consult with their beneficiaries when formulating investment policies. In one of the few legislative mandates for SRI, Ontario's former *South African Trust Investments Act* of 1988 provided that, in the case of pension funds with at least 100 beneficiaries, the trustees could refuse to acquire or dispose of a South African investment once they had made inquiries and had reasonable grounds for believing that most beneficiaries would consent and that they held a majority of the beneficial interests in the pension fund's assets. The concept of a "duty to consult" in fiduciary law has been most strongly developed by Canadian courts in the context of the government's obligations to Aboriginal peoples (Richardson, 2007b). Courts have held that such a duty arises when the government (federal or provincial) contemplates conduct that might adversely affect Aboriginal rights (Lawrence & Macklem, 2000). A duty to consult, however, is not per se tantamount to a duty to accommodate; trustees being required to ascertain the views of beneficiaries do not necessarily have to give effect to their wishes.

A related legislative trend in some jurisdictions is strengthening the informational rights of beneficiaries, by requiring trustees to disclose their investment policies including with regard to SRI. Such reforms have been introduced in several European states and Australia, obliging occupational pension funds to disclose their SRI policies, if any.[24] The regulations however do not *oblige* these funds to follow SRI. Another reform, adopted in Canada and the United States, requires mutual

[24] For example, UK's *Occupational Pension Schemes (Investment) Regulations*, 2005: cl. 2(3)(b)(vi)-(3)(c); Australia's *Corporations Act*, 2001 (Cth), s. 1013D(1)(l); France's *Projet de loi sur l'épargne salariale* (7 February, 2001). No 2001-152, arts 21, 23.

funds to disclose their shareholding proxy voting policies and voting records.[25] Its purpose includes discouraging fund managers from passively colluding with corporate management, and through a more active proxy process to improve the quality of corporate governance. Research on implementation of some of these standards however reveals shortcomings, with mandated disclosures sometimes leading to vague, boilerplate statements that do not illuminate the methodology behind SRI decisions or the quality of their implementation (Gribben & Faruk, 2004; Fair Pensions, 2006).

These legislative reforms, largely confined to the pension fund sector, have been driven by several developments which provide insights into how democratizing decisions can be rationalized. Because occupational pension plans are often an indelible part of the employment relationship, there has been pressure to extend participation of employees in workplace decisions to their pension funds (Gates, 1998; Fung, Hebb, & Rogers, 2001). The shift from defined-benefit (DB) to defined-contribution (DC) pension plans has further strengthened the case for giving members more voice. As beneficiaries are exposed to greater financial risks to their retirement plans, the argument grows that they should have more say in making investment decisions (Monks & Minow, 1991, 223). OECD (2004, 5.16, 5.24) guidelines on occupational pension regulation recommend that beneficiaries in DC plans be allowed to choose their investment options. More voice to beneficiaries is particularly important when beneficiaries have limited ability to transfer their savings elsewhere. Unlike mutual fund investors, members of occupational pension plans often cannot readily withdraw their contributions unless they change jobs and join a different pension plan.

But does democratizing investment decision-making in such a manner make SRI more likely? Are beneficiaries more likely to demand socially responsible decisions if they can be heard? The current anecdotal evidence suggests a modest correlation. More democratically-governed funds sometimes appear to be at the forefront of SRI. A pioneering research program on United States public pension plans and urban revitalization coordinated by Harvard University and Oxford University has documented a wealth of case studies of investors partnering with community development associations and local financial intermediaries to promote urban renewal and community economic development (Clark, Hebb, & Hagerman, 2004). Tessa Hebb's (2008) landmark study on pension fund engagement in North America found that public sector funds such as CalPERS were more committed than private pension funds to engage with companies on SRI issues, partly because of the greater presence of member-nominated trustees and trade union-influence in pension plan governance. An earlier Canadian study on the impact of union representation in pension funds found "some evidence that union involvement is facilitative of social investment" (Quarter & Carmichael, 2001, 108).

[25] Securities Exchange Commission (SEC), "Disclosure of Proxy Voting Policies and Proxy Voting Records by Registered Management Investment Companies" (SEC, January 31, 2003); Canadian Securities Administrators (CSA), *National Instrument 81–106 Investment Fund Continuous Disclosure and Companion Policy 81–106 CP* (CSA, 2005).

Conversely, some empirical research suggests that the views of pension fund members in practice tend to carry little weight in investment decisions (Alexander, 1993, 113). A 2005 survey of British occupational pension fund trustees revealed that 53 percent of respondents attached "no significance" and only 13 percent attached "great significance" to the views of their members when considering ESG issues in their investment policies (Gribben & Gitsham, 2006, 14). Even among dedicated SRI funds in the mutual fund industry, while a few may informally survey their members periodically for their views on SRI, most funds generally do not provide forums for active dialogue among investors nor encourage their participation in investment policy-making (Richardson, 2008, 275).

Such anecdotal evidence perhaps points to the limitations of current participatory mechanisms in fund governance. But it is preferable to give beneficiaries more formal opportunities to be heard than to rely on informal and less transparent and accountable arrangements. Strengthening their voice in fund governance, by legal rights either to be consulted or represented on boards, provides a concrete way to convey their views and to enable trustees to make investment decisions legitimated by the imprimatur of the democratic process. It could even provide a framework for ethical deliberation to guide SRI. Such an approach could herald a significant evolution in the nature of the fiduciary relationship, away from the traditionally subservient role of beneficiaries.

5.4 Options for Legal Reform

The legal framework governing fiduciary finance relationships is unlikely to remain unchanged; this chapter has identified several areas where modest reforms in some jurisdictions are underway already. It is thus worth concluding this chapter by canvassing briefly some further legal measures by which fiduciary finance could accommodate the will of beneficiaries. Ignoring reform is unrealistic given that both the recent global financial crisis and the burgeoning movement for SRI are intensifying pressure for improved social accountability of financial actors. It is becoming increasingly difficult to view fiduciary finance as just value-neutral investment transactions devoid of any ethical, social or environmental ramifications. The following suggestions are not tailored to any specific type of financial institution, but are intended as generic ideas to stimulate debate.

Perhaps the most feasible option, in terms of congruence with existing national fiduciary rules, is to strengthen current reforms to the internal governance of financial institutions. Beyond mandating appointment of more beneficiaries to governing boards and requiring trustees to consult periodically with beneficiaries, such as through surveys when proposing major investment policy decisions, the duty to consult could include a collateral duty on trustees *to consider* or *take into account* the views of beneficiaries. This would not necessarily oblige trustees to follow the opinions of beneficiaries, but would at least oblige trustees to consider carefully their views and to be able justify their final decisions.

The law could also mandate trustees to act, albeit within the purpose of the trust, without express unanimity among beneficiaries. It could authorize such decisions so long as they are satisfied that their decisions do not unduly or materially disadvantage one class of beneficiaries. Beneficiaries might even be able to at least agree on the broad *principles* governing an SRI policy, such as to favour investing in companies which belong to an approved SRI market index or which are certified under a credible sustainability performance standard. Otherwise, legislation could allow trustees to act on the wishes of beneficiaries where a specified substantial majority agreed, such as a large, three-quarters majority.

Such a reform, if it is to dovetail with current trust law, would need safeguards for minority beneficiaries in accordance with the duty of impartiality. Trustees could be required to demonstrate that any such SRI policy still fulfills the duty of care, such as by demonstrating the policy's financial prudence. Yet, because the latter safeguard could thus limit SRI decisions to those viewed as "financially material" to investment performance, it would not greatly improve the mandate for advancing SRI than what is available now. Hence, other mechanisms to safeguard the interests of a minority might be necessary. One option is to oblige trustees to offer alternative investment portfolios to different classes of beneficiaries, covering SRI and other investment approaches.

Legislating duties to consult and accommodate would also desirably need to be supplemented by a duty on trustees to inform beneficiaries and themselves about the nature of SRI and its financial and social effects and risks. Under fiduciary law, any beneficiary consent must be given on the basis of disclosure of all relevant information.[26] As previously mentioned, laws have been enacted in a number of jurisdictions requiring financial institutions to disclose their policies on SRI. They could be extended to require disclosure of how such policies are *implemented*, including evaluation of their impact and effectiveness in promoting socially responsible outcomes. Although such an approach creates additional compliance costs, informed consent perhaps warrants such a comprehensive approach.

Legislation could go further to oblige trustees to invest ethically and responsibly, or at least to clarify whether trustees could take into account certain significant social and environmental issues such as climate change (Woods, 2009). Financial institutions would, by this approach, start to resemble mission-based investors, which have an ethical charter in their trust deed. Similar suggestions have been made to return corporations to their origins in the nineteenth century as civic-minded institutions operating under public charters (Fraser, 1998). Contemporary reform is not unprecedented. In 2007, Oregon amended its *Business Corporations Act* to permit expressly an Oregon company's articles of incorporation to include a provision "authorizing or directing the corporation to conduct the business of the corporation in a manner which is environmentally and socially responsible."[27] While the effect of the Oregon legislation has yet to be ascertained, the law does not oblige companies to

---

[26] *Boardman v. Phipps* [1967] 2 A.C. 46, 101.

[27] Oregon Revised Statutes, 2007 s. 60.047(2)(e).

have such an objective—rather, they may choose to do so. More relevantly, in the financial sector, the managers of the national pension plans of Norway, Sweden and New Zealand are legislatively obliged to follow ethical and responsible investment policies.[28]

Of course, such imposed SRI legislative charters are seemingly at odds with the idea of a bottom-up approach to SRI derived from the unadulterated free will of beneficiaries. The principal justification for such an approach, as I have elaborated elsewhere (Richardson, 2009), is that the freedom to invest includes the responsibility to avoid sponsoring and profiting from environmentally harmful and socially unjust development. Hawley and Williams (2000) have also argued persuasively how it is in the self-interest of "universal" investors to be mindful of such considerations, because as economy-wide investors, they should have no interest in abetting behaviour by any one company that yields a short-term financial advantage while undermining the health of the economic systems in which the firms in which they invest are embedded. Thus, SRI-imposed mandates may be reconciled with the will of beneficiaries as paternalistic regulation to ensure beneficiaries do not advocate investments which in the long-term could be inimical to their own self-interest. Such SRI mandates would also invariably be written broadly, as current examples in Scandinavia and New Zealand are, to offer sufficient latitude for deliberation and choice by beneficiaries.

Alternatively or in addition to this approach, the law could provide new means by which trustees may accommodate social customs or third party interests. One option is to establish an ethics advisory council to provide advice or direction on social expectations for SRI. Trustees following its advice could be deemed to be acting in accordance with fiduciary standards. The government could appoint representatives from key constituencies to the council to ensure it is broadly representative of societal values. This idea is not as far-fetched as it might seem, as ethics councils have already been established for this purpose in relation to national pension plans in Norway and Sweden. The ethics advice of these Scandinavian councils is often based on well established international law. UNEPFI's (2007, 7) survey of the Swedish and Norwegian funds, among other examples of public sector pension plans, found "a range of some of the most advanced and creative approaches to responsible investment." Such an approach has yet to be adopted for private sector funds, and it would certainly be controversial. They might tolerate an ethics panel with a more restrained mandate, such as being responsible for setting general guidance and voluntary standards. Already, institutions such as the United Nations Principles for Responsible Investment to some extent play this role.

Ultimately, even with such reforms, trying to regularize SRI under fiduciary law by appealing to the will of beneficiaries or social customs is challenging. It is unlikely that there would be unanimity among beneficiaries in a large financial

---

[28] Sweden's *Lag om allmänna pensionsfonder (AP-Fonder), Svensk författningssamling* (2000): 192; Norway's ethical investment mandate was issued on December 22 2005 pursuant to *Regulation on the Management of the Government Pension Fund,* 2004; and New Zealand's Superannuation and Retirement Income Act 2001, ss. 58(2)(c) and 61(d).

institution regarding the desirability of SRI; at most, they might agree to some procedural standards or general principles to govern SRI decision-making. This approach, however, could generate new problems if trustees gain too much discretionary power to determine what is "socially responsible." Enhancing opportunities for more democratic deliberation among beneficiaries might also fail to engender change. The voices for ethical change could become drowned in arenas where typically money talks the loudest. Many beneficiaries might wish to eschew SRI altogether if they perceive it as too financially risky. Thus, more "democratic" decision-making might degenerate into an unsavoury battle of competing interests, rather than a harmonious dialogue towards an ethically-guided consensus. The seemingly easy solution would be to impose even more rigid SRI mandates by law, but that could be politically difficult and undermine the democratic basis to SRI.

5.5 Conclusions

Strengthening fiduciary relationships for SRI faces a difficult path. But the considerations canvassed in this chapter are hardly decisive reasons to shun reform or abandon further discussion. If we accept that the financial sector must share responsibility to promote socially just and environmentally sustainable development, as I have previously argued, it is imperative to promote public debate about how the fiduciary relationship can be restructured to promote SRI. While the pioneering Freshfields Report remarked that trustees can act on the will of beneficiaries, it overlooked various legal and practical difficulties.

This chapter has sought to contribute to knowledge of how fiduciary law affects SRI by focusing on the salience of the will of beneficiaries, and analysing the obstacles and opportunities to having trustees act on their will. It has also sought to explain why the voice of beneficiaries matters and how the law could be reformed to create a more democratic and accountable fiduciary relationship. Despite lingering ambiguities in the law, and uncertainties about how they should be reformed, the following conclusions can be reached.

First, trustees are generally not obliged to consult with or take instructions from beneficiaries, though they can be pursuant to specific legislation. It is regulation rather than fiduciary law that mostly enables the voice of beneficiaries to be heard. Only rarely, such as in a small, private trust with few beneficiaries, might they exert their views. Otherwise, trustees are free to interpret what is their "best interests" based on the terms of the governing trust deed.

In practice, unanimity among beneficiaries in a large financial institution on social, environmental and other ethical issues is unlikely to occur. While they might rarely agree on some general principles or procedures to govern SRI, and perhaps even concur to shun exceedingly controversial actions, such as investment in a country associated with genocide, on most SRI issues beneficiaries will have widely different opinions.

Third, trustees must ordinarily treat beneficiaries even-handedly, and thus cannot easily respond to the will of beneficiaries if there is no unanimity among them. Differential treatment is only possible if the trust deed or governing legislation allow it. The position of different classes of beneficiaries spanning several generations (e.g., present and future retirees of a pension fund) is one situation that may allow trustees to invest responsibly for the long-term to protect the interests of a specific group of beneficiaries.

Social customs and third parties may be considered by trustees, but primarily only as an adjunct means of fulfilling the best interests of beneficiaries. Such considerations might include avoiding investing in socially controversial activities posing financial risks. In many cases, however, a widespread social concern such as the threat of climate change will still involve significant disagreement about how to address the problem and at what cost.

A fifth finding of this chapter is that legislated mechanisms that provide for consultation with or appointment of beneficiaries as trustees do not alter the underlying fiduciary rules. Trustees must still treat all beneficiaries impartially, and they do not become an agent of beneficiaries. These statutory mechanisms are valuable primarily as a means to help trustees be better informed of what the interests of beneficiaries are, especially where trustees hold significant discretionary powers over beneficiaries' assets.

Finally, legal reforms are starting to tinker with the fiduciary relationship, and some options to strengthen the voice of beneficiaries in fund governance exist. The principal lesson is that there is a potential tension between, on the one hand, seeking to legislatively impose SRI mandates and, on the other, giving beneficiaries more independence to determine their own investment goals.

Reforming the fiduciary relationship in investment decisions remains worthwhile, because the voice of beneficiaries should be heard. If SRI becomes simply an imposed regulatory prescription or a means for trustees to advance their own social and political ideology, it may lose legitimacy and suffer accordingly.

Chapter 6
Effective Shareholder Engagement: The Factors that Contribute to Shareholder Salience

James Gifford

6.1 Introduction

Institutional investors are increasingly becoming active owners through voting their shares and engaging in dialogue with companies on a broad range of environmental, social and corporate governance (ESG) issues. This includes not only investors that consider themselves socially responsible investors but also mainstream investors. As of 2010, the UN-backed Principles for Responsible Investment (PRI), which contain commitments to active ownership on ESG issues, had over 700 signatories, representing more than USD 20 trillion in assets under management. The majority of these signatories engage in dialogue with investee companies to some extent, either directly or as part of broader investor collaborations, to influence corporate behaviour (PRI Initiative, 2007, 2008, 2009).

This chapter seeks to determine which factors contribute to shareholder salience in improving the environmental, social and corporate governance (ESG) performance of investee companies, and the relative importance of these factors.

6.2 Analytical Framework

Mitchell, Agle, and Wood's (1997) theory of stakeholder salience was selected as the underlying theoretical framework for the analysis of institutional shareholder engagement with investee companies. These authors explore the maze of definitions of agency, stakeholder and institutional theory and propose a simple and coherent model of stakeholder salience. They develop a descriptive model of stakeholder salience, defined as the degree to which company managers give priority to the

This chapter is a republished article that first appeared in Journal of Business Ethics in 2010.

J. Gifford (✉)
PRI, EC2A 3DR London, UK
e-mail: james.gifford@unpri.org

T. Hebb (ed.), *The Next Generation of Responsible Investing*,
Advances in Business Ethics Research 1, DOI 10.1007/978-94-007-2348-1_6,

claims of various stakeholders (including those of their shareholders). They identify three overarching attributes that determine the degree to which managers pay attention to stakeholder demands: power, legitimacy and urgency. The attribute of power mirrors Scott's (2001) regulative pillar (one of the core drivers of corporate change within institutional theory), though Mitchell et al. (1997) define it more broadly, stating that a stakeholder has power "to the extent it has or can gain access to coercive, utilitarian, or normative means, to impose its will in the relationship" (1997, 865). Mitchell et al. (1997) take Suchman's (1995) definition of legitimacy as "a generalized perception or assumption that the actions of an entity are desirable, proper, or appropriate within some socially constructed system of norms, values, beliefs, and definitions" (1995, 574). Legitimacy is central to Scott's (2001) normative pillar within institutional theory, and can also be seen to include the cultural-cognitive pillar, in that once a practice gains widespread legitimacy within the community involved, it becomes "the way things are done". Mitchell et al. (1997) see these two attributes – power and legitimacy – as overlapping and interacting. Both are required in order for the stakeholder claim to be salient in the eyes of the company managers. Urgency is the third of Mitchell's et al. (1997) attributes and represents the "degree to which stakeholder claims call for immediate attention" (1997, 864). This is based on the premise that urgent matters demand and get attention. Agle, Mitchell, and Sonnenfeld (1999) find evidence that the application of urgency is essential to maximise shareholder salience. They find that "although shareholder power, legitimacy, and urgency are all correlated with shareholder salience, we note that for this sample of large public firms, urgency is the best predictor of shareholder salience . . . it is the extra push of shareholder urgency that really gets CEO attention" (1999, 520).

Mitchell et al. argue that stakeholder salience is positively related to the degree to which the three attributes of power, legitimacy, and urgency are "perceived by managers to be present" (1997, 873). Agle et al. (1999) conducted a survey of 80 CEOs in the US and found support for this theory. Ryan and Schneider (2003) take Mitchell's et al. (1997) theory on stakeholder salience and apply it to the "new" reality of large institutional shareholders with massive power in the marketplace and the alignment of shareholder power with stakeholder power (through the ownership of pension funds by millions of citizens). On the basis of power and legitimacy, they find public pension funds are the most salient stakeholders of the listed company. With respect to urgency however, Ryan and Schneider (2003) find that active fund managers (i.e. stock pickers) exhibit a greater degree of urgency in their interactions with companies than do passive shareholders because of their trading activities, and the resulting urgency of their claims as perceived by company managers.

In this chapter, each of Mitchell's et al. (1997) overarching drivers of stakeholder salience – power, legitimacy and urgency – is analysed and further subdivided into sub-attributes and mapped onto the various shareholder engagement practices or characteristics. This mapping process led to the development of a number of propositions that were then tested through three case studies.

Power is categorized – using Etzioni's (1964) framework – into coercive power (through the use of formal shareholder governance powers), utilitarian power (the

Table 6.1 Sources of shareholder power

Level of analysis	Sources of shareholder power
Coercive	■ Use of formal shareholder rights through resolutions ■ Replacement of directors or CEOs ■ Legal proceedings to enforce shareholder rights ■ Successful lobbying for regulation
Utilitarian	■ Provision or withdrawal of capital or other resources from companies (investment, divestment)
Normative	■ Public or private statements, shareholder resolutions or other activities that affect the company's or individual managers' reputations

power to reward or punish through financial means) and normative power (expressed through actions that affect a target company's reputation). Table 6.1 shows Etzioni's (1964) three types of power and the key sources of this power relevant to shareholder engagement.

From this, the following are proposed:

- Proposition 1: In successful engagements, the shareholder request is backed by an implicit or explicit threat of the use of formal shareholder rights (Coercive power)
- Proposition 2: In successful engagements, the shareholder request is backed by an implicit or explicit threat of divestment (Utilitarian power)
- Proposition 3: In successful engagements, the shareholder request is accompanied by public or private activities that have the potential to affect the reputation of the target company or its managers (Normative power)

Legitimacy, drawing on Wood (1991), is further divided into individual legitimacy (relating to the credibility of the engagement of practitioners meeting with the target companies on behalf of the shareholder), organizational legitimacy (driven by the credibility of the shareholder organization in the market) and societal legitimacy (based on the legitimacy of the issue in the eyes of the community). It is proposed that for this analysis, a fourth type of legitimacy – pragmatic legitimacy – should be added, focusing on the legitimacy of the shareholder's argument from the perspective of the company: i.e. the business case. This additional category of legitimacy draws on Suchman's (1995) notion of "pragmatic legitimacy" which rests on "self-regarding utility calculations" of the audience – in this context, the company managers at the receiving end of shareholder requests. While the business case that is put to companies will affect the legitimacy of the shareholder in the companies' eyes, the strength of the arguments themselves as perceived by the company is sufficiently important to constitute a separate level of analysis within "legitimacy". Put together, these four sources of legitimacy provide a complete and appropriate sub-categorization of legitimacy within the shareholder engagement context.

Table 6.2 Sources of shareholder legitimacy

Level of analysis	Sources of shareholder legitimacy
Individual	■ Credibility, expertise, experience and status of the individuals engaging with the company
Organizational	■ Legitimate claim on the company (e.g. large shareholding, high-risk stake) ■ Alignment between shareholders' interests and those of the company (shareholder has the best interests of the company at heart) ■ Perception that the shareholder organization is a credible and respected member of the investment community ■ Consistency of messaging from different parts of the shareholder organization
Pragmatic	■ The shareholder has a strong argument for why the proposed action is in the interests of the company ■ The shareholder provides new information to the company
Societal	■ The shareholder embodies or reflects a position widely accepted in society ■ Existence of norms or codes of conduct ■ Supportive political and policy environment

Table 6.2 combines Wood's (1991) and Suchman's (1995) categorizations of legitimacy and proposes sources of legitimacy that may contribute towards shareholder salience.

The following are proposed:

- Proposition 4: In successful engagements, shareholder representatives are highly credible, evidenced by seniority, experience, expertise and the ability to build trust (Individual legitimacy)
- Proposition 5: In successful engagements, the shareholder institution is seen as "mainstream", aligned with the interests of the company, and internally consistent (Organizational legitimacy)
- Proposition 6: In successful engagements, the shareholder has a strong business case, including providing the company with new information on emerging issues (Pragmatic legitimacy)
- Proposition 7: In successful engagements, the shareholder request has strong societal legitimacy, and the shareholder can make use of standards or norms as a basis for engagement (Societal legitimacy)
- Proposition 8: In successful engagements, the shareholder is engaging within a supportive political and policy environment (Societal legitimacy)

In the propositions above, societal legitimacy was further divided into two propositions to reflect the difference between general support from society as reflected by civil society or consumer movements, and the related but distinct societal legitimacy that comes from public policy makers and the political and regulatory environment. The former can be seen as a precursor to the latter, but it was felt sufficiently important to differentiate situations where there was clear governmental support for an issue compared with only NGO or consumer support.

Urgency is the third of Mitchell's et al. (1997) attributes and represents the "degree to which stakeholder claims call for immediate attention" (1997, 864). They state that "urgency, with synonyms including 'compelling', 'driving', and 'imperative', exists only when two conditions are met: (1) when a relationship or claim is of a time-sensitive nature and (2) when that relationship or claim is important or critical to the stakeholder" (1997, 867).

Mitchell's et al. (1997) attribute of urgency is more problematic than the other two attributes from the instrumental perspective of a shareholder conducting an engagement with an investee company. The time-sensitive nature of the attribute is clear – i.e. deadlines and time pressure tend to focus the minds of managers. However, "criticality", as defined, reflects the subjective importance the investor places on the claim. From an instrumental shareholder perspective, it is unhelpful to suggest that "you will be more influential if you care more". It is proposed therefore, that this factor be interpreted as the presence of shareholder behaviour that illustrates a resolve or determination to address the issue of concern. In the context of shareholder engagement therefore, it is proposed that criticality exists where there is a high level of intensity in the engagement, demonstrated through assertiveness, persistence and the application of resources. Table 6.3 expands the two sub-components of urgency and identifies sources of shareholder urgency.

The following are proposed:

- Proposition 9: In successful engagements, the engagements are time-sensitive (Time sensitivity aspects)
- Proposition 10: In successful engagements, the shareholder is assertive and persistent, and expends resources (Criticality of stakeholder demand)

There are a number of other factors that do not fit neatly into one of Mitchell's et al. (1997) attributes, yet are likely to moderate, positively or negatively, the effects of all three of Mitchell's attributes, and are important from an instrumental shareholder engagement perspective. These include the extent of coalition-building activities by the investor, the relative size of the investor and the company, and the values of the managers of the company, the latter of which was elaborated in Agle et al. (1999).

Table 6.3 Sources of shareholder urgency

Level of analysis	Sources of shareholder urgency
Time-sensitivity	■ Shareholder resolutions at AGMs ■ Benchmarks with deadlines for response ■ Use of other forms of deadline to create time pressure
Criticality	■ Assertiveness of tone ■ Persistence ■ Willingness to apply resources

The first of these moderating variables is related to relative size of the shareholder vis-à-vis the company, and its stake in the company. Presumably, if a shareholder has a large stake in the company, or is itself a large shareholder in the market, it is a more powerful economic actor in relation to the company, and would have more power (through formal shareholder rights) and legitimacy (through being a large, respected market player), and therefore, salience.

The second is coalition building among shareholders, and working with non-governmental organisations (NGOs) and policy makers. Coalition-building is very much related to the size question, as a coalition of shareholders is, in effect, a pooling of their power and legitimacy. Because size of the shareholder or coalition of shareholders enhances all three of Mitchell's et al. (1997) attributes, it is proposed that these factors positively moderate power, legitimacy and urgency, rather than reside within any of them.

The third moderating factor – the values of company managers – comes from the other direction – the subjective attitudes of managers towards the shareholders and their requests. Again, this factor is likely to cut across Mitchell's et al. (1997) attributes and moderate shareholder salience independently from the attributes or characteristics that the shareholder itself possesses. This moderating factor was identified and applied by Agle et al. (1999) when they tested Mitchell's et al. (1997) through surveying company CEOs.

Adding these three factors, the following are proposed:

- Proposition 11: In successful engagements, shareholders have a high degree of relative economic and governance power over the firm
- Proposition 12: In successful engagements, the shareholder builds coalitions with other shareholders and stakeholders
- Proposition 13: In successful engagements, managers' values are broadly aligned with the premise of the investor request

Table 6.4 maps the various levels of analysis of power, legitimacy and urgency against the concrete shareholder engagement characteristics and attributes, which define the propositions to be tested in the case studies.

6.3 Research Design

The research uses qualitative case studies of the shareholder engagement practices within three leading institutional investor organizations, two large mainstream funds in the UK (Hermes and Insight Investment) and one relatively small, but influential, SRI fund in the US (Calvert). These were chosen because of the size of their engagement teams and reputations as leaders in the field. They also represent a variety of approaches and styles of engagement. The research method was designed to

Table 6.4 Factors likely to affect shareholder influence

	Power enhancing			Legitimacy enhancing				Urgency enhancing	
★ indicates the main sub-attribute relevant to that investor practice or characteristic +/– indicates the presence of attributes and the expected sign of influence (positive or negative)	Coercive	Utilitarian	Normative	Individual	Organisational	Pragmatic	Societal	Time sensitivity	Criticality
Power-oriented									
1. Use of shareholder rights: shareholder resolutions, votes against management, director elections	★	+	+		–			+	+
2. Use of economic power: divestment (or investment)		★	+					+	+
3. Use of the media and/or public statements/peer pressure; public shareholder campaigns; threats to reputation			★		–			+	+
Legitimacy-oriented									
4. Credibility of the individuals: seniority, experience and expertise; ability to develop trust and collegiality				★	+	+	+		
5. Status of the engaging organisation: degree to which shareholder is perceived to be 'mainstream'; perceived alignment of interests between the shareholder and the company; organisational alignment and consistent messaging			+	+	★				
6. Strength of the business case: validity of the argument; evidence; extent of new information provided to the company; maturity of the issue				+	+	★	+		
7. Strength of the societal case: social and cultural context; existence of legitimising standards, norms and principles			+			+	★		
8. Political/policy context: supportive political environment; regulatory momentum	+	+	+		+	+	★		
Urgency-oriented									
9. Time-sensitivity: deadlines, benchmarks									+
10. Intensity of private engagement activities: assertiveness and persistence					–			+	
Moderating influences									
11. Relative economic and governance power: size of the stake, investor and firm	+	+	+	+	+				
12. Coalition building: leveraging other investors, NGOs and policy makers	+	+	+		+				+
13. Values of managers: degree of alignment with investor request					+	+			

deliver an in-depth analysis of leading practice, rather than attempting to capture a statistically-valid snapshot of shareholder engagement activities or processes across the sector.

Despite the qualitative nature of the study, a rating system of zero, one, two or three stars was developed for evaluating the strength of support for each proposition across each of the cases studied. Zero stars indicate that the attribute or practice is not present or not relevant. One star indicates that there is some support for the attribute contributing to shareholder salience. Two stars indicate that the attribute is seen as moderately important, and three stars indicate that the attribute is very important and contributes to a large degree to shareholder salience. This approach allows an aggregation of results across the cases and engagements to provide an indication of the relative importance of the various influences identified in the propositions. These ratings were determined by the author and based on responses to specific questions put to the shareholder representatives involved in the engagements, seeking to determine support or otherwise for the propositions in specific contexts, as well as analysis of documentary evidence, such as correspondence to and from the target companies, and the investors' engagement databases which recorded notes and summaries from meetings with companies. The ratings were shared with the practitioners involved and the validity of the conclusions confirmed.

6.4 Analysis of Cases

Hermes is predominantly a corporate governance engager, with a direct goal of improving the financial performance of companies by improving some aspect of governance or strategic performance, often through influencing the boards of companies. Insight Investment, while also a large mainstream investor and very financially oriented, has an additional mandate to seek improvements in corporate behaviour on environmental and social issues, ultimately with the goal of improving long-term financial performance. However, the direct links between many of Insight's engagement activities and the financial returns to the portfolio are not as clear as with Hermes'. Insight engages on a range of environmental and social issues, even where the potential material impact to Insight's portfolio would be difficult to demonstrate. Insight's corporate governance work, however, is similar to Hermes' in style and substance (though not as well-staffed), and indeed the two organizations have worked together on issues of common concern. The major difference, therefore, between Hermes and Insight in this context appears to be the degree to which their engagement is driven by financial criteria, and, resulting from that, Insight's greater willingness to engage on thematic environmental and social issues across a number of companies, contrasting with Hermes' approach of focusing on company-specific, and primarily corporate governance, issues.

In the Insight case, three engagements were studies in depth:

- The sustainability performance of the UK house building sector, based on a sustainability benchmarking exercise
- A biodiversity risk management engagement with extractives and utilities companies
- An engagement on occupation health and safety with UK companies

For Hermes, four engagements were explored:

- A global pharmaceutical company's approach towards access to medicines in developing countries
- Succession planning and remuneration issues in an underperforming UK company
- An oil company's approach to risks associated with operating in Burma
- An issue relating to access to HIV medicines, as well as executive remuneration within another global pharmaceutical company.

Calvert is a relatively small retail fund (though the largest SRI fund), with an explicit social and environmental mandate. It is seeking to sell to a vast number of retail customers of socially-responsible mutual fund products, through a large network of financial advisors. Its shareholder advocacy work is driven not only by Calvert's inherent social commitment, but also by the need for market differentiation within the SRI sector. Examples of successful advocacy campaigns are used repeatedly in Calvert's marketing materials. Calvert also uses a financial rationale for its environmental and social activities on the basis that "good" companies are best equipped to prosper financially through better managing emerging issues. The Calvert engagements studied include:

- Encouraging board diversity within US companies
- Supplier standards and supply chain transparency at The Gap
- A call for systematic ESG disclosure by US companies
- The adoption of a computer take-back and recycling scheme at Dell

Table 6.5 below is a summary of the results from the three cases and lays out the degree of support for each of the propositions. Each proposition, representing a source of shareholder salience, is also mapped against the various level of analysis of Mitchell's et al. (1997) attributes.

Figure 6.1 below shows the average ratings for each of the propositions across all three cases.

The following section takes each proposition and summarises the overall results, drawing on lessons learned from the cases.

Table 6.5 Support for propositions: Analysis of sources of investor influence

		Power enhancing			Legitimacy enhancing				Urgency enhancing	
★ indicates the main sub-attributes that were found to be relevant to that investor practice or characteristic +/– indicates the *proposed* presence of attributes and the expected sign of influence (positive or negative)	Overall	Coercive	Utilitarian	Normative	Individual	Organizational	Pragmatic	Societal	Time sensitivity	Criticality
Power-oriented										
Use of shareholder rights		+	+	+		–			+	+
Insight										
Hermes	★★			★★					★★	★★
Calvert	★★★			★★★					★★	★★★
Divestment			+	+					+	+
Insight										
Hermes										
Calvert										
Actions that affect reputation, media/public statements, peer pressure				+		–			+	+
Insight	★★			★★						★
Hermes	★★			★★						★
Calvert	★★★			★★★						★★

Table 6.5 (continued)

Legitimacy-oriented									
Credibility of the individuals					+	+	+	+	
Insight	★★				★★				
Hermes	★★★				★★ ★				
Calvert	★				★				
Perceived as mainstream, interests aligned, internally consistent				+	+	+			
Insight	★★					★★			
Hermes	★★★					★★ ★			
Calvert	★					★			
Strong business case					+	+	+	+	
Insight	★★★						★★ ★		
Hermes	★★★						★★ ★		
Calvert	★★★						★★ ★		
Strong societal case				+			+	+	
Insight	★			★			★	★	
Hermes									
Calvert	★			★			★	★	
Political/policy context		+	+	+		+	+	+	
Insight	★★					★	★★	★★	★★
Hermes	★★						★★	★★	
Calvert	★						★	★	

Table 6.5 (continued)

Urgency-oriented									
Time-sensitivity								+	
Insight	★							★	
Hermes	★							★	
Calvert	★							★	
Intensity					–				+
Insight	★★★								★★★
Hermes	★★								★★
Calvert	★★★								★★★
Moderating influences									
Relative size		+	+	+	+				
Insight	★			★	★				
Hermes	★			★	★				
Calvert									
Coalition building		+	+	+	+				+
Insight	★★			★★	★★				★★
Hermes	★★			★★	★★				★★
Calvert	★★★			★★★	★★★				★★★
Values of managers					+	+			
Insight	★★★				★★★	★★★	★★★		
Hermes	★★★				★★★	★★★	★★★		
Calvert	★★★				★★★	★★★	★★★		

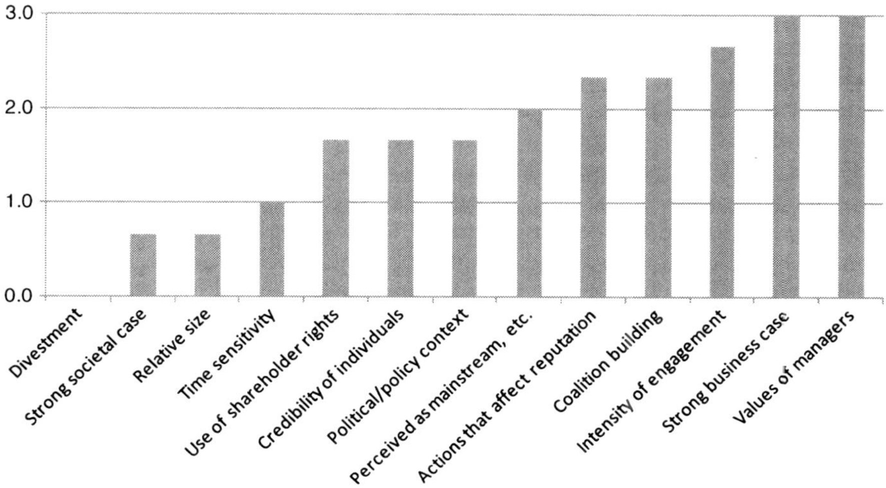

Fig. 6.1 Support for propositions across all three cases

6.5 Power-Related Factors

6.5.1 Use of Shareholder Rights

Insight's thematic engagements did not make use of formal shareholder rights. On corporate governance issues, there was a greater use of voting, but rarely the filing of shareholder resolutions. Hermes frequently used voting (but rarely shareholder resolutions) to send signals to management, and there was strong evidence that the threat of a vote against management was an important motivator for companies to comply with requests. But much of Hermes' use of shareholder rights was subtle, and the threat implicit – though, in a number of cases studied, the threat to vote against management was quite explicit. Of the three cases, Calvert made the greatest use of formal shareholder rights, with the filing of shareholder resolutions (or threat to do so) an integral part of its engagement strategy.

There are a number of possible reasons for these differences. Regarding Insight's thematic engagements based on cross-sector benchmarking exercises, the strategy is not to directly press for specific changes of the type that would be the subject of a shareholder resolution. The goal is to provide a framework for improving corporate performance across a sector and, at the launch of each of these benchmarking reports featuring leaders and laggards, provide a modest normative incentive to improve. Shareholder resolutions were seen as an inappropriate tool for this type of engagement. In addition, these benchmarks are very much legitimacy-oriented, with relationships built up over multiple years. In this case it is concluded that the use of shareholder rights undermines legitimacy, and this can damage the positive, trust-based approach implicit in the benchmarking process.

Like Insight, Hermes itself rarely files shareholder resolutions, though there were many occasions where it votes against management (often relating to remuneration reports). Hermes' and Insight's reluctance to use shareholder resolutions indicates the importance they place on maintaining their legitimacy with companies (and their view that legitimacy-oriented engagement is indeed effective).

Calvert, however, uses shareholder resolutions routinely as a tool to gain management's attention and move an issue forward. This case demonstrates that resolutions can be very effective and need not harm legitimacy, particularly over the longer term. Filing a resolution can bring a firm to the table, allowing Calvert staff to then build relationships and develop legitimacy where none may have existed previously. There is considerable evidence that company management will take significant steps to accommodate investor demands in order to avoid resolutions going to the vote.

The three cases (and indeed direct quotes from interviewees) support the view that there is a cultural difference between the US and the UK on the issue of filing shareholder resolutions, with this tool being much more common in the US due to weaker shareholder rights leaving shareholders with fewer options, as well as a more confrontational corporate culture.

Calvert appears to be able to make use of the shareholder resolution process as a normal part of its interaction with companies, without necessarily damaging its legitimacy. In fact, the withdrawal of a shareholder resolution based on the company's commitment to establishing a long-term dialogue is a sophisticated way of building the "socialising infrastructure" to allow the establishment of legitimacy, trust and strong relationships. That said, in some cases, companies saw the filing of a resolution as a hostile act, which resulted in Calvert losing legitimacy and being unable to make any progress with those companies.

Overall, there is strong support for the proposition that engagement efforts can be assisted by the judicious use (or threat of use) of shareholder rights. But their use is certainly not a prerequisite to successful engagement, and has the potential side effect of undermining organizational legitimacy.

6.5.2 Divestment

The threat of divestment is not a lever that was used in any of the engagements studied. There may be cases where divestment or threat of divestment by large investors could be a driver for shareholder salience , but, in these particular cases, it was not.

Hermes is largely passively managed, so divestment is not seen as an option for them. Insight has a separation between its fund management decision-making on the one hand and its voting and engagement activities on the other. Insight is explicit in its preference for engagement over divestment as a way of addressing environmental and social issues. While Calvert does divest from companies that do not fulfil its social and environmental criteria, it does not use the threat of divestment directly with companies it is seeking to change. Often the companies with which Calvert engages are considered "good" companies overall and are not at risk of being excluded, but have some key areas in which they can improve. One would expect Calvert to make greater use of the threat of divestment for those companies that are on the borderline of being excluded from their index, and therefore from their investible universe.

6.5.3 Actions that Affect Reputation

The clearest example of the use of normative power is "going public" and making strong media statements to put pressure on companies to agree to shareholder demands. The case-study organizations rarely, if ever, use the media to push directly for changes in company behaviour. All three cases indicated that "going public" damages legitimacy and should be avoided if possible. Responses from the Hermes case affirmed companies' distaste for shareholders using the media to make a point. With Insight's environmental and social engagements, the media were not used as a tool to pressure companies directly. However, in their governance work, this approach was taken on occasion. This may reflect the maturity of the corporate governance debate and the confidence that investors feel to go "into the trenches" where they see management taking action that damages shareholders' interests. Calvert avoided direct criticism of companies with which it was engaging, as it felt this would undermine its relationship with the company. Calvert does, however, use the media regularly to raise awareness of the issues themselves (climate change, human rights, etc.).

The evidence points to two conclusions regarding the use of negative publicity generated by shareholders: companies will indeed take steps to avoid it (normative power contributes to salience); and negative public statements emanating from the shareholder will undermine the relationship between shareholder and company.

While avoiding the use of the most negative and confronting forms of normative power, all three organisations applied normative power in more subtle ways, and there is strong evidence that overall, the use of normative power was an important contributor to shareholder salience. Although Insight does not actively court the media, its level of transparency is likely to result in a degree of normative pressure being applied to companies that are named as the targets of engagement and featured in Insight's reports. Insight staff emphasised that normative power need not always be negative, and that giving positive feedback to companies on good work is an effective and under-utilized practice.

Perhaps the most sophisticated and clever use of normative power is evidenced in the sector benchmarking activities conducted by Insight. These benchmarks introduce an element of competition and peer pressure among companies. Because these processes constitute robust and objective assessments of sustainability performance across a sector, and do not involve direct demands (apart from participation), they largely eliminate the harm to legitimacy that more aggressive approaches may risk. They also provide an opportunity for subtle, yet powerful, reputational levers to be applied to companies through the public release of the results. Being judged against peers is an important motivator, particularly when the results are viewed and the process is endorsed by senior government ministers.

Calvert clearly applies normative power as a routine part of its strategy. Companies often see the "tick of approval" from the SRI industry as a reputational asset worth seeking. Inclusion or exclusion from the Calvert Social Index is likely to have reputational impacts for some companies. However, Calvert prefers to build trust over the long term, and recognizes the damage that media statements can have on an engagement. The indirect use of normative power through leveraging peer pressure is another important finding. Calvert has observed that when an industry leader, such as Dell, takes the lead on an issue like computer take-back and recycling, the rest of the industry follows.

Another finding is the importance of the reputation of individuals within the company as a lever for shareholder influence. There was strong evidence that targeting (or at least "playing upon") the reputations of individual managers can be an effective avenue for influencing the entire company.

Given the lack of coercive and direct utilitarian avenues of power available to most investors in most cases, the predominant form of power that investors can apply is normative power, which generally involves actions that affect or threaten to affect the company's or its managers' reputations. While the evidence does not point to the use of normative power as being essential, it is clearly a useful tool.

6.6 Legitimacy-Related Factors

6.6.1 Credibility of the Individuals

At the individual level, there is a range of attributes that could contribute to legitimacy in engaging with companies including personal credibility, experience, seniority, specialized knowledge, contacts and professional background. In all three cases, the engagement staff were relatively young – with the majority being in their late 20s or early- to mid-30s. Most of Insight's investor responsibility team have NGO backgrounds, yet there was no evidence that their backgrounds or age undermined their legitimacy in engaging with companies. The high level of legitimacy awarded to Insight's staff by companies is due in part to their high degree of expertise and specialized knowledge in the areas under discussion. Hermes also has a predominantly young team, but with more mainstream financial sector backgrounds such as financial journalism and corporate governance analysis. Hermes also sends very senior representatives to some engagements, including a former CEO of a listed company, illustrating that seniority and experience is indeed seen as important. Insight also employs a veteran corporate governance expert, with decades of experience in the field. Calvert's social analysts (who also do engagement) are recruited specifically for their environmental and social expertise and research ability. Financial background was not seen as essential, but it was acknowledged that it is becoming more so.

There were important differences in how the individuals from the three teams were likely to be perceived by companies, but these did not necessarily translate into more or less legitimacy. Certainly, Hermes' staff were tasked with discussing the issues of greatest financial and strategic concern to the boards and senior management of the companies and in that sense, expertise in that area would enhance individual legitimacy. However, Insight's and Calvert's staff were able to build legitimacy on a broader range of issues through their expertise in those areas and their ability to develop trust and personal relationships.

Overall, there was strong evidence in support of the proposition that the credibility and reputations of the individuals conducting the engagements is a reasonably important factor.

6.6.2 Perceived As: Mainstream, Interests Aligned, and Internally Consistent

There was strong evidence for the proposition that these factors did enhance organizational legitimacy and therefore shareholder salience. There were important differences between the three cases, with Hermes likely to be perceived as the most mainstream, with Insight following and then Calvert, with its explicit social mandate and small size likely to result in it being seen as a niche fund with a social agenda and therefore having relatively less legitimacy. The differences in organizational legitimacy represent differences in style between the three organizations, with Hermes aligning itself very much with the concerns of company boards, and Calvert, on the other end, focusing almost exclusively on the social and environmental performance of companies. Insight and Hermes are also likely to gain considerable legitimacy simply from their size in the market.

Hermes made the greatest efforts to ensure its organizational legitimacy was protected and enhanced, through being careful not to engage on issues that are not seen as relevant to the company's financial prospects. Hermes' reward for this level of legitimacy is the regular invitations to "go inside" a firm to view and discuss confidential board-level matters. This, in itself, reflects very high levels of organizational legitimacy unavailable to most other shareholders.

Calvert is clearly different from both Insight and Hermes in that it is a small fund, proudly SRI-oriented, and engages almost exclusively on environmental and social issues. Interestingly, Calvert is able to access a different type of organizational legitimacy because it is an SRI fund, but only with those companies that see the SRI "tick of approval" worth pursuing. For other companies, Calvert is unlikely to have the legitimacy that comes with the large assets and mainstream market perceptions of the other two funds. However, it appears that Calvert is able to build legitimacy during its engagements due to the level of expertise and professionalism applied to engagements over a number of years. The goal for small funds such as Calvert should be therefore to get a "foot in the door" and use that to build strong relationships with companies and their staff over the longer term.

6.6.3 Strong Business Case

The source of pragmatic legitimacy in the context of shareholder engagement is the "business case" for taking action, from the company's perspective. It is not surprising that the strength of the business case was found to be the most important of the legitimacy-oriented contributors to shareholder salience. There was very strong evidence in all three cases that the business case is vital to the success of the engagement. There was also strong evidence that providing the company with new information on emerging issues (as a way of building the business case) contributes significantly to the prospects for success. Insight and Calvert both contribute considerable amounts of new information to companies during the engagement process by providing tools, best practice guides and advice.

Hermes is the most financially-oriented of the three engagement operations, and the targeting decisions were based in financial criteria rather than environmental and social. Therefore the business case is somewhat easier to make, given that most targeted companies had poor financial performance to start with, and Hermes' engagement was explicitly attempting to address it. Responses from companies that Hermes engaged with indicated that the companies prefer engagement on what one called "sensible issues" (i.e. financially- or strategically-relevant), and it is likely that the weaker the business case, the greater the risk that the company will perceive the issue as not "sensible", thereby risking the shareholder's organizational legitimacy. Despite Calvert's social agenda, the business case is still a major consideration in its targeting decisions because it recognises that if it cannot make a strong business case, then the engagement will fail.

The more an investor can provide practical tools, frameworks and "how-to's" for companies to address issues in a cost-effective way, the greater the likelihood of the company taking action. One approach used by Calvert is to start with a simple request, such as a feasibility study and a commitment to dialogue. The initial request is not necessarily onerous for a company to undertake, but allows the shareholder to get "in the door" and build trust.

These cases confirm that the business case is probably the most important factor in the success of engagement, and therefore shareholders should spend considerable time and resources in building that case.

6.6.4 Strong Societal Case

The societal case is often seen as the most obvious source of legitimacy of a stakeholder claim. The societal case is represented by, for example, the strength of moral support for an issue within society, often reflected by ethical codes, norms or principles. However, the evidence suggests that the appeal to moral, ethical or broader societal arguments was not considered a major contributor to shareholder salience.

Insight draws on the societal case in many of its documents, but not in its direct discussions with companies. It appears that while societal principles and norms may foreshadow regulation and inevitable change in corporate behaviour, they are not particularly useful in themselves as tools within the engagement process. A societal norm must be related back to the pragmatic legitimacy of the claim, through identifying reputational risks to the company, regulatory momentum, or other consequences to the company of not being aligned with that norm.

Hermes, apart from the one occasion where they used the OECD Guidelines for Multinational Enterprises as a tool for engagement, does not normally draw on norms-based arguments or frameworks. Calvert is driven by the societal case and its targeting is based on where it can create the greatest good for society. However, while it does raise the societal case and make moderate use of various norms and codes, its primary focus – in its interactions with companies – is on how societal trends and attitudes will affect the financial performance or other aspects of company operations.

6.6.5 Supportive Political Environment

Where there is a supportive political environment for an engagement, there is strong evidence that it can indeed enhance shareholder salience. Insight has been the most successful in working directly with policy makers on engagement, using them to enhance the normative impacts of one of their sector benchmarks (involving a Government Minister in the launch) and to fund another benchmark directly. While most of Hermes' engagements were not backed in any direct sense by policy makers or public sector organisations, the examples of Hermes' engagements that did involve participation of government officials demonstrated the importance placed on the political environment by companies. Calvert worked with the Treasurer of the State of Connecticut (who is also the sole trustee of that State's pension scheme) to enhance the legitimacy of an engagement, and also with regulators on other matters of concern.

The involvement of policymakers in engagement can take a number of different forms including actively joining with investors to push voluntary improvements in company performance, endorsing the work of investors through launching benchmarks and the resulting reports, or directly funding the engagement itself (or its research aspects).

6.7 Urgency-Related Factors

6.7.1 Time-Sensitivity

In the three cases, time-sensitivity was seen as only moderately relevant to the success of engagements. It is acknowledged that the benchmarking and shareholder resolution/voting processes involved deadlines that can be leveraged to focus the attention of managers. However, there was no strong evidence that the time-sensitivity factor was an important driver of shareholder salience in the context of engagement. Interestingly, Hermes' staff felt that in many cases, they actually needed time to work through the issue with the company, and that real change rarely occurred in the lead up to an AGM. However, it was also acknowledged that there are opportunities for shareholders to intervene successfully during moments of crisis for the company.

It is likely that most shareholder engagement – particularly relating to environmental and social issues – works to longer timeframes than those envisioned by Mitchell et al. (1997) in their characterization of urgency. Very few of the shareholder requests require "immediate attention" in the "crisis management" sense referred to by Mitchell et al. (1997). Insight's benchmarks are slow, methodical and process-driven activities, conducted over multiple years. Calvert's multi-year dialogues indicate that major changes to corporate practices take time, and it is an incremental process.

That said, the time-sensitive nature of the shareholder resolution process is nevertheless likely to focus the attention of management on the problem and therefore may be a useful tool from time to time.

6.7.2 Intensity of Engagement/Criticality

Criticality in Mitchell et al.'s (1997) model was modified for this context to reflect the level of intensity of engagement. On assertiveness, all three cases support the use of a calm, professional and business-oriented communication style and tone with companies. However, there is also a thread running through the cases around the need to be firm, transparent and direct, and to "up-the-ante" where necessary. Because of the nature of the Insight sector benchmarks, the tone was very much process-oriented rather than request-oriented, and therefore it may not have required the degree of assertiveness that other direct shareholder requests may require. Hermes' tone tends to be more "questioning" than "demanding", indicating their strong preference for legitimacy-based interaction. There was a willingness to "up the ante" where necessary, backed by evidence of some "robust" conversations. Calvert's tone is professional and business-like, but it too is willing to escalate the rhetoric where necessary. It was noted that being overly-assertive can undermine legitimacy, as it adds an adversarial aspect to the interaction, rather than keeping a spirit of working together for mutual benefit. Therefore, assertiveness – when taken too far – can be salience-decreasing because of the harm to organizational legitimacy.

All three cases demonstrated a great degree of persistence, with many engagements continuing over multiple years. All three organizations applied significant resources to their engagements, through the allocation of staff time to company dialogue and, particularly in the case of Insight, the commissioning of third party research.

Another practical tool for increasing the intensity of an engagement is the filing of shareholder resolutions. Shareholder resolutions are inherently attention-grabbing, and demonstrate to the company that the shareholder is willing to expend considerable time and resources on the issue (as well as leveraging normative power). Of the three cases, Calvert files the most shareholder resolutions, by a considerable margin. Again, this reflects the cultural and regulatory context in the US, but also may reflect Calvert's limited ability to gain the attention of management without such action.

6.8 Moderating Factors

6.8.1 Relative Size: Size of the Stake, the Shareholder and the Company

The size of the stake was not found to be as important as might be expected. That said, if the size of the stake means a shareholder is one of the larger shareholders, this status will bring with it additional salience.

The case studies indicate that the total size of the shareholder organization (assets under management) is likely to have a greater bearing on organizational legitimacy and therefore salience than the stake in the company at that particular time (unless the stake is particularly large). For Insight, size of the stake didn't appear to be important, whereas Insight's overall size in the market was felt to be important to organizational legitimacy and therefore shareholder salience. This was affirmed in the Hermes case, where their reputation in the market (organizational legitimacy) was felt to be more important than size of the stake. The Calvert case shows that even a small investor with an insignificant stake in economic or governance terms can effect significant change within these large companies. One company response in the Hermes case indicated that managers only have time to have detailed discussions with a small number of shareholders, so in that sense, being one of the larger shareholders is probably important in gaining a share of that limited access to board-level representatives (depending on how many other shareholders are taking up management's time).

It was suggested that smaller companies, particularly when dealing with governance issues, may be more amenable to change because of the formal leverage and the greater ease with which a shareholder can pull together a coalition in cases where there is a smaller shareholder register. The point was also made that small companies are less used to engagement by investors and may therefore be more responsive.

The lesson is that while relative size clearly can have an impact on salience, small funds should be confident that they too can exert influence, even on large companies, through maximizing their other points of leverage.

6.8.2 Coalition Building

There was strong evidence that building coalitions, not only with other investors but also with NGOs and policy makers, does contribute to the salience of shareholder claims. The cases contained numerous examples of the successful use of coalitions between investors, NGOs and governments. That said, there were numerous cases where no other stakeholders were involved and the engagement nevertheless appeared to be successful. Insight's governance work was conducted, on many occasions, in collaboration with other large investors, but not in the cases of the environmental benchmarks studied. Hermes is very much involved in investor collaborations, particularly on governance issues. It was felt that coalitions are particularly useful in regions where a shareholder has only a small geographical presence and it must rely on local investors, both to understand the local context as well as provide legitimacy in that market. Coalition-building is perhaps most important and most evident with Calvert. Because of its modest size, Calvert needs to gain the support of large investors (most often public pension funds) to ensure its shareholder resolutions receive respectable votes in favour, and therefore add to the legitimacy of the claim. In many cases, they also need the support of other SRI investors and partners to share the workload involved in the most intense and long-running engagements.

Limitations of coalitions were also highlighted. There is considerable overhead involved in investor collaboration. There is also the issue of sharing credit, where engagement outcomes are used as a marketing asset. Another challenge is competitive pressures and the "free rider" problem, where one shareholder expends resources to engage with the company, resulting in benefits for all shareholders.

Coalitions with NGOs can be useful, contributing significant intellectual resources, and increasing the potential for the application of normative power. There are also some examples of effective coalitions with policy makers. Insight's engagement on the CHaSPI process was conducted with a UK-government agency, the Health and Safety Executive. The potential benefits of working in collaboration with policy makers to promote better corporate practice is a key finding of this study, and it is suggested that investors and researchers explore this strategy further.

6.8.3 Values of Managers

Like the business case, the values of managers are universally seen in these cases as a very important contributing factor to the success of an engagement. Insight felt this issue could be one of the most important factors. Calvert claimed the leadership of the firm as the number one variable in its willingness to work with social investors. Examples were given where an issue progressed quickly, once a new chairman or CEO with more closely-aligned views took over. This factor can be particularly important where supportive individuals within the company are having difficulty moving an issue forward internally, and the shareholder can lend support to that individual's efforts. This finding supports the characterization of the firm as a forum for competing stakeholder interests, including internal stakeholders. Similarly, Insight found that an unsupportive individual in a key position can stop an engagement in its tracks.

It was noted that managers' values are very much connected with managers' personal reputations, and that this can be an important point of leverage. One targeting strategy suggested is to write to new CEOs and chairmen when they start, to determine the willingness of the new person to move forward on particular issues, and then target companies accordingly. Another strategy could be to seek out CEOs or board members who have made previous public commitments to sustainability and good governance, and then hold that person to those sentiments.

In addition to having values that are aligned, it was also seen as important that the company and the individuals involved have some level of knowledge and understanding of the issue in order to take it forward. This would seem to contradict the idea that new information will necessarily be well received. The truth lies somewhere in between, in that the provision of new and emerging issues is a driver of salience, but must still be somewhat within the paradigms of the individuals within the firm. If ideas are perceived to be too "radical", then they are likely to be dismissed out-of-hand and are therefore unlikely to be salient.

6.9 Assessing the Relative Importance of the Various Factors

Figure 6.2 below illustrates support for the propositions in each case, grouped by attribute.

From this, we can see that the three cases have different emphases when it comes to power and legitimacy. Insight and Hermes draw less upon power than does Calvert (due mostly to Calvert's use of normative pressure through shareholder resolutions), but the large funds draw more on legitimacy (due to their size and mainstream status). All three engage intensively, with Hermes being slightly more

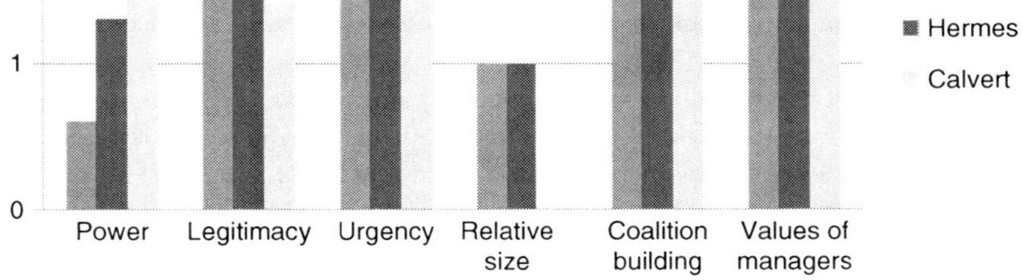

Fig. 6.2 Support for propositions, grouped by attribute

"low-key" than the others, based on its preference for behind-the-scenes engagement. Relative size was not considered important. Coalition-building was important for the large funds and very important for Calvert. The values of managers were seen to be very important to all three.

From a practitioners' perspective, these findings lend support to the notion that the targeting process (driven by an assessment of which managers have aligned values) is the most important aspect to get right. Building coalitions is also very important. However, investors cannot easily change their own size (which was the driver of legitimacy that led to the high scores for this factor). So apart from taking steps to build coalitions (and perhaps engaging with smaller companies), the size challenge is not easily addressed. A commitment to undertake intense engagements with an appropriate level of assertiveness and persistence is important, while ensuring that legitimacy is enhanced as much as possible (particularly relating to the business case). Power is applied as a tool where legitimacy-based attempts fail.

6.10 Conclusion

This chapter supports, with qualifications, Mitchell's et al. (1997) model of stakeholder salience based on the stakeholder's possession of power, legitimacy and urgency, moderated by the values of the target company's managers. The definition of legitimacy is enhanced to include the legitimacy of what a shareholder says (the strength and substance of the arguments), not just who they are (the shareholder's reputation and credibility in the market). Urgency is modified to include a sense of intensity of engagement, which not only includes time sensitivity, but also the persistence, assertiveness and resources applied. Added to the model are moderating factors around relative economic size and coalition building.

This chapter also confirms that shareholders are indeed most salient when there are high levels of power, legitimacy and urgency and the target company managers have values that allow for the accommodating of the shareholders' concerns. However, it is concluded that all three of the overarching attributes need not be present to achieve high levels of salience. The chapter suggests that within the engagement practitioner community, there is a strong preference for legitimacy-based engagement in the first instance, with an appropriate degree of intensity, and power being applied only after legitimacy-based options have been exhausted. This adds a temporal dimension to the stakeholder model, in that the attributes are not drawn upon at the same point in time, but applied sequentially as the engagement escalates.

It is concluded that the business case and the values of the target company managers are the two most important factors contributing to salience. It is hoped that the exploration, modification and expansion of Mitchell's et al. (1997) stakeholder model in the context of shareholder engagement will provide additional explanatory power for those seeking to improve corporate ESG performance through leveraging the influence of perhaps the most important stakeholders of the firm: its owners.

Chapter 7
Measuring the Impact of Engagement in Canada

Tessa Hebb, Heather Hachigian, and Rupert Allen

7.1 Introduction

Large institutional investors in Canada are increasingly seeing the value in mobilizing shareholder rights to affect change in the environmental, social and governance (ESG) standards of companies in their investment portfolios. Engagement activities range from quiet conversations and private consultations, to minority shareholder resolutions and proxy voting battles. The effectiveness of engagement, both in terms of enhancing shareholder value and improving the ESG standards of companies, is often cited as a reason to maintain ownership of a company rather than divest when company ESG standards are below acceptable levels. However, given the often private nature of engagement and the reluctance of companies to admit that their reason for improvement is due to pressure from shareholder engagement, it is difficult to quantify the impact corporate engagement has on corporate ESG standards.

This chapter argues that corporate engagement has the potential to produce a positive change in company behaviour. It asks: what are the factors in engagement that lead to successful outcomes? The chapter seeks to quantify any observed positive change in corporate ESG standards that result from engagement.

The chapter extends the literature on stakeholder engagement. It examines three different types of engagements and sponsoring institutions. It details the impact of power, urgency, and legitimacy on stakeholder salience (Mitchell, Agle, & Wood, 1997). It also builds on the sub-attributes of shareholder saliency demonstrated through a series of engagements (Gifford, 2009). The chapter provides three case studies of engagements between institutional investors and companies in Canada over the past 5 years. It examines the outcomes of each engagement from the perspectives of the investor. It also considers the short term impacts and long term changes in corporate behaviour that resulted from engagement.

T. Hebb (✉)
Carleton University, Ottawa, ON, Canada K1S 5B6
e-mail: thebb@attglobal.net

T. Hebb (ed.), *The Next Generation of Responsible Investing*,
Advances in Business Ethics Research 1, DOI 10.1007/978-94-007-2348-1_7,

The chapter is laid out in the following manner. In the next section we review the existing literature on this topic. The third section builds a theoretical framework in order to understand the salience of shareholders in their ESG engagement with companies. The fourth section of the chapter introduces each of the three case studies and provides data on their engagements and their outcomes. The fifth section of the chapter draws on public information and interviews with each of our three case studies to gain a deeper understanding of their engagement process. The sixth section looks at the implications of this research in terms of our theoretical understanding of corporate engagement. The chapter wraps up with some concluding observations, the limitations of this current research and future research to be undertaken.

7.2 Understanding Corporate Engagement

Responsible Investing (RI), once seen as antithetical to corporate profits, is facing a newly engaged global audience. Post-financial crisis, and with a growing awareness of sustainability issues, mainstream investors are beginning to lend a larger ear to the theme of RI (Hawley, 2009, SIO, 2008). They are increasing their initially tepid acknowledgement of the issues with a growing support seen in the increasing body of literature devoted to the subject (Hoepner & McMillan, 2009). The old mindset of RI as divergent and to some extent adversarial to company and shareholder goals (Friedman, 1970) is eroding (Wood & Jones, 1995; Freeman, 1999). RI is being seen as a performance driver, not as a performance laggard (Porter & Kramer, 2002; SAM, 2010). It is seen as a means of driving shareholder profit through the risk management of environmental, social and governance (ESG) issues.

This fundamental change in mindset is being brought about by the reinforcement of the RI business case that seeks to develop and bind the notions of financial performance with environmental, social and governance indicators. The business case contends that it is not simply a matter of ethics but rather that financial gains, management of risk and corporate responsibility converge in the long run (Hill et al., 2007; Wood, 2009). The RI advantage is one of anticipating and mitigating long-term risks, through the implementation of ESG screens and indicators, not simply moral and ethical considerations (UNEP FI, 2008). However, there are still barriers to larger adoption of RI practices such as a lack of disseminated information linking RI factors to firm performance and a lack of financial incentives for investors.

While mounting attention to RI is new, the overall concept is not. Its not so humble roots were in the anti-apartheid movement and with religious groups who intervened with corporations on specific social and moral issues (Beabot & Schmiesing, 2003; Social Investment Forum, 1995). Beginning in the early 1980s these social activist organizations were joined by two other forces, large individual shareholder activists, such as Robert Monks, and large institutional investors such as CalPERS (Hebb, 2008). These shareholder activists brought pressure to bear on companies concerning governance issues when their interests as shareholders were not aligned with company management (Gillan & Starks, 1998; Useem, 1996).

As corporate decision-making is delegated from shareholders to top managers, problems arise when the interests between managers and shareholders do not coincide. This happens when the basic opportunistic behaviour of individuals means they would rather make choices that maximize their own benefit over that of others (Eisenhardt, 1989; Luft, 1997). Known as the Principal-Agent Problem, the question arises how to get managers to act as loyal agents for shareholders' interests rather than their own (Jensen & Meckling, 1976; Fama & Jensen, 1983; Shleifer & Vishny, 1997).

Whether or not management and shareholder views are likely to coincide depends on a variety of factors and prevailing conditions; personal preference, ethical beliefs, contracts, goals, organizational culture, and manager values (Diltz, 1995; Agle, Mitchell, & Sonnenfeld, 1999; Reinhardt, Stavins, & Vietor, 2008; Howard-Grenville, Nash, & Coglianese, 2006).

The two fundamental mechanisms that a shareholder has to exercise are voice and exit. Voice has the potential to take many forms; private dialogue, public shaming, shareholder proposals and active monitoring. Exit on the other hand, has one simple option, divestiture (Hirschman, 1970). While exit appears to be an alternative to voice, the threat of exit could be used as a form of voice (Palmiter, 2002). The threat of exit can further enable the effectiveness of behind the scenes negotiation. In theory divestment is seen as having a negative impact on firms as it can raise the cost of capital for the firm. In reality, divestment does not often have an impact on the cost of capital but rather, it is the threat to corporate reputation that companies fear. Consequently it is suggested that the threat of exit could possibly speak more authoritatively than conventional voice when used by smaller scale investors (Gallagher et al., 2009). Although, this is difficult to substantiate given the private nature of negotiations.

Full divestiture is still seen primarily as a means of ridding shareholders of poor performing stocks (Alexandrou & Sudarsanam, 2001). Some studies have noted that incentives to divest might not be based solely on performance, but rather that private and political views may force management strategies (Jensen & Murphy, 1990; Wright & Ferris, 1997).

Activist shareholders, those who choose to exercise voice in terms of influencing the direction of corporate strategy, use a variety of methods to signify their displeasure with corporate policies and governance issues (Hebb, 2008). While the positive effects of this type of lobbying by large institutional investors has been noted in some cases, known as the CalPERS effect (Anson, White, & Ho, 2003; Barber, 2006; Smith, 1996) and the Hermes effects (Becht, Franks, Mayer, & Rossi, 2008), there is still some contestation and contradiction in other studies over the positive effects of shareholder activism (Gillan & Starks, 2007; Karpoff, 2001; Romano, 2001).

The differing results of these studies are most likely a result of different metrics used and the single event or stochastic shock under investigation (Karpoff, 2001). Also, the studies which show a lacked correlation between shareholder engagement and financial benefits had access only to public information and due to the private nature of many negotiations it in unlikely that some of the activism was made public

(Carleton, Nelson, & Weisbach, 1998). In contrast Becht et al. (2008), who found a very strong and positive relationship, had access to the material that reflected the behind the scenes negotiations and were able to factor this information into their analysis.

The active nature of voice centered shareholder engagement in terms of monitoring and dialogue with companies can make it prohibitively expensive in terms of potential returns (Bainbridge, 1995). As such it is beyond the means of most mainstream small scale investors who can rationalize leaving engagement to others rather than engaging themselves (O'Barr & Conley, 1992; Hendry, 2004). Generally, only large institutional investors are able to absorb the hefty costs of continuous monitoring and overcome the free-rider problem of small investors receiving the same benefit without the associated costs (Coffee, 1991; Gantchev, 2009). However, the willingness of institutional investors to act in coalition and the increasing block ownership of funds are seen to be making it easier for smaller investors to pursue meaningful engagements over divestment (Hawley & Williams, 1997, 2000; Monks, 2000).

Recent studies of stakeholder theory reinforce the claim that shareholders play an increasingly important role in determining the corporate strategy (Wood & Jones, 1995; Hillman & Keim, 2001; Moneva, Riviera-Lirio, & Munoz-Torres, 2007). In the past, the importance of stakeholder claims was thought to rest solely on the shoulders of whether the particular claim or stakeholder was deemed to be legitimate or not (Clarkson, 1995). Now, stakeholder salience is understood to be the result of a variety of attributes; power, urgency and legitimacy (Mitchell et al., 1997).

7.3 Building a Theory of Corporate Engagement

Shareholders have a particular problem when it comes to interacting with the firms in which they have an ownership stake. That is ensuring that the firms, or rather the decision making managers, are pursuing and making decisions that are in the best interests of the shareholders, not simply representing their own opportunistic ends and needs. This is known as the Principal/Agent Problem and arises when there is a separation of ownership and control (Jensen & Meckling, 1976). The separation occurs when the principal, the shareholders, delegate their responsibilities of decision making to managers at the firm, the agent, who can consequently act in their own self interest and utility maximization which could undermine the interests of the shareholders (Berle & Means, 1932; Galbraith, 1976; Koford & Penno, 1992).

Principals delegate their decision making authority to agents because the agents have a greater knowledge and awareness of day-to-day company operations, and hence will be in a superior position to facilitate and orchestrate profit maximizing decisions and choices, which coincides with the primary goal of shareholders (Friedman, 1970). This means that the actions taken by the agent have the potential to create a significant and hopefully beneficial impact not only for themselves but also for the principals. However, as noted above there are certain risks and conflicts of interest associated with this type of relationship which imbues the agent with decision making capabilities and powers of the principal, as both will try for rational utility maximization (Jensen & Meckling, 1976; Koford & Penno, 1992; Luft, 1997).

The point of contention manifests itself in two ways; moral hazard and adverse selection (Eisenhardt, 1989). Adverse selection addresses the possibility of agents misrepresenting their ability to perform their specific tasks and moral hazard refers to the danger of agents not maximizing their effort to act on the principals behalf. Both arise out of conditions of incomplete and asymmetrical information between the principal and agent. And both of these create residual costs (Eisenhardt, 1989). Therefore it is in the principal's best interest to reduce the asymmetry of information, by determining what the agents are doing and mitigating behaviour that is not in line with the interests of the principal (Skankman, 1999).

Monitoring is one of the control mechanisms that owners are able to exert on firms as a method of realigning their interests and values of the managers and ensuring that their values are being taken into consideration. However, monitoring is a costly exercise, and not something that can realistically be undertaken by a solitary investor because of the prohibitive costs and the propensity of the free rider problem, which undermines the incentives of any one firm to initiate a monitoring program on its own (Coffee, 1991, 1997).

The costly nature of monitoring, originally seen as a barrier to principals exerting a form of control, is slowly being alleviated through the increasing number of large scale shareholders and investors who work in coalitions. These groups are better able to manage and offset the costs of monitoring due to their large size and stake in the firm. This is seen as shifting of the power dynamic between owners and managers (Clark & Hebb, 2004; Hebb, 2008).

But how do firms give priority to the rising number of stakeholder claims? How do they choose who to listen to? Not all stakeholders are treated equally. Some appear to have stronger voices than others (Henriques & Sadorsky, 1999). Mitchell et al. (1997) suggests there are three key attributes that affect stakeholder salience; power, urgency and legitimacy. There must be an accounting for all three, as stakeholder influence will be positively related to the cumulative attribute factors. Gifford (2009) builds on the descriptive framework established by Mitchell and further subdivides the categories into sub-attributes and maps them onto stakeholder engagement practices. He also found that these attributes are most salient when the managers hold values that accommodate the stakeholders' concerns.

Gifford suggests "that within the engagement practitioner community, there is a strong preference for legitimacy based engagement in the first instance, with an appropriate degree of intensity, and power being applied only after legitimacy-based options have been exhausted." This would suggest a temporal element with factors drawn upon in a sequential pattern rather than all at once during shareholder engagement of ESG factors (Gifford, 2009).

Stakeholder theory while still predominantly concerned with the corporate point of view towards business practices (Frooman, 1999) is slowly beginning to take into consideration external factors when dealing with stakeholder relationships (Harrison & Freeman, 1999). Phillips, Freeman, and Wicks (2003) suggest that stakeholder theory must "... incorporate a respect for both the power of managerial action and the constraints and catalysts stakeholders create for managers" if it is to address the nature of stakeholder importance in changing and improving on company strategy. Reconciling the different avenues of stakeholder research; normative, descriptive and instrumental, is difficult, because the different streams function more as alternative approaches to stakeholder theory rather than as complements (Donaldson & Preston, 1995). This represents a serious obstacle in the development of stakeholder theory and will likely keep a unified theory at bay until it is reconciled (Agle et al., 2007).

While addressing the issues of integrated stakeholder theory is important, this chapter seeks to further develop and build upon normative and descriptive areas of stakeholder theory. It examines which factors contribute to shareholder salience in improving ESG standards of investee companies.

7.4 Methodology

In exploring the Canadian experience with shareholder engagement and its impact on corporations, this chapter uses Grounded Theory to develop a framework inductively from the data collected in our case studies (Glaser & Strauss, 1967). Eisenhardt (1989) argues that "multiple cases are powerful means to create theory because they permit replication and extension among individual cases". By replication we are not referring to enhancing chances of statistically significant results by increasing sample size, but rather the possibility of collecting more available observations and design variables to enhance the depth of our comparisons (Yin, 2009). Our research does not focus on specific variables, recognizing that each case as a whole is a set of complex interactions between variables and it is these interactions within the case as a unit that are important rather than the variables themselves (Eisenhardt, 1989). We develop three case studies; two focusing on institutional investors and one on an investment organization. The three cases are selected based on their size (large institutional investors/advisors), reputation for engagement (leaders in Canada), and representation of different types of investment institutions (pension fund, mutual fund and investment advisor).

Each case focuses on a specific area of engagement, representing either an environmental, social and governance issue. Data are collected through semi-structured interviews and document review.

The interviews are designed to uncover the impact of engagement from the perspective of the investor. One interview is conducted in person, while the other two interviews are conducted by telephone. Interview questions are constructed to reflect why the organization chooses to engage, how the organization conducts its engagements and the impact of the engagements on the firms. The interaction between these variables contributes to developing a framework of the engagement experience in Canada and its impacts.

In addition to the interviews, some quantitative data are collected through review of public documents. This data includes voting outcomes on shareholder proposals, forms of engagement, focus areas of engagement, changes in corporations' ESG policies and a time dimension. These data complement the interviews, allowing us to quantify observed positive changes in corporate ESG standards and measure them against what we find in interviews related to the reduction of risk or impact on financial returns in aggregate.

Our analysis relies on a comparative case study approach of Grounded Theory (see Post & Andrews, 1982). This allows us to compare cases that are similar with respect to several variables but with different outcomes (impact) and cases with similar outcomes but many variable differences to examine which conditions they have in common, allowing us to uncover some possible causes in both scenarios (Yin, 2009). It is our intention to piece together the individual patterns to draw a more complete theoretical picture of the engagement process. (Eisenhardt, 1989).

7.5 Three Case Studies of Canadian Corporate Engagement

In this section, we present data on engagement to gain a deeper understanding of the engagement practices of each of our three case studies, CPPIB, SHARE and NorthwestEthical Investments. Each of the three case studies is separate and distinct. Each has different organizational structures, policy frameworks and mandates. As a result, each case study's engagement practices should be viewed as a discreet set of practices. This section of the chapter is drawn from publically available information.

The Canada Pension Plan Investment Board (CPPIB, 2009), which was incorporated in 1997 as a federal Crown corporation, is a professional investment management organization responsible for investing the $123.9 billion in assets of the Canadian Pension Plan (March, 2010). CPPIB is a large asset owner and undertakes direct and collaborative engagements with the companies in which it invests, as well as industry dialogue, and proxy voting. CPPIB currently focuses its engagement on three areas: climate change, extractive industries (oil and gas and mining) and executive compensation. We examine CPPIB's Climate Change engagement, an area the investor believes to have the potential of significantly impacting long-term shareholder value. CPPIB focuses in particular on the energy and utilities sectors, as the increasing regulations on GHG emissions will likely lead to higher costs for firms. The investor's overall objectives with respect to this focus area are to enhance disclosure and corporate reporting on strategies to manage climate change risks and to improve research and analysis on the impact of increased regulation of GHG emissions on long-term shareholder value (CPPIB *Report on Responsible Investing*, 2009).

The Shareholder Association for Research and Education (SHARE) was established in 2000 as a social enterprise with a mandate to coordinate and implement RI practices. It provides services mostly to smaller funds, such as Meritas Mutual Funds, which has combined assets under management (with Qtrade Fund Management) of $350 million ($4 billion under administration). We focus on SHARE's Say on Pay campaign, which promotes the establishment of an advisory vote on executive compensation. The Say on Pay campaign began with the banking sector in Canada and grew to include the energy and oil and gas sectors, among others.

Ethical Funds, a Canadian mutual fund company which has been active in socially responsible investing since the 1980s, established its Shareholder Action Program in 2000. In 2007, Ethical Funds partnered with Northwest Funds, creating Northwest & Ethical Investments L.P. (NEI). NorthwestEthical has close to $4 billion in assets under management (March, 2010). We focus on NorthwestEthical Funds' engagement with Barrick Gold. Areas of engagement with this company have included human rights, environmental justice, biodiversity, climate change, HIV/AIDS. Community Engagement has been a focus of its engagement with Barrick over recent years. In 2006 Ethical Funds submitted a resolution asking Barrick to develop and disclose its Community Engagement and Sustainable Development Guidelines. Unsatisfied with its progress on this issue, the investor filed a second shareholder resolution in 2009 on this issue, which received 17% support.

7.5.1 Breadth and Depth

We note that independent of their asset size, all respondents target their engagements in an effort to balance the depth and breadth of their investments. We also observe that all cover a range of environmental, social and governance (ESG) issues in their focused engagements.

SHARE engages across all three areas. See Fig. 7.1 for a quarterly report of SHARE's 2009 engagements under each ESG category. We see a significant increase in environmental engagements in quarter 3, which is due to SHARE's involvement in the Carbon Disclosure Project's letter campaign (46 letters). Overall, there is some variance between the number of issues addressed under each category.

In 2009 Ethical Funds placed most emphasis on environmental and social issues (38 and 31 engagements respectively) and less on governance (3 engagements). However, from 2006 to 2008 Ethical engaged more heavily on governance issues, writing to all companies on the Toronto Stock Exchange (TSX) Composite Index

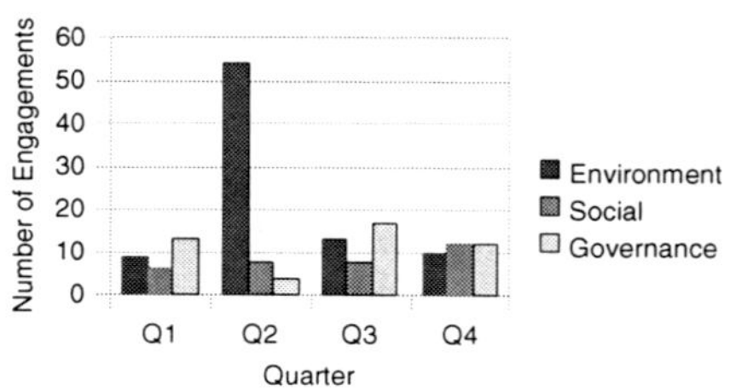

Time Period	Environment	Social	Governance
Q1	9	6	13
Q2	54	8	4
Q3	13	8	17
Q4	10	12	12

Fig. 7.1 SHARE's engagements in 2009

asking them to link executive and director performance evaluations and compensation plans to the achievement of long term ESG objectives, and to disclose this to investors.

In aggregate over 2009, Ethical Funds reported on 72 focus engagements and SHARE reported on 65 (plus 46 letters to companies on CDP). These figures do not reflect number of companies engaged however, because in some cases investors will engage with the same company on several issues.

CPPIB in its annual Report on Responsible Investing highlights its impact across each of the three focus areas; climate change, extractive industries, and executive compensation. Many of CPPIB's engagements are undertaken in collaboration with other concerned investors. The report indicates areas where there have been improvements in corporate standards and disclosure. It also details CPPIB's engagement in other areas beyond the three listed above, including a collaborative engagement on the Global Compact and issues concerning Burma.

From the information available in public reports we are also able to observe the breadth and depth of the specific engagement cases we focus on in the interviews. SHARE's Say on Pay engagement started with the *big five* banks in Canada and has now reached a total of 21 corporations. NorthwestEthical has engaged on 7 issues with Barrick Gold beginning in 2005. CPPIB's focused Climate Change engagement involves both direct engagement with companies and collaboration through the Carbon Disclosure Project. The Climate Change engagement began in 2006. Ethical's engagement with Barrick Gold originated in 2002–2003 demonstrating the level of commitment involved in each of these focus engagements.

7.5.2 Methods of Engagement

Although at this time we do not have specific data on the number of letters, phone calls and meetings for all three cases, this corporate dialogue can be inferred from the residual of the total number of engagements and in some cases shareholder proposals filed for each investor. SHARE and NorthwestEthical both file proposals as part of their engagement program. In 2009, SHARE filed a total of 23 proposals, which made up 36%, (22% when 46 CDP letters are included) of its total engagement activities. NorthwestEthical filed 11 proposals in 2009, constituting 15% of its total engagement activities in 2009. On average, NorthwestEthical filed 12 proposals over the past 5 years and SHARE filed an average of 24.5 over the past 2 years. In contrast, CPPIB has not filed shareholder proposals. However, "where appropriate CPPIB will work with other investors to help draft shareholder proposals (CPPIB *Policy on Responsible Investing*, 2009)."

In 2009, NorthwestEthical filed the majority (eight) of its proposals on issues regarding human rights/indigenous rights and three related to disclosure on environmental performance. In contrast, SHARE's 2009 proposals are concentrated on governance rather than social and environmental issues, with a total of 21 proposals filed on executive compensation, 1 on a social issue and 1 on CDP disclosure. We find similar results in 2008.

With regard to the method used for each case's specific engagements, Say on Pay began with letters and then escalated to filing proposals. NorthwestEthical took a similar escalating approach to its engagement with Barrick Gold, beginning with dialogue in 2002–2003 on a number of issues and has filed two shareholder proposals since this time against the company.

CPPIB uses a number of approaches for engagement including direct engagement, collaborative engagement, industry dialogue and proxy voting. On issues of climate change CPPIB both engages directly with companies and collaborates with the Carbon Disclosure Project (CDP). In 2009 the CDP sent out 3700 questionnaires including 200 in Canada on climate change. Following a request by CPPIB in 2008, the Canadian Institute of Chartered Accountants published guidelines for the inclusion of climate change-related disclosure in the Management's Discussion & Analysis (MD&A) section of companies' annual reports. Additionally, CPPIB actively seeks and encourages third party research that incorporates long-term, material ESG factors.

One common trend we observe between all three cases is the use of collaboration in their focused engagements. For example CPPIB as mentioned above collaborates with the CDP on its Climate Change engagement. SHARE collaborates with the Canadian Coalition for Good Governance (CCGG) and NorthwestEthical collaborates through the UNPRI on its indigenous people and extractive industry engagements.

7.5.3 Divestment

In 2005 Ethical Funds divested from 5 of 45 companies it engaged and in 2006 it divested from 3 companies after attempts of engagement were not successful. Since 2006 however, Ethical Funds has not divested from any companies with which it engages. We find no evidence of any of SHARE's engagements resulting in divestment, nor has there been any divestment at CPPIB as they believe that engagement is more effective than divestment in improving company standards.

7.5.4 Proxy Voting

All three organizations see Proxy Voting as part of their Responsible Investing mandate and see proxy voting as a valuable asset. SHARE divides its services to clients between engagement and proxy voting. CPPIB and NorthwestEthical include it in their engagement activities.

As noted in CPPIB's Report on Responsible Investing, during the 2009 proxy season, CPPIB voted at 3070 meetings on 17,937 agenda items. CPPIB voted against management 15% of the time. CPPIB reviewed on a case by case basis all of the shareholder proposals and voted on 763 shareholder proposals, comprising 4.3% of all resolutions they voted on. "A number of shareholder proposals were withdrawn by their proponents following successful engagement, resulting in companies agreeing to take action in response to the proposals (CPPIB *Report on Responsible Investing*, 2009)". CPPIB supported several shareholder proposals requesting improved disclosure of governance, social and climate change related risks. Examples include disclosure on environmental and social risk (voted for 18/26 proposals) and majority vote for election of directors (voted for 27/28 proposals).

Ethical Funds voted proxies at 634 company meetings in 2009 and opposed management's recommendations to shareholders 46% of the time. Main areas of contention included director independence, options, compensation, auditor independence, and shareholder resolutions. Ethical Funds supported resolutions filed by shareholders 84% of the time. Although SHARE cannot vote proxies, it provides a comprehensive proxy-voting service to help institutional investors exercise their voting rights. "SHARE assesses environmental, social and governance factors to help investors exercise voting rights in a way that builds long-term shareholder value (SHARE, 2010)."

7.5.5 Impacts of Engagement

7.5.5.1 Shareholder Proposals

Compared to the results of corporate dialogue, outcomes of shareholder proposals prove to be much easier to quantify. Of the eleven proposals filed by Ethical Funds in 2009, we observe four positive results, where three were adopted after a vote and one withdrawn before making it on the ballot. Ethical characterizes the outcome of two of its proposals as neutral. These two proposals resulted in votes that did not pass but did gain significant leverage or were withdrawn. We observe negative results from the other five proposals, where the support was poor or the vote was not placed on the proxy circular.

Of the 23 proposals filed by SHARE in 2009, we observe that ten have been adopted or withdrawn before a vote. The other thirteen proposals have not yet been voted on or the results are not available publicly. For all proposals filed by SHARE 2008 and 2009 where results are available, all have been adopted, withdrawn, or raised significant support and were adopted in the following year.

7.5.5.2 General Impacts

We also look at results of all methods engagements in aggregate to capture the impacts of dialogue on corporations' behaviour. In the case of Ethical Funds, the investor has experienced more positive results overtime, with positive results in 39.5% of its total engagements in 2006 to 45.7% in 2009. For SHARE it is more difficult to capture the general trends in engagement in terms of percentage since SHARE presents its data quarterly and engagements stretch across several quarters. But overall it is possible to observe an aggregate of 69 positive trends compared to 34 negative trends over 2008 and 2009. CPPIB's annual Report on Responsible Investing highlights a number of areas where their engagement has been successful.

We now turn to considering the particular outcomes of the three focus engagements. For CPPIB, "Several Canadian companies we engaged improved the quality of their reporting on climate change and sustainability issues, including providing more detail. Ninety-nine Canadian companies provided a response to the CDP information request in 2009" (CPPIB, 2009).

For SHARE, of the "Say on Pay" shareholder proposals that went to a ballot in 2009, the average shareholder support was 53%, (4 votes) which is 12% more votes than were received the previous year at Canada's banks. These majority votes have resulted in "Say on Pay" policies now in place at Canada's major banks. In 2010 SHARE submitted 12 more proposals on "Say on Pay" and already three companies have engaged in discussions with SHARE in an effort to have the proposals withdrawn.

Ethical Funds has engaged with Barrick Gold since 2002–2003 through dialogue and submitted two shareholder proposals over this time. Areas where engagement appears to have an impact include Barrick's establishment of a human rights policy, joining the UN Global Compact on corporate responsibility and providing antiretroviral drugs to employees and their families in Africa. However Barrick has not been responsive to Ethical's request that the company conduct a human rights impact assessment of a project in the Western Shoshone community in Nevada. Ethical Funds filed a shareholder proposal in 2009 in an effort to get the company to improve its human rights and environmental performance. The proposal received 17% support.

7.6 Corporate Engagement: Canadian Experience

Semi-structured interviews were conducted over the winter of 2010 with representatives of engagement teams at CPPIB, SHARE and NorthwestEthical Funds. The interviews were designed to identify each organization's definition and approach to engagement, success indicators and impacts. Interview questions are broadly organized into three categories, yet the variables within these categories are intricately linked. The first set of questions explore why investors use engagement, territory that has been extensively covered in RI literature (Hebb, 2008). The second set addresses the methods of engagement used by these organizations. An understanding of the rationale and methodology of engagement for each case provides a basis for exploring the impacts of engagement, which is our third category of interview questions. These three sets of questions will build on the data we provided in the previous section to deepen our account of the engagement experience and impacts in Canada.

7.6.1 Why Engage?

Interviews begin by asking participants what shareholder engagement means to their organization and how they define the concept. The most apparent theme that emerges in this section of the interviews is that all respondents view engagement as a large part of their responsibility as long-term investors. One respondent describes themselves as "active owners that engage to enhance long-term financial performance" (CPPIB). Another comments that "using the rights associated with share ownership, investors can influence companies to improve their management of environmental, social and governance (ESG) risks and opportunities, helping to build accountability and long-term shareholder value" (SHARE). For our third respondent, "engagement is a very crucial part of what we do as investors. We take ownership very seriously" (NorthwestEthical).

All three engagers see engagement as broader than simply dialogue with companies in their portfolio. Rather, it represents all positive forms of interaction between the shareholder and the company including, dialogue, reports, direct and collaborative engagement, input to regulators, developing codes of conduct, and proxy voting. In the case of SHARE and NorthwestEthical Funds it also includes submitting shareholder resolutions.

There is also a consensus between investors we interviewed that the definition of engagement extends beyond interactions with companies in their portfolios, to include industry associations, regulators and other stakeholders in the process. Only one respondent framed its definition of engagement by comparing it with alternative forms of socially responsible investing, claiming "[engagement] is preferential to screening stocks".

Respondents were then asked to identify the process of selecting firms with which they engage. All investors we interviewed have developed focus areas for their engagement. However, we identified some divergence between each cases' process of selecting focus areas. One investor "engages in a portfolio review to establish its focus areas. ESG issues are prioritized using a risk based approach, including relative risk and size of holding" (CPPIB). Although concern for risk is incorporated into the other two respondent's selection process, they both use a range of factors, including Canadian values, investors' interest and expert opinion, to identify corporations and focus areas for engagement. Both respondents acknowledged their limited resources and suggested that concern for the likelihood of success plays a role in terms of selecting their engagements.

"Some issues are harder to engage on than others. Corporate governance is the easiest because there are mechanisms and support to make this work." (NorthwestEthical Funds). The respondent suggests issues that are more difficult to engage on such as human rights, are often intangible, particularly if there is an absence of credible third parties to promote the cause or the issue is not reflected in legislation. An example of such an issue is "free, prior and informed consent" that impacts communities serving as host to large scale developments around the world (NorthwestEthical Funds).

Engagement can be a costly and resource intensive activity, which raises the question of how it aligns with an investor's fiduciary duties. Two respondents stated that they conduct cost-benefit analysis to determine whether or not to engage with a company. The third respondent suggested that "it is less about costs and more about efficient use of resources and focusing our efforts." (NorthwestEthical Funds). Although engaging with companies internationally was raised as a cost constraint (NorthwestEthical Funds). Two respondents agree that often "it is too costly *not* to engage in many cases" and our third respondent suggests that "compared to what portfolio managers get paid, shareholder engagement is a bargain" (NorthwestEthical Funds).

When asked to consider whether other investors may abstain from engagement to reap the benefits from others undertaking engagement, one interviewee comments that their organization "works with investors who do not raise the free-rider problem as an issue because for them, improving the environmental, social and governance profiles of the companies in which they invest is an endeavour to which they have strongly committed themselves" (SHARE). All respondents referred to collaborative efforts as a strategy to reduce the costs of engagement. One respondent stressed the importance of collaborative efforts such as the UNPRI which has "tilted the tables in our favour" (NorthwestEthical Funds).

7.6.2 How to Engage?

We then ask our respondents to describe how they engage with firms in their focus areas. This is inherently dependent on their rationale for engagement and will contribute to understanding the impacts of engagement. All respondents indicated that they use a variety of engagement methods and that "the method of engagement we use, depends on the issue" (CPPIB). However, there is some divergence in the method that is used most frequently by each organization and how these methods are applied.

In thinking about the methods of engagement they use, we asked our respondents to describe their engagement approach in terms of the three pillars of stakeholder theory; legitimacy, urgency and power. All respondents identify legitimacy as the most important aspect of their engagement. Legitimacy is not only defined by size of the investor, but also by the approach that is taken in the engagement. All respondents agree that power is a last resort and not something that is commonly used. "We are not often a large investor; we don't often fall in the top ten to twenty investors . . . corporations are not responding to us because we have power" (NorthwestEthical Funds).

CPPIB's "engagement involves dialogue with senior executives and board members of companies in which we invest as well as with regulators, industry associations and other stakeholders. Engagement can be direct or collaborative with other investors in order to combine resources and expertise (CPPIB, 2009)." CPPIB first conducts extensive research on the engagement before the company is even approached. CPPIB uses a four step approach in its engagements. First it analyzes the ESG risks of companies in its public equity portfolio using internal and third party research. Then it identifies the engagement focus areas considering materiality, time horizon, resource implications and likelihood of success. It determines the optimum method of engagement: direct, collaborative, proxy voting and/or input to regulators. The fourth step is to develop a list of companies for direct engagement and set specific engagement objectives (CPPIB). With its commitment to disclose its RI activities CPPIB publishes an annual report of its RI activities and achievements.

NorthwestEthical Funds also uses in-person meetings with the progress of these meetings reported in their public documents. Ethical Funds uses minority shareholder resolutions if they do not see significant progress through dialogue. They begin their dialogues with comprehensive research on both the company and the case. Although they lack the size of CPPIB, they gain legitimacy with companies through their engagement approach "We do not treat annual meetings as theatre, we don't embarrass executives through press releases, we do not use the media to make our case. We are solutions oriented (NorthwestEthical Funds)." This speaks to both the use of legitimacy and the use of urgency of the issues in increasing saliency on engagement with companies. However, the fact that they are willing to put forward minority shareholder resolutions does increase the power of this small fund.

Consistent with our findings for the other two respondents, SHARE also uses letters and in-person meetings frequently in its corporate dialogue. Also like the other two engagers, solid arguments backed by in depth research provide the organization with the urgency and legitimacy required to gain saliency with the companies with which it engages. For this respondent, "persistence is a key to successful engagement" (SHARE). Like NorthwestEthical Funds, SHARE is also willing to use minority shareholder resolutions when dialogue falters. For them engagement is issues driven "If we can't make headway on the issue and generate support broadly we generally don't pursue it through the proposal mechanism" (SHARE).

Respondents were also encouraged to discuss their experiences with negative approaches to engagement, including divestment and reputational damage. These investors try to avoid the use of negative media campaigns and cited that reputational damage is not in the best interest of investors or the company.

7.6.3 *Impact of Engagement*

All respondents agree that measuring success is a difficult task, particularly on an annual basis, as in many cases it may take a few years before seeing any change in a firm's behaviour. Additionally there is difficulty when there is a disconnect between a corporations' policy and performance. A third problem identified by a respondent is determining whether a change in behaviour was a direct result of their own engagement actions, because "corporations are loath to admit that our engagement had an impact on them" (Ethical Funds).

CPPIB uses three indicators to measure success: more disclosure, financial performance, and lower risk. A second respondent's definition of success requires a "concrete balance of depth of dialogue with the companies and the breadth of the engagers willing to address the issue" (SHARE). For this respondent, success is about "attention to an issue where there was no attention before and bringing about change where issuer willingness and/or shareholder consensus is found" (SHARE). Our third respondent measures its success by setting objectives for engagement and tracking against these benchmarks. The results of their engagement are measured against key progress indicators and are reported annually.

In addition to commenting on more general trends, we prompted our respondents to provide their perspective on the impact of their specific engagements (Climate Change Say on Pay, and Barrick) and the response they have received from corporations. There was some variance in the degree of positive response to engagement that each of the three cases experienced. One investor reported an overall positive response in its focused engagements. "Several Canadian companies we engaged improved the quality of their reporting on climate change and sustainability issues, including providing more detail about how their strategies are being implemented and about performance on climate change and sustainability-related goals (CPPIB, 2009, 6)".

Our other two cases both reported experience with some negative responses, claiming that response from the firm depends on the issue, and also on whether the firm has previous experience with the engagement process. In the case of the latter, a positive response was more likely when the firm was familiar with the engager, finds one respondent. The "Say on Pay" campaign received a very strong positive response. "The response to our letter was quite good, although it took the banks some time to get into the issue substantively" (SHARE). Our third respondent reported a mix of positive and negative responses from its engagement with Barrick.

In general we find through our interviews that urgency and legitimacy are more critical to successful stakeholder salience and engagement then the attribute of power. In the next section of the chapter we will discuss the implications of our findings.

7.7 Testing the Saliency of Shareholder Engagement

Concern for companies' environmental, social and governance (ESG) standards are becoming increasingly acknowledged by today's investors. In the past, financial data was deemed the primary source of information required to judge the suitability of investment. But a deeper understanding of the impact that ESG performance has on risk over time is making RI a mainstream activity for investors. With company ESG data now available through such dominant information providers as Bloomberg, Thompson Reuters, and MSCI, investors are able to monitor these standards at the company level with greater efficiency.

The mantra of today's investors is one of active ownership. Increasingly these investors directly engage companies in their investment portfolio in an effort to raise their ESG standards. The three cases under investigation all use corporate engagement as their preferred method of RI and active ownership. They see positive corporate engagement as a more effective method of influencing and raising corporate ESG standards than using negative screens or divestment. Increasingly divestment is not being used as a tool to influence positive corporate change, as it is a blunt instrument and doesn't deliver an effective message to company management. The largest of our cases (CPPIB) focuses on engagement rather than on divestment in its climate change engagements. NorthwestEthical has not used it in the past few years, and SHARE is a service provider on engagement rather than an asset owner in its own right.

The question we ask in this chapter is whether such engagement does indeed have a measurable impact on companies' ESG standards. If so, to what can we attribute the saliency of these particular stakeholders? It has been suggested that power, legitimacy, and urgency are the key attributes of stakeholder saliency (Mitchell et al., 1997; Gifford, 2009). Our three cases confirm this central thesis.

We suggest that shareholders are stakeholders of today's corporations. Granted they are a unique class of stakeholder given their legal status as owners of public companies. As a result of their status, the claim of shareholders (also known as principals) on the firm is seen as legitimate with their rights enshrined in law (Jensen & Meckling, 1976; Shleifer & Vishny, 1996). While this is also true of other company stakeholders whose claims are legitimized through legal contracts (employees and suppliers), legitimacy is not so clearly recognized for external agents that represent communities of interest such as customers, NGOs and activists. These external stakeholders must work harder than shareholders to establish legitimacy in their claims.

In contrast, shareholders are encouraged to act as corporate monitors, applying a level of oversight to their actions and decision-making. Though it is fair to say that to date shareholder rights have been restricted to a narrow band of influence. Establishing ESG corporate practices are usually seen as the domain of managers. Such practices are often deemed "ordinary business" and therefore not subject to shareholder intervention. As a result company managers are often unwilling to acquiesce their day-to-day management authority on these issues to shareholders. They resist external interference in setting corporate standards.

Our findings suggest that the power of the shareholder appears to be the least important of the three attributes that contribute to shareholder saliency. Comparing the results of our three cases we find similar impacts on corporations whether the shareholder is large (as in the case of CPPIB), mid-sized (NorthwestEthical) or small (SHARE). Though it should be noted that the two smaller engagers (by asset size) do put forward minority shareholder resolutions if they are unable to achieve satisfactory results with dialogue and therefore bolster their power in their relationship with the firm. In contrast, the largest engager, representing the largest fund in Canada (CPPIB), has not used the threat of public shareholder resolutions to achieve its desired results.

In most cases power strategies of divestment and use of media for negative campaigns have not been used. In fact it was suggested that such campaigns are far less successful in achieving meaningful change with companies as they result in entrenched positions and have a negative impact on the reputation of the engager. Only in the cases of the two smaller engagers was the sub-attribute of shareholder rights used to enhance the power of the engagement. Still, it appears that legitimacy and urgency in corporate engagement are of greater significance in achieving actual change within companies than power.

While shareholders have legitimacy with the firms they hold in their portfolio, it could be argued that when it comes to raising ESG standards, legal status is a necessary but not sufficient condition. Our case study suggests that for shareholders to influence corporate ESG standards other sub-attributes of legitimacy and urgency are required. Here we draw on the work of Gifford (2009) [See Table 6.5 for a detailed description of the sub-attributes of shareholder saliency.] All three cases undertake extensive research on the issues. They use research to establish a strong case for the ESG issue on which they engage. CPPIB first conducts extensive research on the engagement before the company is even approached. This would suggest that while their size and role in the Canadian economy gives them a significant amount of power, they prefer to engage the company through both the urgency of the issue and the legitimacy of their claim.

Strategies to develop legitimacy on issues include white papers, reports, roundtables, and presentations to company managers on the issue. They look for allies, work in coalitions, and point to legislative and regulatory agendas as part of their engagement with the company. All three cases highlight the critical importance of having a solid case to put before management, establishing a reputation, adding value in the discussion, and coming with solution oriented approaches. All three credit their success to their ability to engage management in a positive and constructive manner.

Legitimacy is further enhanced through attributes of knowledge, reputation, and individual values. The status of the engager is also important. Development of the business case for the issue under engagement (as detailed above) was also seen as critical to success in the engagement, as was presenting the societal case and the legal and regulatory framework. All three cases indicated that without building a substantive case on which to engage they doubted that they would have been successful.

Urgency is generated in the engagements but is not the essential driver. All three cases benchmark their engagement outcomes. Several engagements took place over a number of years with successful conclusions. None of the three cases under investigation pointed to the attribute of urgency as a driver of successful engagements nor was the lack of urgency discussed as the cause of unsuccessful engagements. In most cases the ability to bring forward a strong business case to back the ESG concern, combined with a reputation for positive, solution oriented outcomes was given as the key driver in successful engagements.

As suggested by Gifford (2009) each case stressed that the moderating influence of individual values of company management played a role in ensuring successful results from their engagement. In many cases engagers sought out company managers with shared values and a deep understanding of the issue under discussion.

7.8 Conclusion

These three case studies examine shareholder engagement and its ability to raise the ESG standards of firms. We suggest that such engagement is able to raise corporate ESG standards. Our three case studies back this claim. Given that shareholders are able to exert influence on company managers, we ask what attributes contribute to the salience of these particular stakeholders? Here we build on the stakeholder typology developed by Mitchell et al. (1997) and further refined by Gifford (2009). We find that of the three attributes deemed critically important to stakeholder saliency: power, legitimacy and urgency, that legitimacy is the most critical attribute in shareholders' ability to influence managers to raise corporate ESG standards.

We further find that the sub-attributes of legitimacy detailed by Gifford (2009): credibility of individuals, status and reputation of engaging institution, strong business case, strong societal case, and policy and regulatory environment, are critical to successful engagements. While some might assume that the legal status as shareholders would be enough to make these particular stakeholders salient, our case studies indicate that building on this legitimacy through exercising the sub-attributes is critical to successful engagement as measured by meaningful company change.

Currently our research looks at the impact of shareholder engagement from the perspective of the investor. We measure success in engagements using the metrics of the investors rather than from the perspective of the firm. This is a limitation of the research to date. We are unable to focus on impacts of engagement on particular firms using share prices and risk reduction indicators, as this requires significant time to establish a relationship with the firm. In addition, we do not attempt to build an econometric model for measuring the impacts of shareholder engagement. Although the share price, risk and changes in ESG policies of the firm are quantifiable, the independent side of the equation, such as the private conversations between managers and investors and trust building efforts, are complex and would be difficult to assign numerical values to these variables.

Future research will build on our current findings. We will provide a deeper analysis of the underlying externality and its broader social costs that each engagement represents. We will investigate the perspective of corporate managers on the engagement and its impacts. To do this we will interview company managers to capture their understanding of the engagement process and its outcomes in terms of ESG standards at the company level. We will look for their indicators of shareholder saliency and compare these to the investors' perspective detailed in this chapter.

Additionally we will attempt to quantify the changes that occurred in these companies as a result of engagement. What change in policies and practices resulted from the shareholder engagement? How were these implemented? What were the outcomes of these changes? How are they measured? Finally we will look to third party ESG rating agencies to see if the improved ESG standards at the company is captured in this data. We will also examine the financial impacts for the firm and investors of the ESG change.

Shareholder engagement is most often cited by institutional investors as their preferred method of implementing RI policies (PRI Initiative, 2009). To date engagement impacts lack detailed academic research to back the claim of their effectiveness. Further research is needed to address this gap.

Chapter 8
The Good Corporate Citizen

Edward J. Waitzer and Johnny Jaswal

8.1 Introduction

"...being too far ahead of your time is indistinguishable from being wrong." (Marks, 1993, 6)

Many observers view the law and legal scholarship as remarkably self-serving disciplines. Scholars and judges (Posner, 2008) often find a way to ensure that "the law" confirms the view they would otherwise favour for economic, social or political reasons. There are strong incentives built into the political process for those who make laws to engage in (and invite) such circumlocution, by being purposefully general in the language they use to express concepts.

The broad theme of this paper is that judges (by choice or default) often eschew clarity in the law and favour ambiguity in order to achieve a desired outcome (This easily leads to confusion and unintended consequences. One area where this ambiguity is apparent is the law surrounding proper corporate purpose, and the duties, discretion and accountability of directors. Our goal in this paper is not to advance a normative rationale for or against "good corporate citizenship". Rather, our focus is on how courts and legislators have attempted to devise legal norms relating to directors' (and officers') duties, in order to advance a modest notion of corporate social responsibility within the traditional framework of corporate governance.

At the heart of such efforts lies the continuing debate as to the obligation of directors and officers to act in "the best interests of the corporation" (Sunstein, 1995). As discussed later in this paper, translating this duty into clear, operational guidance for directors lies at the heart of one of the great, unresolved debates in corporate law – whether and to what extent the interests of the corporation are limited to those of its shareholders or extend to the "stakeholder" constituencies that contribute to or are impacted by the corporate enterprise. Suffice to say, at this juncture, that the Committee which recommended including such express statutory language

E.J. Waitzer (✉)
Stikeman Elliott, Toronto, ON, Canada M5L 1B9
e-mail: EWaitzer@stikeman.com

T. Hebb (ed.), *The Next Generation of Responsible Investing*,
Advances in Business Ethics Research 1, DOI 10.1007/978-94-007-2348-1_8,

in the Canada Business Corporations Act ("CBCA") specifically declined to offer guidance as to how the words "in the best interests of the corporation" should be interpreted. Instead, they left this task to the courts, while expressing the view that their formulation would allow the courts to escape from the constraints of what (they suggested) has somewhat charitably been described as the "anachronistic" view that has developed in the English courts (Dickerson, Howard, & Getz, 1971 para 241). They were referring to Gower's (1969, 522) complaint that such courts viewed the best interests of the company as that of its shareholders.

The Supreme Court of Canada's recent decision in BCE Inc. v. 1976 Debenture holders (the "BCE Decision")[1] illustrates the hazards of navigating this debate. In getting to a decision that confirmed the prevailing view of the law, and seeking to clarify its own reasons in Peoples Department Stores Inc. (Trustee of) v. Wise (the "Peoples Decision"),[2] the Supreme Court managed to express some strikingly confusing views about the duties of directors and directors' accountability. The near term result will likely be a diminution of the latter. Likewise, the Supreme Court's casual references to good corporate citizenship, in the absence of clear-headed analysis (or legislative norms), will likely serve primarily to add procedural costs to ensure adequate legal cover for board decisions, rather than create new norms and incentives to guide corporate conduct.

The BCE Decision may be welcomed by many. Boards will take comfort in language which suggests that, in the context of change of control transactions, their duty to act in the best interests of the corporation may be discharged by taking reasonable steps to maximize shareholder value. They will also welcome the broad discretion which the BCE Decision appears to confer on them to determine what is in the best interests of the corporation, should they choose to take a course other than maximizing short term shareholder value. Because of the breadth of effect that the Supreme Court has accorded to the concept of the business judgment rule, it will be difficult for corporate stakeholders (including shareholders) to challenge their conduct so long as directors act in a reasoned and informed manner.

Non-shareholder stakeholders and advocates of corporate social responsibility will welcome the Supreme Court's discussion of directors being required to act in the best interests of the corporation viewed as a "good corporate citizen".[3] They will also applaud the Supreme Court's statement that the fiduciary duty of directors is not confined to short-term profit or share value but, rather, where the corporation "is an ongoing concern, it looks to the long-term interests of the corporation".[4]

The BCE Decision provided the Supreme Court with a rare opportunity to articulate and clarify its view with respect to proper corporate purpose and the responsibilities of directors. To do so meaningfully would have required more careful elaboration on stakeholder theory, the director-centric governance model and

---

[1] [2008] S.C.J. No. 37, SCC 69.

[2] [2004] 3 S.C.R. 461.

[3] BCE Decision, supra note 49 at para. 81.

[4] Ibid., at para. 38.

attendant accountability mechanisms. Instead, unreasoned discourse, especially by the Supreme Court, is likely to be interpreted to provide something for everyone; which may mean too little for anyone (Daniels & Morck, 1995).[5] Put another way, the BCE Decision can be read as saying that the best interests of the corporation are the interests of those stakeholders that a particular board deems most worthy of protection provided that due process is adhered to in selecting which stakeholder interests to favour. It is unlikely that this is what the Supreme Court had in mind, rendering its reasoning somewhat suspect.

The first part of this paper reviews the history of ambiguity in the assessment of directors' duties and accountability. Specifically, the extent of uncertainty and public policy debate surrounding the duty of loyalty and good faith, the duty of care, and the business judgment rule, focussing particularly on Anglo-American law, are examined. The second part of the paper focuses on judicial circumlocution as to the role and accountability of directors in the BCE Decision. In the third part of the paper, various well developed legal theories that a court might invoke to meaningfully elaborate the role of directors are presented. In particular, the incorporation into corporate law of trust law principles, the team production approach to corporate law, moral stakeholder theory as a normative principle of corporate governance, the application of the common law duty to act reasonably and prescribing "enhanced" directors' duties in specified circumstances are considered. In addition, statutory reform and shareholder initiated approaches towards focusing director accountability are canvassed. We briefly canvass some relevant precedents, domestic or otherwise, to illustrate such approaches.

As we embark on a consideration of how such legal obligations might be framed, the factors motivating increasing pressure for companies to be "good citizens" are worth noting. At the simplest level, the lack of congruence between those who take a narrow view of corporate social obligations (i.e., to comply strictly with law) and the actual behaviour of corporate managers has become strained. As discussed later in the paper, it is obvious to any serious observer that corporate managers are highly attentive to the interests of various constituencies, beyond those of current shareholders and are constantly weighing competing interests. In this context, recognizing the limitations of legal norms, corporate law has been structured to provide "managerial discretion to respond to social and moral norms and sanctions" (Elhauge, 2005). This has become particularly relevant in a world characterized by connectedness and complexity. Globalization has eroded the power of states to regulate large, multi-national corporations (Wolf, 2001, 178) and market externalities (see for example Teubner, 1997, 3). Likewise, the sheer complexity of contemporary social problems challenges their susceptibility to effective regulation through traditional, national legal instruments. In this environment, corporations (and other

---

[5] See also, Frank Easterbrook and Daniel Fischel, The Economic Structure of Corporate Law (Cambridge, MA: Harvard University Press, 1991) at 38 – "A manager told to serve two masters (a little for the equity holders, a little for the community) has been freed of both and is answerable to neither. Faced with a demand from either group, the manager can appeal to the interests of the other."

effective institutions) are being forced to look farther ahead and farther afield to achieve "sustainable" solutions.

8.2 Statutory Duties

8.2.1 Duty of Loyalty and Good Faith

Some of the confusion regarding the role and accountability of directors can be traced to the conflation of directors' fiduciary and statutory duties. Canadian corporate law imposes two basic duties on directors and officers – a duty of care and one of loyalty and good faith, both of which are shaded by the "business judgment rule". While both are often referred to collectively as "fiduciary duties", it is more typical for the "fiduciary" label to be applied only to the duty of loyalty and good faith. For example, the Supreme Court of Canada in the Peoples Decision specifically referred to the duty of loyalty (in contrast to the duty of care) as a "statutory fiduciary duty".[6] Subsection 122(1)(a) of the CBCA provides that "every director and officer of a corporation in exercising their powers and discharging their duties shall act honestly and in good faith with a view to the best interests of the corporation."[7]

As Flannigan (2004) has pointed out in a series of articles, describing this "duty of loyalty" as a fiduciary obligation is a mistaken characterization. The function of fiduciary duties is to control opportunism and discipline self-interested behaviour in those arrangements in which an actor has "access to the assets of another for a defined or limited purpose".[8] The fiduciary accountability of corporate directors and officers is established through their preferential access to the assets of the corporation. Fiduciary duties are a narrow subset of the duty of loyalty, embracing conflicts between the corporate duties of directors and their personal interests. These typically arise in respect of corporate opportunities, compensation, contracts in which a director or officer has a material interest and change of control transactions. The broader statutory duty of loyalty and good faith imposes on directors and officers the obligation not to exceed their authority and to exercise such authority "in the best interests of the corporation." Considering the interests that directors must take into account in their decisions is a distinct exercise from defining the beneficiaries of their fiduciary duties. Conflating the two issues necessarily involves either the expansion of fiduciary duties or an erosion of the statutory duty of loyalty and good faith.

[6] Peoples Decision, supra note 50 at para. 32.

[7] Supra note 49.

[8] See also "The Boundaries of Fiduciary Accountability" (2004) 83 Canadian Bar Review; "The Adulteration of Fiduciary Doctrine in Corporate Law" (2006) 122 Law Quarterly Review; "Reshaping the Duties of Directors" (2005) 84; Canadian Bar Review; "Book Review: A Romantic Conception of Fiduciary Obligation" (2005) 84; Canadian Bar Review.

The mistaken description of the duty of loyalty and good faith as a "statutory fiduciary duty" is exemplified in the drafting proposals which led to the CBCA (the "Dickerson Report" Vol. 1). In characterizing the proposed duty as "a general statutory formulation of the principles underlying the fiduciary relationship between corporations and their directors (Ibid., p. 81)" the Dickerson Report referred to earlier U.K. (Company Law Committee, 1962) and Ontario law reform initiatives (Province of Ontario, 1967) In fact, a reading of the Ontario reform proposals suggests that the Select Committee on Company Law may have been focusing on the narrower "fiduciary" concern of directors foregoing their personal self-interest:

> The law is clear as to what duties of good faith are owed by a director to the company arising from the fiduciary relationship . . . the Committee has determined that it is not the director's fiduciary relationship to the company which is unclear in law, nor does the precise scope or nature of his duties and responsibilities need clarification (Ibid., p. 53).

While this may be a charitable view of the Ontario Select Committee's analysis, there is no basis for giving the Dickerson Report a similar benefit of the doubt. Making it clear that the statutory provision was intended to embrace common law and equitable principles, the Dickerson Report identified its purpose as giving "statutory support to principles that are as difficult to apply as they are well understood (Wolf, 2001, p. 81.)". By observing that the notion of the best interests of the corporation left "the way free for directors to take into account whatever factors they consider relevant in determining corporate policies (Ibid., p. 82)", they clearly had in mind a broader agency duty – one inconsistent with traditional fiduciary obligations.

The resulting lack of clarity and accountability is not unique to Canadian corporate law. Flannigan (2006a, 2006b) traces how things went astray shortly after the House of Lords' decision in Regal (Hastings) Ltd. v. Gulliver.[9] That decision confirmed the focus of fiduciary regulation on controlling opportunism, indicating strict liability where a conflict exists (or a benefit is obtained), absent consent. In contrast, the following month, the U.K. Court of Appeal in Re Smith & Fawcett Ltd.[10] combined the concept of fiduciary obligation with that of "the best interests of the corporation". Describing the power to register share transfers as a "fiduciary power", Lord Greene stated that directors "must exercise their discretion bona fide in what they consider – not what a court may consider – is in the interests of the company, and not for any collateral purpose".[11]

Likewise, in Howard Smith Ltd. v. Ampol Petroleum Ltd.,[12] in considering whether directors had properly issued shares during a control contest, the Privy Council took a view of fiduciary accountability as extending beyond the objective of controlling opportunism. In rejecting the argument advanced on behalf of the directors (that the issuance of shares was not motivated by self-interest and was

[9] [1942] One All E.R. 378, HL, [1967] 2. A.C. 134n

[10] [1942] 1 Ch. 304.

[11] Ibid., at 306.

[12] [1974] A.C. 821.

within the authority of the board), Lord Wilberforce purported to expand the scope of fiduciary accountability:

> But it does not follow from this, as the Appellants assert, that the absence of any element of self-interest is enough to make an issue valid. Self-interest is only one, though no doubt the commonest, instance of improper motive: and before one can say that a fiduciary power has been exercised for the purpose for which it was conferred, a wider investigation may have to be made.[13]

Nor is the confusion as to the distinction between fiduciary accountability and determining the best interests of the corporation limited to Anglo-Canadian jurisprudence. In credit Lyonnais Bank Nederland N.V. v. Pathe Communications Corp. ("Credit Lyonnais"), in the context of deciding whether there was a breach of fiduciary duties, then Chancellor Allen stated that "where a corporation is operating in the vicinity of insolvency, a board of directors is not merely the agent of the residue risk bearers, but owes its duty to the corporate enterprise."[14] While the decision was initially interpreted to expand directors' duties to include creditors when a corporation is in the so-called "zone of insolvency", subsequent case law has clarified that, rather than extending or expanding duties to creditors, it was intended to create an additional shield for directors against shareholders claiming the company should have taken increased risks for their benefit.[15] In the more recent Gheewalla case, the Delaware Supreme Court made it clear that duties are not owed directly to creditors but that directors continue to owe duties only to the corporate enterprise.[16]

The Supreme Court of Canada addressed the above-mentioned logic in the Peoples Decision. By doing so under the rubric of fiduciary obligations (as in Credit Lyonnais), it may have added to the confusion in Canada. Peoples Department Store Inc. ("Peoples") had been acquired by a subsidiary of Wise Stores Inc. ("Wise") from Marks & Spencer Canada Inc. ("M&S").[17] The three Wise brothers were directors of both Wise Stores and its new subsidiary. To protect amounts due to M&S on account of the purchase price, the purchase agreement restricted the amalgamation of the two corporations.[18] As a result, a joint procurement program was established whereby Peoples did most of the purchasing and transferred to Wise inventory purchased on its behalf.[19]

When Peoples filed for bankruptcy, its trustee claimed that the directors had breached their statutory duties of loyalty and care to Peoples by implementing the joint procurement plan.[20] While the Supreme Court of Canada determined the directors do not have a fiduciary duty to corporate creditors where the corporation is

---

[13] Ibid., at 834.

[14] 1991 Del. Ch. Lexis 215 at 108 (Del. Ch. 1991).

[15] Production Resources Group, L.L.C. v. NCT Group, Inc., 863 A. 2d 772 (Del. Ch. 2004).

[16] Foundation, Inc. v. Gheewalla, 930 A.2d 92 (Del. Sup. Ct. 2007).

[17] Peoples Decision, supra note 50 at para. 8.

[18] Ibid., at para. 11.

[19] Ibid., at para. 18.

[20] Ibid., at para. 23.

approaching insolvency,[21] it framed its analysis in terms of what stakeholder claims are entitled to consideration by directors in determining "the best interests of the corporation".[22] The Supreme Court rejected the notion that the best interests of the corporation means the best interests of its shareholders and stated that the positions of other stakeholders (including creditors – and not merely when a corporation approaches the zone of insolvency) are entitled to consideration by directors:

> It is clear that the phrase the "best interests of the corporation" should be read not simply as the "best interests of the shareholders" . . . in determining whether they are acting with a view to the best interests of the corporation it may be legitimate, given all the circumstances of a given case, for the board of directors to consider, inter alia, the interests of shareholders, employees, suppliers, creditors, consumers, governments and the environment.[23]

The Supreme Court cited with approval the view of Berger J. in Teck Corp. v. Millar: "I appreciate that it would be a breach of their duty for directors to disregard entirely the interests of a company's shareholders. . .But if they observe a decent respect for other interests lying beyond those of the company's shareholders in the strict sense, that will not, in my view, leave directors open to the charge that they have failed in their fiduciary duty to the company."[24]

The stakeholder debate is an important and timely one but the Supreme Court may have done a disservice by characterizing it as an issue of fiduciary obligation. Having done so, the Supreme Court found that both Peoples and Wise had consented to the existence of the conflicting duties that the directors owed to each of them and that the evidence indicated no favouritism but, rather, that the defendant directors had been solely motivated to resolve the problem of managing inventories efficiently.[25] As a result, the Supreme Court concluded that there was no fiduciary breach. By treating the issue as whether directors owed a fiduciary obligation to creditors (as opposed to determining whether the directors had breached their statutory duty to the corporation), the Supreme Court managed to extricate itself from the proper purpose analysis by arguing that creditors (and, presumably other stakeholders) had other remedies – such as oppression and negligence -available to them. Indeed, the Supreme Court suggested that the availability of a broad oppression remedy "undermines any perceived need to extend the fiduciary duty imposed on directors".[26]

Having mischaracterized the issue as one of fiduciary accountability, the Supreme Court might have resolved the issue by finding no evidence of bad faith or negligence. Instead, while observing that directors' fiduciary liability is strict,[27] it immediately stepped back from that position to assert that "all the circumstances

[21] Ibid., at paras. 43–46.

[22] Ibid., at paras. 481–484.

[23] Ibid., at para. 42.

[24] Teck Corp. v. Millar (1972) 33 DLR (3d) 288 at 314.

[25] Ibid., at paras. 480–481.

[26] Ibid., at paras. 485–486.

[27] Ibid., at para. 480.

may be scrutinized to determine whether the directors and officers have acted honestly and in good faith with a view to the best interests of the corporation".[28] The Supreme Court also stated that "the subjective motivation of the director ... is the central focus of the statutory fiduciary duty".[29]

It is not clear how the Supreme Court reconciled "subjective motivation" or scrutiny of "all the circumstances" with strict liability. Nor is it evident how wading into the stakeholder debate was relevant to the issue of fiduciary accountability. Doing so arguably imported the oppression analysis and further diluted the concept of fiduciary accountability – if complainants must produce evidence of improper motivation or culpability "in the circumstances", the likelihood of a court finding directors in breach of their "fiduciary" duty is substantially diminished.[30]

8.2.2 Duty of Care

A review of how the law has evolved with respect to the duty of care further highlights the hazards of ambiguity. Subsection 122(1)(b) of the CBCA provides that "every director and officer of a corporation, in exercising their powers and discharging their duties, shall ... exercise the care, diligence and skill that a reasonably prudent person would exercise in comparable circumstances." The common law standard of directorial care was subjective and (viewed in hindsight) remarkably low. Its classic articulation is found in re City Equitable Fire Insurance Company Limited.[31] In effect, the common law standard did not require of directors (as it did of others under the general law of negligence) to meet the standard of the reasonable person. This approach was rejected by each of the Ontario Select Committee on Company Law and the Dickerson Report.

The Ontario Select Committee recommended that the common law standard of care be elevated to an objective test, requiring that directors exhibit the degree of care, diligence and skill of a "reasonably prudent director in comparable circumstances".[32] The language ultimately adopted in the Ontario Business Corporations Act (the "OBCA") extended the test to officers, as well as directors, and measures their conduct against that of a "reasonably prudent person" (rather than of a "reasonably prudent director") in comparable circumstances.[33]

---

[28] Ibid.

[29] Ibid., at para. 491.

[30] For a more detailed discussion of the frailties of the Peoples Decision, see Ian Lee, "Peoples Department Stores v. Wise and the 'Best Interests of the Corporation'" (2005) 41 Canadian Bus. L.J.; Mohamed F. Khimji, "Peoples v. Wise –Conflating Directors' Duties, Oppression and Stakeholder Protection" (2006) 39 U.B.C. Law Review; and D'Arcy L.MacPherson, "Supreme Court Restates Directors' Fiduciary Duty – A Comment on Peoples Department Stores v.Wise" (2005) 43 Alta. L. Rev.

[31] [1925] 1 Ch. 407.

[32] Sunstein, 1990 at 56, para. 7.2.4.

[33] Business Corporations Act, R.S.O. 1990, c. B.16 s. 134(12).

While the use of the word "person" instead of "director" might have been viewed as a conforming change (given the extension of the duty to officers, as well as directors), it was also viewed as a diminution of the proposed standard from that of a "director" (connoting some degree of expertise or professionalism) to that of a "reasonably prudent person". This was the conclusion of the Federal Court of Appeal in construing virtually identical language in s. 27.1(3) of the Income Tax Act.[34] That Court found the reference to a reasonably prudent (vs. skilled) person suggested a subjective standard of competence, a logic buttressed by the inclusion of the phrase "in comparable circumstances". Accordingly, it concluded that the language in s.227.1(3) created a hybrid test:

> It is not enough for a director to say he or she did his or her best, for that is an invocation of the purely subjective standard. Equally clear is that honesty is not enough. However, the standard is not a professional one. Nor is it the negligence law standard that governs these cases. Rather, the Act contains both objective elements, embodied in the reasonable person language, and subjective elements, inherent in individual considerations like "skill" and the idea of "comparable circumstances". Accordingly, the standard can be properly described as "objective subjective".[35]

Like the Ontario Select Committee, the Dickerson Report sought to raise the common law standard of care in its proposed statutory codification.[36] As it noted, "it is ... cold comfort for a shareholder to know that there is a steady supply of marginally competent people available under present law to manage his investment".[37] Although the Dickerson Report did not propose the phrase "in comparable circumstances", it was included by the legislative drafters. At least until the Peoples Decision, this was viewed by many (including the Federal Court of Appeal) as preserving the common law subjectivity of the duty of care.

Arguably, such ambiguity was put to rest by the Supreme Court of Canada in the Peoples Decision. With respect to the specific issue, the Supreme Court made it clear that the standard had been raised to an objective contextual one:

> The main difference is that the enacted version includes the words "in comparable circumstances", which modifies the statutory standard by requiring the context in which a given decision was made to be taken into account. This is not the introduction of a subjective element relating to the competence of the director, but rather the introduction of a contextual element into the statutory standard of care.[38]

As a result, the duty of care imposed on directors would appear to be identical to that imposed on all other persons. In reaching that result, however, the Supreme Court may have created new uncertainty. Firstly, their reference to the introduction of a "contextual element" into the statutory standard of care is not clear. According to the Supreme Court "The contextual approach dictated by s.122(1)(b)

[34] Soper v. Canada (1998), 1 F.C. 124 (C.A.) at para. 38.

[35] Ibid., at para. 41.

[36] Dickerson Report, supra note 59 at para. 242.

[37] Ibid.

[38] Peoples Decision, supra note 50 at paras. 490–491.

of the CBCA not only emphasizes the primary facts, but also permits prevailing socioeconomic conditions to be taken into consideration."[39]

The Supreme Court did not elaborate on the relevance of such socio-economic conditions or how they might be taken into account - whether by directors or by judges, exercising their discretion in adjusting liability standards after the fact. Nor did it reflect on the justiciability of such issues. Instead, the Supreme Court took an expansive view of the scope of directors' duty of care, observing that:

> ... unlike the statement of the fiduciary duty in s.122(1)(a) of the CBCA, which specifies that directors and officers must act with a view to the best interests of the corporation, the statement of the duty of care in s.122(1)(b) of the CBCA does not specifically refer to an identifiable party as the beneficiary of the duty. ... Thus the identity of the beneficiary of the duty of care is much more open-ended, and it appears obvious that it must include creditors.[40]

As Nicholls points out, it appears that the Supreme Court may have conflated two different concepts – the tort "duty of care", which anticipates many beneficiaries, and the statutory duty. Nicholls argues that it is difficult to understand why a corporate statute would impose additional personal duties on directors other than to the corporation itself.[41]

It has been suggested that this reasoning of the Supreme Court was based on the civil law of Québec.[42] This raises interesting issues with respect to the consistent interpretation of the CBCA – a federal statute, particularly in the context of interpretation by a civil law court. Ontario has subsequently amended its Business Corporations Act to add the underlined words:

> s.134(i): Every director and officer of a corporation in exercising his or her powers and discharging his or her duties to the corporation shall, a) act honestly and in good faith with a view to the best interests of the corporation; and b) exercise the care, diligence and skill that a reasonably prudent person would exercise in comparable circumstances.[43]

In analyzing the Supreme Court's language in the Peoples Decision, it is interesting to consider whether a broader duty of care, theoretically owed to a diverse, undefined group of stakeholders, might serve to defeat the object of the duty of loyalty, thereby creating further confusion and leading to suboptimal board decision-making. For example, would well advised directors eschew risks for fear of attracting creditor liability, even when doing so sacrifices corporate opportunity? If so, the Peoples Decision would serve to encourage self-interested conduct (i.e., the mitigation of exposure to personal liability). This concern has been specifically raised in the context of court-supervised reorganization proceedings under

[39] Ibid., at para. 491.

[40] Ibid., at para. 57.

[41] Christopher C. Nicholls, Corporate Law (Toronto: Emond-Montgomery, 2005) at 298–299.

[42] Bruce L. Welling, Corporate Law in Canada: The Governing Principles, 3rd ed. (London, ON: Scribblers Publishing, (2006) at 331, note 115. Both the Peoples Decision and the BCE Decision were considered by the Supreme Court on appeal from the Quebec Court of Appeal.

[43] Business Corporations Act, R.S.O. 1990, c. B.16, s. 134.

the Bankruptcy and Insolvency Act and the Companies' Creditor Arrangement Act.62 For this reason, Ben-Ishai and Nowak recommend that the oppression remedy should not be available for use by stakeholders of a corporation once it has entered into a court-supervised reorganization proceeding.

Such concerns have risen to the forefront, of late. Increasingly, directors focus on the personal consequences of board service, both in deciding to go (or remain) on a board, in their deliberations (which tend to be highly process driven) and in their aversion to taking higher risk decisions (which are often a characteristic of longer-term strategies). The consequences for firm and systemic innovation and competitiveness are alarming.

8.2.3 The Business Judgment Rule

One final aspect of the Peoples Decision merits comment. This was the first instance in which the Supreme Court of Canada specifically considered and validated the "business judgment rule". In the United States, the courts have formalized the "business judgment rule" as a standard of conduct which, if adhered to, insulates the board from judicial review of their actions. A classic example is found in Stephanie Ben-Ishai and Catherine Nowak's, ("The Threat of the Oppression Remedy to Reorganizing Insolvent Corporations" 2008) Ann. Insolv. Rev.U.S. case, Shlensky v. Wrigley, in which the plaintiff challenged the Wrigley board's refusal to install lights at Wrigley Field when every other major league baseball team played night games. The board defended its actions based on the preferences of Wrigley's majority owner – that baseball is a day game and that lighting the stadium would damage the surrounding community. The court granted the board's motion to dismiss, relying on the "business judgment rule" to preclude the plaintiffs from even inquiring into the basis for the board's decision.[44]

Assuming a board acts in good faith, on an informed basis, in a manner in which it believes is in the best interest of the corporation, and is neither wasteful (in the narrow sense of mounting to "corporate waste") nor engaged in self-interested conduct, they are afforded wide latitude by the U.S. courts under the shield of the business judgment rule.[45] The presumption of judicial deference to the judgment of directors may be rebutted if any of the above-noted conditions are not satisfied, in which case the burden shifts to the directors to show that their actions were rational and taken in good faith. Self interested conduct in the context of control transactions results in the application of a more stringent "entire fairness" test.[46]

---

[44] 237 N.E. 2d 776 (Ill. App. 1968).

[45] Aronson v. Lewis, 473 A.2d 805, 1984 Del. Lexis 305 (Del. S.C. 1984); Kaplan v. Centex Corp., 284 A.2d 119, 1971 Del. Ch. Lexis 143 (Del. Ch. 1971); Robinson v. Pittsburgh Oil Refinery Corp., 14 Del. Ch. 193, 126 A. 46, 1924 Del. Ch. Lexis 21 (Del Ch. 1924); Puma v. Marriott, 283 A.2d 693, 1971 Del. Ch. Lexis 137 (Del. Ch. 1971).

[46] Unocal Corp. v. Mesa Petroleum Co., 493 A.2d 946, 1985 Del. Lexis 482 (Del. S C. 1985).

Former Chancellor Allen justifies the business judgment rule, within the overall context of liability provisions, as intended to protect shareholders by encouraging boards to take risks for their benefit.[47] Elhauge provides a more socially-focused rationale – that allowing managerial discretion may serve to subject corporate decisions to the same social and moral processes that apply to sole proprietors.[48]

In practice the business judgment rule has provided a broad shield. Well advised boards should always have a carefully prepared record to ensure that the business judgment rule protection trumps any statutory duty claim. For example, boards have been protected in taking actions that deliberately benefit creditors at the expense of shareholders, so long as the decision was based in facts, well considered, in good faith, and not conflicted by any personal interests of a majority of directors.[49]

Canadian jurisprudential deference to the "business judgment rule" is less developed. In CW Shareholdings v. WIC Western International Communications Ltd.,[50] the Ontario Superior Court of Justice explained that the rule:

> ... operates to shield from court intervention business decisions which have been made honestly, prudently, in good faith and on reasonable grounds. In such cases, the board's decision will not be subject to microscopic examination and the court will be reluctant to interfere and usurp the board of directors' function in managing the corporation.

The rule was referred to by the Supreme Court of Canada in the Peoples Decision as follows:

> Many decisions made in the course of business, although ultimately unsuccessful, are reasonable and defensible at the time they are made. Business decisions must sometimes be made, with high stakes and under considerable time pressure, in circumstances in which detailed information is not available. It might be tempting for some to see unsuccessful business decisions as unreasonable or imprudent in light of information that becomes available ex-post facto. Because of this risk of hindsight bias, Canadian courts have developed a rule of deference to business decisions called the "business judgment rule", adopting the American name for the rule.[51]

For reasons discussed below, the BCE Decision may serve to either enshrine an overly broad formulation of the business judgment rule or cast doubt as to its relevance and utility. Neither of these outcomes is desirable.

---

[47] William T. Allen, "Modern Corporate Governance and the Erosion of the Business Judgment Rule in Delaware Corporate Law" (2008) Comparative Research in Law and Political Economy Research Paper No. 06/2008, available online at ssrn.com/abstract=1105591.

[48] Supra note 60 at 844.

[49] See S. Bainbridge, Corporation Law and Economics (New York: Foundation Press, 2002) at 414–15.

[50] (1998), 39 OR (3d) 755.

[51] Peoples Decision, supra note 50 at para. 64.

8.3 The BCE Decision

Those who follow Canadian corporate law eagerly awaited the Supreme Court of Canada's reasons in the BCE Decision. Given the uncertainty surrounding directors' duties and to whom they are owed, exacerbated by the Supreme Court in the Peoples Decision, there was a general expectation that the Supreme Court might use the opportunity to revisit and distinguish (or otherwise clarify) its earlier reasoning. Instead, the Supreme Court created additional uncertainty with respect to the manner in which the "fairness" test for a Plan of Arrangement ("Arrangement") and the oppression remedy will be applied, as well as adding to the confusion surrounding directors' duties and the indeterminate nature and scope of their agency obligations.

The facts involved a (then) traditional leveraged buyout (which, at the time, would have been the largest of its kind, had it been consummated) to have been effected by an Arrangement under the CBCA. While it did not purport to arrange the legal rights of bondholders of Bell Canada (a wholly-owned subsidiary of BCE), certain such bondholders contested the fairness of the Arrangement and brought an oppression claim. The trial judge dismissed such claims, finding the Arrangement to be in the best interests of BCE and Bell Canada.[52]

The Quebec Court of Appeal unanimously overturned the trial decision, finding that the Arrangement had not been shown to be fair and that it should not have been approved.[53] The Court of Appeal found that the BCE board of directors (the "Board") was under a duty to consider whether the Arrangement could have been structured in a way that provided a satisfactory price for shareholders while avoiding (or at least mitigating) the adverse effect on bondholders. In the absence of such efforts (and ignoring the trial judge's specific findings that the Board had considered the interests of bondholders), the Court of Appeal determined that BCE had not discharged its onus of showing that the Arrangement was fair and reasonable. Given its lack of linkage to the factual record, the Court of Appeal's decision was troubling in that it suggested a substantive objection – i.e., it was not sufficient to consider extra-contractual interests but, rather, the Board should have done something about them (beyond ensuring that contractual obligations should be honoured). Absent a legal entitlement that could be clearly articulated, the Quebec Court of Appeal left unanswered how a board might go about striking a satisfactory and legally justifiable balance.

On a remarkably expedited basis, the Supreme Court of Canada heard the appeal and unanimously reversed the decision of the Quebec Court of Appeal. In its reasons, the Court reinstated key findings of the trial judge, rejecting the bondholder claims that the transaction was oppressive and confirming that BCE had satisfied the fairness test required for court approval of the Arrangement.

---

52 BCE Inc. and Bell Canada v. 1976 Debentureholders et al. (2008), 43 B.L.R. (4th) 1, 2008 QCCS 9057.

53 72 BCE Inc. and Bell Canada v. 1976 Debentureholders et al. (2008), 43 B.L.R. (4th) 157, 2008 QCCA 935.

In analyzing the manner in which the "fairness" test for an Arrangement will be applied, the Supreme Court noted that the scope of judicial inquiry is generally confined to legal rights. The Supreme Court rejected the "fair and reasonable" test by which courts previously reserved to themselves the discretion to rule against an Arrangement, notwithstanding shareholder approval thereof.[54] Instead, and absent extraordinary circumstances (not found in this case and, therefore, presumably not simply a diminution in the market value of a complainant's securities), the Supreme Court articulated a narrower test for approval, i.e., whether (a) the Arrangement has a valid business purpose and (b) the objections of those whose legal rights are being arranged have been resolved in a fair and balanced way. The Supreme Court recognized that "there is no such thing as a perfect arrangement" and that "although Board decisions are not subject to microscopic examination with the perfect vision of hindsight, they are subject to examination".[55]

The valid purpose prong of the test suggests a fact specific inquiry by the Supreme Court and ties into their discussion of necessity. Presumably, the lower the degree of "necessity" the higher the degree of scrutiny an Arrangement will attract. The fair balancing prong looks at a number of factors (including requisite shareholder approval). It remains to be seen whether this two-part test will facilitate Arrangements or be used by courts as a (different) mechanism to "second guess" shareholder votes when they are so inclined for equitable reasons. Moreover, as noted, the Supreme Court's reasons imply a "necessity" test in order to effect a transaction by way of an Arrangement. In this case, the Supreme Court determined such necessity to have been established, without any elaboration thereon.

The Supreme Court also set out a two-pronged test with respect to their analysis of the oppression remedy. A complainant is required to establish (a) that it had a reasonable expectation which (b) was "unfairly disregarded".[56] The Supreme Court found the concept of reasonable expectations to be objective and contextual in that "the question is whether the expectation is reasonable having regard for the facts of the specific case, the relationships at issue, and the entire context, including the fact that there may be conflicting claims and expectations".[57] It went on to suggest that, where there is a conflict between the views of stakeholders, each are entitled to reasonably expect that they will be treated fairly. In resolving conflicts, the Supreme Court suggested that a board owes a duty to the corporation, not a particular group of stakeholders, and the reasonable expectations of stakeholders are that the directors will act in a disinterested and impartial manner, free from conflict of interest, and in the best interests of the corporation.

The Supreme Court elaborated various factors useful in determining whether reasonable expectations exist (and are protected), including general commercial practice, the nature of the corporation, the relationship between the parties, past

---

[54] BCE's common shareholders approved the Arrangement by a vote of over 97%.

[55] BCE Decision, supra note 49 at para. 164.

[56] Ibid., at para. 56.

[57] Ibid., at para. 62.

practice, steps the claimant could have taken to protect itself, representations and agreements, and the fair resolution of the conflicting interests of different stakeholders.[58] With respect to the last factor, while the Supreme Court noted that directors can resolve conflicts between different stakeholder groups in a way that favours one group at the expense of another, it articulated a cornerstone of fair treatment – "the corporation and shareholders are entitled to maximize profit and share value, to be sure, but not by treating individual stakeholders unfairly".[59] The BCE Decision fails to provide guidance as to when permissible favouritism crosses over the line into the zone of unfairness.

The Supreme Court's approach to the oppression remedy illustrates the circular logic of its reasoning. Reasonable expectations arguments are, by their nature, somewhat circular, insofar as expectations are likely to reflect extant legal norms. To compound (for confound) that the Supreme Court, in effect, suggests that reasonable expectations can be breached, so long as doing so is not unfair. This challenges the law since Ebrahimi,[60] under which "reasonable expectations" defined fairness. Moreover, in setting out several factors for determining the "reasonableness" of expectations, the Supreme Court may have changed their relative significance. For example, did the Supreme Court, in listing the existence of a contract alongside the other factors, intend to diminish its relative importance? More generally, by touching on various theories of what might form the basis for a judicially recognized "reasonable expectation" the Supreme Court created uncertainty as to the assessment thereof.[61]

The Supreme Court's analysis regarding how a board should weigh "the fair resolution of conflicting interests between corporate stakeholders" appears to link oppression to the duty of loyalty owed by directors and that "reasonable expectations" are now relevant to such duty. The Supreme Court stated that:

> directors, acting in the best interests of the corporation, may be obliged to consider the impact of their decisions on corporate stakeholders, such as the debenture-holders in these appeals. This is what we mean when we speak of a director being required to act in the best interests of the corporation viewed as a good corporate citizen. However, the directors owe a fiduciary duty to the corporation, and only to the corporation.[62]

Earlier in its reasons, the Supreme Court asserted:

> . . .this case does involve the fiduciary duty of the directors to the corporation, and particularly the "fair treatment" component of that duty, which, as will be seen, is fundamental to the reasonable expectations of stakeholders claiming an oppression remedy.[63]

---

[58] Ibid., at paras. 69–84.

[59] Ibid., at para. 64.

[60] In Ebrahimi v. Westbourne Galleries Ltd., [1973] AC 360 (H.L).

[61] Jeffrey G. MacIntosh, "BCE and the Peoples' Corporate Law: Learning to Live on Quicksand" [Insert upcoming CBLJ cite].

[62] BCE Decision, supra note 49 at para. 66.

[63] Ibid., at para. 36.

Merging the duty of loyalty (one owed to the corporation) with the oppression remedy (intended to redress personal harm to a security holder, creditor, director or officer of a corporation) can only serve to create uncertainty as to both.

In effect, the Supreme Court suggests that fair treatment in respect of alleged corporate or personal harms is whatever stakeholder groups are entitled to reasonably expect, without further elaboration on the nature (or reasonableness) of such expectations or the distinction between various remedies.[64] The Supreme Court appears to designate the board as a referee and, so long as it observes appropriate process, to afford it the protection of what appears to be an extraordinarily expansive business judgment rule.

The Supreme Court's "fiduciary duty" analysis is the most problematic. It states that the content of the duty varies with the situation at hand[65] and, in effect, relegates it to one of the listed factors to be considered in the context of considering oppression relief – i.e., entailing a factual "fairness" determination rather than a determination of whether a decision was made on a good faith basis. Reaffirming the Peoples Decision (i.e., that the duty is to act in the best interests of the corporation, which may include considering the impact of corporate decisions on particular groups of stakeholders), and rather than simply confirming directorial discretion to consider stakeholder interests, the Supreme Court went on to speak of an affirmative (if ill-defined) "fiduciary duty to act in the best interests of the corporation, viewed as a good corporate citizen".[66] In resolving conflicting interests, the Supreme Court suggested that there is "no principle that one set of interests – for example, the interests of shareholders – should prevail over another set of interests. Everything depends on the particular situation faced by the directors and whether, having regard to that situation, they exercise business judgment in a responsible way."[67] Such observations are unhelpful in clarifying norms of directorial conduct. The Supreme Court also noted that the "fiduciary duty" of the directors to the corporation is not confined to short-term profit or share value. "Where the corporation is an ongoing concern, it looks to the long-term interests of the corporation."[68]

Although the stakeholder debate is an important and timely one, the Supreme Court may have done it a disservice by characterizing its premise as an issue of fiduciary obligation. The challenge of judicial monitoring of competing stakeholder interests is even more daunting than that of monitoring shareholder value maximization. Judges are ill-suited to either task.

---

[64] For an interesting and somewhat prescient contextual analysis, written after the Supreme Court's decision and in anticipation of its reasons, see Peer Zumbansen and Simon Archer, "The BCE Decision: Reflections on The Firm as a Contractual Organization" (2008) Comparative Research in Law and Political Economy Research Paper No. 17/2008, available online at ssrn.com/abstractid=1160094. See also MacIntosh (supra note 128) for a discussion of how the BCE Decision further confuses derivative and personal actions.

[65] BCE Decision, supra note 49 at para. 37.

[66] Ibid., at para. 8.

[67] Ibid., at para. 84.

[68] Ibid., at para. 38.

The BCE Decision also adds uncertainty to the nature and scope of directors' agency obligations. Looking to the facts of the case, the Supreme Court vindicated the trial judge. The Supreme Court found that evidence both supported a reasonable expectation that the Board would consider the position of the bondholders and, in fact, did consider their interests in an appropriate manner, given the circumstances. The repeated references to the interests and fair treatment of stakeholders, and to long-term corporate citizenship, suggest a rejection of the Delaware model, which expressly recognizes and explicitly resolves the conflict directors face in a change-of-control context, establishing as a principle that once a board of directors makes a decision to sell a company, they (i) have a duty to maximize the value that shareholders receive and (ii) are subject to an "intermediate standard of review" – their decisions receive less deference than under the normal business judgment rule.[69]

That said, having framed the issue in terms of stakeholder theory (in contrast to a duty to maximize value for shareholders while respecting obligations to other stakeholders), the Court provided no guidance as to the priority of any constituency claims, other than to suggest that boards focus on the "best interests of the corporation". For example, the Supreme Court did not address (because they were not called upon to do so) the treatment of preferred shareholders. Ontario's Divisional Court decision in Carling O'Keefe[70] effectively protected such shareholders by holding that the directors' duty is to act in the best interests of shareholders as a whole, including holders of preferred shares. The BCE Decision posits preferred shareholders as just another stakeholder group whose interests (arguably more akin to debt then common equity) must be balanced.

Even the question of whether directors may, should or are obliged to consider stakeholder interests (and, if the latter, when) was not addressed clearly by the Supreme Court. Early in its reasons, the Supreme Court notes that in the Peoples Decision "...this Court found that although directors must consider the best interests of the corporation, it may also be appropriate, although not mandatory, to consider the impact of corporate decisions on shareholders or particular groups of stakeholders."[71] Later the Supreme Court states "the duty of directors to act in the

---

[69] See Revlon, Inc., v. MacAndrews & Forbes Holdings, Inc., 506 A. 2d 173 (Del. S.C. 1986); subsequent Delaware cases have addressed fact specific issues concerning how directors should approach value maximization when selling a company. In each of Maple Leaf Foods Inc. v. Schneider Corp. (1998), 42 O.R., (3d) 177 and Ventas Inc. v. Sunrise Senior Living Real Estate Investment Trust (2007), 85 O.R. (3d) 254, the Ontario Court of Appeal held that when there is a change of control, directors should take reasonable steps to maximize shareholder value. Other Canadian courts have taken a similar view. This principle is also reflected in Canadian Securities Administrators' National Policy 62202, which states: (2) The primary objective of the take-over provisions of Canadian securities legislation is the protection of the bona fide interests of the shareholders of the target company.

[70] 89 Palmer v. Carling O'Keefe Breweries of Canada Ltd. (1989), 67 O.R. (2d) 161, 56 D.L.R. (4th) 128.

[71] BCE Decision, supra note 49, at para. 39.

best interests of the corporation comprehends a duty to treat individual stakeholders equitably and fairly."[72] Is this duty mandatory in nature?

Having waded into stakeholder theory, the Supreme Court retreated (without so acknowledging). In searching for an accountability mechanism, the Supreme Court recognized as a practical matter that, with a change of control being imminent, the Board had a duty to maximize value for shareholders (even while stating that the Revlon duty does not displace the fundamental rule that the duty of directors cannot be confined to particular priority rules). This reasoning was buttressed by finding the buy-out would have a beneficial impact on BCE. Absent any finding of conflict of interest or bad faith, and providing that its decisions were within a range of reasonable choices they could have made in weighing conflicting interests, the Supreme Court was not prepared to exercise hindsight as to whether the Board's decision was the perfect one.

In effect, by deferring to directors' determinations as to how to resolve conflicts between stakeholder groups in a fair manner that reflects the best interests of the corporation, the Supreme Court appears to have broadened the jurisprudential relevance and protection afforded by the business judgment rule. What previously afforded protection from directorial negligence arguably now extends to determining directors' statutory duties and whose interests should, may or must be considered in resolving conflicts in a "fair manner".[73] Taking the Supreme Court's logic to its extreme, boards would be accorded broader deference than administrative tribunals. In the case of the Ontario Securities Commission, this recently was held to include "the right to be wrong"[74] (but, in the case of boards, presumably not the right to be "unfair", whatever that may mean).

This may reflect a fundamental divergence of Canadian and U.S. legal norms with respect to review of directors' conduct. For example, in contrast to the "entire fairness" test[75] which informs judicial review of directors' conduct (at least when allegations of self-interest are made) in the U.S., Canadian courts have tended to defer to process-oriented requirements[76] imposed by securities regulators, largely in response to the historical prevalence of controlled public companies in Canada. Securities regulation, in effect, has "occupied the field", leaving the courts less inclined to invoke the extraordinary breadth of the oppression remedy in the face of self-interested or control transactions.

However, the Supreme Court's reasons leave it open for the opposite to be argued as well. By engaging in a detailed review of the factual circumstances, the Court

[72] Ibid., para. 82.

[73] Alternately, the context may have supported a conclusion that shareholders had a reasonable expectation, in a sale of control, that the board would act to maximize value for them.

[74] Sears Holdings Corporation et al. v. Ontario Securities Commission et al. (2006), 84 O.R. (3d) 61 at para. 13.

[75] See, e.g., Weinberger v. UOP, Inc., 457 A.2d. 701 (Del. S.C. 1983), requiring defendants to demonstrate that the impuned transaction was "entirely fair" to the corporation.

[76] Ontario Securities Commission Rule 61-501 – Insider Bids, Issuer Bids, Business Combinations and Related Party Transactions.

may be interpreted to have been paying lip-service to the business judgment rule (or using it as a device to extricate itself from the analytical swamp it had waded into). Such a lack of deference and implied willingness to second guess director decisions, made with care and in good faith, would suggest a radical narrowing of the business judgment rule!

While many had hoped the BCE Decision would be the Supreme Court's opportunity to clarify and narrow some of the open-ended pronouncements in the Peoples Decision, one can speculate on a range of fact situations in respect of which the law may now be highly uncertain. How does a board of directors deal with a bidder whose stated intentions may be prejudicial to non-shareholder constituencies (or whose reputation is for not honouring certain contractual commitments) when their offer is the best value for shareholders? All other things equal, should a board be prepared to accept a lower bid in order to ensure a better capitalized acquiror (at least at the time the acquisition is effected)? In a broader context, how would one advise a board of directors which decides to relocate operations offshore, with a view to ensuring the corporation's long-term commercial viability, given the conflicting effects on creditor, employee, shareholder and other constituencies? Traditional notions of fiduciary duties, oppression and the business judgment rule have been confused in a casual discourse on corporate citizenship and directorial accountability – remarkable both in its lack of analytical rigour and of necessity to reach the Supreme Court's ultimate decision.

Ironically, the oppression claim (in respect of which relief only extends to conduct prejudicial to the interests of security holders, creditors, directors or officers) was abandoned by the bondholders and not argued by their counsel before the Supreme Court. This renders the effect of the Supreme Court's discussion of these issues even more uncertain.

8.4 Alternative Paths to Corporate Citizenship

While not an excuse for casual reasoning by the Supreme Court of Canada in the Peoples and BCE Decisions, the debate about imposing corporate citizenship or social responsibility obligations through corporate law is long-standing. It is fair to say that courts and legislators have, overall, tended to follow and respond to the incremental manner in which societal expectations have increased over time. The following section of this paper considers ways in which this process might be accelerated and clarified.

No one disputes the proposition that corporations may only pursue their economic mission through lawful means.[77] That said, legal and political debates about the role of the corporation in society extend back close to a century. The political

[77] Robert C. Clark, Corporate Law (Little Brown 1986) at 17–18, stating that a corporation's purpose is to "maximize the value of the company's shares, subject to the constraint that the corporation must meet all its legal obligations to others who are related to or affected by it".

debate has intensified with the success of the corporation as a vehicle for mobilizing capital and, accordingly, its impacts on society. As noted by US President Obama in his inaugural address:

> Nor is the question before us whether the market is a force for good or ill. Its power to generate wealth and expand freedom is unmatched, but this crisis has reminded us that without a watchful eye, the market can spin out of control and that a nation cannot prosper long when it favours only the prosperous.[78]

Debates as to how to tweak the market's "watchful eye" tend to run aground when (and to the extent) they are disconnected from effective legal frameworks. Robert Reich characterizes these phenomena as a kind of "faux democracy", suggesting that the message that companies have social responsibilities tends to divert public attention from the task of establishing such laws and rules in the first place.[79] This, in turn, feeds into the legal debate over corporate social responsibility, generally characterized by competing theories as to the duties of directors and managers – to "owners" or to a wider range of "stakeholders". While, as discussed below, there have been occasional law reform initiatives to address this issue, the debate has been highly theoretical and repetitive.

Advocates of corporate social responsibility have embraced words in the Peoples Decision that accepted "as an accurate statement of law" the legal proposition that it may be legitimate for directors to consider, inter alia, the interests of shareholders, employees, suppliers, creditors, consumers, governments and the environment in determining whether they are acting with a view to the best interests of the corporation.[80] There was little Canadian law on this issue prior to the Peoples Decision.[81] Rather than providing clarification, the BCE Decision reaffirmed the Peoples Decision, stating that:

> The fiduciary duty of the directors to the corporation is a broad, contextual concept. It is not confined to short term profit or share value."[82] and that: "In considering what is in the best interests of the corporation, directors may look to the interests of, inter alia, shareholders, employees, creditors, consumers, governments and the environment to inform their decisions. Courts should give appropriate deference to the business judgment of directors who take into account these ancillary interests, as reflected by the business judgment rule.[83]

---

[78] Barack Obama, Inaugural Address, January 20, 2009, available online at: http://www.pic.org/pressroom/entry/president_obamas_inaugural_address/.

[79] Robert B. Reich, "The Case against Corporate Social Responsibility" (2008) Goldman School of Public Policy Working Paper No. GSPP08-003, available at ssrn.com\abstract=1213129.

[80] BCE Decision, Supra note 49, para. 34.

[81] As noted earlier in this paper, in Teck Corp. Ltd. v. Millar (1973), 33 D.L.R. (3d) 288, (B.C.S.C.) at 97, Justice Berger stated: "I appreciate that it would be a breach of their duty for directors to disregard entirely the interests of a company's shareholders in order to confer a benefit on its employees ... But if they observe a decent respect for other interests lying beyond those of the company's shareholders in the strict sense, that will not, in my view, leave directors open to the charge that they have failed in their fiduciary duty to the company."

[82] 101 BCE Decision, supra note 49 at para. 38.

[83] Ibid., para. 40.

As discussed, such statements add little to the law, other than to conflate concepts and provide cover for directorial discretion, assuming appropriate process is adhered to. The resulting uncertainty concerning proper corporate purpose could lead to a diminution in directorial accountability and potential liability. There are, however, a range of alternate legal theories that courts may choose to focus on to more meaningfully elaborate on the "social" or "stakeholder-related" duties of directors. Some are canvassed below. In addition, we briefly note several opportunities for legislative or shareholder-initiated reform.

8.5 Trust Law

The Supreme Court's language, particularly in the BCE Decision, is somewhat suggestive of theories of corporate responsibility advanced by Berle and Dodd in the nascent stage of the corporate responsibility/accountability debates. In 1931, Berle advanced the notion that corporate directors would become subject to the implied oversight of a court's equitable jurisdiction[84] and that, in the future, corporate law would become "in substance, a branch of the law of trust".[85] He argued that directors' powers are subject to equitable limitations to ensure that their grant of power is used for "the ratable benefit of all the shareholders as their interest appears".[86] Berle was reacting to the broad powers directors exercised "on behalf of" owners. In effect, he engaged in the same sort of aspirational logic as the Supreme Court of Canada, concluding:

> In every case, corporate action must be twice tested: first, by the technical rules having to do with the existence and proper exercise of the power; second, by equitable rules somewhat analogous to those which apply in favor of a cestui que trust to the trustee's exercise of wide powers granted to him in the instrument making him a fiduciary.[87]

The Supreme Court of Canada might have embraced and expanded on Berle's proposal to incorporate trust law principles into corporate law. Berle's argument was taken to its logical (for those who advocate stakeholder responsibility) conclusion by Dodd the following year.[88] Dodd treated the corporation as a separate legal person and characterized directors as trustees, not for the shareholders but for the separate legal entity. He then argued that directors could "employ [corporate] funds in a manner appropriate to a person ... with a sense of social responsibility without thereby being guilty of a breach of trust".[89] Put otherwise, Dodd suggested that any

---

[84] A.A. Berle, Jr., "Corporate Powers as Powers in Trust" (1931) 44 Harv. L. Rev. 1049.

[85] Ibid.

[86] Ibid.

[87] Ibid.

[88] E. Merrick Dodd, Jr., "For Whom Are Corporate Managers Trustees?" (1932) 45 Harv. L. Rev. 1145.

[89] Ibid., at 1161.

notion of social responsibility by directors, on behalf of corporations, is voluntary but permissible.

Berle quickly responded,[90] arguing that Dodd's proposal effectively replaced the notion of shareholder primacy with nothing but the discretion of management, doing away with any legal accountability mechanisms. He characterized this as simply handing power over to management "with a pious wish that something nice will come out of it".[91] He went on to note that:

> [Lawyers] must meet a series of practical situations from day to day. They are not … in a position to relinquish one position – here, the idea of corporate trusteeship for security holdings – leaving the situation in flux until a new order shall emerge. Legal technique does not contemplate intervening periods of chaos; it can only follow out new theories as they become established and accepted by the community at large.[92]

However, as Berle became more concerned about corporate power he became more enamoured with the stakeholder theory of corporate governance, as evidenced by his directive to lawyers to "provide for the new interests as they successively appear".[93] In his best known work, he suggested "that the 'control' of the great corporation should develop into purely neutral technocracy, balancing a variety of claims by various groups in the community and assigning to each a portion of the income stream on the basis of public policy rather than private cupidity".[94]

Dodd continued to provide the counterpoint as his thinking evolved. In reviewing Berle and Means' book, he seized on the hazard Berle had initially focused on in their exchange – that duties to "the corporation" weakened duties to shareholders without putting anything effective in their place and argued that "If corporations generally are to be conducted in such manner as to give due regard to the interests of all classes in society … it is primarily through legislation that the change can be brought about."[95]

The conclusions of both Berle and Dodd are not as incompatible as they may at first seem. Berle suggested that the stakeholder debate should be incorporated into corporate law through trust law principles. Dodd argued that it should only be recognized through legislation. In contrast, the Supreme Court's analysis in the BCE Decision fails to even suggest a workable framework.

Before leaving the trust law characterization, it should be noted that courts have meaningfully wrestled with the extent to which non-shareholder interests should be considered by directors. For example, several years before the Credit Lyonnais

---

[90] A.A. Berle, Jr., "For Whom Corporate Managers are Trustees: A Note" (1932) 45 Harv. L. Rev. 1366.

[91] Ibid., at 1368.

[92] Ibid., at 1371.

[93] Ibid., at 1372.

[94] A.A. Berle, Jr. and Gardiner Means, The Modern Corporation and Private Property (New York: Macmillan Company, 1932) at 312–313.

[95] E. Merrick Dodd, "The Modern Corporation and Private Property" (1933) 81 U.Pa. L. Rev. at 785.

decision in Central Ice Cream,[96] a bankrupt company's only asset was a $52 million judgment it had obtained against McDonald's. In response, McDonald's offered to settle for $16 million - which would have satisfied all of the creditor claims and left $4 million for the shareholders. The creditors favoured the settlement while the shareholders opposed it. Stopping short of the suggestion in Credit Lyonnais that, in the zone of insolvency, directors may need to make choices other than those that shareholders would make, the judge (Easterbrook) suggested that bankruptcy law requires the trustee to maximize the value of the estate. By this logic, directors duties might be analogized to the trust law principle of "impartiality" – the duty of trustees to consider the trust as a whole, with due regard for the diverse beneficial interests created by the terms of the trust.[97]

As with Berle and Dodd, Judge Easterbrook's thinking evolved. Viewing the corporation as a "nexus of contracts" between various stakeholders relegated corporate law to a set of default rules[98] designed to reduce transaction costs (by obviating the need for individual contracts). Such a construct considerably diminishes (if not eliminates) the notion of the corporation as a distinct entity. Easterbrook and Fischel argue that if the corporation is simply a web of contracts, it becomes "a financing device and is not otherwise distinctive".[99]

The limits of this conceptualization were highlighted in the bid by Rupert Murdoch's News Corporation for Dow Jones, Inc. About 64% of Dow Jones was held in various trusts for descendants of the Bancroft family. Some family members preferred the premium cash offer, while others were prepared to sacrifice monetary value in order to ensure continued "journalistic integrity". According to press reports, in considering the various interests involved, the first several months of negotiations were spent arguing over principles (resulting in various "commitments" to protect and invest in the quality and integrity of the Dow Jones publications and news services), while the last several days were spent negotiating price. The final "sweetener" was News Corporation and Dow Jones agreeing to pay the family's advisors' fees – estimated at US$40 million (or an additional US$2 a share for family members on top of the US$60 per share final bid price).[100] Faced with a conflict between money and idiosyncratic preferences, the outcome was not surprising (and the law was not particularly relevant). To the extent that fiduciary duties serve as a proscription on self-interest, it tends to be obscured by the contractual approach to corporate law.

---

[96] In re Central Ice Cream Co., 836 F. 2d 1068 (7th Cir. 1987).

[97] For example, where the interests of beneficiaries conflict, the trust should try to maximize the value of the trust as a whole – to "act impartially and with due regard for the diverse beneficial interests created by the terms of the trust". See s.79(1), Restatement of the Law, Trusts, 3d ed. (St. Paul MN: American Law Institute 2003).

[98] Frank Easterbrook and Daniel Fischel, supra note 55 at 75.

[99] Ibid., at 10.

[100] Andrew Ross Sorkin, "Murdoch and Dow Jones: How the Deal Got Done" The New York Times (1 August 2007).

A contrasting contractual analogy to trustee powers in a corporate law context was illustrated in the merger of Reuters Plc and the Thomson Corporation. There, as a part of a business combination that gave the controlling shareholder of the Thomson Corporation control over the combined entity (initially a dual listed structure of Thomson Reuters Corporation and Thomson Reuters PLC), Thomson and its controlling shareholder undertook to support the Reuters Trust Principles in relation to the combined entity. These principles include the preservation of integrity, reliability of news, development of the news business and related principles and are enforced by the Reuters Founders Share Company Limited, which was to hold a special "founders share" in each of the dual listed entities, enabling it to exercise an overriding vote where a third party has obtained prescribed holdings of voting shares in excess of specified limits.

Alces has recently argued that efforts to define and enforce corporate fiduciary duties, where the relationship isn't a fiduciary one, has led to the atrophy of such duties to the point of obsolescence.[101] Instead, she recommends contractually-based disciplinary regimes, including provision for an "equity trustee" which might serve a similar function for shareholders as does an indenture trustee for bondholders. Perhaps there is some basis in such mechanisms for enshrining the "long term" focus averted to by the Supreme Court in the BCE Decision, should a board and/or a corporation's shareholders so choose. The notion of enshrining overriding principles into the corporation's constating documents merits more careful review, and is discussed below.

8.5.1 Team Production Theory

Blair and Stout significantly advanced Dodd's trustee analogy in proposing the "team production" approach to corporate law as the basis for describing the existing legal duties of directors (rather than arguing, as did Dodd and Berle at various stages in their thinking, about what the board's responsibilities should be in the future).[102] They argue that the board's economic and legal role is to balance competing interests of various stakeholders, all of which are essential to the success of the enterprise. In describing it as a "mediating hierarch" between competing constituencies within the corporation, Blair and Stout see stakeholders as voluntarily ceding control to the board, which, in promoting a team enterprise, is then obliged to and responsible for balancing competing interests.[103]

[101] Kelli A. Alces, "Debunking the Corporate Fiduciary Myth" [insert cite], available at ssrn.com/abstract = 135 2595.

[102] Margaret N. Blair and Lynn A. Stout, "A Team Production Theory of Corporate Law" (1999) 85 Va. L. Rev. 2.

[103] Ibid., at 28. Margaret N. Blair and Lynn A. Stout, "A Team Production Theory of Corporate Law" (1999) 85 Va. L. Rev. 2.

One can read much of this reasoning into the BCE Decision. The Supreme Court stated that the duty of directors to act in the best interests of the corporation:

> comprehends a duty to treat individual stakeholders affected by corporate actions equitably and fairly. There are no absolute rules and no principle that one set of interests should prevail over another. In each case, the question is whether, in all the circumstances, the directors acted in the best interests of the corporation, having regard to all relevant considerations, including – but not confined to – the need to treat affected stakeholders in a fair manner, commensurate with the corporation's duties as a responsible corporate citizen.[104]

Until recently, such notions rarely caused legal confusion. Indeed, ambiguity in statutory duties allowed for constructive tension and responsive judicial interpretation in egregious cases.

Any dissonance between the legal duties of directors to "owners" and their broader obligations has tended to be one of theory and behaviour. In practice the day-to-day conduct of effective managers generally reflects an implicit view of corporate obligations to a variety of constituents as being more immediate (if not important) to the enterprise than are its obligations to shareholders. Convergence is achieved, as the Supreme Court implied, by taking a longer-term view of value (and wealth) maximization.

The difficulty arose in the face of systemic behaviour challenging the incumbency of management and rewarding the immediate realization of shareholder value, often to the detriment of other constituents. As is generally the case, market forces (including the short-term focus of incentive structures, the opportunity for deception arising from financial innovation, the limited attention span of politicians and the overwhelming urge to manage public expectations) trumped legal theory. At that point that a legal construct, which professes to balance multiple interests, breaks down, insofar as it provides neither coherence, consistency, nor organizational focus.

Those who advocate team production (or other-than-shareholder primacy) recognize this limitation. For example, Ellsworth argues in favour of customer primacy as providing the most effective discipline on corporate management.[105] Blair and Stout do not address this challenge of keeping accountability focused. Nor did the Supreme Court of Canada. While reaffirming the "stakeholder" model of directors' duties they had endorsed in the Peoples Decision (and, hence, largely accepting the bondholders' argument as to directors' duties), the Supreme Court ruled against the bondholders in the BCE Decision, concluding that they had no reasonable expectation to anything more than the contractual rights provided to them in the trust indentures pursuant to which their bonds were issued.

Examples of new stakeholder-based governance models (in addition to more traditional models such as cooperatives and employee-owned firms) are rapidly

---

104 BCE Decision, supra note 49 at para. 82.

105 Richard R. Ellsworth, Leading with Purpose: The New Corporate Realities (Stanford: Stanford University Press, 2002). This would have been an ironic test to apply to BCE which, until relatively recently, enjoyed monopoly status in Canada.

emerging. A recent survey of such experiments in substituting social-benefit for profit-maximization as the dominant organizational principle around which ownership, governance, capitalization and compensation structures are designed identified three dominant models.[106] The first are stakeholder-owned companies, such as the Rabobank Group in the Netherlands, the Vanguard group of mutual funds or John Lewis Partnership PLC. The latter is the largest department store chain in the U.K., wholly-owned by its 69,000 employees. It is overseen by a traditional board as well as an employee-elected governing body (which, in turn, elects 5 of the 12 board members and has the power to dismiss the chairman). The second are mission-controlled companies, such as Thomson Reuters Plc (discussed above). Upstream 21 Corporation is a holding company established in Oregon to buy local companies focused on building social and economic capital within the region and facilitated by recent reforms to Oregon's corporate law, described below. Finally, there are public-private hybrids, which deliberately blur the lines between for-profit and non-profit modes of operation.

Google.org, which manages Google's annual philanthropic budget of about U.S. $2 billion,[107] terms itself "for-profit philanthropy" and operates as a division of Google - eschewing the traditional tax-exempt foundation organizational structure in order to embed itself within and draw fully on the resources of Google.

8.5.2 Moral Stakeholder Theory

The team production approach to corporate law fails to address the issue of immediate accountability. Most directors are anxious to meet all prescribed legal norms and are reluctant to stray much further. The proliferation of new governance standards (and consequential liability) has exacerbated their proclivity to risk averse behaviour.

It has been argued that moral stakeholder theory ("MST") may "hold the key to giving the board a more useful, comprehensive framework of the firm's utility and purpose to society."[108] MST can be summarized as upholding the beliefs that "fiduciary obligations go beyond short term profit and are in any case subject to moral criteria in their execution; and...mere compliance with the law can be unduly limited and even unjust."[109]

---

[106] Marjorie Kelly, "Not Just for Profit", strategy & business (Booz & Co.) Issue 54, Spring 2009, p. 49.

[107] See Dana Brakman Reiser, "For-Profit Philanthropy" (2008) available online at http://works.bepress.com/dana_brakman_reiser/14. In Google's IPO, discussed later in this paper, the company announced its intention to contribute 1 percent of equity and 1 percent of profits to charity.

[108] Rookman Mahavaj, "Critiquing and Contrasting 'Moral' Stakeholder Theory and 'Strategic' Stakeholder: Implications for the Board of Directors" (2008) 8 Corporate Governance 2 at 115.

[109] K.E. Goodpaster "Business Ethics and Stakeholder Analysis" (1991) 1 Business Ethics Quarterly 1 at 70.

Like the team production approach, MST implies that a board's role is to balance the competing interests of various stakeholders. While the team production approach fails to provide a workable framework for stakeholder identification and how their interests should be balanced, MST, through the identification of relational attributes, seeks to provide insight with respect to the relative manner in which stakeholders' interests should be considered by directors.

For example, Mitchell, Agle and Wood[110] seek to narrow the definition of stakeholder on the basis of "power to influence the firm; legitimacy of the stakeholder relationship with the firm; and urgency of the stakeholder claims." Mapping stakeholders using such criteria might better enable directors to recognize, prioritize and thereby manage various stakeholder interests more efficiently, thereby enabling boards to effectively move away from market induced short term incentives. In response to Friedman's concern that "few trends could so thoroughly undermine the very foundations of our free society as the acceptance by corporate officials of a social responsibility other than to make as much money for their stockholders as possible,"[111] MST mapping arguably benefits corporations financially, even though directors may not have anticipated financial gain at the time of stakeholder identification. For example, in an interview regarding an energy company that suffered financial loss and long term costs because of its inability to identify and prioritize stakeholders interests, a company executive stated "I think that the stakeholder risks that developed... were not ones that we could have seen before, perhaps because of our lack of knowledge and understanding about a bunch of church groups."[112]

It is often the case that stakeholders will have unique insights to contribute to the success of an enterprise. For that reason (and a desire to promote effective stakeholder engagement) corporate reporting is increasingly viewed as a process through which to meaningfully engage stakeholders (rather than simply an outcome required by regulation). Put otherwise, the identification of stakeholder interests, according to MST, may provide more focused accountability.

A similar mapping exercise might be beneficial at a societal (i.e., country or regional) level. While the "virtues" of responsibility, accountability, fairness and transparency are widely accepted and implicit in most corporate governance frameworks, their application is highly contextual and there is (or should be) a legitimate debate as to whom and how far such "virtues" should be applied. West recently proposed such a research agenda to address the question of whether corporate governance convergence between various jurisdictions is appropriate.[113] He noted that, irrespective of the answer to the question he posed, such an inquiry might inform

[110] R.K. Mitchell, B.R. Agle, and D.J. Wood, "Toward a Theory of Stakeholder Identification and Salience: Defining the Principle of Who and What Really Counts" (1997) 22 The Academy of Management Review 4 at 853–886.

[111] Milton Friedman, Capitalism and Freedom (Chicago: University of Chicago Press, 1962) at 133.

[112] Supra note 142 at 119.

[113] Andrew West, "Corporate Governance Convergence and Moral Relativism" (2009) 17 Corporate Governance: An International Review 1 at 107.

governance frameworks (including accounting practice, managerial approaches and business education).[114]

8.5.3 Obligation to Act Reasonably

We have previously noted how, in an early effort to defer to the business judgment of directors, courts have exempted directors from general tort law principles, reducing the threshold for liability (as regards to their statutory duties of care and loyalty) to one of gross negligence. Canadian jurisprudence was further muddled following the Federal Court of Canada's decision in Mentmore Manufacturing Co. Ltd. v. National Merchandise Manufacturing Co.,[115] where Justice LeDain asserted a conflict between the principles of tort law and corporate law.[116] Leaving aside confusion regarding the argument that directors should be subject to the same application of tort law as are others,[117] there is a broader argument that, in all basic areas of law governing market conduct (including tort, contract and property law), there is a fundamental duty to act reasonably.

Singer characterizes this as an "obligation of attentiveness",[118] arguing that directors, in their oversight of corporate conduct, are subject to the same equitable obligations as others to attend to the effects of their (in this case the corporation's) actions on others. These obligations apply to those with whom the corporation has continuing relationships (i.e., stakeholders) as well as to the interests of strangers. Beyond specific laws that create clear limits on corporate conduct, Singer suggests that this obligation to attend to the interests of others is based in the common law duty to act reasonably:

> This obligation. . .requires us to temper our self-interest by attending to the needs of others. We are required to abide by clear statutory and regulatory limitations on our freedom. But we are also under a continuing duty not to act negligently; we are not free to act unreasonably so as to cause significant harm to others. ... we have an obligation to balance their interests against our own to determine whether we can justify the harm we may cause them. Can we explain to a neutral third party why we acted as we did? Can we explain to those who suffer the consequences of our actions why they suffered a tragedy but not an injustice?[119]

---

[114] Ibid., at 117.

[115] (1978), 89 D.L.R. (3d) 195 (F.C.A.).

[116] Robert Flannigan, "The Personal Tort Liability of Directors" (2002) 81 The Canadian Bar Review 2.

[117] There are currently operating in Canada a number of arguably inconsistent judicial approaches to the question of when directors may be found liable to third parties for tortious corporate acts. See, for e.g., Nicolas Juzda, "The Tort Liability of Directors to Parties Outside the Corporation", LL.M. Thesis, Osgoode Hall Law School, November 2007.

[118] Joseph W. Singer, "Corporate Responsibility in a Free and Democratic Society" (2008) 58 Case Western Law Review 1, accessible at ssrn.com\abstract=1278133.

[119] Ibid., at 6.

In the environmental field, the precautionary principle has now been embraced, both in international law and in domestic Canadian and U.S. statutes and jurisprudence.[120] By mandating precautionary measures in the face of threats of serious or irreversible environmental harm, the principle may serve to elaborate on directors' duty of care. A similar concept has been advanced by Ruggie in his efforts to operationalize a "protect, respect and remedy" framework as regards the issue of human rights and transnational corporations.[121] He argues for a "corporate responsibility to respect all human rights or, put simply, to not infringe on the rights of others."[122]

The concept of a "duty to consult and accommodate" has been well developed by the Supreme Court of Canada in the context of the Crown's obligations to Aboriginal peoples. It has held that such a duty arises when the Crown (federal or provincial) contemplates conduct that might adversely affect Aboriginal rights or title.[123] Likewise, trust scholars have suggested that financial fiduciaries might be subjected to a statutory duty to consult with their beneficiaries when formulating investment policies.[124]

Given this judicial history, it would not have been a significant leap for the Supreme Court in the BCE Decision to explicitly develop a directorial "duty to consider", as has been suggested by Sneirson.[125] Under such a theory, fulfilling the statutory duty of care would require directors to consider all reasonably available material information. A broad view of materiality would include the consideration of potential impacts on various stakeholders. Failure to do so could lead to decisions being invalidated by the courts.[126] Such a notion comports with the Supreme Court's reasoning that, once stakeholder interests have been considered, directors can reach whatever decision they believe is in the best interests of the corporation. It

[120] For a full discussion of the development and extended relevance of the precautionary principles, see Michael Kerr, Richard Janda and Chip Pitts, Corporate Social Responsibility: A Legal Analysis, LexisNexis Canada, 2009 at Chapter 9.

[121] John Ruggie, Special Representative of the U.N. Secretary-General, "Business and Human Rights: Towards Operationalizing the Protect, Respect and Remedy Framework" U.N. Document A/HRC/11/13 (April 22, 2009).

[122] Ibid., at paras. 45–55.

[123] See Kent McNeil, The Crown's Fiduciary Obligations in the Era of Aboriginal Self-Government [upcoming] Canadian Bar Review; Sonia Lawrence and Patrick Macklem, "From Consultation to Reconciliation: Aboriginal Rights and the Crown's Duty to Consult" (2000) 79 Can. Bar Rev. 252.

[124] Gary Watt, Trusts and Equity, 2nd ed. (Oxford: Oxford U. Press, 2006) at 437. This proposal raises interesting issues as to how the views of future or contingent beneficiaries are to be taken into account.

[125] Judd F. Sneirson, "Doing Well by Doing Good: Leveraging Due Care for Better, More Socially Responsible Corporate Decision-Making" (2007) 3 Corp. Gov. Law Rev. 438.

[126] Although, absent gross negligence, directors would generally remain affectively immune from personal liability as a result of indemnification provisions.

would also be consistent with management literature which suggests that a broader stakeholder assessment framework will lead to better corporate decision-making.[127]

Here, again, the challenge is one of accountability. While the duty of loyalty can be utilized to limit the pursuit of self-interest by individual directors/managers, there is no equivalent construct for the corporation itself. It is unrealistic to hold directors accountable to the level of moral reasoning implicit in a "duty of attentiveness" for the "reasonableness" of corporate actions and their effects on others without the elaboration of clear standards by the courts or legislators.

8.5.4 Enhanced Duties

Another approach would be to articulate "enhanced duties" analogous to, but broader than, the "Revlon" duty in U.S. jurisprudence, which the Supreme Court purported to reject in the BCE Decision (but then, as a practical matter, appeared to embrace). For example, Shanfman recently proposed a standard of conduct for public company boards when dealing with excessively risky decisions. In such circumstances, he would require that boards specifically consider the company's liquidity, capital adequacy, funding risk and the like before getting to a determination of whether it is in the best interests of the corporation to proceed with such a decision.[128]

Creating such a standard of review would be consistent with the approach to board oversight taken by then Chancellor Allen in the Caremark Decision,[129] in which he identified a new affirmative duty to monitor corporate compliance with "applicable legal standards" whether or not the board had been given any notice of the wrongdoing on the part of the company's employees. It should be noted that Allen has recently expressed reservations about the effect on risk taking of directorial liability, absent a conflict of interest.[130] He describes how shareholders seek to shift risk to directors whenever things go wrong, thereby discouraging subsequent risk-taking. Providing guidance might serve to clarify the manner in which directors fulfill their duties of care and loyalty in the context of specified decisions. The Delaware Supreme Court noted in Stone v. Ritter that "Where directors fail to act in the face of a known duty to act, thereby demonstrating a conscious disregard for their responsibilities, they breach their duty of loyalty by failing to discharge that fiduciary obligation in good faith."[131] While this judicial observation was made in

---

[127] Michael C. Jensen, "Value Maximization, Stakeholder Theory, and the Corporate Objective Function", (2001) 14 J. Applied Corp. Fin. 8.

[128] Bernard S. Sharfman, "Enhanced Duties for Excessively Risky Decisions" (Draft of February 26, 2009), available at ssrn.com/abstract=1337124.

[129] Re Caremark International Inc. Derivative Litigation, 698 A.2d 959 (Del. Ch. 1996).

[130] 237 N.E. 2d 776 (Ill. App. 1968).

[131] 911 A. 2d.362 (Del. S.C. 2006) at 370.

the context of a board accused of not having a system in place to monitor violations of law, it might be applied to an articulation of other fact situations.

If anything has been learned from the most current financial crisis, it relates to the interconnectedness that characterizes global policy-making and enterprise.[132] Leaders (private and public) now realize (although they may still resist) the need to extend their horizons – temporally, sectorally and geographically. With the growing recognition that social issues have profound effects on long-term business prospects, notions of corporate citizenship become more consonant with traditional fiduciary norms.[133]

8.5.5 Statutory Reform

Prescribing standards for corporate citizenship may not lend itself to the narrowness (and shallowness) which characterizes the evolution of common law in small, incremental steps. It behooves us to also canvass legislative initiatives to develop and clarify such norms. Recent efforts in this regard tend to focus on more expansive conceptions of directors' duties and on reporting standards aimed at encouraging more responsible corporate conduct.

8.5.5.1 Director's Duties Redefined

As noted above, the ambiguity inherent in statutory directorial duties began to break down in the 1980s, as hostile, leveraged control transactions challenged the incumbency of managers and rewarded the immediate realization of shareholder value, often to the detriment of other constituents. The ensuing "corporate constituency statutes" adopted by many U.S. states from the 1980s onwards, empower (but, generally, do not require) directors to consider a wide range of interests in their decision-making, including those of employees, customers, creditors and local communities.[134] While such statutes have proven challenging for practitioners advising boards (because, like the BCE Decision, they are so open-ended), most are

---

[132] See, for e.g., John M. Broder "Climate Change Seen as Threat to U.S. Security: N.Y. Times, August 8, 2009". In commenting on the geo-political impacts of climate change General Anthony Zinni, former head of the U.S. Central Command, is quoted, "We will pay to reduce greenhouse emissions today, and we'll have to take an economic hit of some kind. Or we will pay the price later in military terms and that will involve human lives."

[133] Benjamin J. Richardson, "Putting Ethics Into Environmental Law: Fiduciary Duties for Ethical Investment" (2008) 46 Osgoode Hall Law Journal 243 at p. 271. For analogous arguments concerning the fiduciary obligations of institutional investors see United Nations Environment Programme & Financial Initiative (UNEP FI) Asset Management Working Group, "Fiduciary Responsibility: Legal and Practical Aspects of Integrating Environmental, Social and Governance Issues Into Institutional Investment" (2009) UNEP FI: Geneva.

[134] See, for example, E. Orts, "Beyond Shareholders: Interpreting Corporate Constituency Statutes" (1992) 61 George Washington Law Review 4.

permissive and do not expose directors to liability if they choose to disregard non-shareholder interests.[135] So, too, with the Delaware case law permitting directors to consider the interests of non-shareholder constituents in the context of hostile takeovers.[136] In this respect, they differ from the arguments of Blair and Stout (and, possibly, the theory of the BCE Decision), which suggest that a board must (or at least should) take such non-shareholder interests into account.

The impetus for such legislative reform was anti-takeover protection, based on the popular sentiment of ensuring that local (i.e., state) interests would not be adversely affected as a consequence of such transactions (and the cost-cutting and asset-disposals which often follow). The conflict between these objectives and shareholder wealth maximization (as well as the obvious conflict of interest in incumbent directors/management using such statutory provisions to secure their own position) may be the reason that the "corporate citizenship" goals suggested in these statutes have not been realized upon.[137] It should be noted that most such statutes are not limited in their application to control transactions.[138]

This conflict was belied in the 1990s, as compensation schemes responded to and exacerbated the increasingly short-term focus of market participants. The transformation was profound and overwhelming. For example, the U.S. Business Roundtable -which, with the advent of hostile take-overs, had stressed the social role that corporations play in their communities revised its position in 1997 to re-focus on the paramount duty of management to shareholders.[139] Corporate executives who had portrayed raiders as vandals now embraced the very same values – a process of reinvention which characterizes (and is often both a strength and Achilles' heel of) our enterprise system. Yet, even without constituency statutes, broad managerial discretion has been recognized in U.S. corporate law.[140]

Law reform initiatives in each of Canada and Australia have, in recent years, considered and rejected as unnecessary proposals to amend corporate law to permit (or require) directors to take into account the interests of constituencies, other

---

[135] An exception is the constituency statute of Connecticut, 117 Conn. Gen. Stat. 33-S.131(e) (2003). It only applies in respect of control transactions and requires (rather than permits) directors to consider stakeholder interests in determining the best interests of the corporation. The Indiana and Pennsylvania statutes require that directors not focus solely on the interest of shareholders as determinative.

[136] See Unocal Corp. v. Mesa Petroleum Co., 493 A. 2d 946 (Del. 1985) and Paramount Communications, Inc. v. Time Inc., 571 A. 2d 1140 (Del. 1990).

[137] Alternatively, it is widely viewed that these laws simply confirm, in change of control situations, the broad discretion conferred upon directors under the business judgment rule.

[138] Supra note 184.

[139] Business Roundtable, Statement on Corporate Governance (September 1997).

[140] See, e.g., 1 Am. Law Inst., Principles of Corporate Governance: Analysis and Recommendations, (1994)s.2.01(b)(2)–(3) and cmt.d. which states that: Even if corporate profit and shareholder gain are not thereby enhanced, the corporation, in the conduct of its business: (1) Is obliged, to the same extent as a natural person, to act within the bound regarded as appropriate to the responsible conduct of business; and (3) May devote a reasonable amount of resources to public welfare, humanitarian, educational, and philanthropic purposes.

than shareholders, in their actions. In the process leading to the most recent (2001) amendments to the CBCA, Industry Canada published a discussion paper on directors' liability.[141] While noting that the term "best interests of the corporation" is far from clear, and citing a previous survey of case law suggesting that "where [the] relationship between the short-term and longer-term or broader-based interests is incapable of precise definition. . .Canadian directors have few guidelines",[142] the paper suggested that "the circumstances are not prevalent, and thus, the absence of guidelines in these cases is not a major issue."[143] While considering various options (particularly in response to control transactions) the report recommended that no legislative changes be made in this area and that the courts be left to develop the concept of the "best interest of the corporation".[144]

In Australia, each of a Parliamentary Joint Committee on Corporations and Financial Services[145] and a federal governmental committee on corporations and markets[146] concluded that Australian corporate law already affords sufficient basis for directors to consider the interests of stakeholders, including shareholders. Both rejected the desirability of legislative reform. The latter group noted that including a non-exhaustive list of interests to be taken into account, in the absence of guidance as to how such interests are to be prioritized and reconciled, could "make directors less accountable to shareholders without significantly enhancing the rights of other parties."[147]

In contrast, the United Kingdom's 2006 Companies Act introduced a new statutory duty of loyalty which requires that directors look to "promote the success of the company for the benefit of its members as a whole" and, in doing so, take account of a range of statutorily prescribed considerations, including "the likely consequences of any decision in the long term", "the interests of the company's employees", "the need to foster the company's business relationships with suppliers, customers and others", "the impact of the company's operations on the community and the environment", "the desirability of the company maintaining a reputation for high standards of business conduct" and "the need to act fairly as between members of the company".[148]

---

[141] Industry Canada, CBCA Reform: Background Papers, Directors' Liability (November 1995) Available at www.ic.gc.ca/bic/site/cilp-pdci.nsf/eng/h_cl00388.html.

[142] Mindy Paskell-Mede and John Nicholl, "Directors' Liability from Private Rights of Action" Final Report, May 25, 1994 at 60, note 3.

[143] Supra note 170 at 16.

[144] Ibid., at 18.

[145] Parliamentary Joint Committee on Corporations and Financial Services (PJCCFS) "Corporate Responsibility: Managing Risk and Creating Value" (2006) available on-line at www.aph.gov.au/Senate/committee/corporations_ctte/corporate._responsibility/report\report.pdf.

[146] Corporations and Markets Advisory Committee (CAMAC), "The Social Responsibility of Corporations" (2006) available on-line at www.camac.gov.au.

[147] Ibid., at 111–112.

[148] Companies Act 2006 (U.K.), 2006, c. 46, s.172.

In fact, there has been little judicial consideration of state constituency statutes in the last several decades. We are only aware of one instance in which such a statute has been referred to in finding in favour of a decision by an incumbent board.[149] It is not surprising that courts have shied away from the juridification of stakeholder interests – the BCE Decision illustrates the challenge. Insofar as the U.K. statutory standard, while requiring (rather than permitting) directors to consider stakeholder interests, ultimately adjudges their deliberations based on whether their decisions "promote the success of the company for the benefit of its members [i.e., shareholders] as a whole", the most one can reasonably expect is to see judicial validation for long-term wealth creation, rather than finding a new locus for directorial accountability. Even those firmly wedded to shareholder value would concede this point.[150]

In 2007 Oregon amended its Business Corporations Act (effective January 1, 2008) to expressly permit an Oregon corporation's Articles of Incorporation to include a provision "authorizing or directing the corporation to conduct the business of the corporation in a manner which is environmentally and socially responsible."[151] While apparently intended to address "sustainability" concerns, the amending legislation does not purport to define "environmentally and socially responsible" conduct. Presumably, those utilizing this provision will take care in doing so, so as to avoid uncertainty or conflict with other corporate objectives.

8.5.5.2 Reporting Requirements

An expected corollary of the new statutory duty in the U.K. Companies Act was to have been substantially enhanced social transparency through a requirement for "major companies"[152] to provide an annual "operating and financial review" (OFR) and would have required directors to consider including in such review material relevant to the interests of stakeholders -such as the company's policies relating to employment, environmental issues and social and community issues relevant to

[149] Georgia-Pacific Corp. v. Great Northern Nekoosa Corp., 727 F. Supp. 31; 1989 U.S. Dist. Lexis 15725 (U.S. Dist. 1989) referred to in Richard Marens and Andrew Wicks, "Getting Real: Stakeholder Theory, Managerial Practice, and the General Irrelevance of Fiduciary Duties Owed to Shareholders" (1999) 9 Business Ethics Quarterly 2 at 284.

[150] For example, Henry Hansmann and Reinier Kraakman in "The End of History For Corporate Law" state that there is "no longer any serious competitor to the view that corporate law should principally strive to increase long-term shareholder value" (2001) 89 Georgetown Law Journal at 440–441. See also Michael Jensen, "Value Maximization, Stakeholder Theory and Corporate Objective Function" (2001) 7 European Financial Management 3 at 309.

[151] ORS 60.047 (2)(e), reported on by Perkins Coie, available online at www.perkinscoie.com/news/pubs_detail.aspx?publication=1553&op=updates.

[152] Department of Trade and Industry, Government White Paper, "Modernizing Corporate Law", (2002) Command Paper CM 5553-1 at clauses 77 and 78 (which set out the criteria for "major companies"). Available on-line at www.dti.gov.uk/companiesbill/whitepaper.htm.

the company's business.[153] However, as the Companies Bill went through parliamentary debates, the OFR requirement was deleted, leaving only the requirement to include in a company's Annual Business Review (for public companies) "information about environmental matters, the employees of the company and social and community matters".[154] According to the statute, the purpose of the business review is "to inform members of the company and help them assess how the directors have performed their duty under s.172".[155] Information about environmental, employee and community matters is not required if, in the view of the directors, it does not assist in understanding the business of the company. Nor is there a requirement to state why such disclosure is not provided. The deletion of the OFR requirement in the U.K. Companies Act was a disappointment to those who view social transparency as a way to influence norms of corporate conduct.[156]

There remains, however, ample ground for optimism, both as to the imposition of new social transparency requirements and their effect on corporate conduct. For example, the European Parliament's recent resolution on corporate social responsibility anticipates more expansive social transparency, "so that social and environmental reporting is included along side financial reporting requirements".[157] This observation was made having regard for the shortcomings of voluntary social reporting in which "only a minority of the reports use internationally accepted standards and principles, cover the company's full supply chain or involve independent monitoring and verification".[158]

In South Africa, the King Report (a voluntary governance code first published in 1994, revised in 2002 and with proposed revisions outstanding) advocates an integrated approach taking into account the "triple bottom line"-people, profits and planet.[159] The King Report recommends that companies move away from profit maximization and, in developing business strategies, focus on a broad range of stakeholders.[160] It recommends disclosure of the nature and extent of a company's commitment to social, ethical, safety, health and environmental practices, as well

---

[153] Ibid., at 149.

[154] Companies Act 2006 (U.K.), 2006, c.46, s. 417(5).

[155] Ibid., at s. 417(2).

[156] 176 See, for example, Cynthia A. Williams, "The Securities and Exchange Commission and Corporate Social Transparency" (1999) 112 Harv. L. Rev. and Cynthia A. Williams & John Conley, "An Emerging Third Way? The Erosion of the Anglo-American Shareholder Value Construct" (2005) 38 Cornell Int'l L.J., available on-line at http://papers.ssrn.com/sol3/papers.cfm?abstract_id=632347.

[157] European Parliament Resolution of March 13, 2007 on "Corporate Social Responsibility: A New Partnership", available at eruoparl.europa.eu/sides/getDoc.do?type=TA&reference=P6-TA-2007-0062&language=EN.

[158] Ibid.

[159] Institute of Directors in South Africa, King Report on Corporate Governance for South Africa (first published in 1994, revised in 2002). Its most recent draft Report on Governance for South Africa (King III) was released for public comment on February 26, 2009 and can be found at www.iodsa.co.za.

[160] Ibid.

as organizational integrity. While compliance is voluntary, most South African public companies follow the King Report's recommendations as a result of initiatives by various external sources to track and publish performance. For example, the Johannesburg Stock Exchange launched the first Socially Responsible Investment (SRI) index in May, 2004, based on proprietary criteria, in keeping with the framework promoted by the UN Principles for Responsible Investment.[161] Major South African companies, including SAB Miller, AngloGold Ashanti and Mondi actively report social responsibility initiatives on their websites. The King Report was also referred to by a South African court in finding that directors had breached environmental orders. The court specifically noted that the corporate community within South Africa has widely accepted the recommendations of the King Report, stressing that one of the characteristics of good corporate governance is social responsibility.[162]

The French Commercial Code was amended in 2001 to require all French corporations listed on its primary stock exchange to report annually on social and environmental impacts.[163] This requirement was elaborated upon the following year by a Decree which specifies categories of social, community-related and environmental information that must be disclosed.[164]

Under the new "Social Responsibility for Large Businesses" law, which amended the Danish Financial Statements Act as of January 1, 2009, an estimated 11,000 of the largest Danish companies (both listed and state-owned) are now required to include information on their corporate responsibility policies and practices in their annual financial reports. An absence of such corporate responsibility policies must also be reported. A stated objective of the legislation is to encourage large businesses "to work actively on ways they can contribute to solving social challenges". This links to a longer term governmental strategy, outlined in the May 2008 government "Action Plan on Corporate Social Responsibility".[165] The Action Plan stated the government's intention "to promote social responsibility and help Danish businesses reap more benefits from being at the global vanguard of corporate social responsibility".

In 2008 the Australian Stock Exchange ("ASX") adopted a new set of corporate governance principles which frame corporate citizenship issues within the notion of "material business risks". Such risks are defined as follows:

> Material business risks have the potential to create value and protect established value. The following examples of material business risk categories are identified in Principle 7: operational, environmental, sustainability, compliance, strategic, ethical conduct, reputation or

---

[161] For further Information about the JSE SRI index, see www.jse.co.za/sri.

[162] Minister of Water Affairs & Forestry v. Stilfontein Gold Mining Co., 2006 (5) SA 333 (W).

[163] Loi no. 2001-420 (15 May 2001), J.O., May 16, 2001, 7776, art. 116.

[164] See L.J. Dhooge, "Beyond Voluntarism: Social Disclosure and France's Nouvelles Regulations Economiques" (2004) 21 Ariz. J. Int'l & Comp. L. 441.

[165] Available online at www.eogs.dk/graphics/Samfundsvar/dk/documenter/action_plan_GSR.pdf.

brand, technological, product or service quality, human capital, financial reporting, market-related risks.[166]

Listed companies need to establish policies concerning "material business risk management" and disclose a summary thereof. According to the Corporate Governance Council, "where a company has risks relating to sustainability or corporate social responsibility that are material to its business, they should be considered in the context of [the revised reporting requirement]".[167]

Australia recently announced support for the establishment of the Responsible Investment Academy, designed to mount education and training programs to enable the investment community to better assess ESG considerations.[168] It also appointed a senior Australian Treasury official to the Global Reporting Initiative Governmental Advisory Group, with the Minister for Superannuation and Corporate Law noting: "it's clear to me that the true value of corporate responsibility crystallizes around effective reporting".[169]

Another recent example of a similar approach was that proposed by the Canadian Securities Administrators (CSA) in their request for comments on proposals to replace their existing corporate governance regulatory regime.[170] The proposed new CSA National Policy 58–201, Corporate Governance Principles, articulates nine core "high-level corporate governance principles and provides guidance to issuers on their corporate governance structures and practices". In connection with the draft commentary to "Principle 5 – Promote Integrity", the CSA provides examples of generally recommended practices, including adoption of a code of conduct.[171] It then goes on to suggest that, in connection with the adoption of such a code of conduct, issues to be addressed should include "the issuer's responsibilities to security holders, employees, those with whom it has a contractual relationship and the broader community".[172]

---

[166] ASX Corporate Governance Council, Review of the Principles of Good Corporate Governance and Best Practice Recommendations (2007, Principle 4.).

[167] Ibid., Australian Stock Exchange Corporate Governance Council, Supplementary Guidance on Principle 7: Recognize and Manage Risk (2007).

[168] Australian Minister for Superannuation & Corporate Law, Media Release No. 009 of 05/02/2009.

[169] Australian Minister for Superannuation & Corporate Law, Media Release No. 008 of 05/02/2009.

[170] CSA press release, December 19, 2008; and request for comment – proposed repeal and replacement of NP 58-201 Corporate Governance Guidelines, NI 58-101 Disclosure of Corporate Governance Practices, and NI 52-110 Audit Committees and Companion Policy 52-110CP Audit Committees (2008) 31 OSCB 12158 (December 19, 2008).

[171] Ibid., at 12176.

[172] Ibid., at 12177. Curiously, CSA National Policy 62-202 "Take-Over Bids – Defensive Tactics" purports to remove many of the tools that a self-entrenching board might seek to invoke to favour non-shareholder constituencies.

Increasingly public companies and their counsel are facing difficult judgment calls as to whether non-financial information concerning a company's environmental policies or social practices might be viewed as "material" under relevant securities laws.[173] For example, over the last several years, a number on investor groups, lead by CERES,[174] have sought to pressure the U.S. Securities and Exchange Commission ("SEC") to mandate climate change disclosure in public filings. CERES, along with the New York Attorney General, a number of state treasurers, pension fund managers and others petitioned the SEC on September 18, 2007 to provide interpretive guidance on climate risk disclosure.[175] A supplemental filing on June 12, 2008 described subsequent developments from the date of the original petition.[176] The request was reiterated in an October 28, 2008 submission to the SEC in connection with its "21st Century Disclosure Initiative".[177]

To date, the SEC has not officially responded to these submissions, however the New York Attorney General (who was a signatory to the original CERES petition) issued subpoenas to five energy companies on September 14, 2007 questioning the adequacy of their climate change disclosure under the New York securities law.[178] The subpoenas (and subsequent investigations) resulted in settlements with two of the companies, Xcel and Dynegy, in August and October, 2008, respectively. Each company agreed to provide more detailed climate disclosure in their future SEC annual reports, including descriptions on financial risks present and probable regulation relating to greenhouse gas emissions, litigation, physical impact associated with climate change and strategies to reduce climate change risks.[179] Pressure on the SEC continues.[180] Most recently, the SEC's Investor Advisory Committee has indicated

---

[173] See, for example, David Monsma and Timothy Olson, "Muddling Through Counterfactual Materiality and Divergent Disclosure; the Necessary Search for a Duty to Disclose Material Non-financial Information" (2007) 26 Stan. Envtl L.J.

[174] CERES is a coalition of investors and public interest groups focused on improving corporate, environmental and social performance. See www.ceres.org.

[175] Petition for Interpretive Guidance on Climate Risk Disclosure (September 18, 2007), available at www.incr.com//Document.Doc?id=187.

[176] Letter form California Public Employees' Retirement System et al., to Nancy M. Morris, SEC Secretary (June 12, 2008), available at www.ceres.org//Document.doc?id=358.

[177] See "Investors call on SEC to require better disclosure on climate change and other risks" Ceres (23, October, 2008), available at www.ceres.org/Page.aspx?pid=951. This letter also calls on the SEC to consider how material, environmental, social and corporate governance data can be integrated into public filings.

[178] N.Y. General Business law No. 352, commonly referred to as the Martin Act, which allows investigation of any "fraudulent practice" related to investments.

[179] See in re Xcel Energy Inc, Assurance of Discontinuance Pursuant to Executive Law No. 63(15), aod#08-012 (August 26, 2008), available at www.oag.state.ny.us/media_center/2008/aug/xcel_aod.pdf; in re Dynegy Inc, Assurance of Discontinuance Pursuant to Executive Law No. 63(15), aod# 08-132 (October 23, 2008), available at www.oag.state.ny.us/media_centre/2008/oct/dynegy_aod.pdf.

[180] See, for e.g., Social Investment Forum July 21, 209 letter to SEC requesting increased ESG disclosure (available online at www.socialinvest.org/documents/ESG_letter_to_SEC.pdf) and similar June 12, 2009 letter from CERES' Investor Network on Climate Risk (available online at

its intention to establish a subcommittee to focus on disclosure of environmental, social and governance ("ESG") factors.[181]

While the SEC has yet to issue guidance, the Canadian Institute of Chartered Accountants recently did so.[182] This was followed by an Ontario Securities Commission ("OSC") Staff Notice on environmental reporting which, based on a review of the continuous disclosure documents of 35 issuers, found a number of common deficiencies and issued guidance in respect thereof. The Staff Notice explicitly considers the materiality of environmental matters both from a financial statement and continuous disclosure perspective.[183] This approach may signal a convergence of legal and aspirational requirements, focusing on the "materiality" of non-financial information.

On April 9, 2009 the Ontario Legislature voted unanimously to support a private member's resolution calling for the OSC to consult and report back to the Minister of Finance on best practices on corporate social responsibility and environmental, social and governance reporting standards.[184]

At the federal level, a private member's bill currently before the Standing Committee on Foreign Affairs and International Development would require companies in the resource sector and receiving federal government support to "act in a manner consistent with international environmental best practices and with Canada's commitments to international human rights standards."[185]

The Public Accountability Statements Regulations, which apply to Canadian banks, insurance companies and trust and loan companies, with equity of $1 billion or more, pursuant to[186] subsections 459.3(4) of the Bank Act, 489.1(4)[187] of the Insurance Companies Act[188] and 444.2(4) of the Trust and Loan Companies Act respectively,[189] require the annual filing of a public accountability statement, which must describe the entity's contribution to Canada's economy and society, including

www.incr.com/Page.aspx?pid=1107). For a useful survey of ESG policies recently compiled by the U.S. Environmental Protection Agency, see www.asria.org/news/press/lib/Global%20ESB%20Survey.pdf.

[181] Reported on in Global Proxy Watch (July 31, 2009).

[182] Canadian Institute of Chartered Accountants, "Building a Better MD&A – Climate Change Disclosures" (2008), available online at http://www.cica.ca/download.cfm?ci_id=48027&la_id=1&re_id=0.

[183] OSC Staff Notice 51-716, Environmental Reporting February 21, 2008, (2009) 31 OSCB2228.

[184] Laurel Broten, M.P.P. motion on April 2, 2009, 1st Session, 39th Parliament, Legislative Assembly of Ontario (available online at www.ontla.on.ca).

[185] House of Commons of Canada, Bill C-300, An Act respecting Corporate Accountability for the activities of Mining, Oil or Gas Companies in Developing Countries, John McKay, M.P., Second Reading, May 25, 2009.

[186] SOR/2002-133 [Regulations].

[187] S.C. 1991, c.46.

[188] S.C. 1991, c.47.

[189] S.C. 1991, c.45.

"detailed examples ... of their participation ... in activities for the purpose of community development ... of activities undertaken on their behalf during the period by their employees on a voluntary basis for the purpose of community development ... of their philanthropic activities and an overview of initiatives undertaken ... to improve access to financial services for low-income individuals, senior citizens and disabled persons."[190]

In each of the above-noted instances, demands for disclosure reflect broader efforts to influence corporate conduct and governance. This approach is exemplified in a recent PricewaterhouseCoopers report, "Recasting the Reporting Model – How to Simplify and Enhance Communications".[191] In advancing the case for "making sustainability mainstream", the report suggests that:

> the interdependent relationship between existing financial data and other data (including social, customer, supplier and environmental indicators) must be made clear and, that doing so could have a transformational impact on reporting by ensuring companies' decision-making and strategy and investors' valuations are based firmly on a more complete picture of performance.[192]

8.5.5.3 Reforming Regulatory Paradigms

While beyond the scope of this paper, it is worth noting the shifting role of what traditionally have been viewed as "economic" or "market" regulators to one that includes proactively advancing social goals. For example, Ontario's Green Energy Act[193] adds to the mandate of the Ontario Energy Board the objectives of promoting conservation and renewable energy. The Act fundamentally shifts the focus of regulation from ensuring cost and environmentally efficient supply to regulating the energy sector as a contributor to the "green economy", focusing on advancing environmental and social values and outcomes.

8.5.6 Shareholder Initiated Approaches

As public norms (and expectations) shift, corporations may chose to pro-actively clarify directors' duties, thereby conditioning the "reasonable expectations" of stakeholders. One Canadian example of such an exercise is Magna International Corporation. In 1984, its shareholders ratified a "corporate constitution" which set out certain principles, including guidelines for the allocation of profits as between

[190] Supra note 235 – (remembered).

[191] PricewaterhouseCoopers, "Recasting the Reporting Model – How to Simplify and Enhance Communications: Opportunities for Discussion" (2008), available from nfo@corporatereporting.com.

[192] Ibid., at 5.

[193] Bill 150, An Act to enact the Green Energy Act, 2009 and to build a green economy, to repeal the Energy Conservation Leadership Act, 2006 and the Energy Efficiency Act and to amend other statutes S.O. 2009, C.12. (Royal Assent received May 14, 2009).

employees, shareholders and management, the allocation of at least 7% of pre-tax profit for research and development "to ensure [Magna's] long-term viability", and the allocation of not more than 2% of pre-tax profit for "charitable, cultural, educational and political purposes to support the basic fabric of society".[194] The constitution also provides that any amendments thereto require shareholder approval with each class of shares (Magna is controlled through 300 vote shares) voting separately. Magna (arguably in an effort to mitigate attempts to unionize plants) also adopted an "Employee's Charter", which focuses on job security, workplace safety, competitive compensation and equity/profit participation.[195]

Such initiatives are not unique to Magna. For example, Casio has established a "charter of creativity for Casio and Casio common commitment",[196] as described in Casio's 2008 Corporate Report.[197] This Charter embraces a number of norms, including corporate social responsibility, which is "said to be a matter of a company fulfilling its responsibility to all stakeholders in all economic, environmental and social respects".[198]

A more recent (and widely publicized) example was the initial public offering of Google. The prospectus included a letter from the founding shareholders which articulated a number of principles on which Google was based and which would continue to be maintained after the public offering (by the use of a dual class share structure through which the board and executive management team would control 61.4% of the voting power). Commitments to serving end users, a long-term focus ("a management team distracted by a series of short-term targets is as pointless as a dieter stepping on the scale every half hour") and "making the world a better place" were set out in some detail in an effort to ensure that prospective investors would understand that "Google is not a conventional company. . .[and they] do not intend to become one."[199]

The Google vision was expressed succinctly as: "We believe strongly that in the long term, we will be better served – as shareholders and in all other ways – by a company that does good things for the world even if we forego some short term gains."[200]

Such disclosure (arguably reinforced by shareholder approval or other validation) has proven to be consequential in determining director liability. In Greenlight Capital Inc. v. Stronach,[201] a case involving the conduct of Magna's controlling

---

[194] Available online at www.magna.com/magna/en/responsibility/constitution/pdf/Corporate_constitution.pdf.

[195] Available online at www.magna.com/magna/en/employees/charter/default.aspx.

[196] Available online at http://world.casio.com/corporate/principle/charter.html.

[197] Larry Page and Sergey Brin, "An Owner's Manual for Google Shareholders", available online at http://investor.google.com/ipo_letter.html.

[198] Ibid.

[199] Ibid.

[200] Ibid.

[201] 2008 CarswellOnt 4093, 91 O.R. (3d) 241, 47 B.L.R. (4th) 215, 240 O.A.C. 86.

shareholder in respect of a Magna spin-off company under identical control, the trial judge found such disclosure to be directly relevant to a determination of the subjective expectations of the shareholder plaintiff in the context of an oppression claim.[202] Given the BCE Decision, boards are likely to be advised to deliberately condition stakeholder expectations in order to insulate themselves in respect of oppression (and other) claims.

In recent years, shareholder activists have tested the limits of corporate law with by-law proposals that attempt to constrain the authority of boards of directors. It has been argued that, to the extent such proposals attempt to usurp authority for shareholders (who do not owe duties to advance the interests of the corporation) they should not be allowed.[203] Conversely, one law firm recently proposed that corporations amend advance notice by-laws governing shareholder proposals to include new, continuous disclosure obligations (beyond those contained under U.S. securities laws) relating to beneficial ownership interests (intended to prevent activist shareholders from secretly accumulating a significant interest without disclosure).[204] The Dutch Parliament is currently considering legislation which would codify recommendations of a Corporate Governance Code Monitoring Committee appointed by the Minister of Finance. The bill would impose substantive responsibilities on institutional shareholders, such as a requirement on holders of at least 3% public company's voting shares to notify the regulatory authority as to whether they agree with the firm's strategy.[205]

Lord Myners, the U.K. Finance Secretary, recently argued that voting rights might vary in proportion to the length of time shares are held.[206] Such a proposal would follow the French model, under which ordinary shares double their voting rights if they are held by the same owner for a period of time specified in the company's charter (typically several years).[207] While the focus (attacking "short-termism") is laudable, we are not aware of evidence that such measures have been effective. The risk, again, is a diminution in board accountability.

Another approach to extending authority to shareholders would be through the use of unanimous shareholder agreements ("USAs"). Though, at common law, the

---

[202] Greenlight Capital Inc. v. Stronach (2006), 22 B.L.R. (4th) 11 at para. 23.

[203] Frederick H. Alexander and James D. Honiker, "Power to the Franchise of Fiduciaries" (2008) 33 Delaware J. of Corporate Law 749.

[204] Phillip A. Gelston and James C. Woolery, "Beneficial Ownership – By-law Disclosure Proposal" (2008) Cravath, Swaine & Moore LLP; Michael J. de la Merced, "Shedding Light on Hidden Activists" New York Times (9 September 2008).

[205] See Global Proxy Watch (July 31, 2009).

[206] The Economist, "Short of Ideas – The Rights of Shareholders and the Wrong Done to Clients". August 6, 2009, available online at www.economist.com/businessfinance/displaystory.cfm?story_id=14174485.

[207] Tatiana Nenova, "How to Dominate a Firm with Valuable Control? Dual Class Firms Around the World: Regulation, Security-Voting Structure and Ownership Patterns", World Bank (April 2001) available online at papers.ssrn.com/sol3/papers.cfm?abstract_id=1017603 at p.3.

discretion of directors in respect of their duties cannot be fettered,[208] a USA is a statutory exception to the common law principle. Arguments have been raised as to whether USAs can be used in public companies. This issue was analyzed in a 1996 discussion paper, [209] which concluded that there is nothing in the statute that says USAs cannot be used in the context of a public corporation. Section 146(1) of the CBCA states:

> An otherwise lawful written agreement among all the shareholders of a corporation, or among all the shareholders and one or more persons who are not shareholders, that restricts, in whole or in part, the powers of the directors to manage, or supervise the management of, the business and affairs of the corporation is valid.

As noted, there is no restriction with respect to the number of shareholders or type of corporation; if shareholders can reach a sufficient agreement, why should legislation interfere? Further, Section 146(5) of the CBCA states:

> To the extent that a unanimous shareholder agreement restricts the powers of the directors to manage, or supervise the management of, the business and affairs of the corporation, parties to the unanimous shareholder agreement who are given that power to manage or supervise the management of the business and affairs of the corporation have all the rights, powers, duties and liabilities of a director of the corporation, whether they arise under this Act or otherwise, including any defences available to the directors, and the directors are relieved of their rights, powers, duties and liabilities, including their liabilities under section 119, to the same extent.

The USA would likely have to be created a company is first set up and would have to be in place at the time of the initial public offering. The prospectus would provide full disclosure and state that the shares are subject to the USA which prescribes a different governance framework than the statute. Share certificates would have to be legended according. Section 146 (4) of the CBCA provides that transferees of shares subject to a USA are deemed to parties to the USA if they have notice of the agreement or a "reference to it is noted conspicuously on the security certificate".[210]

Thus, as a matter of corporate law, if the agreement is written, otherwise lawful and unanimous, the afore-mentioned sections should be effective in creating a limited access arrangement between the corporation, directors and shareholders. It is interesting to consider whether shareholders exercising some or all of the powers of directors through such an agreement would be then subject to statutory duties as traditionally understood.[211]

Shareholders might also impose their will *ab initio* or, arguably at least, at any time by including in the articles of incorporation provisions intended to provide guidance to directors in the exercise of their duties. While under the CBCA this

---

[208] Kennerson v. Burbank Amusement Co., 260 P. 2d 823 (Calif. C.A. 1953); Sherman & Ellis v. Indiana Mutual Casualty, 41 F.2d 588 (7th Cir. 1930).

[209] Canada Business Corporations Act Discussion Paper: Unanimous Shareholder Agreements (1996).

[210] CBCA, supra note 58, s. 49(8).

[211] It is difficult to reconcile a duty of directors to consider stakeholders' interests with the ability of shareholders to restrict the powers of directors.

would not serve to relieve directors of their statutory obligations (and potential liability), it might, at least, colour "reasonable expectations". In contrast, Delaware law generally allows corporate charters to contain "any provision ... for the conduct of the affairs of the corporation, and any provision creating, defining, limiting and regulating the powers of the corporation, the directors, and the stockholders ... if such provisions are not contrary to the laws of this State."[212] Moreover, Delaware allows charter provisions that eliminate managerial duty of care liability in damages.[213]

Each of the Australia and New Zealand corporation statutes contain a provision providing for a corporate constitution of a wholly-owned subsidiary to permit its directors to act in the best interests of the parent company.[214] Quaere whether this represents a sanctioned departure from shareholder primacy or simply clarifies the identity of interests?

There is also growing evidence of the potency of shareholder advisory votes, particularly in respect of executive compensation practices. This is but one manifestation of the seminal and growing role of institutional investors in campaigning for improvements in corporate governance and conduct.[215] Various voluntary codes of conduct and business self-regulation have emanated from (and are directed to) such investors.[216] John Bogle recently referred to the challenge of establishing a "fiduciary society" based on statutory duties to focus on long-term investment, appropriate due diligence and "ensuring that managers/agents act in a way that reflects their ethical obligations to society".[217] Indeed, such manifestations of shareholder (and other popular) sentiment are now informing legislative processes.[218]

---

[212] See DEL. CODE. ANN. tit. 8, s. 102(b)(1) (1974).

[213] Ibid., s. 102(b)(7).

[214] New Zealand Companies Act 2006, s. 131(2), Australia Corporations Act 2001, s. 187.

[215] See, for example, Gordon Clark and Tessa Hebb, "Why Should They Care? The Role of Institutional Investors in the Market for Corporate Global Responsibility" (2005) Environment and Planning A 2015; Gordon Clark and Darius Wojcik, The Geography of Finance: Corporate Governance in the Global Marketplace (New York: Oxford University Press 2007); Stephen Davis, Jon Lukomnik and David Pitt-Watson, The New Capitalists: How Citizen Investors are Reshaping the Corporate Agenda (Boston: Harvard Business School Press 2006).

[216] See, for example, International Corporate Governance Network, "Statement on Global Corporate Governance Principles" (2005) available online at www.icgn.org; United Nations Environment Program Finance Initiative, "Fiduciary Responsibility – Legal and Practical Aspects of Integrating Environmental, Social and Governance Issues into Institutional Investment" (July 2009) available online at www.unepfi.org/fileadmin/documents/fiduciaryII.pdf.

[217] John C. Bogle, "A Crisis of Ethic Proportions", Wall Street Journal (20 April 2009) also part of a longer article by him entitled "Building a Fiduciary Society" in the July/August 2009 issue of The Corporate Board.

[218] For example, the Australian Treasurer recently announced his government's intention to amend the Australian Corporations Act to require shareholder approval for termination payments that exceed average annual base salary. See Rachel Pannett, "Australia to Rein in Executive Pay", Wall Street Journal, March 19, 2009, p. C2.

8.6 Conclusion

Allen suggested long ago that "anyone trying to understand how our law deals with corporations must have in mind that they are the locus of many conflicting claims, and not all of those claims are wholly economic."[219] He noted how the long-term/short-tem distinction preserved the norm of shareholder oriented property theory, while affording directors considerable latitude to deal with other groups or institutions having an interest in, or who are affected by, the corporation.

As he concluded:

> ... in defining what we suppose a public corporation to be, we implicitly express our view of the nature and purpose of our social life. Since we do disagree on that, our law of corporate entities is bound itself to be contentious and controversial. It will be worked out, not deduced. In this process, efficiency concerns, ideology, and interest group politics will commingle with history (including our semi-autonomous corporation law) to produce an answer that will hold for here and now, only to be torn by some future stress and to be reformulated once more. And so on, and so on, evermore.[220]

In other words, the legal and economic frameworks of corporate governance are embedded in more basic values, attitudes and beliefs. As former U.S. Supreme Court Justice Earl Warren noted, "the law floats on a sea of ethics".[221]

Likewise, Elhauge has forcefully argued that corporate law does and should confer managerial discretion to consider and, within reason, respond to social and moral sanctions because of the fact that "there are residual areas beyond the reach of even optimally framed legal duties".[222] Once framed in this manner, the challenge shifts to one of determining when, absent self-interested conduct, courts should constrain the exercise of such discretion.[223]

It has been argued that, in each of the Peoples and BCE Decisions, the Supreme Court of Canada may have reached to achieve a desired outcome – one arguably consonant with societal norms – without carefully articulating the underlying legal reasoning, arguably leading to a diminution in both judicial clarity[224] and directorial

[219] William T. Allen, "Our Schizophrenic Conception of the Business Corporation" (1992) 14 Cardozo Law Review at 280.

[220] Ibid., at 281.

[221] Quoted in Noel Preston, Understanding Ethics 3rd edition (Annandale: The Federation Press, 2007) at 21.

[222] Einer Elhauge, "Sacrificing Corporate Profits in the Public Interest" (2005) 80 N.Y.U.L. Rev. 733 at 804. at 743.

[223] For example, the American Law Institute suggests that courts should sustain decisions to sacrifice profits for ethical principles when such principles are reasonable because they "have significant support although less-than-universal acceptance". Supra note 208 at s. 2.01 cmt.h. See also David L. Engel, "An Approach to Corporate Social Responsibility" (1979) 32 Stan. L. Rev. at 27–34 (he suggests a more stringent standard – one based on a clear broad social consensus).

[224] Ian Lee, supra note 71 points out that the court's approach in the Peoples Decision "obscures the choice actually faced by the court and the normative considerations relevant to that choice. In this way, it is an example of the kind of reasoning that realist scholars persuasively critized in the

accountability. Some of the existing legal theories that the Supreme Court might have focused on to elaborate the responsibilities of directors have been presented, along with a consideration of potential legislative and shareholder initiated reforms, any of which might add clarity to the law.

A reader reviewing the recommendations presented in this paper may reasonably assume that clarification with respect to the role and accountability of directors necessarily involves a shift towards greater scrutiny in terms of the interests that directors should consider and directors' commitment to long term value maximization. While this reflects the authors' bias, it need not be the case. For example, clarity with respect to the role and accountability of directors could involve establishing that the role of directors should be a singular focus on maximizing wealth creation for the benefit of the current shareholders, with the safeguarding of other interests to be left to political and social forces and agencies.[225]

Ultimately, the determination of proper corporate purpose, duties of directors and directors' discretion accountability depends on an understanding of the role of the corporation in our society. Is a legal construct that has and continues to hold the potential to transform our world really one that we want to hinder? If not, how best can we focus the role of directors (or others assigned with legal duties and accountability) on ensuring that corporations generate wealth within the context of broader societal values? Equally, how do we focus the "watchful eye", referred to by President Obama, to ensure an effective oversight role and ultimate responsibility for wealth distribution?

Never before have the duties owed by directors attracted such political currency. Sadly, the Supreme Court of Canada has now missed two opportunities to address these issues in the context of corporate law. Perhaps, in venturing into the realm of social responsibility, it was "being too far ahead" of its time. If so, only by not "going deep". Others, hopefully, will soon provide greater clarity.

---

last century". See, e.g., F. Cohen "Transcendental Nonsense and the Functional Approach" (1935), 35 Col. L. Rev.

[225] See for e.g., Reich, Supra note 117.

Chapter 9
Misdeeds Matter: Long-Term Stock Price Performance After the Filing of Class-Action Lawsuits

Rob Bauer and Robin Braun

9.1 Introduction

A company can obtain external financing via a contract between itself as a legal entity and its prospective financiers. In the process of raising external capital, the company pledges its assets vis-à-vis control rights for the investors (Hart, 1995). If the company violates the terms of the agreement, the claimholders can legally enforce their rights in court. In the United States, shareholders—as one major group of external financiers—have the right to resort to class-action lawsuits if they believe that their agents (i.e., company management) have violated the duty of loyalty or the duty of care (Shleifer & Vishny, 1997). Typically, U.S. regulators are fairly strict in their interpretation of managers' duty of loyalty. Our study was an attempt to answer the question, what happens to shareholders if these duties are (allegedly) violated?

Recent developments in financial markets have accelerated the rate of filings of class-action lawsuits. Significantly above fundamental levels between 1998 and 2001, stock market valuations burst the internet bubble, which resulted in a large number of unhappy shareholders. Allegations during this period included inflated stock prices, shareholder-wealth-destroying mergers and acquisitions, false IPO prospectuses, and managerial insider trading. After 2001, the widely publicized cases of Enron Corporation, Tyco, WorldCom, Global Crossing, and Adelphia Communications Corporation led to a considerable number of governance-related lawsuits. In 2005, the founder of Adelphia and his son were sentenced to prison, and a settlement fund of $2.5 billion was established for the plaintiffs. More recently, the subprime crisis has produced option-backdating scandals and excessive risk taking. According to the Economist, shareholders filed class-action lawsuits at an "annual pace of around 270 between August and October 2007 (Economist, 2007)." In 1995, the U.S. Congress enacted the Private Securities Litigation Reform Act,

---

This chapter is a republished article that first appeared in the *Financial Analysts Journal* in 2010.

R. Bauer (✉)
ECCE, 6211 LM Maastricht, The Netherlands
e-mail: r.bauer@maastrichtuniversity.nl

T. Hebb (ed.), *The Next Generation of Responsible Investing*,
Advances in Business Ethics Research 1, DOI 10.1007/978-94-007-2348-1_9,

which enables (private) shareholders to allege any violation of Rule 10b-5 of the Securities Exchange Act of 1934. This rule prohibits, *inter alia*, any manipulative and deceptive practices by managers and corporations and prescribes managerial duties. According to Romano (1991), these duties can be subdivided into duty of care and duty of loyalty. The latter term describes fiduciaries' conflicts of interest and requires them to put the corporation's interest ahead of their own. Typically, the duty of loyalty includes self-dealing and related party transactions. In our study, we focused on the duty of care, which requires the execution of "reasonable skills, diligence and especially taking care in board actions (Romano, 1991, p. 56)". The allegation of self-interested managerial misconduct and the post-evaluation of poor business decisions both fall under the violation of duty of care (Loss & Seligman, 2004).

Becht, Bolton, and Röell (2003) classified the threat of shareholder litigation as a governance mechanism. As such, shareholders can exert control by initiating lawsuits. An unresolved issue is the actual credibility of the threat and its reputational and financial costs for managers. Given that equity-linked incentives constitute a major part of U.S. directors' and officers' total compensation (Hall & Liebman, 1998), shareholder litigation also materially affects their overall pay package. According to Fich and Shivdasani (2007), a significant amount of reputational risk is also at stake for managers of sued corporations. Do managers fear shareholder litigation because of substantially longer-term adverse stock price reactions?

In our study, we analyzed various types of allegations brought forward in class-action lawsuits and their short- and long-term effects on shareholder value. In particular, we addressed the following questions. When are class-action lawsuit filings likely to occur, and what are the immediate stock price reactions to them? Can we discriminate between different types of allegations, and do they differ in returns across event windows? How do sued companies perform over the long term, and what is the role of a triggering event before the filing of a lawsuit? Can shareholder litigation discipline managers *ex post*, and should they fear the *ex ante* threat? We adopted the perspective of an investor in a company who has become disgruntled with the company's stock price performance and/or who suspects illegal corporate conduct and must decide whether to allege violations of Rule10b-5 in a lawsuit. Under what circumstances does it pay for the investor to file a lawsuit, and how much time must elapse until the company's performance improves and the investor profits in the long term?

9.2 Data and Methodology

Our primary source of data was the Securities Class Action Clearinghouse maintained by Stanford Law School in collaboration with Cornerstone Research.[1] In existence since 1995, the database includes more than 2800 companies that are listed

[1] This database is available at http://securities.stanford.edu.

on the NYSE, Amex, or NASDAQ. The database also includes private and OTC-traded companies, as well as foreign issuers (who also fall under U.S. securities regulations). We hand-collected case-by-case information and identified seven main reasons for shareholders to go to court against the corporation (Table 9.1). The appendix provides a sample of companies to clarify our coding and grouping methods. These allegations are not mutually exclusive and can amount to a theoretical maximum of seven allegations at the same time. We deliberately decided to retain cases on insider trading and related party transactions. Allegations of this type fall under the violation of duty of loyalty and are less likely to affect the whole company. Our source of data for daily and monthly stock returns was CRSP. We obtained market benchmark return and SMB, HML, and momentum factors from Kenneth French's website.[2]

For the purpose of isolating a true "filing effect," we also identified whether any triggering event preceded the filing of the lawsuit. We classified triggering events as events in which a material correction of management's earnings forecasts took place before the filing date of the class-action lawsuit. Alternative triggering events can be the initiation of a U.S. SEC investigation, self-disclosure of accounting problems, resignation of key executives, or severe problems in the auditing process. In our final sample of 650 companies for 1996–2007, a triggering event preceded the filing in more than 55% of the cases. In one analysis, we discriminated between companies with and without triggering events.

As can be seen in Table 9.1, the annual number of class-action lawsuits peaked in 2002 after the bubble burst. This finding gives a first indication that class-action lawsuits are a response to decreasing stock markets. It is also in line with Povel, Singh, and Winton (2007), who stated that managers' incentives to manipulate are largest in boom times because shareholders are less vigilant. After 2002 and the enforcement of the Sarbanes–Oxley Act, a sharp increase occurred in lawsuits related to corporate governance. False and misleading statements, often coinciding with stock price manipulation, were the prime allegations brought forward by shareholders in class-action lawsuits.

Panel B shows in which industries class-action lawsuits were most prevalent. The four most litigation-vulnerable sectors were shops (FF9), manufacturing (FF3), consumer durables (FF2), and energy (FF4), which tend to be mostly large, capital-intensive industries. Because the business equipment sector (among other high-tech companies) is usually highly dependent on growth opportunities, it surprisingly did not show up as an exposed sector in terms of litigation risk. A possible explanation is that high growth typically does not coincide with companies being large in terms of assets. Typically, large companies are sued for their deep pockets (DuCharme, Malatesta, & Sefcik, 2004). Note that our sample did not discriminate between *ex post* meritorious and frivolous lawsuits, which tend to be lawyer driven. Our objective was to find any pure effects on companies of the *filing* of lawsuits and to find out whether the filing had merits beyond the aimed settlement amount. Therefore, an analysis of *ex post* successful lawsuits only, as in Fich and Shivdasani (2007), could bias our results downward.

---

[2] Available at http://mba.tuck.dartmouth.edu/pages/faculty/ken.french.

Table 9.1 Sample description and allegation types by industry

	Annual no. of class-action lawsuits	Stock price manipulation	Accounting fraud/errors in financial statements	Illegal business practices	Insider trading of directors and officers	False, misleading statements/failure to disclose	SEO, IPO, or acquisition related	Governance or compensation related
A. Types of allegations brought forward								
1996	25	5	6	3	4	18	3	1
1997	37	21	4	19	12	28	4	6
1998	36	20	6	10	9	23	8	5
1999	66	36	8	19	14	47	13	8
2000	46	32	4	13	7	35	10	6
2001	54	32	8	10	21	44	15	8
2002	92	49	8	34	13	42	12	15
2003	76	36	18	26	6	35	3	11
2004	67	25	17	24	7	40	9	14
2005	70	35	9	31	14	40	6	24
2006	33	19	1	18	11	12	3	14
2007	48	21	6	13	9	27	4	12
Total	650	331	95	220	127	391	90	124

Table 9.1 (continued)

	Shops	Manufacturing	Consumer durables	Energy	Other	Money	Business equip-ment	Health	Consumer non-durables	Chemicals	Business utilities	Telecoms	Sum
B. Class-action lawsuits per year and industry type													
All years	22.77%	20.46%	13.38%	10.77%	10.31%	4.92%	4.77%	4.31%	4.15%	1.85%	1.38%	0.92%	
	148	133	87	70	67	32	31	28	27	12	9	6	650
1996	24.00%	20.00%	12.00%	16.00%	24.00%	0.00%	4.00%	0.00%	0.00%	0.00%	0.00%	0.00%	
	6	5	3	4	6	0	1	0	0	0	0	0	25
1997	35.14%	10.81%	5.41%	16.22%	2.70%	2.70%	5.41%	13.51%	2.70%	2.70%	2.70%	0.00%	
	13	4	2	6	1	1	2	5	1	1	1	0	37
1998	25.00%	16.67%	27.78%	5.56%	11.11%	2.78%	5.56%	0.00%	5.56%	0.00%	0.00%	0.00%	
	9	6	10	2	4	1	2	0	2	0	0	0	36
1999	27.27%	18.18%	9.09%	7.58%	15.15%	0.00%	13.64%	3.03%	3.03%	0.00%	1.52%	1.52%	
	18	12	6	5	10	0	9	2	2	0	1	1	66
2000	28.26%	15.22%	8.70%	10.87%	4.35%	6.52%	2.17%	6.52%	8.70%	4.35%	4.35%	0.00%	
	13	7	4	5	2	3	1	3	4	2	2	0	46
2001	44.44%	7.41%	9.26%	0.00%	12.96%	5.56%	3.70%	9.26%	7.41%	0.00%	0.00%	0.00%	
	24	4	5	0	7	3	2	5	4	0	0	0	54
2002	15.05%	19.35%	11.83%	10.75%	9.68%	16.13%	4.30%	9.68%	0.00%	0.00%	0.00%	3.23%	
	14	18	11	10	9	15	4	9	0	0	0	3	93
2003	18.42%	25.00%	17.11%	13.16%	7.89%	5.26%	5.26%	2.63%	2.63%	0.00%	2.63%	0.00%	
	14	19	13	10	6	4	4	2	2	0	2	0	76
2004	13.43%	38.81%	8.96%	16.42%	8.96%	4.48%	2.99%	1.49%	1.49%	0.00%	1.49%	1.49%	
	9	26	6	11	6	3	2	1	1	0	1	1	67
2005	15.71%	20.00%	18.57%	11.43%	7.14%	1.43%	2.86%	1.43%	10.00%	8.57%	1.43%	1.43%	
	11	14	13	8	5	1	2	1	7	6	1	1	70

Table 9.1 (continued)

	Shops	Manufacturing	Consumer durables	Energy	Other	Money	Business equip-ment	Health	Consumer non-durables	Chemicals	Business utilities	Telecoms	Sum
2006	24.24%	12.12%	18.18%	6.06%	18.18%	0.00%	3.03%	0.00%	9.09%	6.06%	3.03%	0.00%	
	8	4	6	2	6	0	1	0	3	2	1	0	33
2007	19.15%	29.79%	17.02%	14.89%	10.64%	2.13%	2.13%	0.00%	2.13%	2.13%	0.00%	0.00%	
	9	14	8	7	5	1	1	0	1	1	0	0	47

Notes: Panel A shows the sample size of our analysis. The different types of allegations stem from the case-by-case information at the Securities Class Action Clearinghouse (http://securities.stanford.edu). In this table, inclusion criteria are the availability of common sample data for company characteristics of the concerned companies. Allegations are coded according to the information listed in the "original complaint allegations" section on the aforementioned website. Panel B breaks down class-action lawsuits by year and by industry type into the 12 Fama–French (FF) industries as listed on Kenneth French's website (http://mba.tuck.dartmouth.edu/pages/faculty/ken.french). FF1 and FF2 are consumer nondurables (food, tobacco, textiles, apparel, leather, toys) and consumer durables (cars, TVs, furniture, household appliances), respectively. FF3 is manufacturing (machinery, trucks, planes, office furniture, paper, commercial printing). FF4 is energy (oil, gas, and coal extraction and products). FF5 is chemicals (chemicals and allied products). FF6 is business equipment (computers, software, and electronic equipment). FF7 is telecoms (telephone and television transmission). FF8 is business utilities. FF9 is shops (wholesale, retail, and some services). FF10 is health (health care, medical equipment, and drugs). FF11 is money (financial institutions). FF12 is all others. Industry groups are sorted in descending order of occurrence of class-action lawsuits over 1996–2007

9.2.1 Testable Hypotheses

We tested whether class-action lawsuits have long-term disciplining effects on the CEO and the company. Shareholders use class-action lawsuits as a punishing device in response to underperformance and managerial malfeasance. We hypothesized that shareholder wealth effects (over both short and long horizons) differ among the types of allegations brought forward. If stock price performance does not recover from a short-term dip, then investors that sue a company are better off to dispose of their shares and to take only the settlement amount instead of holding on to their shares. According to Fich and Shivdasani (2007), an out-of-court settlement is proposed in 91% of the cases. Out of these settlements, the amounts range between $3 million and $40 million for the 25th and 75th percentile, respectively, whereas the average settlement amounts to $22 million. If performance recovers and outperforms the market after adjusting for risk over long horizons, then the lawsuit has merits beyond the settlement amount that the plaintiffs originally aimed for. Long-term stock performance is highly sensitive to the type of allegations that the corporation faces. We discriminated between unlawful activities, which are likely to systematically affect the whole entity (violation of duty of care), and allegations charging individuals (violation of duty of loyalty). We argued that individuals are more likely to be disciplined for their behavior than the whole company as a legal entity. In the case of a whole company, a lawsuit filing is a more disruptive and adverse event, which erodes investor confidence over a long period. For this group of companies, (rather than for the group of companies in which individuals were charged with a violation of duty of loyalty), we hypothesized a significant long-term underperformance. On the basis of this reasoning, we hypothesized that only companies whose individual directors were charged with a violation of duty of loyalty would experience a disciplining effect from lawsuits, which translates into long-term reversal.

We also tested whether class-action lawsuits have similar negative stock price effects irrespective of whether the company was already facing problems before the filing date—a triggering event such as voluntary self-disclosure. The filing of a lawsuit, therefore, resembles a material loss of investor confidence, which manifests itself as inferior stock price performance. In this case, we hypothesized that the actual filing of the lawsuit would cause long-term performance effects rather than self-disclosure before the filing.

9.3 Long-Term Wealth Effects in Class-Action Lawsuits

We used several methods to evaluate the effects on shareholder wealth of class-action lawsuit filings. Our general approach was to use event studies for various purposes. We evaluated short-term announcement effects of class-action lawsuit filings on daily returns in the classic style of Brown and Warner (1980). For longer horizons (up to 36 months), we used monthly data. We also proposed the implementation of calendar time portfolio returns with a Fama and French (1993) risk correction in accordance with Kothari and Warner (2007) and others. We further suggested the importance of augmenting the risk correction with a momentum factor in accordance with Carhart (1997).

9.3.1 Short-Term Announcement Effect

Cumulative abnormal returns best depict the immediate stock price reaction of a class-action lawsuit filing. Using various methods, we documented a consistent decline in stock price on the filing of a class-action lawsuit. More importantly, we observed a significant dip in stock prices before the actual filing, which points to either rumors hitting the market or repercussions from triggering events (Fig. 9.1).

Following the sharp stock price drop, we failed to observe a significant recovery within 2 months following the event (up to 40 trading days). This finding hints at the importance of analyzing long-term shareholder wealth effects. Substantial short-term wealth effects can be documented. Even though we saw a recovery of 200–300 bps from shortly after the filing until Day 40, the cumulative abnormal returns over the whole event window were constantly negative. This robustness in negative performance stems from the almost monotonous decrease in stock price before the filing date. We could attribute the sharp decline in stock prices before

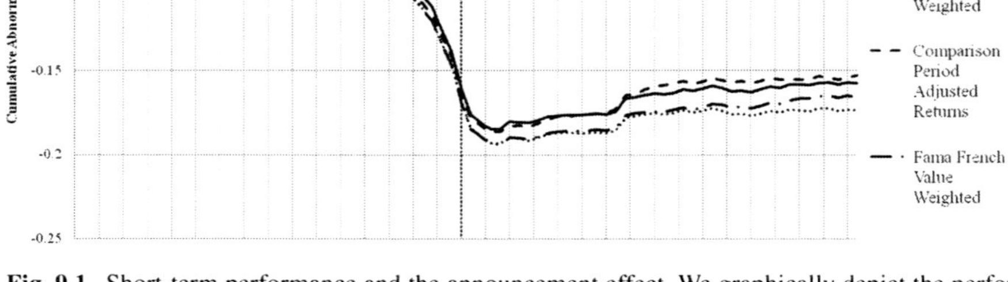

Fig. 9.1 Short-term performance and the announcement effect. We graphically depict the performance of cumulative abnormal returns during the event period of our firms in the class-action lawsuit sample. Our sample size is 650. Our estimation window ranged from maximum 255 (minimum 60) trading days before the event period. Our event date is day zero (lawsuit filing day), where we draw a vertical line for convenience. Fama-French Momentum (Fama-French 4 Value-Weighted) abnormal returns have been estimated using Kenneth French's data library, whereas the beta was estimated versus the value weighted market benchmark of the CRSP universe. The "Comparison period" subtracts the firms' average returns from the estimation window in order to derive abnormal returns. The "Market adjusted returns" are derived from subtracting the contemporaneous equally weighted market return in the CRSP universe of stocks

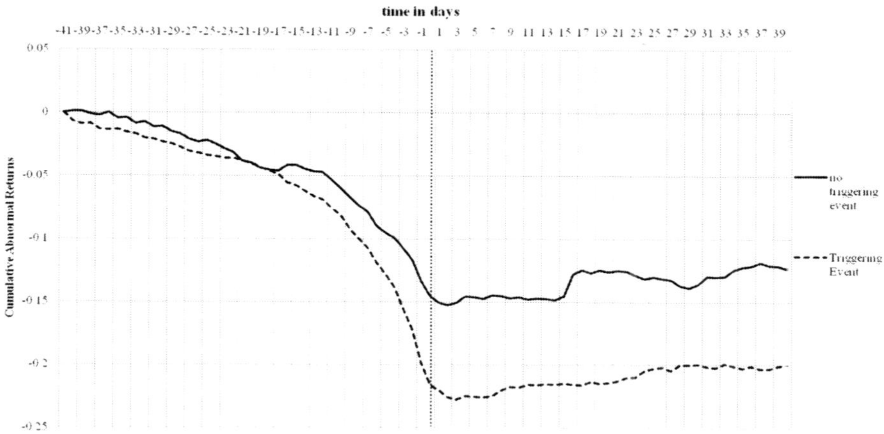

Fig. 9.2 The role of triggering events. The graph below depicts the same Fama-French 4-Factor event study as in Fig. 9.1 with the exception that the sample is split into firms, in which a triggering event (in the form of self-disclosure, SEC investigations, etc.) has preceded the actual filing of the lawsuit, and into firms where such a triggering event is absent. The dashed vertical line represents event day zero (the day of the lawsuit filing)

the event day purely to triggering events. But we split the sample into companies in which a triggering event preceded the filing of the lawsuit and companies in which it did not and compared the shapes of the graphs (Fig. 9.2).

Figure 9.2 shows clearly that companies in which a triggering event preceded the filing were not the only cases with a pre-event-day decline in performance. Though somewhat weaker in magnitude, companies' share price performance declined correspondingly before the event if a lawsuit came as a surprise to the market. This case implies that we did not purely examine companies that had already suffered from adverse events before the lawsuit. Our findings were robust to all types of specifications in event study methods. We obtained qualitatively similar results when using equally weighted benchmarks. An attractive property of event studies that follow the Fama and French (1993) two-step procedure is that one can use the estimated coefficients and their loadings on the factors from the estimation period of daily return data. We used these coefficients for the computations of the expected returns during the event window in order to further characterize sued companies by their factor loadings. We did so to distinguish between companies by their exposure to conventional risk factors. Next to these coefficients, we also used data from Compustat to verify our inferences with balance sheet data (Table 9.2).

We further broke down the sample by the type of violation that each company was charged with. Companies accused of accounting fraud (Panel C) had by far the lowest loading on HML, which we interpreted as being extremely high-growth companies before the filing. This stellar growth might have been fueled by allegedly wrong accounting data. Similarly, companies facing insider-trading allegations (Panel E) had a negative exposure to small-company risk (SMB coefficient

Table 9.2 Exposure to risk factors during estimation period

	Mean	Median	Std. Dev.	Max.	Min.	N
A. Entire class-action lawsuit sample						
Beta	1.307***	1.290***	0.601	4.100	−1.060	649
SMB	−0.562***	−0.440***	1.100	2.990	−5.210	649
HML	−0.433***	−0.510***	0.675	1.920	−1.980	649
UMD	−0.032	0.030	0.696	2.280	−3.420	649
B. Stock price manipulation						
Beta	1.267***	1.260***	0.596	3.110	−1.060	327
SMB	−0.625***	−0.460***	1.159	2.050	−5.210	327
HML	−0.351***	−0.460***	0.676	1.920	−1.980	327
UMD	−0.043	0.020	0.750	2.280	−3.120	327
C. Accounting fraud						
Beta	1.486***	1.435***	0.566	2.900	−0.180	92
SMB	−0.457***	−0.445***	1.007	1.970	−4.830	92
HML	−0.705***	−0.790***	0.615	1.060	−1.960	92
UMD	0.071	0.130*	0.449	1.270	−1.140	92
D. Illegal business practices						
Beta	1.342***	1.360***	0.547	3.140	−0.410	217
SMB	−0.516***	−0.330***	1.103	2.050	−4.630	217
HML	−0.286***	−0.390***	0.678	1.920	−1.710	217
UMD	−0.065	−0.060	0.643	1.540	−2.360	217
E. Insider trading						
Beta	1.208***	1.235***	0.670	2.970	−1.060	128
SMB	−0.980***	−0.665***	1.272	1.290	−5.210	128
HML	−0.412***	−0.510***	0.630	0.910	−1.980	128
UMD	−0.086	−0.005	0.744	1.780	−3.120	128
F. False and misleading statements						
Beta	1.250***	1.210***	0.576	4.100	−0.660	393
SMB	−0.569***	−0.480***	1.102	2.060	−4.830	393
HML	−0.447***	−0.530***	0.649	1.720	−1.980	393
UMD	−0.014	0.040	0.679	2.280	−2.860	393
G. IPO, SEO, or acquisition related						
Beta	1.275***	1.240***	0.566	2.710	−0.040	92
SMB	−0.355***	−0.265***	0.953	2.050	−4.340	92
HML	−0.414***	−0.545***	0.648	1.540	−1.710	92
UMD	0.009	0.040	0.635	2.180	−3.120	92
H. Governance related						
Beta	1.451***	1.390***	0.548	3.140	0.330	127
SMB	−0.398***	−0.450***	1.009	1.970	−4.340	127
HML	−0.325***	−0.440***	0.732	1.540	−1.840	127
UMD	−0.071	−0.090	0.669	2.180	−2.150	127

*Significant at the 10% level

***Significant at the 1% level

Notes: This table reports the statistics of the exposures to the Fama–French risk factors and momentum. The market benchmark for beta is the equally weighted CRSP universe of stocks. For details on the construction of the variables, refer to Kenneth French's website of –0.98). This observation can be attributed to the fact that directors and officers in large-cap companies have steeper incentives (Core, Holthausen, & Larcker, 1999). That is, if directors and officers can capture more upside potential from inside information, they are also more likely to use it. Overall (Panel A), one can conclude that sued companies are growth companies, which tend to be large. The latter finding is consistent with the literature on litigation, which states that shareholders target companies with deep pockets. Turning to the average company characteristics per allegation type in the calendar year before the filing of the lawsuit corroborates most of the previous findings. The right-hand side of Table 9.3 also points to sharp changes in company characteristics and a decline in operating performance and valuation subsequent to litigation. Still, an institutional investor is likely to place greater emphasis on exposures to risk factors than on stale accounting data. Later in the chapter, we will discuss our investigation of whether these coefficients experience a transformation and whether stock characteristics change subsequent to the litigation.

In the next step to distinguish between types of allegation, we looked at the same subsamples. Table 9.4 reports five different event windows ranging from (–1, +1) to (–10, +10). Because average abnormal returns are likely to be affected by extreme values (upward or downward), it also reports median values (in parentheses). We checked for the statistical significance of the difference of mean (median) values from zero with t-statistics (z-values).

In Panel 9A, note that "illegal business practices" showed the most negative abnormal returns in all settings. Allegations that are related to governance or compensation, as well as insider-trading allegations, also result in a nontrivial negative announcement return. Over longer horizons, abnormal returns become increasingly negative. These findings are likely the result of shareholders losing confidence in the company they invest in as soon as corporate governance failures or a manager taking advantage of private knowledge is disclosed to the investing public. Panel 9B highlights that for the two broadest event windows, the stock price reaction to an increasingly severe lawsuit (approximated by the number of allegations brought forward) was more negative. We conclude that a more negative stock price reaction with more allegations brought forward can yield harsher personal consequences for the CEO and for the company. If we focus on the first three rows (up to three allegations), the picture of decreasing cumulative returns is consistent among all event windows. In most of the cases, mean and median abnormal returns are highly significant below 1%.

To determine which allegations drove the return during our event periods, we conducted a cross-sectional regression of our event window cumulative abnormal returns on a number of control variables and dummies of the types of allegations with "stock price manipulation" as the base level. We also controlled for company characteristics, which have been shown to drive abnormal returns (Campbell, Lo, & MacKinlay, 1997). Because all the companies in our sample experienced an event, we needed a base level of allegations for comparing results. We identified the base variable in allegations of "stock price manipulation." The fact that the correlation between allegation dummies did not exceed 0.32 allowed us to include these multivariately. Results are reported in Table 9.5.

Table 9.3 Key pre- and post-lawsuit financial and performance characteristics

	Pre-lawsuit				Post-lawsuit			
	Mean	Median	Std. Dev.	*N*	Mean	Median	Std. Dev.	*N*
A. Entire class-action lawsuit sample								
Market cap	$19,320.47	$4,293.25	$41,950.30	612	$18,154.75	$3,474.54	$41,162.77	514
Book-to-market ratio	0.4368	0.3668	0.3420	610	0.4624	0.4724	0.8440	512
EBIT/assets	0.0729	0.0693	0.1101	533	0.0278	0.0483	0.1636	450
Dividend yield	6.93	0.04	20.65	609	9.17	0.00	27.24	514
Price/earnings	10.46	8.57	50.06	607	12.95	6.90	75.15	509
B. Accounting fraud								
Market cap	$29,481.90	$5,585.67	$55,615.39	89	$33,914.86	$5,177.73	$65,748.71	79
Book-to-market ratio	0.4409	0.4121	0.3084	89	0.4862	0.4656	0.8266	79
EBIT/assets	0.0760	0.0638	0.1175	72	0.0556	0.0439	0.1129	63
Dividend yield	11.91	0.98	27.35	89	17.42	0.93	45.41	79
Price/earnings	2.01	7.17	93.99	88	25.76	6.02	175.26	78
C. Illegal business practices								
Market cap	$12,059.62	$2,632.04	$31,505.14	201	$11,943.47	$2,042.18	$34,944.52	164
Book-to-market ratio	0.4601	0.3900	0.3235	199	0.5022	0.5129	0.7761	163
EBIT/assets	0.0789	0.0721	0.1004	174	0.0071	0.0474	0.1958	149
Dividend yield	4.20	0.00	13.92	200	4.55	0.00	15.06	163
Price/earnings	12.15	8.85	37.84	200	6.65	7.13	34.79	162
D. Insider trading								
Market cap	$15,870.10	$4,703.75	$35,338.93	121	$9,973.44	$3,788.69	$18,750.84	94
Book-to-market ratio	0.3585	0.2880	0.3011	119	0.4411	0.4396	0.8441	94
EBIT/assets	0.0869	0.0949	0.1213	114	0.0194	0.0588	0.1878	87
Dividend yield	1.28	0.00	3.47	118	3.55	0.00	11.94	94
Price/earnings	22.36	11.32	46.89	120	13.69	7.09	32.17	93

Notes: This table reports financial and company information before and after the filing of the lawsuit. It shows mean and median values, the variables' standard deviations, and the sample size (*N*). EBIT is earnings before interest and taxes. The data sources are CRSP and Compustat. Market capitalization is computed at the end of the calendar year before the filing year of the lawsuit and is the number of shares outstanding (Item #25) multiplied by the closing stock price (#199). Book-to-market ratio is computed as the book value of common equity (#60) divided by market capitalization. EBIT/assets is computed as ([Item #18 + Item #16 + Item #15]/Item #6) and price/earnings as (#199/[#18/#25])

Table 9.4 Cumulative average abnormal returns

Type of allegation	(−1, +1)	(−1, 0)	(0, +1)	(−5, +5)	(−10, +10)	N
A. Abnormal return per type of allegation						
Average of all allegations	−4.33***	−3.86***	−2.03***	−8.52***	−11.57***	648
	(−1.07)***	(−0.89)***	(−0.63)***	(−4.22)***	(−5.74)***	
Stock price momentum	−5.17***	−4.65***	−2.53***	−8.80***	−13.46***	327
	(−1.49)***	(−1.17)***	(−0.85)***	(−4.52)***	(−7.71)***	
Accounting fraud	−2.99***	−2.43**	−1.11*	−5.69***	−6.44***	92
	(−0.43)	(−0.58)	(0.11)	(−3.44)***	(−3.80)***	
Illegal business practices	−6.87***	−5.95***	−3.56***	−12.64***	−14.17***	217
	(−2.41)***	(−1.89)***	(−1.30)***	(−6.12)***	(−7.29)***	
Insider trading	−4.91***	−4.39***	−2.23**	−9.44***	−14.22***	127
	(−1.42)***	(−1.46)***	(−0.32)**	(−4.20)***	(−5.26)***	
False/misleading statements	−3.86***	−3.86***	−1.71***	−8.79***	−12.96***	392
	(−0.67)***	(−0.83)***	(−0.56)***	(−4.00)***	(−6.92)***	
SEO, IPO, or acquisition related	−2.78**	−2.90***	−1.26*	−2.64	−3.94	92
	(−0.31)	(−0.87)**	(−0.59)	(−1.30)	(−2.14)	
Governance problems	−4.58***	−3.73***	−1.55**	−9.42***	−10.65***	128
	(−1.00)***	(−0.82)***	(−0.45)**	(−3.30)***	(−4.43)***	
B. Average abnormal returns per total number of allegations						
1	−2.92***	−2.37***	−1.73***	−7.35***	−9.42***	167
	(−0.32)	(−0.27)	(−0.42)	(−3.56)***	(−4.75)***	
2	−4.47***	−3.97***	−1.95***	−8.61***	−11.76***	268
	(−1.34)***	(−1.19)***	(−0.79)***	(−4.63)***	(−6.54)***	
3	−5.83***	−5.28***	−2.54***	−9.52***	−13.74***	169
	(−1.74)***	(−1.49)***	(−0.45)**	(−4.23)***	(−6.79)***	
4	−3.20	−2.77	−2.22	−9.28*	−11.42*	34
	(−0.95)	(−0.50)	(−0.92)	(−3.66)*	(−3.91)	
5	−5.38	−9.19	−1.68	−10.43	−9.82	5
	(0.70)	(−0.12)	(−0.19)	(−3.77)	(−5.25)	

*Significant at the 10% level for a test (*t*-stat. for mean and *z*-stat. for median) for abnormal returns different from zero

**Significant at the 5% level for a test (*t*-stat. for mean and *z*-stat. for median) for abnormal returns different from zero

***Significant at the 1% level for a test (*t*-stat. for mean and *z*-stat. for median) for abnormal returns different from zero

Notes: Panel A reports the same abnormal return windows for the seven types of allegations (defined in Table 9.1). Note that these types of allegations are not mutually exclusive. For the event study, we required an estimation period window of at least 60 trading days and a maximum of 255 days for the estimate of the R_m–R_f, HML, SMB, and momentum coefficients. Day 0 is defined as the day of the class-action lawsuit filing. Panel B distinguishes between the numbers of allegations filed in the lawsuit. Median values are reported in parentheses

Table 9.5 Cross-sectional regressions and single allegations

Type of allegation	(–1, +1)	(–1, 0)	(0, +1)	(–5, +5)	(–10, +10)	
A. Cross-sectional regression of cumulative abnormal return over different event windows on control variables						
ROA	–0.0200	0.0006	–0.0196	–0.0079	–0.0095	
	(–0.6655)	(0.0207)	(–0.9549)	(–0.1537)	(–0.1616)	
Log MB	–0.0379***	–0.0419***	–0.0189**	–0.0742***	–0.0731***	
	(–3.1754)	(–3.8359)	(–2.3249)	(–3.6638)	(–3.1553)	
Log TA	–0.0027	–0.0029	–0.0020	0.0042	0.0166**	
	(–0.7437)	(–0.8745)	(–0.8103)	(0.6806)	(2.3214)	
Change in sales	0.0333	0.0108	0.0421**	0.0568	0.0505	
	(1.1526)	(0.4079)	(2.1426)	(1.1586)	(0.8993)	
Change in price	0.0514***	0.0423***	0.0283***	0.0506**	0.0836***	
	(3.4202)	(3.0748)	(2.7610)	(1.9809)	(2.8616)	
Dividend payer	0.0193	0.0168	0.0001	–0.0074	–0.0465	
	(1.2744)	(1.2093)	(0.0054)	(–0.2864)	(–1.5750)	
Stock price manipulation						
Accounting fraud	0.0042	0.0012	0.0093	0.0109	(0.0222	
	(0.2189)	(0.0679)	(0.7112)	(0.3352)	(0.5972)	
Illegal business practices	–0.0296**	–0.0328***	–0.0132	–0.0593***	–0.0300	
	(–2.2757)	(–2.7609)	(–1.4916)	(–2.6914)	(–1.1885)	
Insider trading	0.0175	0.0107	0.0175*	–0.0056	–0.0304	
	(1.2037)	(0.8062)	(1.7680)	(–0.2256)	(–1.0778)	
False/misleading statements	–0.0001	–0.0154	0.0077	–0.0297	–0.0516**	
	(–0.0077)	(–1.2380)	(0.8285)	(–1.2861)	(–1.9556)	
SEO, IPO, or acquisition related	–0.0013	–0.0091	–0.0020	0.0443	0.0759**	
	(–0.0782)	(–0.5954)	(–0.1771)	(1.5628)	(2.3395)	
Governance problems	–0.0025	–0.0077	0.0119	–0.0199	–0.0119	
	(–0.1657)	(–0.5521)	(1.1458)	(–0.7649)	(–0.3994)	
Industry controls	Y	Y	Y	Y	Y	
Year controls	Y	Y	Y	Y	Y	
Adjusted R^2	0.0900	0.0930	0.0525	0.0936	0.1460	
N	512	512	512	512	512	
Type of allegation	(–1, +1)	(–1, 0)	(0, +1)	(–5, +5)	(–10, +10)	N
B. Average CARs of the subsample of companies with only one allegation (N = 167)						
Stock price manipulation	–3.43%	–0.83%	–4.88%**	–10.21%**	–12.93%**	13
	(–3.51%)**	(–1.17%)	(–2.86%)**	(–6.68%)*	(–8.48%)*	
Accounting fraud	0.28%	0.42%	0.50%	–2.60%	–2.93%	28
	(0.30%)	(0.04%)	(0.48%)	(–4.24%)*	(–2.12%)*	
Illegal business practices	–8.14%**	–6.76%*	–3.54%	–15.91%**	–13.06%**	20
	(–2.08%)	(–0.84%)	(–0.52%)	(–5.77%)**	(–5.99%)	
Insider trading	–2.27%	–1.05%	–3.56%	7.34%	–13.38%	1
	(–2.27%)	(–1.05%)	(–3.56%)	(7.34%)	(–13.38%)	

Table 9.5 (continued)

Type of allegation	(–1, +1)	(–1, 0)	(0, +1)	(–5, +5)	(–10, +10)	
False/misleading statements	–2.42%**	–2.53%**	–1.32%	–6.76%***	–10.20%***	96
	(0.23%)	(0.02%)	(–0.29%)	(–1.74%)	(–4.37%)**	
SEO, IPO, or acquisition related	NA	NA	NA	NA	NA	0
	NA	NA	NA	NA	NA	
Governance problems	–6.32%	–1.97%	–4.62%	–6.70%	–7.45%	8
	(–2.55%)	(–0.94%)	(–2.27%)	(–6.09%)	(–8.25%)	

*Significant at the 10% level
**Significant at the 5% level
***Significant at the 1% level
Notes: Panel A reports the coefficients of cross-sectional regressions of the abnormal returns for the five different event windows. Every regression controls for return on assets (ROA), growth opportunities (Log MB), size (Log TA), change in sales over the prior calendar year, change in stock price over the calendar fiscal year, whether the company is a dividend-paying company, and industry (Fama–French 12) and year effects; *t*-statistics are reported in parentheses in Panel A. Panel B restricts our sample to those companies facing only one allegation to isolate overlapping effects between allegations that are not mutually exclusive; we report results of tests of mean and median being different from zero in parentheses in Panel B

In a multivariate setting, we still observe that "illegal business practices" resulted in significantly lower CARs (cumulative abnormal returns) than for the base case, especially for very short-term event windows. For "insider trading," however, the pattern is reversed. Coefficients on control variables like company size (log of total assets) and growth opportunities (log of market-to-book ratio) were in line with the event study literature. The latter as a control variable was consistently negative, which points to a short-term correction of fundamental values. Company size has a mitigating effect on abnormal returns because large companies are more likely to be diversified and have a larger shareholder base than small companies. After controlling for other factors, we found that allegations of this type do not result in significantly lower CARs than in the base case; for longer periods, however, they bear more negative announcement returns.

Because allegations are not mutually exclusive, overlap between the allegation types might blur our findings. To isolate any overlapping effects of allegations, we decided to proceed differently. For that purpose, we also focused on the group of companies (167 in total) that faced only one allegation and distinguished between those allegations. We stuck to a univariate analysis of mean and median values. Thus, we were able to isolate the allegation types from each other so that we could discriminate more easily. For the 20 companies charged with only illegal business practices, CARs during event windows (–5, +5) and (–10, +10) turned out to be very significant (–16% and –13%, respectively). Insider trading was inconclusive because it almost constantly coincided with an allegation of either stock price manipulation or false and misleading statements. Therefore, the sample size was very low and did not allow for statistically reliable inferences. We conclude that shareholder wealth effects differ significantly with respect to the various allegations brought forward.

9.3.2 Long-Horizon Results

We were unable to observe a clear pattern of short-term (2 months) recovery of the stock price for sued companies. To gain more insight into this result, we conducted the same analysis by using monthly data and an event window of up to 36 months. Figure 9.3 graphically depicts the development of monthly cumulative abnormal returns with several methods.

The development from the event Month 0 to Month 3 approximately confirms the image from Fig. 9.1—namely, an indication of a slight recovery of the stock price, which sharply reverses thereafter. After Month 3, we see a gradual decline down to a minimum of –23% CAR in less than 3 years. For the entire sample of 650 sued companies (irrespective of allegation type), this is quite puzzling. On average, shareholder litigation does not seem to pay off in terms of stock price recovery. If we take the statistical validity in this case for granted, we can infer that shareholders aim for the settlement amount and dispose of any equity share in the company that they sued in the first place. We acknowledge potential statistical biases, however, for this type of analysis. Still, this preliminary result can serve as a crude indication of long-term shareholder wealth effects.

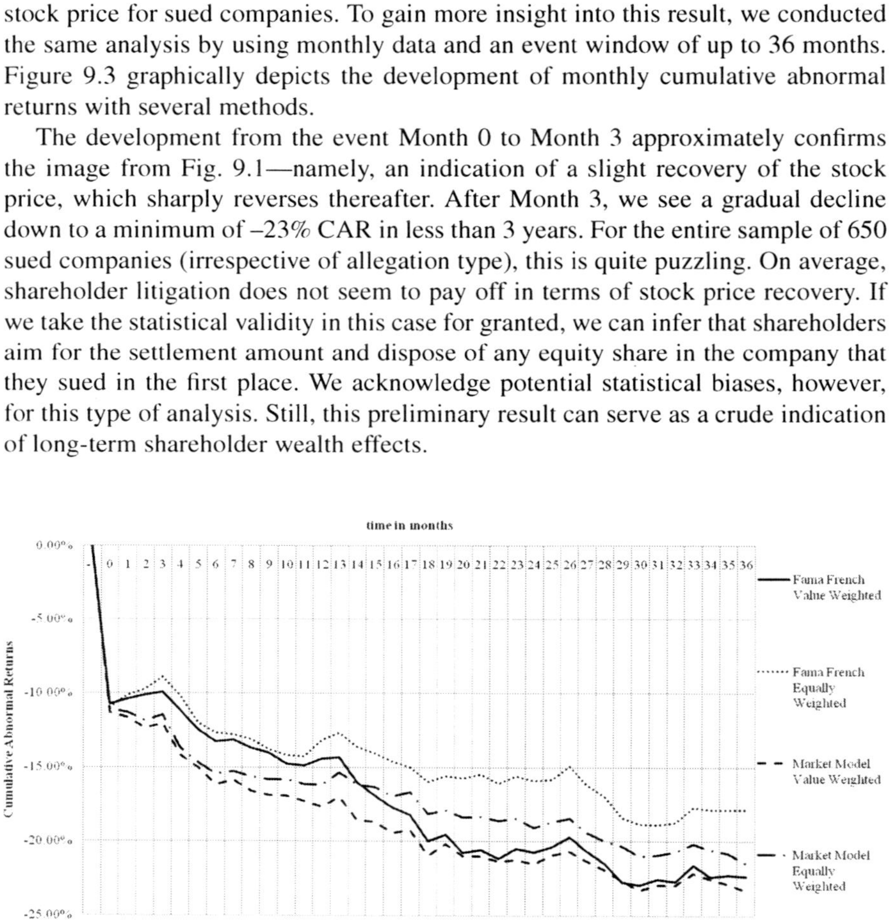

Fig. 9.3 Long term performance—monthly cumulative abnormal returns. Below, we show long term monthly cumulative abnormal returns of firms that experienced a class-action lawsuit between 1996 and 2007. We use the same event window of [0; +36] months and distinguish between four estimation methods: Fama-French 4 Factor Abnormal Returns use the CRSP Value-weighted (equal-weighted) market return, SMB, HML, and Momentum premia as a benchmark during the estimation window. The estimation period stops 6 months before the event. The market model (CAPM) estimation suppresses the use of SMB, HML, and Momentum

9.3.3 Abnormal Returns in Calendar Time

Long-horizon event studies are not unproblematic with respect to statistical validity because potential misspecification of daily expected returns accumulates over long horizons to sizable estimation errors. Moreover, cross-correlation becomes greater over long horizons (Kothari & Warner, 2007). The buy-and-hold abnormal return approach of Daniel, Gimblat, Wermers, and Titman (1997), therefore, uses matching companies/portfolios to calculate abnormal return for each company and holding period t. Here, risk adjustment takes place via characteristic-based measures. The difficulty in using this approach is that it is not a feasible investment approach because the total number of event companies is not known in advance (Eckbo, Masulis, & Norli, 2000). So, if we want to compute long-term shareholder wealth effects from the time of the filing date and how these shareholders perform on a risk-adjusted basis compared with the market and conventional risk factors, we must proceed differently.

We used a calendar time portfolio approach (Fama, 1998), which works as follows. Suppose that a group of companies experience some common corporate event. In the sample period, companies are facing events that might be spread over time (T = months). Further assume that we want to compute price performance over period T following the occurrence. To do so, in each calendar month over the entire sample period, we construct a portfolio containing securities that experience an event during the previous time T. Owing to the nature of the construction, the number of companies in the portfolio is not constant: Companies exit and new companies enter each month. In this way, we account for all the cross-correlations of event company abnormal returns in the portfolio variance. The net of risk computation of abnormal returns takes place differently. We regress the resulting time series of monthly returns on the Fama–French factors plus a momentum factor (Carhart, 1997):

$$R_{pt} - R_{ft} = a_p + b_p \left(R_{mt} - R_{ft}\right) + s_p SMB_t + h_p HML_t + u_p UMD_t + e_{pt}, \quad (9.1)$$

where

R_{pt} = either the equal- or value-weighted return for calendar month t for portfolio p, which has experienced an event during the prior time T

R_{ft} = the risk-free rate

R_{mt} = the return on the CRSP value-weighted market portfolio

SMB_t = the differential return between a portfolio of small stocks and a portfolio of big stocks

HML_t = the return differential between value and growth stocks (high versus low book-to-market ratio)

UMD_t = the difference in returns between the prior year's winners and losers

a_p = the average monthly abnormal return on our portfolio of event companies over the T post-event period (the equation's critical variable)

b_p, s_p, h_p, and u_p = the sensitivities to market, small-company risk, value premium, and momentum, respectively

This type of risk correction spans the method that was originally proposed by Fama and French (1993); and Fama, French, Booth, and Sinquefield (1993). Mitchell and Stafford (2000) and Brav and Gompers (1997) prominently applied this approach. We adopted seven different holding periods ranging from 0–6 months to 0–48 months. This setup reflects the fact that performance does not include the announcement return of the class-action lawsuit filing. The first return of an included company is always between the end of the filing month and the end of the subsequent month. The results are shown in Table 9.6.

Table 9.6 Long-term performance in calendar time

	(0, 6)	(0, 12)	(0, 18)	(0, 24)	(0, 30)	(0, 36)	(0, 48)
A. All lawsuits ($n = 648$)							
Alpha	−0.017	−0.006	−0.007	−0.001	−0.002	−0.002	−0.002
	−4.46***	−1.71**	−2.02**	−0.330	−0.720	−0.650	−0.600
Beta	1.305	1.256	1.213	1.058	1.089	1.117	1.133
	13.10***	15.30***	16.92***	9.91***	14.10***	17.64***	19.62***
SMB	0.617	0.558	0.554	0.489	0.578	0.597	0.598
	5.00***	5.09***	5.91***	4.37***	7.15***	7.93***	8.13***
HML	0.353	0.341	0.396	0.140	0.208	0.241	0.241
	2.07**	2.16**	3.28***	0.850	1.83**	2.39***	2.42***
UMD	−0.569	−0.516	−0.463	−0.427	−0.414	−0.401	−0.393
	−5.63***	−5.55***	−5.97***	−5.34***	−5.53***	−5.14***	−4.79***
Adjusted R^2	0.730	0.725	0.750	0.728	0.782	0.795	0.804
B. Accounting fraud ($n = 92$)							
Alpha	−0.023	−0.013	−0.013	−0.010	−0.008	−0.002	−0.003
	−2.88***	−2.06**	−2.29**	−2.18**	−1.88**	−0.470	−1.050
Beta	1.761	1.644	1.641	1.508	1.303	1.141	1.193
	8.34***	10.44***	11.78***	11.70***	12.43***	9.04***	10.50***
SMB	0.639	0.607	0.604	0.621	0.642	0.664	0.616
	2.89***	3.92***	4.57***	4.98***	5.63***	6.23***	7.70***
HML	0.310	0.615	0.772	0.714	0.517	0.545	0.532
	0.920	2.97***	4.06***	4.48***	3.61***	3.84***	3.82***
UMD	−0.712	−0.719	−0.591	−0.527	−0.436	−0.402	−0.396
	−4.08***	−4.79***	−4.07***	−5.30***	−5.04***	−4.36***	−6.80***
Adjusted R^2	0.555	0.683	0.678	0.653	0.703	0.640	0.770
C. Illegal business practices ($n = 218$)							
Alpha	−0.015	−0.007	−0.007	0.001	0.001	0.002	0.002
	−2.33***	−1.240	−1.45*	0.270	0.250	0.580	0.590
Beta	1.372	1.333	1.274	1.176	1.184	1.167	1.186
	7.39***	8.18***	11.03***	6.82***	13.23***	12.69***	14.47***
SMB	0.616	0.756	0.681	0.498	0.673	0.681	0.691
	2.79***	4.10***	4.57***	2.63***	5.13***	5.58***	5.74***

Table 9.6 (continued)

	(0, 6)	(0, 12)	(0, 18)	(0, 24)	(0, 30)	(0, 36)	(0, 48)
HML	0.633	0.606	0.578	0.183	0.310	0.290	0.246
	2.12**	2.50***	3.38***	0.690	2.17**	2.17**	1.86**
UMD	−0.482	−0.528	−0.482	−0.444	−0.447	−0.456	−0.447
	−4.17***	−4.87***	−5.18***	−4.78***	−5.10***	−5.02***	−4.55***
Adjusted R^2	0.464	0.562	0.621	0.616	0.722	0.736	0.760
D. Insider trading (n = 128)							
Alpha	−0.009	0.011	0.006	0.012	0.009	0.010	0.009
	−1.050	1.33*	0.940	2.15**	1.94**	2.10**	1.93**
Beta	1.488	1.065	1.115	0.850	0.939	0.997	1.033
	6.57***	5.54***	7.95***	5.59***	7.51***	8.85***	10.53***
SMB	1.007	0.628	0.549	0.468	0.535	0.539	0.596
	3.93***	2.74***	3.32***	2.88***	4.19***	4.39***	5.06***
HML	0.821	−0.127	0.015	−0.359	−0.192	−0.129	−0.071
	1.99*	−0.340	0.060	−1.36*	−0.970	−0.700	−0.420
UMD	−0.754	−0.798	−0.649	−0.607	−0.561	−0.535	−0.466
	−3.26***	−3.04**	−3.82***	−4.38***	−5.12***	−4.77***	−4.71***
Adjusted R^2	0.453	0.460	0.525	0.546	0.598	0.611	0.621
E. Governance problems (n = 107)							
Alpha	−0.042	−0.022	−0.011	−0.003	−0.002	−0.003	−0.004
	−3.04***	−2.40***	−1.90**	−0.470	−0.280	−0.510	−0.810
Beta	1.661	1.533	1.326	1.161	1.192	1.185	1.269
	4.85***	6.79***	8.95***	6.33***	9.37***	9.30***	13.34***
SMB	0.679	0.706	0.737	0.487	0.635	0.623	0.585
	1.53*	2.91***	3.75***	2.23**	3.50***	4.16***	4.21***
HML	0.530	0.757	0.733	0.430	0.504	0.556	0.575
	1.060	2.39***	2.95***	1.35*	2.30**	2.65***	3.13***
UMD	−0.264	−0.131	−0.351	−0.235	−0.321	−0.269	−0.327
	−0.920	−0.570	−2.82***	−2.00**	−3.22***	−3.21***	−4.41***
Adjusted R^2	0.243	0.371	0.453	0.388	0.517	0.525	0.592

*Significant at the 10% level
**Significant at the 5% level
***Significant at the 1% level

Notes: In this table, we perform Fama–French calendar time portfolio return regressions as advocated by Fama (1998). Panel A uses 132 observations from January 1996 to December 2006. Panel A restricts our sample to all the companies sued during the period. Panel B involves companies sued for accounting fraud. In Panel C, the sample is the companies sued for illegal business practices. Panel D involves companies facing allegations of insider trading. Panel E includes companies with governance problems. Characterizations are illustrated in Appendix. Our return windows are depicted in the table's column heads. Alpha represents the intercept of a regression of abnormal returns of a strategy that invests in sued companies versus the market benchmark, size, book-to-market, and momentum factors. The dependent variable is the equally weighted monthly percentage return on a portfolio of companies facing litigation during the prior 6, 12, 18, 24, 30, 36, or 48 months. The *t*-statistics (below the coefficients) have been adjusted for heteroscedasticity by using the White correction

Panels 9B–9E of Table 9.6 break down our sample into four allegations: accounting fraud, illegal business practices, insider trading, and governance problems. In the case of accounting fraud allegations, companies' negative abnormal returns persisted significantly for up to 30 months (and stayed negative afterward, although not significantly so). We do not observe this result for companies in Panels 9C and 9D. On the contrary, alpha reversed so long as the stocks were held longer than 24 months for companies facing charges of illegal business practices. Although not statistically significant, the monthly risk-adjusted alpha for a strategy of investing in companies sued for illegal business practices was mildly positive. For companies and directors charged with insider trading, abnormal returns look even more prosperous. Initially (i.e., over a holding period of 0 to 6 months), the monthly alpha was negative but not significant. Shortly afterward, the strategy started generating positive and significant monthly alphas of up to 1.2%. A further striking feature is this group's exposure to HML. Over short holding periods, the coefficient was still positive (being exposed to value stocks), and it switched signs after 18 months (being exposed to growth stocks with low book-to-market ratios). In comparison, allegations of governance problems were also more likely to have a systematically negative effect on performance: Alpha over a maximum period of 1 year was significantly negative. We conclude that for these groups of companies, the filing of a class-action lawsuit has a disciplining effect in terms of stock market performance.

9.3.4 The Role of Triggering Events Before the Filing Date

Does it make a difference if an event before the actual filing of the lawsuit triggers shareholder litigation? In other words, if the investing public is already aware that the company is in a "problematic" situation before the filing of the lawsuit, does the filing of the lawsuit still make a difference for these types of companies? And if so, what returns can be expected on these types of companies? Thus, we investigated whether any disciplining effect stems from the actual litigation or whether shareholders were already monitoring these companies. Recall that we were unable to identify differences in short-term pre-event performance before the lawsuit between the aforementioned two groups. To investigate this "true filing effect," we split our sample into those companies that experienced triggering events before the filing and those companies for which such an event was not documented by the shareholder litigation database and court documents. We continued to rely on the calendar time portfolio approach, and we also checked for differences in average portfolio alphas by using the following formula:

$$\frac{\bar{\alpha}_{p1} - \bar{\alpha}_{p2}}{\sqrt{\frac{\sigma_{p1}^2}{\sqrt{n_{p1}}} + \frac{\sigma_{p2}^2}{\sqrt{n_{p2}}}}}, \tag{9.2}$$

where p_1 and p_2 resemble the average alphas of the individual portfolios (triggering event: yes or no) and n_1 [n_{p1}] and n_2 [n_{p2}] are the sample sizes of the two portfolios. Note that these two sample groups are mutually exclusive and share only the common feature of being sued by their shareholders. The results are shown in Table 9.7.

Table 9.7 Long-term performance in calendar time with triggering events

	(0, 6)	(0, 12)	(0, 18)	(0, 24)	(0, 30)	(0, 36)	(0, 48)
A. Triggering event (n = 359)							
Alpha	−0.019	−0.007	−0.008	0.000	−0.002	−0.002	−0.002
	−2.88***	−1.35*	−1.73**	−0.050	−0.390	−0.550	−0.500
Beta	1.294	1.180	1.098	0.920	0.983	1.035	1.031
	7.54***	9.00***	10.37***	7.06***	10.15***	11.64***	11.69***
SMB	0.650	0.720	0.699	0.634	0.694	0.734	0.759
	3.68***	4.94***	5.59***	4.44***	5.75***	6.59***	7.17***
HML	0.164	0.208	0.234	−0.102	0.057	0.125	0.110
	0.650	0.940	1.38*	−0.480	0.390	0.970	0.840
UMD	−0.425	−0.493	−0.488	−0.463	−0.448	−0.446	−0.416
	−3.81***	−4.23***	−5.76***	−4.41***	−4.65***	−4.55***	−4.21***
Adjusted R^2	0.447	0.530	0.564	0.559	0.597	0.620	0.623
B. No triggering event (n = 290)							
Alpha	−0.012	−0.002	−0.004	−0.002	−0.002	−0.001	−0.001
	−2.07**	−0.360	−1.040	−0.530	−0.630	−0.200	−0.290
Beta	1.305	1.197	1.270	1.199	1.141	1.109	1.148
	8.21***	11.88***	13.28***	12.27***	12.30***	12.20***	15.63***
SMB	0.600	0.435	0.469	0.417	0.472	0.482	0.497
	3.50***	3.64***	4.69***	4.28***	5.99***	6.31***	6.63***
HML	0.447	0.361	0.494	0.345	0.267	0.247	0.267
	1.93**	2.25**	3.99***	2.90***	2.25**	2.12**	2.51***
UMD	−0.744	−0.587	−0.478	−0.427	−0.415	−0.391	−0.397
	−4.86***	−7.14***	−5.37***	−5.95***	−6.02***	−5.45***	−5.05***
Adjusted R^2	0.615	0.671	0.687	0.721	0.743	0.746	0.774
Difference, triggering event vs. no triggering event	−0.007	−0.005	−0.004	0.002	0.000	−0.001	−0.001
t-Statistic	−0.502	−0.255	−0.078	0.479	0.000	−0.150	−0.166

*Significant at the 10% level
**Significant at the 5% level
***Significant at the 1% level
Notes: We conducted the same calendar time portfolio regression as in [Table 9.6] but distinguished between class-action lawsuits that were preceded by "triggering events" (Panel A) and those that were not (Panel B). We tested for the significance of the differences in the estimated average alpha coefficients in the portfolio depending on holding period. The t-statistics (below the coefficients) have been adjusted for heteroscedasticity by using the White correction

Note that our results were highly sensitive to the incorporation of momentum.[3] As can be seen in Table 9.6, u_p was significant and negative on momentum in all the regressions, which seems straightforward. Our portfolio is strongly tilted toward prior losers, which, in the light of sued companies' negative performance history, is logical. For Panel A, note that underperformance diminished over time after 18 months but still persisted. For holding periods of 6 months, note the strongly negative monthly alpha, which translates into an annualized alpha for the investment strategy of almost –20%. For longer periods, underperformance was less negative. Concerning SMB and HML coefficients, we observe a remarkable pattern. We compare these to our previous method in Table 9.2, which estimated pre-event window coefficients for the computation of expected returns during the event window. The coefficients from the pre-event window estimate were both still negative, which suggests that sued companies were large companies with low book-to-market ratios (growth companies). After the event, however, these coefficients turned positive for our portfolio of sued companies. An intermediate conclusion that emerges from this observation is that subsequent to the litigation filing, sued companies behaved like small companies with high book-to-market ratios (these companies could be "fallen angels" in the context of Rauh & Sufi, 2009). Hence, we observe not only a significant effect on stock prices but also a change in company risk with respect to exposures to market factors.

Although initial short- and medium-term holding period alphas were more negative for companies with triggering events before the lawsuit, the alphas of companies without a past triggering event had no statistically significant difference. Hence, we fail to reject the hypothesis of similar long-term returns for companies whose self-disclosure of accounting problems or SEC investigations, rather than shareholder dissidence, triggered the filing. According to our analysis, fundamental events before the filing did not cause investors to lose faith in the company and its directors. Even though both groups of companies started at different levels after 40 trading days, this difference did not result in differences in expected long-term returns between the groups. The official filing of a lawsuit by shareholders appears to be the cause of an erosion of confidence. On the basis of this finding, we conclude that a "true filing effect" does exist.

9.3.5 Possible Explanations and Practical Implications

How can we reconcile our findings with shareholders' motivations to sue companies and possible long-term disciplining effects? According to Coffee (2005), class-action lawsuits occur more often in the United States than in other countries because of the differences in ownership structure and shareholder base. Peng and Röell (2008a) found that litigation is the primary punishment device available to

[3] In unreported results (available upon request), we ran calendar time portfolio regressions based on both the Fama–French three-factor model and the capital asset pricing model.

shareholders in the United States and distinguishes the U.S. capital market from other markets. The question then becomes, who benefits from this punishment, and what are its effects? Are there any long-term merits in terms of disciplining and learning for both shareholders and companies, or do claims center on only the settlement amount and potential damages? With respect to claims of illegal insider trading, our analysis provides clear evidence of a disciplining effect. If selected individuals rather than the whole company are sued, the effect lessens and even reverses into positive abnormal returns over the long term.

Several issues are worth addressing with respect to insider trading arising from stock price manipulation. We acknowledge that the communication of company information to investors is essential to signal a healthy condition to the market. When this communication is taken to deceptive extremes, however, managers violate their duty of loyalty. For this process to work requires the assumption that stock prices do not fully reflect leeway for manipulation (Peng & Röell, 2008b). Investors, however, tend to be uncertain about managers' ability to move stock prices effectively. This uncertainty does not hold if accounting fraud as a company-wide systematic malpractice is alleged. Illegal business practices and accounting fraud are *de facto* systematically adverse events that affect the entire company and seem to erode investor confidence over the long term.

Any discussion about costs of shareholder litigation brings us back to the initial question of the management-borne costs of shareholder litigation. Because top management is truly responsible for triggering the loss in investor confidence in our cases of shareholder litigation, an efficient managerial labor market should replace the incumbents. Ultimately, whether this event is the result of the actions of individuals (as in our cases of litigation), systematic economic shocks, or industry factors determines the future viability of the enterprise. Our long-term performance differential between companies sued for insider trading versus companies sued for company-wide malpractices can be explained in the following way. Insider trading can generally be pinned on a few individuals, whereas accounting fraud and/or illegal business practices are more likely to be the product of a group of people. In the case of insider trading, the filing of the lawsuit and reputational costs discipline the existing managers or a more efficient and ethical management replaces them. In the latter case, new managers are aware of the lawsuit that their predecessors faced, and this information deters them from any self-dealing actions.

We further documented shareholder wealth effects for companies that face accounting fraud allegations. In a recent study, Kedia and Philippon (2009) demonstrated that subsequent to the disclosure of fraud (implicitly, the filing of the lawsuit in our case and, eventually, the final verdict), companies typically shed labor and capital to become more productive. This action results from the high-growth period (also shown by our strongly negative HML loading in Table 9.2) in which false accounting data encompass high levels of investment and the hiring of additional employees. In general, by comparing Tables 9.2 and 9.6, we encounter the same pattern as predicted by Kedia and Philippon's model. Balance sheet data in Table 9.3 further corroborate this theoretical prediction. Companies in our sample experienced a transformation from a negative to a positive SMB coefficient. Moreover, most of our sample companies developed into fallen angels. The HML coefficient turned from a strongly negative into a positive coefficient. Still, at least in our analysis, the true long-term economic effects of accounting fraud and higher productivity did not materialize into higher expected returns. Therefore, institutional investors initiating or joining a class-action lawsuit can, to some degree, expect substantial reorganizations in the sued company, which can result in medium- to long-term outperformance.

If the company has already been facing problems before the filing date in terms of self-disclosure or legal investigations by third parties, it suffers additionally from the filing of the lawsuit by its shareholders. This result is documented by the lack of significantly different alphas between this group and a group without a pre-filing triggering event and by the fairly isomorphic pre-filing patterns. Even though these two groups may be fundamentally different, they still share the common feature that both are being sued by their shareholders. Therefore, we conclude that the lawsuit *per se* and not any pre-filing event drives the long-term post-event performance.

We also documented a few limitations. Despite the appealing simplicity of using calendar time portfolios in our analysis, the asset pricing literature is not unanimous with respect to an accepted model of risk-adjusted performance (Ritter & Welch, 2002). Therefore, any research on long-term post-event performance is likely to be sensitive to the methods used. Whether liquidity and investor recognition subsequent to materially adverse corporate events play a role, is a subject for further research.

9.4 Conclusion

In this chapter, we have provided the first credible evidence of the costs and gains for shareholders from litigation against companies accused of violating the duty of care or the duty of loyalty. The question of performance subsequent to the filing of a class-action lawsuit ultimately determines whether shareholders hold on to their shares and bet on a recovery of the stock price. The alternative is to sell off the equity stake in the company and either accept an out-of-court settlement or await a final verdict. Our analysis reveals that stock price recovery strongly depends on the type of allegation brought forward, the time horizon, and the estimation technique for long-term performance. Whether a stock price recovery kicks in and how potential shareholder losses materialize have important policy implications for security market regulators. Answering this question is essential for institutional investors as lead plaintiffs. Our analysis shows that investors should not be deterred from resorting to lawsuits that allege violations of the duty of loyalty.

We conclude that allegations involving the corporate entity as a whole are highly disruptive. In the short run, the filing of a class-action lawsuit is a materially adverse corporate event whose long-term economic and financial effects depend on the nature of the allegations. How the role of class-action lawsuits as a governance mechanism will evolve and whether shareholders will continue to resort to this disruptive mechanism remain to be seen.

Appendix: Sample of Original Allegation Types

Keywords for our coding into seven allegation types are in italic font.

Insider Trading Allegations (Violation of "Duty of Loyalty")

Ascend Communications Inc. (CUSIP: 043491). Filing date: 2 December 1997

... The original Complaint charges defendants with violating federal securities and state laws, including Section 10(b) of the Securities Exchange Act of 1934 and Section 11 of the Securities Act of 1933, by engaging in an *illegal scheme and deceptive course* of conduct designed to inflate Ascend's stock price through positive statements concerning Ascend's business, earnings and its growth prospects, despite the fact that, at the time the statements were made, defendants knew, or recklessly disregarded, but failed to disclose to investors, that sales of Ascend's advanced modem products would all but cease because of, among other things, serious software and firmware problems. The defendants' scheme allowed *Ascend's officers and directors to sell their Ascend shares at enormous gains, exceeding $40 million in proceeds.*

Retrieved from: http://securities.stanford.edu/1011/ASND97

Accounting Violations/Illegal Business Practices (Violation of "Duty of Care")

Symantec Corporation (CUSIP: 871503). Filing date: 7 January 1997

... The original complaint alleges that during the Class Period, defendants engaged in a fraudulent scheme and course of business that operated as a *fraud or deceit* on all persons who purchased or otherwise acquired Symantec stock. As set forth hereafter, these false and misleading statements included statements about (1) Symantec's new Windows 95-related utility software products known as Norton Navigator, Norton AntiVirus and Norton Utilities; (2) Symantec's Enterprise products; (3) Symantec's sales in Europe; and (4) other aspects of Symantec's business. Furthermore, Symantec's financial statements for its first and second quarters of fiscal 1996 (ended 30 June and 29 September 1995) were *false and misleading in violation of Generally Accepted Accounting Principles.*

Taken from: http://securities.stanford.edu/1013/SYMC97

Illegal Business Practices/Governance Problems (Violation of "Duty of Care")

Duke Energy Co. (CUSIP: 26441C). Filing date: 23 May 2002

. . . The original complaint alleges that Duke failed to disclose that it was engaging in electricity trades involving simultaneous purchases and sales of power at the same price, overstated Duke's revenues in its public SEC filings and elsewhere by including in such revenues sums received in connection with such simultaneous purchases and sales of power, and failed to disclose that Duke did not have in place *sufficient management controls* to prevent Duke's traders from engaging in simultaneous purchases and sales of power at the same price. The complaint further alleges that *Deloitte & Touche violated the common law by certifying Duke's financial statements and by allowing its unqualified opinion to be incorporated by reference into Duke's filings with the SEC despite the fact that such financial statements and filings were materially misleading in that they materially overstated Duke's revenues by counting as revenue sums received in connection with simultaneous purchases and sales of power at the same price*. After the foregoing became known to the public, the complaint alleges, Duke stock tumbled to as low as $32.89 on 21 May 2002, down from a class period high of $47.74.

Taken from: http://securities.stanford.edu/1024/DUK02-01

Chapter 10
Targeted Responsible Investing

Tom Croft

10.1 Introduction

Even though the "Great Recession" in the United States has officially ended and the economies of other countries are slowly recovering, the global credit crisis impaired the ability of banks and investors to provide a sufficient amount of long-term capital required to finance important economic sectors. The areas which were impacted by these difficulties include the manufacturing industry, affordable housing projects, commercial development, and renewable energy schemes. While the credit markets crunch appears to be easing, questions remain as to whether new investments, as well as hiring, will occur soon enough to achieve a broad recovery.

Corporations, banks, financial institutions, venture and private equity firms in the US, Britain and the Euro Zone were still "hoarding" trillions of dollars in assets by the beginning of 2011. This limits the level of equity and debt capital which is available to new and expanding businesses and development projects, research and development (R&D), training, and similarly important investment platforms. As *The Economist* (2010) has put it, "If cautious firms pile up more savings, the prospects for recovery are poor."

Administrations in the United States, Canada, and elsewhere are struggling to achieve a real economic mending. Serious capital gaps remain from this recession hangover and future capital needs, such as addressing long-delayed infrastructure investments or meeting the global climate crisis, remain unmet. What is further lacking is a long-term plan for the scale of capital investment which would reduce

---

Disclaimer The purpose of this report is not to provide advice on investing in any particular investment product. The report may not be construed as being the primary basis for an investment decision or as reflecting recommendations for individuals or institutions. The author disclaims any liability for actions you may take as a result of reading this report. Please talk to your lawyers, consultants and fund managers, etc., before making any investment decision.

T. Croft (✉)
Steelvalley Authority, Swissvale, PA 15218, USA
e-mail: t.w.croft@steelvalley.org

T. Hebb (ed.), *The Next Generation of Responsible Investing*,
Advances in Business Ethics Research 1, DOI 10.1007/978-94-007-2348-1_10,

greenhouse gas emissions and our dependence on fossil fuels and capture the opportunities for growth in clean energy and green technologies.

Many countries face similar challenges in terms of green economy. Capital gaps are common for funding wind and solar farms, green construction, energy efficiency and efficient transportation systems, and manufacturing supply chains which feed these new frontiers. As Kirsten Spaulding, the California Director of CERES noted in her talk at the US-Canada Blue/Green Alliance Conference (2/9/11), many institutional investors, pension policy leaders and labor's "capital stewards" have focused instead on developing strategies which mitigate risks associated with climate change and other sustainability issues. They are simultaneously looking for opportunities to invest in sustainable solutions that will create green jobs and build durable value for funds.

An important question to ask is this: How can we ensure that workers' capital and other common trusts, including the tens of trillions of dollars of retirement assets and institutional investments owned by citizens globally, can invest in opportunities created by clean economy while, at the same time, creating union and family-sustaining jobs? In order for a real green jobs boom to take place, our workers need to manufacture, construct, assemble and manage these projects.

Some innovative institutional investors are exploring options which would allow a portion of their capital to help create long-term, sustainable wealth for workers, communities, and shareholders. And a number of such "worker-friendly" funds in the US, Canada, Europe, Australia and South Africa are already producing positive returns and jobs. They do so by investing in areas such as renewable energy, manufacturing, housing, and infrastructure. These institutional investment approaches can be prudently made within the spectrum of what is known as "alternative investments."

However, in the last decade or so, many global investment managers bet heavily on the wrong alternatives. These unfortunate moves included short-term speculative investments in sub-prime mortgages and obvious property bubbles, mega-hedge/buyout funds, derivatives, credit swap schemes, and others and have contributed to the crash on the global financial markets.

Noted above are only a few of the "crack finance" habits which incarnate the irresponsible finance capital model that was principally hatched on Wall Street. In the last 4 years, financialization brought widespread damage to the American, Canadian, and other national economies. This model led to mismanagement of many savings and assets; it threatened the stability of many jobs and homes, retirement futures and the education of our children as the working families and communities across the world suffered the consequences. In 2011, 15 million workers in the US alone remained unemployed. There are also fears of permanent joblessness affecting older and younger workers alike in other countries.

Rather than investing in the creation of green and affordable housing, too many banks and real estate managers bought and sold mortgage-backed securities consisting of worthless sub-prime loans. Securities were also sold to pension funds and other trusts and endowments. The seriousness of this practice was reflected, among others, in the US Securities and Exchange Commission's fraud case against Goldman Sachs. Instead of building and growing companies, many mega-hedge/buyout managers invested workers' pensions to over-leverage and/or "strip and flip" otherwise viable firms. This, of course, lead to destroying jobs and the economic value of the companies as is demonstrated by the unfortunate outcomes for such companies as Simmons Mattress, now bankrupt, and innumerable similar cases across North America, Europe and elsewhere.

As citizens dust themselves off from this traumatic aftermath which ravaged their savings and retirement assets, they are also searching for answers and alternatives to the reckless mismanagement and ultra-risky bets, many of which turned out to be fraudulent. It is not enough for investment houses and corporate entities to cloak themselves in sweet-sounding, sustainable investment nostrums. Companies such as Goldman Sachs, BP, and many other blue-chip corporations had long boasted of their commitments to responsible investments and green and sustainable business practices. It is nearly impossible to reconcile these assertions with the actual companies' practices which helped trigger the financial markets crash, pushed millions of people into poverty, destroyed the value of retirement and trust assets, and severely damaged the economy and eco-systems (in the case of the 2010 BP spill in the Gulf of Mexico).

What is needed is a way to ensure that investment streams are flowing, responsibly and profitably and without compromising retirement security and the collectively-owned assets of the people, to critical economic needs and essential opportunities. This entails investments in the "real" economy, the "Main Street" economy.

Up from Wall Street: The Responsible Investment Alternative (Croft, 2009) and a companion report authored by the International Trade Union Confederation's Committee on Workers' Capital (ITUC–CWC) (*The Global ETI Report: Helping Workers' Capital Work Harder,* Croft, 2009) made the case that there are strategic and responsible investment paths that have the capacity to rebuild our economy and infrastructure, reinvigorate our cities, and create green jobs of the future. These two sources, among others, documented the fact that the assets in retirement accounts and mutual funds, insurance companies, university, hospital and foundation endowments, college savings funds, and others trusts—in effect, *our money*, —actually own the lion's share of the economy. Further, it is *our* money that can begin to help turn our economies around. *Up from Wall Street* and the *Global ETI Report* can serve as a field guide to responsible capital. They demonstrate how workers' capital is already providing many of the crucial long-term investments needed in all parts of the economy, across the world. Finally, this research, and that of my colleagues, showed that most of the responsible capital strategies also yielded competitive returns on investment.

Working people should encourage trustees and managers of these critical assets to make prudent investments in market activities that yield good jobs and a more energy efficient future. Banks and companies, especially those that have received bailouts, should be goaded along by shareholders and governments. In so doing, the assets can bankroll strategies to rebuild our communities and cities as well as mobilize long-term capital for a cleaner climate.

Many corporations, banks, trust institutions, and unions have already joined the UN Principles for Responsible Investment (PRI), the Investors Summit on Climate Change, and other similar initiatives. They committed billions of dollars toward common-purpose responsible investment (RI), primarily in the public equities arena.

The purpose of this chapter is to illustrate how responsible investment of workers' savings and assets can also be invested in the *private* economy to generate specific social, economic and environmental (ESG) benefits, along with the necessary financial returns. Investments undertaken with these benefits in mind are also known as "economically-targeted investments" (ETIs). ETIs have the ability to generate the following types of collateral benefits: increasing the availability of affordable housing; developing small and medium enterprises (SMEs); revitalizing inner cities and spurring rural economic development; aiding the growth of underserved markets (including emerging and developing countries); and catalyzing the growth in non-traditional industries such as renewable energy.

ETIs undertaken within the guiding ethos of RI allows pension and other trust funds to utilize investment strategies that—if managed prudently—truly serves beneficiaries and their communities in the long-run. Further, it also demonstrates that ETIs offer the capital stewards of these funds another opportunity to join the PRI movement and sustain a triple bottom line without foregoing portfolio diversification.

Responsible investment paths are creating positive and significant impacts on the lives of workers, retirees and their communities. These initiatives include:

- Creating new and renovated living spaces (especially affordable and workforce housing) and workplaces, along with commercial and community facilities;
- Saving or creating hundreds of thousands of living-wage jobs, many of them permanent;
- Supporting SMEs (small/medium-sized enterprises), co-ops, and other employee-ownership models, and providing micro-finance to democratize the availability of capital;
- Developing renewable energy sources and efficient transportation systems, along with the supply chains and power projects linked to those systems;
- Retaining and modernizing other strategic industries;
- Providing green infrastructure, products and services.

The chapter concludes by looking to the future and to the "third wave" of responsible investment. The third wave strategy combines responsible real estate, private equity and project finance (and other ETI strategies) to envision a more comprehensive regional redevelopment model and to connect practical and prudent investments in enterprises and housing with co-investments in human capital, renewable energy and efficient transportation.

Capital stewards can seize the moment, re-create and renew parts of urban cities, redevelop poor rural areas, and invest in sustainable developments that benefit all. Capital stewards can also demand, with their investments, aggressive actions toward climate solutions. Many of these ideas could embody the next generation of targeted investing.

10.2 A Short Background to Targeted Investing

The sheer size of global pension and institutional funds and the role they play in influencing investment at an international level opens the door to leadership in the area of capital stewardship and active ownership. Trustees and managers of common trusts who were meant to care for working people, retirees, and other citizens need to consider the long-term interests of their beneficiaries. These interests include those of the beneficiaries' communities.

Capital stewardship refers to the actions taken by pension fund trustees and other fiduciaries to use workers' retirement savings to achieve the twin goals of the best possible risk-adjusted rate of return on investments and the interests, broadly defined, of the plan's participants and beneficiaries (Kusnet, 2002). Active ownership refers to an engagement with companies on issues of importance. Some approaches to capital stewardship which are presently promoted within the labor movement can be categorized in the following way: (1) negative or positive asset screening, (2) asset managing, and (3) asset targeting.

Economically Targeted Investments (ETIs) fall within the category of asset targeting— they seek to address unwanted capital gaps and direct investments to generate socially desirable benefits and competitive financial returns. Asset targeting approaches include investments which expand employment opportunities in a particular geographical region, increase the availability of affordable housing, strengthen capital infrastructure, revitalize urban neighborhoods, help rural economies, develop SMEs, and support green industries.

Pension funds and similar trusts invariably turn to alternative pension investments to diversify their asset allocation portfolio. Stocks and bonds are usually heavily represented in these portfolios. Alternative investments include private equity, venture capital, real estate, hedge funds, and others.

Internationally, a growing movement, including labor, progressive companies and their allies support the mobilization of government resources and domestic savings for the purposes of investment in sustainable development and poverty reduction. Special attention is paid to protecting core labor standards (*ICFTU Statement*, 2001) There are important linkages between the goals of responsible investing and the investment of workers' savings that must be considered to ensure that these investments truly reflect the interests of workers globally.

Targeted investment and responsible investment of common trust assets, such as pension funds, can be used to generate specific social, economic and environmental benefits, along with the necessary financial returns. This asset targeting approach is often referred to as ETIs. It is also known as alternative investment, socially-targeted investment, and undercapitalized market investment. This approach has historical roots, including the work of John Wesley, an 18th century English religious reformer.

10.3 Economically-Targeted Investments

As mentioned earlier in this chapter, ETIs are responsible investments which make use of workers' capital savings and assets to generate specific social, economic and environmental benefits along with the necessary financial returns. To be considered an ETI, an investment must:

- Aim to provide a competitive risk-adjusted rate of return;
- Target a capital gap or opportunity resulting from a market failure; and
- Be associated with a social, economic or environmental benefit.

According to pension expert Jayne Zanglein (2001), collateral benefits obtained through ETIs can be applied broadly and "create new jobs, provide capital to replace loan funds no longer rolling through the bank pipelines, provide startup businesses with access to capital, finance low-cost housing and improve the infrastructure of the nation, all without sacrificing a return on investments or otherwise jeopardizing the pensions of future retirees."

The first duty of a pension trustee is to oversee the prudent investment of plan assets, solely in the interests of plan participants and beneficiaries. In crafting their particular fund's investment strategy, pension trustees must make workers' retirement security their first priority and must never jeopardize investment returns in order to promote non-financial goals. However, asset allocation is a part of a prudent investment strategy for diversifying investments.

Trustees and principals of common trusts and pensions have an interest in exploring these asset classes in ways that advance the interests of beneficiaries more broadly and which do no harm. They should explore the opportunities presented by ETIs (which preceded the current popularity of the responsible investment movement) which also offer a useful methodology for RI.

ETIs fill identified capital gaps in alternative asset classes. They include real estate, private equity and venture capital, private debt placement, fixed income, infrastructure, and credit enhancement. ETIs also allow pension and institutional funds to promote positive economic development as well as target under-capitalized regions.

All investors want to have a measure of influence over employment and labor relations as well as the environmental practices of portfolio businesses and projects. Responsible investors target companies and construction projects that:

- Provide job security;
- Adopt responsible contractor policies and adopt "high-road" workplace practices;

- Follow responsible environmental standards; and
- Treat workers with respect and provide for neutrality in labor relations.

When investors look to this "high performance" investment agenda, rather than investing in lowest-cost or anti-union firms, they are also following a worker-friendly investment policy. Investing in high performance strategies can generate stable profits through increased labor and management productivity and higher levels of employee participation, including worker ownership. It better allows investors to monitor and manage the potential risk and liabilities which arise from firms or projects and from such outcomes as, for example, dangerous products or delayed project completion.

10.3.1 US Legal Guidelines for ETIs

This section relies on the relevant US legal framework, because the investment approach used there is consistent with the fiduciary duties of trustees from other countries (Carmichael & Quarter, 2003). ETIs have been defined by the US Department of Labor (DOL) as "investments selected for the economic benefits they create apart from their investment return to the employee benefit plan" (*DOL Bulletin*, 1994).

DOL's Interpretive Bulletin 94-1 clarified that a pension plan may choose an investment which has collateral benefits if the investment has a risk-adjusted market rate of return which is equal or superior to alternative investments. The DOL has consistently construed the Employee Retirement Income Security Act's (ERISA) requirement that a fiduciary act "solely in the interest of," and "for the exclusive purpose of providing benefits to participants and their beneficiaries" as "prohibiting a fiduciary from subordinating the interests of participants and beneficiaries in their retirement income to unrelated objectives" (Zanglein, 2001).

However, the DOL's bulletin stated that a fiduciary may invest plan assets in an ETI "if the ETI has an expected rate of return that is commensurate to rates of return of alternative investments with similar risk characteristics that are available to the plan, and if the ETI is otherwise an appropriate investment for the plan in terms of such factors as diversification and the investment policy of the plan" (Zanglein, 2001).

According to another DOL report, prudent investments exist in an inefficient market and remain unfunded due to information gaps and high administrative costs of consummating and monitoring deals. In the words of the report:

> To the extent that capital markets are judged to be tradition-bound, rigid or incapable of funding all 'worthy' investments, making funds available from the pension investment pool is seen as addressing capital gaps that would otherwise impede local economic development (*DOL Advisory Council*, 1992).

On October 16, 2008, the DOL, which was then in the waning weeks of the Bush administration, and under prodding by the US Chamber of Commerce, published an interpretive bulletin that modified and superseded the DOL's prior guidance regarding ETIs. It is generally held that, while the DOL expressed concerns about ETIs (and the risk to fiduciaries of not making investment decisions based on what is in the interest of plan participants), the bulletin did not reflect a substantive change in the law on this issue.

The new rule stated that before a fiduciary selects an ETI (over another investment), it must first conclude that the investment alternatives under consideration are "economically indistinguishable," that is, "truly equal, taking into account a quantitative and qualitative analysis of the economic impact on the plan (*DOL Interpretative Bulletin 08-1*, 2010)." This analysis must include consideration of an investment opportunity's level of diversification, degree of liquidity and potential risk and return as compared to other investments that would fill a similar role in the plan's portfolio. Importantly, the ETI Bulletin cautions that any fiduciary who considers factors outside the economic interests of the plan should maintain a contemporaneous written account of the economic analysis concluding that the investment opportunities considered were of equal economic value. Specifically, the DOL notes that fiduciaries "will rarely be able to demonstrate compliance with ERISA" in the absence of such a written record (ibid).

10.4 From ETIs to RI

Today, many countries encourage responsible pension investments in the "real economy:" in local companies, SMEs, affordable housing, and others. Some national governments have encouraged infrastructure projects and other investment initiatives that promote the public good as well as have provided financial incentives to reduce the risk of those investments. A number of pension and other trust fund trustees have designed pension investment policies that promote the use of ETIs and RI approaches within their pension fund.

Large common trusts, including labor-sponsored pension funds, are investing around the globe in a broad range of targeted and responsible investment strategies (UNEP FI, 2007). Many existing targeted investment vehicles, including those in this chapter, serve as models for pension trustees looking to develop well-rounded and prudent ETI and RI policies.

In December 2007, Global Unions approved a statement on responsible approaches to the stewardship of workers' capital that calls on investors to take into account the broader social and environmental consequences of their investment decisions.

> In particular, the Global Unions urge trustees and institutional investors to embrace this responsible approach to investment decision-making as promoted by initiatives such as the Principles for Responsible Investment (Committee on Workers' Capital, 2010).

The Principles for Responsible Investment (PRI), launched by the United Nations Environment Program Finance Initiative (UNEP FI), inspired investors around the globe to think more long-term and strategically about risk and opportunity. The RI re-frames the investment decision to better ensure that investors account for the real risks on their investments, which otherwise might appear profitable. Investors are urged to understand the present and future impacts of business activities on social issues, the wider society and the natural environment.

These principles should also be applied to pension and trust investments in the private sphere. There is also an increasing recognition by trade unions globally that the investment of workers' capital should reflect the intrinsic interests of workers, not only by bringing competitive financial returns, but also by contributing to the long-term vitality of economies, social standards, societies and environments.

Responsible capital stewards invest around the world and contribute to the giant pools of private capital and institutional investments flowing through global markets. In many countries, besides owning an outsized share of corporate stocks, institutional investment allocations to alternative investment classes, including venture and private capital and real estate, provide a large share of private investment in those categories. As previously mentioned, market failures result in capital gaps, a systemic lack of access to capital by microenterprises, isolated regions, inner-cities, labor-intensive sectors as well as ethnic minorities, the unemployed and women.

Smart capital stewards, however, are also increasingly aware that the capital gaps created by these market failures can yield significant investment opportunities. Competitive long-term financial returns and ESG benefits do not have to be mutually exclusive. It is instructive then, to reflect on the experiences of professional managers of responsible funds.

> Managers of responsible funds make decisions using more information than available to most investors. They take into account the quality of labor relations, the impact on environmental quality and sustainability, and effect on communities as clues to potential risk and profit. They aim to earn large and sustainable returns by considering factors other investors are missing from ordinary analysis (Croft, 2010).

10.5 Successful Targeted Responsible Investment

This section categories ETIs under two headings: Real Estate and Businesses and Places and Industry Sectors, each divided into sub-categories. While numerous institutional investors have developed targeted investment programs, or RI policies, this section will focus on the more muscular approaches undertaken by pension funds and labor-sponsored savings programs.

10.5.1 Investments in Real Estate and Businesses

The use of ETIs to achieve financial returns and collateral benefits has most often been applied to real estate. Building trades pension trusts have long invested in real estate projects which create housing and jobs for union members and other members of society. Real estate investment vehicles can include pooled funds which make equity and debt investments, mortgage vehicles (mortgage-backed securities)

Table 10.1 Responsible funds and economically targeted investments

Canada and the U.S.	Type of fund/project
AFL-CIO Investment Trust Corporation: HIT and BIT (US)	Real estate/Fixed income
Union Labor Life Insurance Company (ULLICO): J for Jobs and new infrastructure fund (US)	Private placement/Real estate, and Infra fund
Concert Properties (Canada)	Real Estate
Fédération des travailleurs et travailleuses du Québec: *Fonds de solidarité* (Canada)	Private/Venture capital
KPS Special Situation Funds (US)	Private equity
Multi-Employer Property Trust (MEPT) and NewTower Renewable Energy Trust (NRET)	Real estate, Project finance (PF is fixed income)
The GESD Fund (US)	Private equity
Cycle Capital (Canada)	Venture and Project finance
Yucaipa Companies, and Yucaipa Grand Fund (US)	Private equity and Infra fund
Blue Wolf Capital	Private equity
The Global South	Type of fund/project
Public Investment Corporation (SA)	Broad ETIs: Venture capital, Private equity, Real estate
PIC: Isibaya Fund (SA)	Private equity, Infrastructure, Empowerment transaction
Futuregrowth Asset Management (SA)	Real estate and Infrastructure
PIC & Futuregrowth: Community Property Fund (SA)	Real estate
Europe and Australia	Type of fund/project
Hermes (UK)	Real estate
Caisse de Prévoyance du Personnel Enseignant de l'Instruction Publique et des Fonctionnaires de l'Administration du Canton de Genève (CIA) (Switzerland)	Real estate
Stichting Pensioenfonds ABP (Netherlands)	Clean energy and microfinance
Industry Fund Services/Industry Funds Management (IFS and IFM) (Australia)	Private equity and Project finance

Source: Author.

and fixed-income funds. Fixed-income funds are a debt-based real estate product used for investing in affordable housing. Trusts can also invest in credit enhancements products and union-sponsored pension fund can loan its credit rating to a municipality or a state agency for a fee.

Real estate ETIs can fill capital gaps in areas which would not otherwise be funded, such as low-income housing, for example. Further, funding partnerships can be forged with governments and other investors to secure guarantees and to lessen risk. Investors in the real estate market finance, purchase, and develop land and property. Property development pertains to financing and undertaking of construction of new stock of real estate. Property re-development, on the other hand, refers to improvements, upgrades and expansions to the existing stock. Properties and development transactions can be either residential (owner-occupied or rental housing) or non-residential (commercial, industrial or retail sites) (Falconer, 1999). Investors and lenders can also make loans to residential and commercial borrowers who finance and develop their own properties.

Pension trustees who are new to ETIs may wish to start their fund's ETI programs by investing in well-established pooled real estate funds or property-related fixed-income projects. These programs are liquid, easy to evaluate, and offer competitive returns.

Examples of such investments include the MEPT Fund (US) which re-built a burned and abandoned hospital on the north tip of Roosevelt Island, New York, and converted it into a green housing community with 500 units, a daycare center, and essential amenities. Known as "the Octagon," this remarkable green construction project has won the New York City's Green Apple Award for such renewable advances as the solar roof panels and great amenities. The project generated an estimated 1.5 million job hours for union construction workers.

Additionally, the US-based AFL-CIO Housing Investment Trust (HIT) invested over $750 million in large-scale housing and related projects in New York City following the city's downturn after 9/11. This included some of the first multi-family housing built after that date—one of HIT's ambitious community investment initiatives in the US which generated housing opportunities and thousands of jobs. Over $1.5 billion in home mortgage loans have been provided to NTC union members and city employees through the HIT's HIT HOME homeownership program, making 6320 loans to workers in the city's five boroughs. As part of the AFL-CIO's response to the Great Recession, HIT launched its "Construction Jobs Initiative" with the goal of financing 10,000 union construction jobs by 2011.

A further fund example is the AFL-CIO Building Investment Trust (US) which recently invested in Ballard Park, an $86.7 million residential and retail building currently under construction in one of Seattle's historic neighborhoods. Ballard Park generated approximately 560 union construction jobs, mainly employment for members of construction unions.

10.5.2 Direct Real Estate Investments

Many union-sponsored pension funds invest directly in real estate, meaning that they purchase a property directly rather than through a pooled fund. They require an expertise of an in-house or external investment manager. Direct investments are generally more time-consuming, administratively costly, and higher risk. Direct real estate investments may also expose a fund to decreased liquidity and limited diversification. However, direct investments also offer more control, flexibility, and higher potential returns than do passive investments.

10.5.3 Private Equity and Venture Capital

An increasing number of union-sponsored pension funds are making ETI investments in the field of private equity (PE), which involve investments in smaller, non-public companies. Pension funds are attracted to this class of alternative assets due to potential multiple benefits such as good investment returns and good jobs. PE funds typically have a measure of control in the management of companies in which they invest, and can optimally ensure that either the existing or new management teams focus on operating the company more efficiently.

PE funds can include venture capital funds, private capital funds, and buyout and turnaround funds (including special situation funds) (Falconer, 1999). Pension funds also source investment partnerships which provide debt financing and variations of debt, including senior-term and subordinated debt. Many private capital funds target small and medium-sized enterprises (SMEs), because of their importance in economic growth, social cohesion, employment and local development. SMEs drive research and development, technological innovation and new products. They account for over 95% of enterprises and 60% to 70% of employment, and generate a large share of new jobs the economies of OECD countries (OECD, 2002). Despite their smaller size, these firms can be a part of an important supply chain or strategic to the economy, particularly in sectors such as advanced manufacturing, clean technology, and other cutting-edge industries. SMEs are particularly important to emerging economies and also have a potential to reduce poverty.

Some banking experts fear that many of the traditional problems facing SMEs—lack of financing, difficulties in exploiting technology, constrained managerial capabilities, and low productivity become even more acute in a globalized environment. Many SMEs are located in the Latin American and other developing markets that lack the capacity and the necessary resources with which to carry out R&D activities. To tackle this problem, sub-hemispheric initiatives were developed; FIDEs in Chile provides a model of these efforts.

Specific examples of the impact of these specialized funds include the KPS Special Situations Fund (US) that restructured a bankrupt transportation company with factories in Winnipeg, Manitoba, and St. Cloud and Crookston, Minnesota. The workers of New Flyer Industries design and manufacture energy efficient and hybrid transit buses and parts for cities and institutions across North America. The investment has saved 1800 union jobs, and the return on investment was multifold.

Another example is GrowthWorks Funds (Canada) that invested in Xantrex, a company which pioneered new inverters and chargers for wind and solar energy systems. The VC fund is owned by 50,000 workers in British Columbia and has affiliated headquartered in other provinces. With 500 employees, GrowthWorks Funds has locations in California, Washington State, and Indiana.

A third example is the GESD Fund (US) that rebuilt a part of the historic Fisherman's Wharf area in San Francisco and provided dozens of union jobs and benefits for local residents. It created a 26,000 square-foot Boudin Sourdough Bakery, Bistro and Café with a demonstration bakery which has become a popular shopping destination.

10.5.4 Private Placements

Pension funds also invest in private placements –stocks or bonds issues sold by a corporation directly to an investor. These investments tend to be riskier because they do not include registration under securities regulations. Private placements are generally made by pension funds, insurance companies (as separate accounts), and other trusts.

Union Labor Life's J for Jobs Fund (ULLICO J for Jobs) in the US which has primarily invested in real estate, is a case in point. However, one of ULLICO's most successful developments was the 1990s Newport News shipyard in which an ancillary fund financed double-hull tankers. The first deal invested in the construction of five environmentally safe, double-hulled oil tankers at a total cost of $280 million. ULLICO's $10 million equity stake gave it enough leverage to achieve an agreement that the ships would be constructed in the US at one of the nation's few remaining unionized shipyards. The project provided work for 12,000 steel workers over a 28-month period. ULLICO's exit recovered 100% of invested capital and an internal rate of return reached 20.4% (Calebrese, 2001).

10.5.5 Worker-Ownership and Empowerment Transactions

In the US and Canada, Employee Stock Ownership Programs (ESOPs) and similar owner structures which provide tax advantages for worker-owners. *Sub-chapter S ESOPs* (in reference to a provision in US tax law that further reduces tax liability) have unique potential as ETIs. Some worker-friendly funds have undertaken buyouts and employed an ESOP as an exit strategy. As a result, workers obtain partial ownership in a newly economically viable company.

In South Africa (SA), Brazil, and other emerging economies, there have been a series of empowerment transition initiatives with an objective to share the ownership of in-country corporations (sometimes owned by foreign companies) with historically-disadvantaged citizens. These initiatives are known as empowerment transactions. South African investors have actively pursued Black Economic Empowerment (BEE), which is meant to increase black ownership and control of targeted companies. Pension funds utilized by PE firms have sometimes provided the capital to enable these transactions by backing or partnering with indigenously-owned firms to purchase a company's stock and thus yielding partial or full control.

In 2005 for example, through the Isibaya Fund, PIC paid Rand 6.6 billion to foreign shareholders to acquire a 15.1% stake in Telkom, South Africa's largest telecommunications company (Bonorchis & Bridge, 2004). PIC stepped into the deal at the last moment in order to shore up the Elephant Consortium, a woman-owned group, as the consortium's efforts to purchase the stock had faltered. PIC later restructured the deal and sold 6.7% to the Elephant group.

10.6 Investments Targeting Places and Industry Sectors

10.6.1 Geographic Targeting

A common ETI approach employed by pension funds is commuting a proportion of investments to initiatives within the geographic boundaries of a political entity, such as a nation, a province, or a state. Geographic targeting can be urban or rural. By pooling investments, a number of investors can build a more scalable framework for geographic targeting. While this type of investment focuses mainly on private-side investments, some labor-sponsored pension funds also invest in in-country or in-state public corporations whose headquarters are located in that jurisdiction (potentially as part of an "empowerment transactions" strategy). South Africa's PIC has utilized this strategy.

ETIs can also occur in urban areas, often undertaken by large institutional investors, particular union-sponsored pension funds, that have the potential to revitalize communities and create good jobs, unionized workplaces, and affordable housing. For example, a brownfield redevelopment can lead to inner-city urban revitalization. Once an urban area is revitalized, businesses will grow or return, which in turn leads to job creation. According to Tessa Hebb (2008), urban pension investments can also yield positive environmental impacts.

Pension funds can use a range of ETI strategies in urban areas. Examples include brownfield redevelopment, venture and private capital investments which generate jobs, affordable housing, and other commercial improvements and opportunities. These positive ancillary benefits can be found in Concert Properties (Canada), for instance. In 1993, Concert undertook a CAD$200 million investment in Collingwood Village, a large urban redevelopment project involving 27.6 acres of industrial brownfields in a lower-income neighborhood in Vancouver. The final project planned to include 2800 residential units, of which 15% will be affordable and 20% designed for families with children. Collingwood is a model of community-based planning that benefits local residents through a unique cooperative planning process with Concert, the development team and the City of Vancouver. A significant range of community amenities have been provided, and included a neighborhood house, a community gymnasium, childcare facility, elementary school, neighborhood parks and Community Policing Office. An estimated 1.7 million construction work hours are attributed to Concert's investments, generating CAD$56.7m in wages and benefits (Carmichael, 2005).

Hermes (UK) provides another example of these types of double bottom line investments. In 2000, Argent St. George, mainly owned by BTPS, began planning the King's Cross Regeneration Project in London (www.argentkingscross.com), one of the largest city renewal projects in Europe. This immense multi-dimension urban renewal strategy aims to revitalize 67 acres of brownfield land on one of the most derelict and dangerous parts of London, along the Regent's Canal. The project will cost £2 billion, and take 12 to 15 years to complete. The development will include 8 million sq. ft of mixed use, including up to 25 large, new office buildings, 20 new streets, 10 new major public spaces, the restoration and refurbishment of 20 historic buildings and structures, and up to 2000 homes and serviced apartments. Some 500 homes will be classified as affordable housing, 250 more dedicated to shared equity, homebuy purchase and key worker rent, and another 650 units for student accommodation. The project will create 30,000 jobs. It will be enhanced by open space, new park lands along the canal, cultural and arts amenities and a commitment to sustainable development, renewable energy, and mass transit hubs.

Investments can also take place in targeted rural areas. Such investments can positively impact the local economy, build needed infrastructure and housing, and generate industries and therefore employment. In emerging markets, rural areas suffer more emphatically from under-capitalization, often as a result of colonialism. The degree of rural de-capitalization—a degree to which a region keeps up or lags behind the level of national economy—will determine the types and extent of suitable ETI strategies. However, even in the more mature economies, venture capital tends to congregate in higher growth areas, such as the Pacific and Atlantic coasts in the US, for example. To counter this trend, regional investment strategies in otherwise mature economies have been used in North America in such places as Appalachia in the US and in parts of northern and eastern Canada.

The Futuregrowth Fund's Community Property Fund in South Africa provides another good example. This fund invested Rand 80 million in a first major shopping complex in the township of KaNyamazane. The undertaking was expected to create some 700 jobs (60% of which was designed to hire women) and 70% of products sold should be South African. The 14,000 m^2 shopping centre is 20 km east of Nelspruit, on a main road which passes through rural towns off the N4 between Kruger National Park and Malelane—transport has been incorporated into the development. The KaNyamazane shopping centre is the 17th centre to be funded by the Futuregrowth Fund in disadvantaged areas of South Africa (Mirror, 2005).

10.6.2 Sectoral Targeting: Clean-Tech and Green Building Investments

The green movement and the push for clean energy technologies is a growing industry that should attract all institutional investors. As the world diversifies its energy sources away from fossil fuels, the level of investments in new energy technologies is expected to quadruple to $167 billion by 2015. Increasingly, pension funds and common trusts are not only demanding that investments comply with global climate change agreements and avoid negative environmental impacts but are also exploring innovative opportunities in clean technology and green building. Labor-sponsored pension funds from around the world, including the Netherlands, Denmark, UK, Canada and Australia, are making major investments in this field.

Cycle Capital (Canada) is a venture capital fund launched by the Solidarity Labor Sponsored Investment Fund (LSIF) and Fondaction another Quebec-based LSIF. Its mission is to finance and develop successful businesses which contribute to sustainable development, and its investment strategy is targeted to clean technologies and renewable energy infrastructure projects. Cycle uniquely employs a "life cycle approach" both in the investment process and as a tool to add value to business enterprises. Cycle's investment philosophy calibrates environmental criteria such as resource usage, waste management, environmental management system and social criteria such as employment creation, labor conditions, and relations with stakeholders. Cycle has also made a number of unique investments in green ventures.

10.6.3 Project Finance and Infrastructure

There is a unique opportunity for union-sponsored pension funds to explore energy, transit-related project financings, and, particularly, renewable energy project finance, such as windmill and solar projects, where financing plans can be structured to benefit from national incentive programs to facilitate projects. There are also opportunities to ensure project labor agreements, so that fair labor outcomes can be envisioned at all levels of the project: construction, facility management, and sourcing of energy products.

The infrastructure financing strategy is growing in both mature and emerging markets. Types of infrastructure include traditional transport infrastructure with user fees (roads, rail and airports); regulated infrastructure—with a regulated service contract and an availability fee (water, energy and gas distribution); and social infrastructure where governments pay an availability fee over a 20–30 year term (schools and hospitals) (Torrance, 2007). Pension-funded vehicles such as South Africa's Futuregrowth Fund and the PIC, have further defined infrastructure to include churches, health clinics and other institutions that are part of a community's social fabric.

Infrastructure has historically been financed by municipal bonds which often yielded favorable tax treatment. The most prudent approach to this asset class is to invest in safe and sound infrastructure bond investment vehicles. More recently, infrastructure funds have been organized as equity and quasi-equity funds. It is important to note, however, that these sorts of financing arrangements raise valid concerns, not the least of which is that workers' pensions may be used to replace the legitimate role of governments or be lured into risky privatization schemes. Many public-private partnerships have also been criticized because of the lack of appropriate fiduciary oversight and due to anti-unionization drives which resulted from the projects.

On the other hand, these infrastructure investments can provide opportunities for responsible contracting, anti-privatization, opt-out and other provisions to protect their investment and the interests of their members.

> Several public sector pension funds have also adopted Privatization Policies as part of their investment management. [This type of] policy strongly discourages private equity managers from investing in a company or its affiliates, if any have converted or replaced existing public jobs in schools, public authorities or prisons with institutions staffed by private sector employees, including units such as mailrooms, and food, waste collection, health care, and security guard services (Hebb & Beeferman, 2009).

Examples of such activity include the Industry Fund Service (IFS) and Industry Fund Management (IFM), owned by a number of Australia's superannuation funds, such as the Industry Fund Service, the ABP (2007) pension fund's investment in the Ampere Fund in the Netherlands, and South Africa's PIC has also helped lead the capitalization of Pan-Africa infrastructure fund, designed to serve the capital needs in the southern parts of the continent.

Some responsible funds are exploring interesting hybrid projects. Blue Wolf Capital, for example, has led the purchase of a sustainable paper company Finch Paper in the Adirondacks. The company has transitioned large forestlands formerly owned by Finch to the Nature Conservancy and its partners thus ensuring that the forestlands would be sustainably harvested. The project also contributed to preserving conservation and recreation uses as part of an overall forest stewardship plan. Some of the organizations carrying out new finance and infrastructure initiatives include ULLICO, NewTower, a partnership between Towpath Partners and Landon Butler, and Yucaipa Companies.

ULLICO's new infrastructure investment business assists in the investment, maintenance and refurbishment across the US. For its first closing, it aims to raise approximately $200 million. Structured as an open-ended fund, it will have a strong responsible contract policy (RCP). The NewTower Renewable Energy Trust (NRET) is the result of a partnership between Towpath Partners and Landon Butler funds (such as MEPT). Organized as a bank collective trust, NRET will be a specialized lender providing efficient long-term financing through the US Department of Energy's incentives program for clean energy generation. Its goal for the first closing is just under $200 million. Like ULLICO's project, NRET also has a strong RCP.

The Yucaipa Companies' Grand Fund is a large infrastructure and real estate asset investment partnership with the Ontario Municipal Employees Retirement System (OMERS). The Fund, which raises investments from US pension plans, would participate in OMERS' Global Strategic Investment Alliance. The alliance will charge investors a fee of only a little over 1% of invested capital. OMERS has over 20 years of experience in direct investments in infrastructure.

Further examples of innovation in infrastructure investing include ABP's Investment in Ampère Equity Fund (Netherlands), IFS/IFM (Australia), and Futuregrowth (US).

In partnership with PGGM and others, ABP is investing up to €0.5 billion in dozens of sustainable energy projects through a new sustainable investment vehicle called the Ampère Equity Fund. Evelop, of the Econcern group in Europe, will develop the majority of the projects funded through the Fund and the financial and legal frameworks for the fund were worked out with Evelop's participation. The projects include wind parks on land and at sea and biomass power stations in some Western European countries. The development, construction and operation of these projects will be financed by the Fund. Evelop supervises the creation of the "Koegorspolder" wind park in the province of Zeeland, claimed to be one of the largest wind-power sites in the Netherlands. "Koegorspolder" is the first such project to be financed by the Ampère Fund.

In Australia, IFM acquired Pacific Hydro (PH), one of the world's largest independent renewable energy companies, with hydro and wind assets in Australia and overseas. PH is manages more than 1800 MW of hydroelectric and wind farm projects at varying stages of development, involving construction and operations across Australia, the Asia-Pacific and Latin America. In addition to prioritizing profit growth and rewarding investors and financial partners, PH claims it is committed to innovative renewable energy projects that respect the environment and benefit communities. PH directly employs a staff of 100 and many more are engaged through the company's partnerships and projects. One of PH's new wind projects is the four-part Portland Wind Energy Project, which will ultimately increase Australia's wind energy capacity by 20%. When construction of the farm commenced, it also marked the opening of a nearby blade factory by Danish wind turbine maker Vestas. The plant has created many new jobs in the region.

Through its Infrastructure Bond Fund, Futuregrowth invested and led the development of a multi-purpose center in Soweto, the Grace Bible Church in 2001. The building accommodates 5000 people and is used for church services, courses in adult education, computer skills, and promoting HIV/AIDS awareness. Initially, having saved R6million, the members of the church approached banks for an R13million loan to build the centre. Their request, however, was rejected and Futuregrowth stepped in. The center, now one of the largest private community centers in Soweto, was further expanded in 2008. Futuregrowth participated in a new R30million sports and educational facility which was built on a 13,000 m^2 site. Futuregrowth partnered with the National Urban Reconstruction and Housing Agency to finance the project.

10.7 Towards the Third Wave, or Next Generation of Responsible Targeted Investment

Pension and other trust funds around the world have succeeded in achieving positive financial returns, as well as tremendous environmental, social and governance (ESG) returns from making targeted responsible investments. They have succeeded in promoting more egalitarian growth while earning healthy, sustainable profits. With the use of workers' capital, capital stewards are creating new models of responsible and innovative investment, beyond investment in property and businesses.

Some have called this system "an emerging third wave investment strategy".[1] This third wave strategy combines real estate, PE and other ETI strategies to launch

[1] Stephen Coyle, President, AFL-CIO Housing Investment Trust, personal communication with the author.

at-scale regional redevelopment efforts, comprising multi-use complexes of affordable housing, commercial workplaces and public facilities, jobs-producing firms, and renewable energy and efficient transportation infrastructure. Some of these projects build bridges to the broader community (and the public sector) by creating alliances with training and social services. This approach is being deployed in London, Vancouver, Montreal, South Africa, the Netherlands, and in rebuilding the US Gulf Coast, to name a few examples.

It is clear that Targeted Responsible Investment provides new tools to engage in the economy, a pertinent finding at a time when the "gospel of market efficiency" has failed working people and communities in many parts of the world. The most salient finding is that each fund emphasizes its ability to meet standards for traditional financial success while advancing a goal that benefits, rather than harms, working families and communities.

There will be a greater benefit to workers, citizens and regions, and also the employer community, if investments result in long-term positive outcomes, such as the development and diffusion of environmental technology, rising living standards by encouraging collective bargaining, and the conservation and growth of well-paid jobs in a region (as opposed to irrational downsizing or company off-shoring.)

It is evident that the most progressive investment practices in workers' capital are not distributed evenly across the globe. However, capital stewards, union leaders, and responsible fund managers have an opportunity to build the third wave and make investments to "manifest a worker-friendly, sustainable marketplace" that crosses borders and is financed by a growing network of responsible funds. Partnering and collaborating with other responsible investors and public bodies, pooling and levering resources, capital stewards *could* deploy hundreds of billions of dollars as part of an "international solidarity capital network."

Responsible capital stewards have shown that they can make responsible, long-term investments that earn a good rate of return but also yield important collateral benefits. Thus pension managers *can* align investments with the interests of pension beneficiaries and their communities.

In dramatic form, responsible capital stewards invest in and own not only enterprises, housing and commercial stock (in many cases in a transitory way), but have also taken control of new energy, technology and efficient transportation enterprises and infrastructures. Thus, capital stewards are ensuring that investment streams are flowing to critical economic needs and essential opportunities, while and at the same time being deployed in the triple-bottom line. In other words, responsible capital stewards are investing in a responsible future—our future—and investing in a vision of the economy that's more humane and sustainable.[2]

[2] Leo Gerard, International President, United Steelworkers, in Croft T., Hebb T. (2003) "Collaboration between labor, academics and community activists to advance labor/Capital strategies: The origins of heartland network", In Carmichael, I., Quarter, J. (eds.). *Money on the line: Workers' capital in Canada*. Ottawa: Canadian Centre for Policy Alternatives.

Acknowledgements The author borrowed heavily from *Up from Wall Street*, and a report written for the Global Unions Committee for Workers' Capital (CWC) for this the opportunity to write this report. The book was commissioned by the Heinz Endowments, and published by Cosimo. The author wishes to thank Heinz, Cosimo and the CWC for the opportunity to share his work. In addition, he is extremely thankful to innumerable advisors and contributors to both projects. The book, and therefore this chapter, received valuable input from collaborating consultant Dr. Teresa Ghilarducci, the Irene and Bernard L. Schwartz Professor of Economic Policy Analysis and Director of the Schwartz Center for Economic Policy Analysis at the New School for Social Research in New York City. The author wants to express again his deepest appreciation to Teresa.

Chapter 11
Social Investment and Responsible Investment: Their Relationship and Intersections in the Mining Industry

Caitlin McElroy

11.1 Introduction

Mining is historically linked with national development. Advanced mineral exploration and processing techniques have marked epochs of human civilization from the Iron Age and Bronze Age forward, leading to the rise of powerful nations. Today, while technological advancements in geology and metallurgy are still important for success in mining, access to capital for operations is the most important variable. Small, or more commonly called junior firms, conduct explorations and small-scale projects wherever mineral deposits are found. Increasingly such deposits are found in developing countries. Most often, when these sites promise large deposits, the junior firms sell or partner with one of a handful of international mining corporations, called majors. These firms are generally based in the United States, Canada, Australia and South Africa – countries that have successfully monopolized their own mineral resources and possess the tremendous capital necessary to commence large-scale mining operations elsewhere. For generations the wealth created by these firms has provided a critical component of their respective national GDPs. The operations of these firms abroad are also historically interlaced with colonial aspirations. But, with the combination of the growth of capital in many large developing and mineral economies such as Chile and the BRIC countries (Brazil, Russia, India, China), a rise in national mining corporations, increasing international political will for equitable distribution of the wealth from national natural resources, and stricter investment criteria based on responsible corporate practices, competition for capital and access to sites of mineral deposits is heightened. Rather suddenly for the traditional structure of the international mining industry, the relationship between access to mineral deposits and access to capital is now fraught with complicated intersections.

C. McElroy (✉)
School of Geography and the Environment, Oxford University, OX1 3QY Oxford, UK
e-mail: caitlin.a.mcelroy@gmail.com

T. Hebb (ed.), *The Next Generation of Responsible Investing*,
Advances in Business Ethics Research 1, DOI 10.1007/978-94-007-2348-1_11,

The establishment of corporate foundations is a recent trend to address these changing circumstances. These are institutions of various governance structures established by mining corporations to deliver social investment funds and development assistance to communities surrounding mining operations. Corporate foundations are a mechanism to distribute the development benefits of mining at the intersection of multinational corporations and communities with fledgling social infrastructure. The rapid replication of corporate foundations within the mining industry speaks to the urgent need to hold corporations responsible for distributing the ongoing power, wealth and development potential of mining. From 1950 to 1980 only five foundations, trust or fund models for the distribution of social benefit from mining existed. However, from 1980 to today there are now forty-one foundations, trusts and funds connected to mining operations in developing nations alone, twenty-seven of these established after 2000 (Nelson, Bannerman, Colwell, & Yaeger, 2010). Some of these institutions are designed to meet tremendous societal inadequacies including basic sanitation and infrastructure while others work in partnerships with development organizations, local, and national governments for specific education and business development programs. Majors in the mining industry have tried to attend to the diversity of their operations by establishing specific foundations at different mine sites in order to address the needs of the communities ranging from those in remote locations, to areas of dense population undergoing swift development.

However, the increasingly diverse and rapid establishment of corporate foundations muddles the multitude of demands for the responsible performance of international mining firms and makes it difficult to determine the relationship between specific drivers and enacted responses. This chapter explores the relationship between the increasing importance and prevalence of corporate social investing as a response to responsible investing initiatives in the multinational mining sector. It does so through the development of a conceptual framework of the relationship and current intersections between social investment and the responsible investment initiatives in the mining industry. Corporate foundations in the mining industry are then interrogated against this framework. This tests the utility of the framework and draws out useful nuances in the relationship between social investment and responsible investing initiatives performed by corporate foundations.

Corporate social investing under many different names has always been part of the mining industry. Company towns, supplying homes and goods to employees – as well as large philanthropic donations – have historically been methods of management for the communities that large mining operations require. However, social investing in its current incarnation, and what is now under adoption by mining corporations, stems from the field of development work. In this sense social investing places the emphasis on "investing" in communities, with funds going to projects and individuals to enhance local community development. Strong examples of social investment are found in the abundance of microloan and microfinance organizations for development. Social investing is strategic in the choice of projects, and often requires returns on the original investment. It adheres to the hand-up rather than the now tainted, corporate philanthropy handout. Most social investment programs are driven by development ideals and the normative values of social responsibility. In contrast, it could be said that responsible investment initiatives have had a reverse evolution. Socially motivated investment choices began in the 1970s to screen out investment in corporations involved in weapons and tobacco for the interest of certain groups of investors and spread to screens applied as political statements such as divestment from South African corporations in protest to apartheid. In the past forty years responsible investing has shed the emphasis of its normative social value origins in favor of promotion through arguments for its business logic. There is now considerable empirical evidence that responsible investment, which takes into account the environmental, social and governance performance of a firm as part of its financial picture, also contributes to good financial returns. This has created a "business case" for responsible investment and established a large industry movement for doing well financially by doing good for society and environment (Waddock & Smith, 2000). Both social investment and responsible investing integrate the need for efficient business and social development. But, it is unclear now that both are taken seriously by major corporations and receive attention from a diverse range of society, what relationship and effect each has upon the other.

The conceptual framework developed in this chapter presents the dichotomy between the logic for responsible investing rooted in an empirically based "business case" for corporate social responsibility (CSR) with that of the normative values for CSR driving corporate social investment as an extension of achieving the social license to operate. In delineating the dichotomy between performances of social investment and responsible investment it then highlights emerging conflicts. These conflicts are identified as divergences between the original intent versus the current aspirations of performing social investment and responsible investing. Through an understanding of these conflicts, suggestions for future integration are made.

Corporate foundations in the mining industry are interrogated by this framework. The basis for analysis they provide confirms the validity of the conceptual framework. This chapter concentrates on evaluating social investing and responsible investing initiatives in the mining industry's use of corporate foundations through the broadest spectrum of available literature and select examples of empirical research. This chapter achieves this starting with an elaboration of the analytical context. First, mining in developing countries is discussed and academic theories that shape our issues of interest are presented. Second, the development and operations of corporate foundations in the mining industry are explained in relation to our interest in social investment and responsible investing initiatives. The chapter moves on to elaborate the need for and significance of the research. The second half of the chapter proceeds to define the argument for the conceptual framework and presents the conceptual framework as applied to corporate foundations by the international mining industry.

11.2 Mining in Developing Countries and Corporate Foundations

The long history of extensive mining operations in developing countries and the conflict it has often produced has prompted the development of many theories to explain the relationship between mining and development. These theories have structured the discourse about mining and development and in doing so created spaces of interest for social investment and responsible investing initiatives. To illustrate this we briefly focus on three bodies of academic theory: economics and development, the "resource curse", and corporate governance. Each of these areas will demonstrate how the theory explains the phenomena of corporate foundations and questions the relationship between the increasing importance and prevalence of corporate social investing as a response to responsible investing initiatives.

Each of these theories is based on some similarities in the circumstances of multinational mining corporations and operations in developing countries. While each mine and country's relationship is unique, a generalization of typical conflicts of particular interest to this research question include: inadequate infrastructure, poor governance of the distribution of resource wealth, and power imbalance between the corporation, community and state. Inadequate infrastructure includes the road and transportation networks necessary to operate the mine, as well as systems for the health and education of the community in order to provide a healthy and educated workforce. In order for the mine to operate it must construct the necessary transportation. However, outside labour brought to the mine was frequently more efficient than investing in the needs of the surrounding population. International attention to development needs and the role of the private sector is now forcing mining corporations to rethink this operating model and face local challenges. But, in doing so they encounter the problem of poor governance of the distribution of resource wealth. Often due to weak government infrastructure or regional priorities, communities most impacted by mining activities receive the least benefit. Under pressure to act as responsible members of the community, mining corporations must address ways of redirecting wealth to local communities that currently goes to national or regional governments in the form of taxes and royalties. Mining companies must find ways to deliver social benefit directly to communities without overstepping and serving a governmental role themselves. It is here we find the third conflict in power imbalances between the corporation, community and state. How can the community voice its needs, the corporation not take on the role of the state, and the state balance its need for revenue with its ability to responsibly manage the wealth for the well-being of the population?.

These problems align well with the objectives of social investment and responsible investing. Internal problems requiring the corporation to invest in the community gravitate to solutions in social investment programs. However, the need for a balance of power between the corporation and other actors is critical to assessments of the responsibility of the firm from an investor perspective. How does a corporation manage the expectation of corporate social investment as one essential part of its responsibility and the requirement to moderate its control of development needs as another? It appears corporate foundations are being established to bridge these conditions. The following areas of academic theory illustrate ways different aspects of the common problems faced by mining corporations in developing countries are structured as part of large systemic explanations. They also reveal the link between systemic arguments faced by mining companies and the construction of certain choices to address problems.

First engaging with theories of economics and development, we concentrate on theories particular to the globalization of multi-national corporations. Cast within this discourse we see the identified problems between mining corporations and communities structured as issues of power relationships. For example, it is common within the mining industry for a multinational corporation (MNC) to operate in a remote area of a developing country. Prior to a more global concern for the responsibility of the corporation to the country where it is operating, mining corporations could operate in isolation, moving both the resource and its value out of the country with little to no interaction with the society surrounding it (Ferguson, 2005). In this model the mining industry operated through a series of networks particular only to it and related industries (Barry, 2006). Some political and economic discourses (Scott, 1998; Harvey, 2005) discuss the costs and benefits of isolating powerful institutions or seeking improvement in international development through more encompassing activities of powerful, and often corporate, institutions. For the mining industry, the costs of continuing with a model of strict neoliberal expansion posed risks to future financial performance because the societies and governments in developing countries increasingly responded to inadequate distribution of resource value by taking measures to withdraw the corporation's social license to operate.[1] Further, in order to be accountable to the interests of responsible investors, and demonstrate a positive relationship in their community, this isolated operation model was no longer sustainable.

There are many different corporate responses now used to facilitate engagement with the societies in which mining companies operate, including the establishment of corporate foundations.[2] Although just alluded to here, one can see how analysis

[1] Social License to Operate (SLTO) refers to any collection of activities by communities or government that allow corporations to continue to practice and without which their business activities in the location are in peril. Loss of social license to operate can occur through the formal revoke of mining rights or the informal protest strike or violence from the community. For some further discussion please see: Gunningham, N., Kagan, R. A., & Thorton, D. (2004). Social license and environmental protection: Why businesses go beyond compliance. *Law & Social Inquiry, 29*, 307–341. Nelson, J., & Scoble, M. (2006). *Social license to operate mines: Issues of situational analysis and process* vancouver. Canada, University of British Columbia.

[2] See also information about processes of negotiated agreements with communities. These are practices both conducted as legal formalities and arguably informally through commitments to social investment and participation as with the establishment of corporate foundations. For an example of a role of negotiated agreements in mining see O'Fairchellaigh, C., & Corbett, T. (2004). Indigenous participation in environmental management of mining projects: The role of negotiated agreements. *Environmenal Politics, 14*, 629–647.

of the corporate foundation situated in theories about systems of globalization in relationship to development allow for extrapolation to explain the rise of corporate foundations in larger theoretical discourses.

Another theory from the disciplines of economics and policy particularly pertinent to this investigation is the "resource curse" (Autry, 1993; Auty & Mikesell, 1998; Bridge, 2008). It proposes that, counter-intuitively, developing countries with considerable mineral wealth develop less rapidly than those without. Evidence for the persistent truth of this claim is controversial. However, it is a well-known argument and therefore challenges the scope of the responsibility of the mineral industries. Analysis of the causes of the resource curse focus on the role of government policy and the reinvestment of mineral wealth, but leaves open the role of corporations to also manage productive economic wealth distribution – especially in contexts with weak and corrupt governments. It is under the umbrella of the theory of the resource curse that much of the argument for the social investment role of corporate foundations is structured. Discussed in greater detail later, the Extractive Industries Transparency Initiative (EITI), a global initiative of responsible investors seeking a reduction in corruption and bribery in extractive industries, is clearly related to addressing the resource curse. Awareness of the influence of the resource curse theory on the mining industry, and the ways it challenges the social responsibility of its practices, helps extends the analysis of corporate foundations back to their role as manifestations of social investment objectives.

A final area of academic literature crucial to the investigation of corporate foundations and institutions for managing mining and development is corporate governance theory. CSR literature presents many ways to perform and measure corporate behavior toward the environment and society. While it stresses management systems, it is limited in its discussion regarding the structure of corporate governance by its insistent advocacy of the complete integration of responsible practices throughout a corporation (Davies, 2003; Waddock & Smith, 2000; Kaplan & Norton, 1996). The distinguishing hybridism of the internal and external relationship of corporate foundations to mining corporations calls for reference to broader theories of the structure of corporate governance outside the CSR discourse.[3] There is a long legacy of theories about the structure of corporate governance. Some are directed to guide business professionals (Monks & Minow, 2001) and many others address the consequences of corporate governance for the achievement of specific objectives (Mackenzie, 2007; Gillan, 2006; Aguilera & Jackson, 2003; Clark & Urwin, 2008a, 2008b, 2008c). Using this literature as a guide to the structures of the many models of governance for corporate foundations, we can postulate the consequences of these structures on the performance of the institution beyond the scope of their current operation. By doing so, it becomes possible to marshal empirical data

[3] The external and internal relationship of the corporate foundation to the corporation roughly align with: the independent performance of social investment by corporate foundations as an external relationship between the corporation foundation and corporation and the governance of the foundation and use as a corporate response to responsible investing initiatives as the internal relationship.

about corporate foundations into a forward-looking estimation of the changes they put in motion, in this case specifically changes in the relationship between social investment and responsible investing.

These different theoretical focuses are academic in nature, but each have had effects on the creation of institutions, policy and the logic of organizations that manage the relationship between mining corporations and developing communities. There is also a body of instrumental academic literature that speaks directly to the performance of the institutions and policies structured by the larger theories discussed. Instrumental literature often speaks to the particulars of practices within certain contexts. In relation to corporate foundations in the mining industry, this is evident in work that investigates the way in which practices of social responsibility are conducted. An example is the work of Esteves (2008a, 2008b; Esteves & Vanclay, 2009) concerning social impact assessment and community needs assessment used by corporate foundations to determine what projects require investment. In this work she analyzes the particulars of performing these practices for development and argues for the use of multi-criteria decision analysis (MDCA) as a systematic approach for the practice of social assessment.

Instrumental academic literature also makes significant contributions to understanding the specific context of social responsibility practices. For example, in seeking to understand the spread and performance of corporate foundations in the Chilean copper industry, there is much academic research about specific events in the copper industry and national policy formation that draws upon operating theories of development policy, economics and technology (Lagos, 1997; Newbold, 2006; Jara, Lagos, & Tilton, 2008; Aroca, 2002; Altimirano, 2001; Bartos, 2002) and helps provide context for the analysis of corporate foundations. Similarly, in Southern Africa an academic research team working in tandem with the Benchmarks Foundation is conducting sociological research about the social impacts of the mining industry (Van Wyk, 2007). These reports provide data about the context in which corporate social responsibility practices, including corporate foundations, operate. This type of instrumental literature about the contexts in which corporate foundations are performing, provides a tremendous amount of information to further our understanding of the nature of the problems faced by mining corporations in developing countries with which corporate foundations engage.

In contrast to the broad scope of literature that contributes to our understanding of the dynamics affecting the operation and structuring the choices of mining corporations operating in developing countries, there is little to no literature concerning corporate foundations themselves. The most comprehensive work now available is the World Bank sourcebook on Mining Foundations, Trusts and Funds (Wall, 2010) which provides case studies representing a range of corporate foundation designs and regions of operation. This recent development aside, dedicated attention to corporate foundations only comes from their own reports, such as the comprehensive history and performance review of the Rossing Foundation in Namibia (Grobler, 2008). As a result academic literature only creates a map of the environs and origins of corporate foundations – a shell constructing the space that corporate foundations occupy.

Recent empirical research about the operations of corporate foundations in the mining industry (conducted for the larger research project this chapter is drawn from) investigated several cases of corporate foundations in the mining industry. To establish a common understanding of the general parameters of what is considered a corporate foundation in the mining industry, what they do, and why these corporate foundations are particularly significant to investigate the relationship between corporate social investment and responsible investing, some examples are drawn from this research.

The Rossing Foundation in Namibia illustrates the evolution of the corporate foundation and a sampling of corporate foundations in the mining industry in Chile provides examples of their different structures and objectives. The Rossing Foundation, in operation for thirty-two years, is likely the first of its kind within the industry. Located in Namibia, the Rossing Foundation was created by the Rio Tinto Rossing Uranium mine. The foundation was established to deliver social benefit to the people of Namibia before it became the nation of Namibia. It continues to operate throughout the entire country. Established because of normative values for participation in society, the Rossing Foundation's mission has evolved into advancing Namibian education, particularly in English and Mathematics. This has included building schools, creating curriculum, and training teachers. The foundation receives its funding as three percent of the mine's annual profit before taxes. Due to the balance of independent operation and dependence of the corporation's funding, the foundation is also involved in assisting the mine to secure the sustainability of the mining town originally built for mine employees beyond the life of the mine. While not specifically the foundation's mission, it possesses the expertise and connections to the community to help facilitate this transition, the success of which is very important to the reputation of the corporation. Failure to leave a stable community after mine closure could impact future impressions of the firm's responsibility and affect the firm's social license to operate, thereby limiting access to new mine sites.

In Chile, mining is a cornerstone of not just the economy, but also society. There is tremendous pressure for corporations, particularly international corporations, to contribute to Chilean society beyond taxes and royalties. Several different types of corporate foundations have been established to serve the interests of different firms and the particular circumstances of the areas they operate. The Anglo American Company operates several mines in Chile, and runs a national foundation focused on community building through small business and medium enterprise development systems. They make extensive use of small social investment loan programs. While BHP Billiton is recognized in Chile for the staggeringly large Escondida copper mine near the city of Antofagasta in Northern Chile, the Escondida Foundation affiliated with the mine focuses on social development projects to better the region and draws in government programs through funding partnerships. Several other models of foundations are also in operation, such as Collahuasi's recently established foundation to focus on education in the area of Iquique and indigenous communities surrounding the mine. Each of these organizations requires funds from the mine, expertise beyond it, and is critical in meeting the expectations of participation in Chilean society. As employment opportunities become more limited due to increased mine mechanization and the requirement of specific educational qualifications, these programs maintain contact between the community and the mine.

11.3 The Relationship Between Corporate Social Investing and Responsible Investing Initiatives: The Need for a New Conceptual Framework

The need for mining corporations operating in developing countries to address their role in contributing to development, and to meet the standards of responsible corporate performance expected by investors, is clear. The increasing prevalence of corporate foundations appears to serve as a response to these needs. But little is understood about the performance of corporate foundations as a response to social investment and responsible investment initiatives. Can corporate foundations address both social investment and responsible investing concerns? Further, which is the driving interest?

Addressing this question first requires clarifying the relationship between the problems faced by the mining industry in developing countries and the concerns of investors with the fields of social investment and responsible investing. Why have these fields become the default or choice areas of engagement for these problems? The logical, rather than reactionary, arguments for the necessity of these practices are not well articulated. Reflection and analysis of what has made these practices important to adopt, beyond a response to pressure from organizational initiatives, is conspicuously absent. As a result, it is important to examine what CSR means as an explanatory entity for the logic of so much change in practice.

The vast body of CSR literature can be organized as the establishment of customs that structure the fields of responsible investing and social investment, and as the deployment of a discourse that is becoming a CSR industry. The field of CSR is the current manifestation of a large and generally self-referencing discourse on the responsibilities of corporations to society. In its many forms, the CSR field challenges Friedman's (1970) assertion that corporations serve society strictly through conducting their business without additional consideration of the businesses' responsibility to society. While many scholars have tried to organize the volume and diversity of CSR literature (Cramer, Jonker, & Heijden, 2004; Pava & Kruasz, 1997; Whitehouse, 2006; Margolis & Walsh, 2003; Garriga & Mele, 2004) it is primarily reducible to two arguments. First, the normative argument where explanatory reasons and evidence align along normative beliefs for the social imperative of responsible behavior (Carroll, 1996) and stakeholder inclusion (Donaldson & Dunfee, 1994; Donaldson & Preston, 1995). Second, the business case argument with instrumental and strategic arguments demonstrating the competitive, managerial, and financial benefits related to improved CSR practices (Porter & Kramer, 2006; Waddock & Graves, 1997; Peloza & Papania, 2008; Lin, Yang, & Dian-Yan,

2009). These arguments encompass the logic of CSR, an entity of explanation for the uptake of new responsible practices.[4] While acknowledging the utility of the collective reference to the logic of CSR, it is more useful to our investigation of the precipitation of corporate foundations to move beyond it and focus on the way CSR is conducted both through the actual procedures of its practices and through the perception of these operations. These two levels – the actual practices and the business of spreading the practices – continuously inform each other in the development of what we consider "performing CSR".

The fields of social investment and responsible investing are structured through the combination of perceptions and customs of CSR. Intimately related to development work, social investment is more closely associated with the normative argument for CSR. Corporations have particularly struggled with the concept of stakeholders (Donaldson & Preston, 1995; Metcalfe, 1998) when facing issues of employees and communities impacted by corporate presence and practices. Questions about to whom corporations are responsible, and to what extent, are difficult to address in order of risk to corporate operations. However, more consistent with the normative value driver for social investment, the corporation must take action if there is community need or face negative perceptions about its responsibility. Corporations in developing areas are further challenged to attend to the needs of stakeholders without institutional structures to facilitate benefit from the economic presence of the corporation. As a result, corporate social investment projects develop structures to direct economic benefits of the corporation's operations to local stakeholders. These have become institutions of social investment – such as corporate foundations and the many types of social investment programs they manage. Decisions regarding how to structure and manage these practices adhere to many of the practices of CSR management and measurement systems.

The tenets of responsible investing revolve around the business case argument for CSR. Responsible investing initiatives have adopted three established customs of CSR practice: systems for risk management; processes of external review, including audit and transparency; and managing reflective processes such as reputation, accountability and legitimacy. Following the logic that "you manage what you measure" (Lowenstein, 1996), traditional assessments of financial performance are evaluated with the addition of consideration of the social, environmental and governance practices of the firm. In response, as we will see in the mining industry literature, the measurement of these issues can produce management responses and new practices, such as corporate foundations, within the firms. The operation of the

[4] There is a broad literature investigating the institutional drivers for corporate responsibility particularly well represented by Campbell, J. L. (2007). Why would corporations behave in socially responsible ways? An institutional theory of corporate social responsibility. *Academy of Management Review, 32*, 946–967. As well as a stream of literature seeking to explain the spread of corporate responsibility values and practices within and beyond corporations well represented by Aguilera, R. V., Rupp, D. E., Williams, C. A., & Ganapathi, J. (2007). Putting the S back in corporate social responsibility: A multilevel theory of social change in organizations. *Academy of Management Review, 22*, 836–863.

two levels of CSR are visible in the structure of responsible investing initiatives in both the customs of CSR employed for responsible investing practices, and the influence of these practices as they are perceived by investors and other firms. It is further apparent that responsible investing practices themselves operate at two levels as well: in the assessment of firms as potential investment vehicles and in the decision making within the firm regarding its own investments and how they are perceived.

Within the mining industry, the logic of CSR and its normative advocacy for responsible practices are fulfilled by corporate social investment in developing areas through their use of corporate foundations. Corporate foundations also serve the corporation's interest to maintain its legitimacy as a responsible corporation in which to invest, and thus fulfills the logic of CSR business case advocacy for responsibility. Through this analysis of CSR we can also see rationales for the methods of responsible practices and how they reinforce each other. However, while it contributes to understanding the relationship between corporate social investing and corporate mining foundations, and the relationship between responsible investing initiatives and corporate foundations – it does not extend far enough to inform the relationship *between* social investing and responsible investing initiatives. The obstacle to understanding this relationship is the strong logical dichotomy between the normative reasons for social investment and the business case argument for responsible investing. Because of these shortcomings, the CSR explanation is insufficient for this investigation. New evaluative mechanisms are therefore necessary.

To tackle this need, a new conceptual framework is proposed. It argues that there is a dichotomy between the origin of responsible investing in the business case argument for CSR and the origin of corporate social investing in the normative values argument for CSR. However, in delineating this dichotomy in the performance of CSR practices, certain conflicts arise. These conflicts are divergences between the original intent versus the current aspirations of social investment and responsible investing.

11.4 Corporate Foundations and Their Partnerships in the Mining Industry

Testing the new conceptual framework relating social investment and responsible investing can help answer whether the relationship between the increasing importance and prevalence of corporate social investing is a response to responsible investing initiatives in the multinational mining sector. By interrogating the rise of corporate foundations in the mining industry – and their apparent performance of responsibility in response to social investment and responsible investing pressures – against the framework, the relationship between social investment and responsible investment is also better understood. This offers a perspective from which to better understand what is happening with corporate foundations in the mining industry and tests the utility of the conceptual framework.

The framework is evaluated against corporate foundations as presented by corporations, the ways they are discussed across the industry, and their relationship with other practices and movements for corporate responsibility in developing countries. The beginning of this investigation of corporate foundations starts with the underpinning of industry literature: corporate reports. These reports include financial statements, annual reviews, and sustainability reports.[5] It is important to acknowledge that these reports are all public, and written to inform and communicate corporate operations to others in the industry, investors, and performance review organizations. As a result they speak in response to the interests and pressures of the receiving organizations and potentially raise questions about the level of attention reported issues receive within the internal dialogue of the organization. Nonetheless, it is from these reports that industry and global forums can evaluate the corporate internalization of new practices to demonstrate responsibility.

Issuing corporate reports on the state of the business informs investors and analysts and is consistent with the business case argument supporting responsible investing. The Global Reporting Initiative (GRI) is an excellent example of corporate reporting designed to direct corporations to account for and provide information about issues of concern to responsible investors.[6] The GRI (now considered mainstream) has made industry specific supplements, including the mining and minerals supplements, part of their assessment criteria. Firms must complete these supplements in order to apply for the highest grade of evaluation. But, in spite of the benefits of standardization of the issues addressed in the reports, it is debatable that focusing accountability on particular issues is really motivation for responsible practices or consistent with the holistic operation interests of the responsible investment initiatives. It does demonstrate the time and expense corporations are devoting to reporting their social and environmental activities, and as a result reflects the increasing significance of responsible investing initiatives.

Concern over the performed and perceived responsible practices throughout a firm's operations is addressed further by the International Council on Mining and Metals (ICMM), who work to improve responsible practices and the reputation of the mining industry. The ICMM was born from crisis in the mining industry over a series of environmental and social fiascos in the early 1990s that drew attention to an industrial legacy of environmental damage and negative social impacts. Simultaneously there was a rise of more public and powerful interests directing investors to consider the social and environmental responsibility of firms. The need to address damaging practices and the risk to current and future investments led the largest international mining firms to support the ICMM as a forum capable of providing best practice information, responsible performance standards, and a platform for engagement with other international organizations.

[5] Examples of such reports include: http://www.bhpbilliton.com/bb/sustainableDevelopment.jsp and http://www.angloamerican.com/aal/development/. There is variability in the style, division, and emphasis of content between corporations, but these are representative of the depth of information offered and tone of communication.

[6] Global Reporting Initiative: www.globalreporting.org.

The ICMM now works on several fronts to collaborate with member firms on responsible practice research, offering guidance on issues and practices related to corporate responsibility. It makes this information and the successes within the industry regarding responsibility, public through its website and distribution networks. Three of their nine work areas address the social impact of mining operations, particularly in developing areas. These include a focus on contributions to socio-economic development, the resource endowment initiative directed to mitigating circumstances associated with what is considered the resource curse, and research dedicated to partnerships for development.[7] Each of these work areas includes information about corporate foundations within the mining industry and covers a range of the social investment programs they often administer. This significant attention to practices and the corporate performance of social investment is a noteworthy acknowledgment of the importance of social investment to the ICCM in the promotion of both the improvement of corporate responsibility and to achieve its aims to enhance the reputation of the mining industry for responsible investment. For example, the ICMM website celebrates the listing of one of its member companies, Newmont, for a fourth year on the Dow Jones sustainability index. There is a clear string of connections linking corporate social investment in practice by corporations and the assessed performance of responsibility in developing countries for responsible investing. It is unclear if this advocacy is equivalent to the creation of social investment programs for business reasons. In time, could the promotion of corporate social investing in this way alter the dominant normative drivers credited for the adoption of social investing practices?

The ICMM conducts many of its projects in collaboration with other international organizations – primarily linked to development and standards of responsible performance. With the latter, including the International Labor Organization (ILO), International Standards Organization (ISO), and United Nations Conference on Trade and Development (UNCTAD), the cooperation regards the implementation and regulation of standards. These activities are closely aligned with the business case approach and practices of corporate responsibility.

With the development organizations, the ICMM collaboration is perhaps more complicated. The World Bank with its Oil, Gas, Mining Sustainable Community Development Fund (CommDev), and the International Finance Corporation (IFC) are each arguably organizations of different forms of social investment. The World Bank is regularly criticized for lending to projects in the interest of industrial gain and not, or perhaps even to the detriment of, the societies in which these projects take place. Lending to the mining industry is a particular target of this criticism. The partnerships with the ICMM projects for social responsibility in the mining industry illustrate the strategic interests of each organization. The mining industry can mobilize the partnership to demonstrate the social benefit of development banks that are lending to the industry and their own corporate social responsibility. An example of this includes the creation of the corporate foundation at the Escondida

[7] International Council on Mining and Metals: www.icmm.com.

mine in Northern Chile. This corporate foundation was established in part to fulfill stipulations of IFC funding of the mine on conditions of returning value to the region surrounding the mine. The IFC's inclusion of social investment managed by the corporate sector highlights the growing role of the private sector in development, and the increasing attention to maintaining social license to operate for the success of the venture. This situation offers evidence of change in the value and importance of social investment practices to the considerations of and reaction to the more empirically-based responsible investing. The inclusion of social investment here is not driven by the normative CSR argument and is complicit in the adoption of responsible practices for the success of the business.

Some other international initiatives go further in their missions and work to integrate social investment and responsible investing initiatives. The Extractive Industries Transparency Initiative (EITI) is an example of this.[8] Started in 2002, the EITI works to certify the transparency of payments made by the oil, gas and mining sectors to the government in the countries where they are operating. This sector specific process is a manifestation of a greater movement for financial transparency to reduce corporate and government corruption. It is a slow process of civil society engagement where implementing countries provide transparent records of the revenues received from the extractive sector. It has not been uncommon that corrupt officials take bribes from corporations for access and security at a mine site, or that the government does not report the full extent of the taxes and royalties it is receiving from the mining industry. For example, checking the transparency of payments from corporations to government could make visible the absence of funds that are directed to personal coffers, indirectly funding civil war, or to buying special access for particular corporations. The implications of these events ranges from civil conflict, such as that funded by the diamond industry prior to the Kimberly Process, to quietly hindering the development and opportunities of populations that never see the value of mineral activities returned to society. The resource curse theory presented earlier argues that with or without corruption, poor redistribution of mineral wealth impedes national development. It is hoped that while not part of the performance of the EITI program, implementing countries are made more aware and critical about inquiries into where and how their revenues are invested.

The ICMM is actively involved in supporting and promoting the EITI and through it the responsibility and responsible reputation of the mining industry. The process of implementing countries agreeing to abide by the principles of the EITI, and then be subject to its review, is most similar to the framework of some of the leading organizations for responsible investing, such as the Principles of Responsible Investing (PRI) – the United Nations' investor initiative publicly committing signing firms to the practice of six principles for responsible investment in their business. However, these procedures explicitly protect against investment that perpetuates negative environmental and social impacts. In contrast, the EITI also implicitly promotes the normative value of accounting for the social investment of

[8] Extractive Industries Transparency Initiative: www.EITI.org.

mining revenues. In this instance responsible investment initiatives operate at an aspirational level to use their leverage to promote the normative responsible social values.

Rather than through the specifics of information in this material, but in the nature of its presentation, intended audience, and internal referencing, a rather dialectical discourse lurks. Its cumulative existence alludes to the influences of responsible investing in the promotion of social investment practices. It highlights industry response to them as an increasingly important consideration in the conduct of business for MNCs in developing countries. It also begins to map the process of creating and institutionalizing enactments of corporate social investment, such as corporate foundations, to meet the challenges presented by responsible investing initiatives.

In each example evaluated here, responsible investing initiatives are the instigating forum for attention to the mining industry's involvement in social investment. However, with each degree of separation from the corporation, the original drivers for the promotion of social investment as a response to pressure from responsible investing initiatives are altered by their application to a new aspirational role. For example, the promotion of social investment practices by the ICMM and the World Bank are closely aligned with the original intentions of the responsible investment initiative and call upon social investment as evidence of the successful business practices of the corporations. In contrast, with the EITI, the principles of responsible investing are utilized to address the aspirational goal of promoting the responsible social investment of mineral wealth. At this distance from corporations, responsible investing still provides the advocacy for social investment, but has broken away from the dichotomous tradition of the association of its drivers with the business case for responsibility.

Outside the literature and policy organizations of the mining industry the conceptual framework is applied to the actual operations of corporate foundations. How are social investment and addressing the concerns of responsible investing initiatives executed? Is it different than the changes that are occurring in the discourses structuring the policy and promotion of responsible investing and social investment practices?

Based on the empirical research conducted at the corporate foundations introduced earlier in this chapter, concern over social investment practices dominates in contrast to concern with responsible investing initiatives in the industry and policy dialogues. But, as hinted at in the introduction to the evolution of social investment as CSR, social investment is now performed through business conscientious practices of management and measurement. The growing use of micro-loans, such as with the Anglo American Chilean Foundation's support of small business, demonstrates extensive use of lending standards with strict requirements and attention to the return on the investment. Further, Escondida's corporate foundation has developed an inclusive business plan for the communities in the high altitude desert region of San Pedro de Atacama. This plan has measured which aspects of possible community business can contribute to the mine's supply needs and could be developed to provide goods and services beyond the needs of the mine.

The normative value of corporate social responsibly, and communities' adopted expectations of the social responsibility of mines, still appears to drive the establishment of social investment programs. This is especially true inside the corporate foundation, rather than from the corporation's perspective of the social investment projects conducted by corporate foundations. Reasons for the shift to embrace the business case arguments and practices in the performance of social investment have several possible causes. First, good management is good management. Delivering benefit is more successful when managed for success. Second, the recipients of social investment programs aspire to embrace all the best practices for running their own successful businesses. And third, the attention to issues necessary to meet the expectations of responsible investors is perhaps reflected into internal decisions of the corporation or foundation aspiring to make their own sound investment decisions.

11.5 Conclusion

After our investigation of the relationship between the increasing importance and prevalence of corporate social investing in the mining industry as a response to responsible investing initiatives in the multinational mining sector there are several conclusions. The conditions of operation for mining corporations in developing countries presents many challenges to the degree and method of involvement in development, however; to ensure the continued operation they must somehow be addressed. Here we saw that different approaches to social investment existed prior to and continue to exist independent of responsible investing initiatives in the mining industry. However, the current significance of social investment in the discourse of the social responsibility of the mining industry in developing countries is the result of its promotion as a response to meeting concerns of responsible investment initiatives. The direction of influence in the relationship between social investment and responsible investing initiatives is consistent. Social investment is presented as a response to the interests of responsible investing initiatives.

Other distinguishing features of the relationship between these two fields were constructed first from analysis of their evolution as fields of corporate social responsibility practices. This presented a dichotomy between the original CSR drivers for each field. Social investment is constructed from normative arguments for the performance of CSR, while responsible investing initiatives are built on the business case argument for CSR. However, this dichotomy alone failed to provide further insight into the functional relationship between social investment and responsible investing practices in the mining industry. A new conceptual framework was proposed to continue the investigation. It argues that while there is a clear dichotomy in the drivers for social investment and responsible investing, tracing them in operation reveals emerging conflicts. These conflicts are identified as divergences between the original intent versus the current aspirations of performing social investment and responsible investing. The conceptual framework proposes that through an understanding of these conflicts suggestions for future integration are possible.

When applied to the practice of social investment through corporate foundations in the mining industry the conceptual framework served as a useful tool to identify other facets of the relationship between social investing and responsible investing initiatives. It highlighted a general trend of the extension of the business case argument to social investment when it was promoted as a response to responsible investing. It also illustrated that the dichotomy between attachment to normative and business case CSR drivers was broken in instances where social investing and responsible investing were used in ways that were aspirational and not restricted to the original goals of either social investment or responsible investing.

The implications of this analysis are broad. The conceptual framework presented an interesting distinction between the examination of drivers for CSR performances and the intent of CSR performances. This suggests the need for further investigation and elaboration. It also revealed that in the conflicts between social investment and responsible investing there are spaces where the two fields are integrating. This could be a very important time of transition in these fields and critical area for empirical research. Both social investment and responsible investing have undergone previous evolutions; are we witnessing the next? Will we soon see, as in the example of corporate foundations in the mining industry, that responsible investment practices have now become practices used in the execution of internal corporate investment decisions and their management?

Returning to the specific context of the mining industry, and the use of corporate foundations as site of integrating the performance of social investment with a response to responsible investing initiatives, this current model appears well suited to bridge the problems of maintaining access to both locations of mineral deposits and access to capital. Given the delicate relationship between independence from and dependence on the corporation in the governance structure of corporate foundations, perhaps corporations should practice care in promoting their corporate foundations as the answer to their social responsibility. The expertise in the social investment practices of corporate foundations is slowly adopting some of the practices of business case CSR, but would lose its ability to bridge the social challenges the mining industry faces if they are used as palliative pawns for responsible investing reports.

Looking forward from this investigation there are many related research avenues to expand upon. However the most pressing question: How are the issues raised in this chapter particular to responsible investing engaging with development to be addressed? This question requires more empirical research and has the potential to illuminate the course of future research regarding social investment and responsible investment as a distinct field specifically related to development.

References

ABP. (2007). *ABP, PGGM and Evelop launch the Ampere Fund*. Retrieved October 8, from www.evelop.com/index.php?option=com_content&task=view&id=155&Itemid=39

Adams, E., & Knutsen, K. (1995). A charitable corporate giving justification for the socially responsible investment of pension funds: A populist argument for the public use of private wealth. *Iowa Law Review, 80*, 211–256.

Agle, B. R., Donaldson, T., Freeman, R. E., Jensen, M., Mitchell, R., & Wood, D. (2007). Dialogue: Towards superior stakeholder theory. *Business Ethics Quarterly, 18*(2), 153–190.

Agle, B. R., Mitchell, R. K., & Sonnenfeld, J. A. (1999). What matters to CEOs? An investigation of stakeholder attributes and salience, corporate performance, and CEO values. *Academy of Management Journal, 43*(5), 507–525.

Aguilera, R. V., & Jackson, G. (2003). The cross-national diversity of corporate governance: Dimensions and determinants. *Academy of Management Review, 28*, 447–465.

Aguilera, R. V., Rupp, D. E., Williams, C. A., & Ganapathi, J. (2007). Putting the S back in corporate social responsibility: A multilevel theory of social change in organizations. *Academy of Management Review, 22*, 836–863.

Akerlof, G. A. (1970). The market for 'lemons': Quality uncertainty and the market mechanism. *Quarterly Journal of Economics, 84*(3), 488–500.

Akerlof, G. A., & Shiller, R. J. (2009). *Animal spirits, how human psychology drives the economy and why it matters for global capitalism*. Princeton: Princeton University Press.

Alexander, G. (1993). Pensions and passivity. *Law and Contemporary Problems, 56*(1), 111–140.

Alexandrou, G., & Sudarsanam, S. (2001). *Shareholder wealth experience of buyers in corporate divestitures: Impact of business strategy, growth opportunities and bargaining power*. Paper presented at the European Financial Management Annual Meeting, Lugano, Switzerland, June 27–30.

Altimirano, N. (2001). Copper marketing with forward and future contracts: State-owned and private Chilean firms during the 1990s. *Resources Policy, 27*, 261–272.

Ambachtsheer, K. (2007). Why we need a pension revolution. *Financial Analysts Journal, 63*(1), 21.

Ambachtsheer, K. (2009). Overcoming the global financial crisis: What role should pension funds play? *Rotman International Journal of Pension Management, 2*(1), 1–4.

Ambachtsheer, K. P. (1997). Dedicated governance a 'win-win' solution. *Pensions & Investments, 25*(16), 14.

Ambachtsheer, K. P., Capelle, R. G., & Lum, H. (2007). Trustee competency. *Pensions & Investments, 35*(12), 18–18.

American Law Institute. (2003). *Restatement of the law, trusts* (3rd ed.). Philadelphia: American Law Institute.

T. Hebb (ed.), *The Next Generation of Responsible Investing*, Advances in Business Ethics Research 1, DOI 10.1007/978-94-007-2348-1,

Anand, P., & Cowton, C. (1993). The ethical investor: Exploring dimensions of investment behaviour. *Journal of Economic Psychology, 14*(2), 377–385.

Anson, M. (2008). What do we do now? *Pensions & Investments, 36*(20), p. 12.

Anson, M., White, T., & Ho, H. (2003). The shareholder wealth effects of CalPERS' focus list. *Journal of Applied Corporate Finance, 15*(3), 102–111.

Arness, K., & Howcroft, B. (2001). Corporate governance structures and the comparative advantage of credit unions. *Corporate Governance: An International Review, 9*(1), 59–65.

Aroca, P. (2002). Impacts and development in local economies based on mining: The case of Chilean II region. *Resources Policy, 27*, 119–134.

Augar, P. (2006). *The greed merchants*. London: Penguin.

Augar, P. (2009). *Chasing alpha*. London: The Bodley Head.

Autry, R. (1993). *Sustaining development in mineral economies, the resource curse thesis*. London: Routledge.

Auty, R., & Mikesell, R. (1998). *Sustaining development in mineral economies*. Oxford: Clarendon Press.

Bainbridge, S. (1992). Interpreting non-shareholder constituency statutes. *Pepperdine Law Review, 19*, 991–1025.

Bainbridge, S. (1995). The politics of corporate governance: Roe's strong managers, weak owners. *Harvard Journal of Law and Public Policy, 18*, 671–734.

Barber, B. (1984). *Strong democracy: Participatory policies for a new age*. Berkeley, CA: University of California Press.

Barber, B. M. (2006). Monitoring the monitor: Evaluating CalPERS' activism. *Journal of Investing, 16*(4), 66–88.

Barry, A. (2006). Technological zones. *European Journal of Social Theory, 9*, 239–253.

Bartkus, B. (2000). Mission statements: Are they smoke and mirrors? *Business Horizons, 43*(6), 23.

Bartos, P. J. (2002). SX-EW copper and the technology cycle. *Resources Policy, 28*, 85–94.

Basiago, A. D. (1995). Methods of defining sustainability. *Sustainable Development, 3*(3), 109–119.

Bauer, R., Koedijk, K., & Otten, R. (2005). The eco-efficiency premium puzzle in US equity markets. *Financial Analysts Journal, 61*(2), 51–63.

Bazerman, M. (2006). Climate change as a predictable surprise. *Climate Change, 77*(1–2), 179–193.

Beabot, G., & Schmiesing, K. E. (2003). Socially responsible investing: An application of Catholic social thought. *Logos, 6*(1), 66–99.

Beal, D. J., Goyen, M., & Phillips, P. (2005). Why do we invest ethically? *Journal of Investing, 14*(3), 66–77.

Becht, M., Bolton, P., & Röell, A., (2003). Corporate governance and control. In G. Constantinides, A. Harris, & R. Stulz (Eds.), *Handbook of the economics of finance, Volume 1A: Corporate Finance*. Amsterdam: North-Holland Publishers.

Becht, M., Franks, J. R., Mayer, C., & Rossi, S. (2008). *Returns to shareholder activism: Evidence from a clinical study of the Hermes U.K. focus fund*. ECGI Finance Working Paper, 138/2006.

Ben-Ishai, S., & Nowak, C. (2008). The threat of oppression remedy to reorganizing insolvent corporations. *Annual Insolvency Review, 429.*

Berle, A. A., & Means, G. C. (1932[1967]). *The modern corporation and private property*. New York: Brace and World.

Bernstein, P. L. (2007). *Capital ideas evolving*. Hoboken, NJ: Wiley.

Birks, P. (2002). The content of fiduciary obligation. *Trust Law International, 16*(1), 34–52.

Black, B. (1992). Agents watching agents: The promise of institutional investor voice. *UCLA Law Review, 39*, 811–893.

Blodget, H. (2007). *The wall street self-defense manual*. New York: Atlas Books.

Bogle, J. (2008, March/April). Black Monday and Black Swans. *Financial Analysts Journal, 64/2*, 30–40.

Bogle, J. C. (2005). *The battle for the soul of capitalism*. New Haven: Yale University Press.

Bonorchis, R., & Bridge, S. (2004). PIC buys 15% stake in Telkom. *Business Report*, Johannesburg, South Africa, November 17.

Brav, A., & Gompers, P. A. (1997, December). Myth or reality? The long-run underperformance of initial public offerings: Evidence from venture and nonventure capital-backed companies. *Journal of Finance*, *52*(5), 1791–1821.

Bridge, G. (2008). Global production networks and the executive sector: Governing resource-based development. *Journal of Economic Geography*, *8*, 389–419.

Broder, J. M. (2010). S.E.C. Adds climate risk to disclosure list. *New York Times*, January 27.

Brown, B. J. (1987). Global sustainability: Toward definition. *Environmental Management*, *11*(6), 713.

Brown, S. J., & Warner, J. B. (1980, September). Measuring security price performance. *Journal of Financial Economics*, *8*(3), 205–258.

Buffett, W. (2009). The greenback effect. *New York Times*, August 19.

Burr, B. B. (2009). High-yield timing poor, but funds stick with it. *Pensions & Investments*, *37*(2), 40–41.

Calebrese, M. (2001). Building on success: Labor-friendly investment vehicles and the power of private equity. In A. Fung, T. Hebb, & J. Rogers (Eds.), *Working capital: The power of labor's pensions* (pp. 93–127). Ithaca, NY: Cornell University Press.

Campbell, J. (2007). Why would corporations behave in socially responsible ways? An institutional theory of corporate social responsibility. *Academy of Management Review*, *32*, 946–967.

Campbell, J., Lo, A.W., & MacKinlay, C. (1997). *The econometrics of financial markets*. Princeton, NJ: Princeton University Press.

Canadian Pension Plan Investment Board (CPPIB). (2009). *Report on responsible investing*. Retrieved June 1st, 2010, from http://www.cppib.ca/files/PDF/CPPIB_RRI09_Eng.pdf

Carhart, M. M. (1997, March). On persistence in mutual fund performance. *Journal of Finance*, *52*(1), 57–82.

Carleton, W. T., Nelson, J. M., & Weisbach, M. S. (1998). The influence of institutions on corporate governance through private negotiations: Evidence from TIAA-CREF. *The Journal of Finance*, *53*(4), 1355–1362.

Carmichael, I. (2005). *Pension power: Unions, pension funds and social investment in Canada*. Toronto, ON: University of Toronto Press.

Carmichael, I., & Quarter, J. (Eds.). (2003). *Money on the line: Workers' capital in Canada*. Ottawa: Canadian Centre for Policy Alternatives.

Carroll, A. B. (1996). *Business for society: Ethics and stakeholder management*. Cincinnati: Southwestern Publishing.

Chan, M. (2009). *Subprime carbon? Re-thinking the world's largest new derivatives market*. New York: Friends of the Earth International.

Chapple, A. (2009). *Rethinking capital: The larger lessons of the financial crisis*. London: Forum for the Future.

Chugh, D., & Bazerman, M. (2007). Bounded awareness: What you fail to see can hurt you. *Mind and Society*, *6*(1), 1–18. Reprinted in *Rotman: The magazine of the Rotman School of Management* (2007), 20–25.

Clark, G. L. (2007). Expertise and representation in financial institutions: UK Legislation on pension fund governance and US regulation of the mutual fund industry. *Twenty-First Century Society*, *2*(1), 1.

Clark, G., Hebb, T., & Hagerman, L. (2004). *U.S. public sector pension Funds and urban revitalization: An overview of policy and programs*. Working paper, School of Geography and the Environment, University of Oxford, Oxford, 04/12.

Clark, G., & Monk, A. (2008). Vermont pension investment committee: Effectiveness and governance assessment a consultancy project for the office of the state treasurer. *Vermont*, 1–19.

Clark, G. L. (2008). Governing finance: Global imperatives and the challenge of reconciling community representation with expertise. *Economic Geography*, *84*(3), 281–302.

Clark, G. L., & Hebb, T. (2004). Corporate engagement: The fifth stage of capitalism. *Relations Industrielles/Industrial Relations*, *59*, 142–170.

Clark, G. L., & Urwin, R. (2008a). Best-practice pension fund governance. *Journal of Asset Management*, *9*(1), 2–21.

Clark, G. L., & Urwin, R. (2008b). *A resource-based approach to collective decision-making under risk and uncertainty: Implications for investment management and pension fund governance*. Oxford: University of Oxford.

Clark, G. L., & Urwin, R. (2008c, Fall). Making pension boards work: The critical role of leadership. *Rotman International Journal of Pension Management, 1*(1), 38–45.

Clark, G. L., & Urwin, R. (2010). Innovative models of pension fund governance in the context of the global financial crisis. *Pensions*, *15*(1), 62–77.

Clarkson, M. B. E. (1995). A stakeholder framework for analyzing and evaluating corporate social performance. *Academy of Management Review*, *20*(1), 92–116.

Clary, I. (2009). Fixing a broken system. *Pensions & Investments*, *37*(7), 11–12.

Coffee, J. C., Jr. (1991). Liquidity versus control: The institutional investor as corporate monitor. *Columbia Law Review*, *91*, 1277–1368.

Coffee, J. C., Jr. (1997). The folklore of investor capitalism. Book review of *Investor capitalism: How money managers are changing the face of corporate America* by Useem, M. (1996). *Michigan Law Review*, *95*, 1970–1989.

Coffee, J. C., Jr. (2005, Summer). A theory of corporate scandals: Why the USA and Europe differ. *Oxford Review of Economic Policy*, *21*(2), 198–211.

Committee on Workers' Capital. (2010). International confederation of free trade unions, Retrieved January 29, 2011, from http://www.icftu.org/default.asp?Language=EN

Company Law Committee. (1962). *Report*. London: HMSO, Cmnd. 1749.

Connelly, S. (2007). Mapping sustainable development as a contested concept. *Local Environment*, *12*(3), 259–278.

Core, J. E., Holthausen, R. W., & Larcker, D. F. (1999, March). Corporate governance, chief executive officer compensation, and firm performance. *Journal of Financial Economics*, *51*(3), 371–406.

Cowton, C. (1999). Playing by the rules: Ethical criteria at an ethical investment fund. *Business Ethics*, *8*(1), 60–69.

Cramer, J., Jonker, J., & Heijden, A. (2004). Making sense of corporate social responsibility. *Journal of Business Ethics*, *55*, 215–222.

Croft, T., & Hebb, T. (2003). Collaboration between labor, academics and community activists to advance labor/Capital strategies: The origins of heartland network. In I. Carmichael & J. Quarter (Eds.), *Money on the line: Workers' capital in Canada* (pp. 193–218). Ottawa, ON: Canadian Centre for Policy Alternatives.

Croft, T. (2009). Helping workers' capital work harder: A research report on global Economically Targeted Investments (ETIS). *A research report prepared for the Committee on Workers' Capital*. Working Paper, Steel Valley Authority, Pittsburgh, PA, USA. http://www.workerscapital.org/images/uploads/Helping%20Workers%20Cap%20Work%20Harder.pdf

Croft, T. (2010). *Up from wall street: The responsible investment*. New York: Cosimo, Inc.

Cullity, M. (1985–86). Liability of beneficiaries—a rejoinder. *Estates and Trusts Quarterly*, *7*, 35–52.

Daniel, K., Gimblat, M., Wermers, R., & Titman, S. (1997, July). Measuring mutual fund performance with characteristic-based benchmarks. *Journal of Finance*, *52*(3), 1035–1058.

Daniels, R. J., & Morck, R. (1995). *Corporate decision-making in Canada* (p. 8). Calgary: University of Calgary Press.

David, F. R. (1989). How companies define their mission. *Long Range Planning*, *22*(1), 90–97.

Davies, R. (2003). The business community: Social Responsibility and corporate values. In J. H. Dunning (Ed.), *Making globalization good: The moral challenges of global capitalism* (pp. 301–319). New York: Oxford University Press.

Davis, S., Lukomnik, J., & Pitt-Watson, D. (2006). *The new capitalists: How citizen investors are reshaping the corporate agenda*. Boston: Harvard Business School Press.

De Graaf, F. J., & Williams, C. A. (2009). The intellectual foundations of the global financial crisis: Analysis and proposals for reform. *University of New South Wales Law Journal, 32*(2), 390–415.

Deringer, F. B. (2005). *A legal framework for the integration of environmental, social and governance issues into institutional investment*. Geneva: United Nations Environment Programme Finance Initiative.

Dickerson, R., Howard, J., & Getz, L. (1971). *Proposals for a new business corporations law for Canada*. Ottawa: Information Canada.

Diltz, J. D. (1995, Spring). Does social screening affect portfolio performance? *Journal of Investing, 4*, 64–69.

Disney, R. (2000). Crises in public pension programmes in OECD: What are the reform options? *The Economic Journal, 110*(461), 1.

Dobris, J. C. (2008). SRI—Shibboleth or Canard (socially responsible investing, that is). *Real Property and Trust Journal, 42*, 755–797.

DOL. (1992). *Advisory council on pension welfare and benefit plans*. Report of Department of Labor, US Government.

DOL. (1994). *Interpretive Bulletin 94–1*. US Federal Register, June 23.

DOL. (2010). *Interpretive Bulletin 08–1, 29 C. F.R. § 2509.08–1*. Report of Department of Labor, US Government.

Donaldson, T., & Dunfee, T. (1994). Towards a unified conception of business ethics: Integrated social contracts theory. *The Academy of Management Review, 19*, 252–284.

Donaldson, T., & Preston, L. (1995). The stakeholder theory of the modern corporation: Concepts, evidence and implications. *Academy of Management Review, 20*(1), 65–91.

Doyle, R. J. (1998). *Advisory opinion to W.M. Tartikoff on behalf of pension and welfare benefits administration (PWBA)*. Washington, DC: Office of Regulations and Interpretations. Retrieved May 28 from http://www.dol.gov/ebsa/programs/ori/advisory98/98--04a.htm

Drucker, P. (1976). *The unseen revolution: How pension fund socialism came to America*. London: Heinemann.

DuCharme, L. L., Malatesta, P. H., & Sefcik, S. E. (2004, January). Earnings management, stock issues, and shareholder lawsuits. *Journal of Financial Economics, 71*(1), 27–49.

Eaton, L. (1991). Corporate couch potatoes: The awful truth about boards of directors. Barron's, 22–24.

Eckbo, B. E., Masulis, R.W., & Norli, Ø. (2000, May). Seasoned public offerings: Resolution of the 'new issues puzzle.' *Journal of Financial Economics, 56*(2), 251–291.

Economist. (2007). The crime in subprime. *The Economist Magazine*, December 19.

Economist. (2010). Show us the money: For the recovery to proceed smoothly, firms must stop hoarding cash. *The Economist* (July 1). Retrieved September 29, 2011 from http://www.economist.com/node/16485673

Eisenhardt, K. M. (1989). Agency theory: An assessment and review. *Academy of Management Review, 14*(1), 57–74.

El-Erian, M. (2008). *When markets collide: Investment strategies for the age of global economic change*. New York: McGraw-Hill.

Elhauge, E. (2005). Sacrificing corporate profits in the public interest. *New York University Law Review 80l733*, 804.

Epstein, G. (2010). China's US debt quandary. *Forbes Beijing Dispatch*.

Esteves, A. M. (2008a). Evaluating community investments in the mining sector using multi-criteria decision analysis to integrate SIA with business planning. *Environmental Impact Assessment Review, 28*, 338–348.

Esteves, A. M. (2008b). Mining and social development: Refocusing community investment using multi-criteria decision analysis. *Resources Policy, 33*, 39–47.

Esteves, A. M., & Vanclay, F. (2009). Social development needs analysis as a tool for SIA to guide corporate-community investment: Applications in the minerals industry. *Environmental Impact Assessment Review, 29*, 137–145.

Etzioni, A. (1964). *Modern organizations*. Englewood Cliffs, NJ: Prentice-Hall.

Exley, D. (2009). Comment: Westminster – view the bigger picture. *Pensions Management*. Retrieved September 29, 2011 from http://www.pensions-management.co.uk/news/fullstory.php/aid/5203

Fair Pensions. (2006). *UK pension scheme transparency on social, environmental and ethical issues*. London: FairPensions. Retrieved from http://www.fairpensions.org.uk/research

Falconer, K. (1999). *Prudence, patience and jobs: Pension investment in a changing Canadian economy*. Ottawa, ON: Canadian Labour Market and Productivity Centre.

Fama, E. F. (1970). Efficient capital markets: A review of theory and empirical work. *Journal of Finance, 25*, 383–417.

Fama, E. F. (1998, September). Market efficiency, long-term returns, and behavioral finance. *Journal of Financial Economics, 49*(3), 283–306.

Fama, E. F., & French, K. R. (1993, February). Common risk factors in the returns of stocks and bonds. *Journal of Financial Economics, 33*(1), 3–56.

Fama, E. F., French, K. R., Booth, D. G., & Sinquefield, R. (1993, January/February). Differences in the risks and returns of NYSE and NASD stocks. *Financial Analysts Journal, 49*(1), 37–41.

Fama, E. F., & Jensen, M. C. (1983). Separation of ownership and control. *Journal of Law and Economics, 26*, 301–325.

Ferguson, J. (2005). Seeing like and oil company. *American Anthropologist, 107*.

Fich, E. M., & Shivdasani, A. (2007, November). Financial fraud, director reputation, and shareholder wealth. *Journal of Financial Economics, 86*(2), 306–336.

Flannigan, R. (2004). Fiduciary duties of shareholders and directors. *Journal of Business Law*, 277–302.

Flannigan, R. (2006a). The political path to limited liability in business trusts. *Advocates Quarterly, 31*(3), 257–292.

Flannigan, R. (2006b). The adulteration of fiduciary doctrine in corporate law. *Law Quarterly Review, 122*, 449–469.

Flannigan, R. (2009). The core nature of fiduciary accountability. *New Zealand Law Review, 3*, 375–429.

Fox, J. (2009). *Myth of the rational market: A history of risk, reward, and delusion on Wall Street*. New York: HarperCollins Publishers.

Fraser, A. (1998). *Reinventing aristocracy: The constitutional reformation of corporate governance*. Farnham: Ashgate.

Freeman, R. E. (1999). Divergent stakeholder theory. *Academy of Management Review, 24*(2), 222–227.

Friedman, M. (1970). The social responsibility of business is to increase its profits. *New York Times Magazine*, pp. 122–126.

Frischmann, B. (2005). Some thoughts on short sightedness and intergenerational equity. *Loyola University Chicago Law Journal, 36*(2), 457–468.

Frooman, J. (1999). Stakeholder influence strategies. *Academy of Management Review, 24*(2), 191–205.

Fung, A., Hebb, T., & Rogers, J. (Eds.). (2001). *Working capital: The power of labor's pensions*. Ithaca, NY: Cornell University Press.

Galbraith, J. K. (1976). *Money: Whence it came, where it went*. London, England: Penguin Books.

Galbraith, J. K. (1990). *A short history of financial Euphoria*. London: Penguin Business.

Gallagher, D. R., Gardner, P., & Swan, P. L. (2009). *Institutional swing trades and subsequent firm performance*. EFA 2009, Bergen Meetings Paper.

Gallie, W. B. (1956, March 12). *Essentially contested concepts*. Presented at the Meeting of Aristotelian Society. Retrieved September 30, 2011 from http://commonsenseatheism.com/wp-content/uploads/2011/05/Gallie-Essentially-Contested-Concepts.pdf

Gantchev, N. (2009). *The costs of shareholder activism: Evidence from a sequential decision model*. Finance Department Paper, The Wharton School, University of Pennsylvania.

Garriga, E., & Mele, D. (2004). Corporate social responsibility theories: Mapping the territory. *Journal of Business Ethics, 53*, 51–71.

Gay, G., & Klaassen, J. (2005). Retirement investment, fiduciary obligations, and socially responsible investing. *Journal of Deferred Compensation, 10/4*, 34–49.

Gifford, J. (2004). Measuring the social, environmental, and ethical performance of pensions funds. *Journal of Australian Political Economy, 53*, 139–141.

Gifford, J. (2009). Effective shareholder engagement: The factors that contribute to shareholder salience. In T. Hebb (Ed.), *The next generation of responsible investing* (forthcoming).

Gillan, S. L. (2006). Recent developments in corporate governance. *Journal of Corporate Finance, 12*, 381–402.

Gillan, S. L., & Starks, L. T. (1998). A survey of shareholder activism: Motivation and empirical evidence. *Contemporary Finance Digest, 2*, 310–334.

Gillan, S. L., & Starks, L. T. (2007). The evolution of shareholder activism in the United States. *Journal of Applied Corporate Finance, 19*(1), 55–73.

Glaser, B. G., & Strauss, A. L. (1967). *The discovery of grounded theory: Strategies for qualitative research*. New York: Aldine.

Gompers, P., Ishii, J., & Metrick, A. (2003, February). Corporate governance and equity prices. *Quarterly Journal of Economics, 118*, 107–156.

Gower, L. C. B. (1969). The *principles of modern company law* (3rd ed.). London: Stevens.

Graham, B. (1949). *The intelligent investor*. New York: Harper Collins.

Gray, J. (2009). Rethinking investment beliefs in a time of crisis: The calming hand of philosophy. *Rotman International Journal of Pension Management, 2*(1), 6–11.

Greenspan, A. (2008). We will never have a perfect model of risk. *Financial Times*, March 16, p. 9.

Gribben, C., & Faruk, A. (2004). *Will UK pension funds become more responsible? A survey of trustees – 2004*. Report, UK Social Investment Forum, London.

Gribben, C., & Gitsham, M. (2006). *Will UK pension funds become more responsible: A survey of trustees*. Report, UK Social Investment Forum.

Grobler, J. (2008). 30, *The Rossing foundation 1978–2008*. Report, Windhoek, Namibia: The Rossing Foundation.

Gunningham, N., Kagan, R. A., & Thorton, D. (2004). Social license and environmental protection: Why businesses go beyond compliance. *Law & Social Inquiry, 29*, 307–341.

Gutmann, A., & Thompson, D. (2002). Deliberative democracy beyond process. *Journal of Political Philosophy, 10*(2), 153–174.

Guyatt, D. (2008, Fall). Pension collaboration: Strength in numbers. *Rotman International Journal of Pension Management, 1*(1), 46–52.

Halbach, E. C. J. (1992). Trust investment law in the third restatement. *Real Property, Probate and Trust Journal, 27*(3), 408–466.

Haldane, A. G. (2009). *Rethinking the financial network*. A speech presented at the Financial Student Association, Amsterdam, April 2009. Retrieved September 30, 2011, from http://www.bankofengland.co.uk/publications/speeches/2009/speech386.pdf

Hall, B. J., & Liebman, J. B. (1998, August). Are CEOs really paid like bureaucrats? *Quarterly Journal of Economics, 113*(3), 653–691.

Harrison, J. S., & Freeman, R. E. (1999). Stakeholders, social responsibility, and performance: Empirical evidence and theoretical perspectives. *Academy of Management Journal, 42*(5), 479–487.

Hart, O. (1995). *Companies, contracts, and financial structure*. London: Oxford University Press.

Harvey, D. (2005). *A brief history of neoliberalism*. Oxford: Oxford University Press.

Hawley, J. (2009). *An exploration into corporate governance, risk analysis and the financial crisis: What did universal owners do, and not do, to contribute to the crisis*? Conference paper, UNPRI academic Network, Ottawa, Canada, October.

Hawley, J. P. (1995). Political voice, fiduciary activism, and the institutional ownership of U.S. corporations: The role of public and noncorporate pension funds. *Sociological Perspectives, 38*(3), 415–435.

Hawley, J. P., & Williams, A. T. (1997). The emergence of fiduciary capitalism. *Corporate Governance, 5*(4), 206–213.

Hawley, J. P., & Williams, A. T. (2000). *The rise of fiduciary capitalism: How institutional investors can make corporate America more democratic*. Philadelphia: University of Pennsylvania Press.

Hebb, T. (2008). *No small change: Pension funds and corporate engagement*. Ithaca, NY: Cornell University Press.

Hebb, T., & Beeferman, L. (2009). US pension funds' labour-friendly investments. *Journal of Comparative Social Welfare, 25/2*, 109–117.

Hendry, J. (2004). Beyond self-interest: Agency theory and the board in a satisficing world. *British Journal of Management, 16*(1), 55–63.

Henriques, I., & Sadorsky, P. (1999). The relationship between environmental commitment and managerial perceptions of stakeholder importance. *Academy of Management Journal, 42*(1), 87–99.

Hess, D. (2005). Protecting and politicizing public pension fund assets: Empirical evidence on the effects of governance structures and practices. *University of California-Davis Law Review, 39*(1), 187–227.

Hill, R., Ainscough, T., Shank, T., & Manullang, D. (2007). Corporate social responsibility and socially responsible investing: A global perspective. *Journal of Business Ethics, 70*(2), 165–174.

Hillman, A. J., & Keim, G. D. (2001). Shareholder value, stakeholder management and social issues: What's the bottom line? *Strategic Management Journal, 22*, 125–139.

Hirschman, A. O. (1970). *Exit, voice, and loyalty: Responses to decline in firms, organizations, and states*. Cambridge, MA: Harvard University Press.

Hoepner, A. G. F., & McMillan, D. G. (2009). *Research on 'responsible investment': An influential literature analysis comprising a rating, characterisation, categorisation and investigation*. Working Paper, School of Management, University of St. Andrews.

Howard-Grenville, J., Nash, J., & Coglianese, C. (2006). Constructing the license to operate: Internal factors and their influence on corporate environmental decisions. *Law and Policy, 30*(2), 93–107.

Hudson, A. (2007). The regulation of trustees. In M. Dixon & G. Griffiths (Eds.), *Contemporary perspectives on property, equity, and trusts law* (pp. 163–180). New York: Oxford University Press.

International Confederation of Free Trade Unions (ICFTU), International Trade Secretariats (ITS), and Trade Union Advisory Committee to the OECD (TUAC). (2001). *The role of the international financial institutions in a globalized economy*. A Statement to the 2001 Annual Meetings of the IMF and World Bank.

International Finance Corporation (IFC). (2009). *Sustainable investment in brazil*. A paper prepared for the IFC, Washington, DC.

Jacobs, M. (2006). Sustainable development as a contested concept. In A. Dobson (Ed.) *Fairness and futurity: Essays on environmental sustainability and social justice* (pp. 21–45). Oxford: Oxford University Press.

Jara, J., Lagos, G., & Tilton, J. (2008). Using exploration expenditures to assess the climate for mineral investment. *Resources Policy, 33*, 179–187.

Jensen, M. C., & Meckling, W. H. (1976). Theory of the firm: Managerial behavior, agency costs, and ownership structure. *Journal of Financial Economics, 3*, 305–360.

Jensen, M. C., & Murphy, K. J. (1990). Performance pay and top management incentives. *Journal of Political Economy, 98*(2), 225–264.

Johnson, K. L., & Jan de Graaf, F. (2009). Modernizing pension fund legal standards for the twenty-first century. *Rotman International Journal of Pension Management, 2*(1), 44–51.

Jones, R., & Wood, D. (1995). Stakeholder mismatching: A theoretical problem in empirical research on corporate social performance. *International Journal of Organizational Analysis, 3*, 229–267.

Jurvale, C., & Lewis, A. (2008). Identifying impediments to SRI in Europe: A review of the practitioner and academic literature. *Business Ethics: A European Review, 17*(3), 285–310.

Kanzer, A. (2009). The use of shareholder proposals to address corporate human rights performance. In H. C. de Bettignies & F. Lépineux (Eds.), *Finance for a better world: The shift toward sustainability* (pp. 71–89). Basingstoke: Palgrave Macmillan.

Kaplan, R., & Norton, D. P. (1996). Using the balanced scorecard as a strategic management system. *Harvard Business Review, 74*, 75–85.

Karpoff, J. M. (2001). *The impact of shareholder activism on target companies: A survey of empirical findings*. Working Paper, University of Washington.

Kay, J. (2009). *The long and short of it: A guide to finance and investment for normally intelligent people who are not in the industry*. London: Erasmus Press.

Kedia, S., & Philippon, T. (2009, June). The economics of fraudulent accounting. *Review of Financial Studies, 22*(6), 2169–2199.

Keynes, J. M. (1952). *Essays in persuasion*. London: Rupert Hart-Davis.

Keynes, J. M. (1978). *The general theory of employment, interest and money*. London: Macmillan.

Kiernan, M. (2009). *Investing in a sustainable world: Why green is the new color of money on Wall Street*. New York: AMACOM.

Knight, F. H. (1921). *Risk, uncertainty and profit*. Boston: Houghton Mifflin.

Koedijk, K., & Slager, A. (2007). Investment beliefs: Every asset manager should have them. *Journal of Portfolio Management, 33*(3), 77–84.

Koedijk, K., & Slager, A. (2009). Do institutional investors have sensible investment beliefs? *Rotman International Journal of Pension Management, 2*(1), 12–19.

Koford, K., & Penno, M. (1992). Accounting, principal-agent theory, and self-interested behaviour. In N. E. Bowie & R. E. Freeman (Eds.), *Ethics and agency theory: An introduction* (pp. 127–142). New York: Oxford University Press.

Kok, N. (2008). *Corporate governance and sustainability in global property markets*. PhD Thesis, European Centre for Corporate Engagement, Maastricht, ND.

Kothari, S. P., & Warner, J. B. (2007). Econometrics of event studies. In B. E. Eckbo (Ed.), *Handbook of corporate finance, Volume 1: Empirical corporate finance*. Amsterdam: North-Holland Publishers.

Krosinsky, C., & Robins, N. (Eds.). (2008). *Sustainable investing: The art of long term performance*. London: Earthscan.

Kusnet, D. (2002). *The challenge and promise of cross-boarder capital stewardship*. Washington, DC: Centre for Working Capital.

Kynaston, D. (2000). *The city of London: Illusions of gold 1914–1945*. London: Pimlico.

Lagos, G. (1997). Developing national mining policy in Chile: 1974–96. *Resources Policy, 23*, 51–69.

Langbein, J. H. (2005). Questioning the trust law duty of loyalty: Sole interest or best interest. *Yale Law Journal, 114*(5), 929–990.

Langbein, J. H., & Posner, R. A. (1980). Social investing and the law of trusts. *Michigan Law Review, 79*(1), 72–112.

Lawrence, S., & Macklem, P. (2000). From consultation to reconciliation: Aboriginal rights and the crown's duty to consult. *Canadian Bar Review, 79*, 252–279.

Lewis, A., & Mackenzie, C. (2000). Morals, money, ethical investing and economic psychology. *Human Relations, 53*(2), 179–191.

Lewis, A., & Webley, P. (1994). Social and ethical investing: Beliefs, preferences and the willingness to sacrifice financial return. In A. Lewis & K. E. Wärneryd (Eds.), *Ethics and economic affairs* (pp. 171–182). London: Routledge.

Lin, H. C., Yang, H. L., & Dian-Yan, L. (2009). The impact of corporate social responsibility on financial performance: Evidence from a business in Taiwan. *Technology in Society, 31*, 56–63.

Llewellyn, D. (2004). *Issues in the governance of mutuals in the financial sector*. A paper commissioned for the Myners enquiry into Governance of Life Mutuals, H. M. Treasury, London.

Lo, A. (2005). Reconciling efficient markets with behavioral finance: The adaptive markets hypothesis. *Journal of Investment Consulting, 7*, 21–44.

Loss, L., & Seligman, J. (2004). *Fundamentals of securities regulation* (5th ed.). New York: Aspen Publishers.

Louche, C., & Lydenberg, S. (2006). Investissement sociallement responsible: Differences entre Europe et Etats Unis. *Revue d'Economie Financiere, 85*, 81–105.

Lowenstein, L. (1996). Financial transparency and corporate governance: You manage what you measure. *Columbia Law Review, 96*, 1335–1362.

Luft, J. (1997). Fairness, ethics, and the effect of management accounting on transaction costs. *Journal of Management Accounting Research, 9*, 199–216.

Lunn, P. (2009, Spring). The descent of rational man. *RSA Journal*.

Lydenberg, S. (2009, June). Markets at risk: The limits of modern portfolio theory. In A. White (Ed.), *Restoring the primacy of the real economy* (pp. 42–50). Paper series, Summit on the Future of the Corporation.

Mackenzie, C. (2007). Boards, incentives and corporate social responsibility: The case for a change of emphasis. *Corporate Governance, an International Review, 15*, 935–943.

Mainelli, M., & Giffords, B. (2009). *The road to long finance: A systems view of the credit scrunch*. London: Centre for the Study of Financial Innovation. Retrieved from http://www.zyen.com/PDF/Road%20to%20Long%20Finance.pdf

Marcoux, A. (2005). A fiduciary argument against stakeholder theory. *Journal of Business Ethics, 13*(1), 1–24.

Margolis, J. D., & Walsh, J. P. (2003). Misery loves companies: Rethinking social initiatives by business. *Administrative Science Quarterly, 48*, 268–305.

Markowitz, H. (1959). Portfolio selection. *The Journal of Finance, 7/1*, 77–91.

Marks, H. S. (1993). The value of predictions, or where'd all this rain come from? *Financial Analysts Journal, 49*(6).

Martin, W. (2009). Socially responsible investing: Is your fiduciary duty at risk? *Journal of Business Ethics, 90*, 549–560.

McKinsey & Co. (2010, March). How companies manage sustainability: McKinsey global survey results. *McKinsey Quarterly*.

McLachlan, J., & Gardner, J. (2004). A comparison of socially responsible and conventional investors. *Journal of Business Ethics, 52*, 11–25.

Mercer Investment Consulting. (2005). *A climate for change - A trustee's guide to understanding and addressing climate risk*. Toronto: Mercer Investment Consulting. Retrieved from http://www.iigcc.org/__data/assets/pdf_file/0010/262/A_climate_for_change.pdf

Merton, R., & Bodie, Z. (2005). The design of financial systems: Towards a synthesis of function and structure. *Journal of Investment Management, 3*(1), 1–23.

Metcalfe, C. E. (1998). The stakeholder corporation. *Business Ethics, 7*, 30–36.

Minsky, H. (1992). *The financial instability hypothesis*. A working paper for the Jerome Levy Economics Institute of Bard College, p. 74.

Mirror, M. (2005, November 7). Shopping changes forever. *A piece prepared for the future growth fund*.

Mitchell, M. L., & Stafford, E. (2000, July). Managerial decisions and long-term stock price performance. *Journal of Business, 73*(3), 287–330.

Mitchell, R. K., Agle, B. R., & Wood, D. J. (1997). Toward a theory of stakeholder identification and salience: Defining the principle of who and what really counts. *Academy of Management Review, 22*(4), 853–886.

Moffat, G., Bean, G., & Dewar, J. (2005). *Trusts law: Texts and materials* (4th ed.). Cambridge: Cambridge University Press.

Moneva, J., Riviera-Lirio, J., & Munoz-Torres, M. (2007). The corporate stakeholder commitment and social and financial performance. *Industrial Management & Data Systems, 107*, 84–102.

Monk, A. (2009). The geography of pension liabilities and fund governance in the United States. *Environment and Planning A, 41*(4), 859–878.

Monks, J. (2000). The returns to individual and college characteristics: Evidence from the national longitudinal survey of youth. *Economics of Education Review, 19*(3), 279–289.

Monks, R. A. G. (2001). *The new global investors*. Oxford: Capstone Publishing Ltd.

Monks, R. A. G., & Minow, N. (1991). *Power and accountability*. New York: Harper Collins.

Monks, R. A. G., & Minow, N. (2001). *Corporate governance*. Oxford: Blackwell Business.

Montier, J. (2009). Efficient markets theory is dead. *Financial Times*, June 24.

Myners, P. (2001). *Institutional investment in the UK; A review.* A report for the HM treasury.

Nelson, J., Bannerman, D., Colwell, A., & Yaeger, R. (2010). *Experiences with mining foundations. Business for social responsibility*. Unpublished Document, Version 3, February.

Nelson, J., & Scoble, M. (2006). *Social license to operate mines: Issues of situational analysis and process Vancouver*. Unpublished paper, Canada: University of British Columbia.

Newbold, J. (2006). Chile's environmental momentum: ISO 14001 and the large-scale mining industry – Case studies from the state and private sector. *Journal of Cleaner Production, 14*, 248–261.

Nilsson, J. (2009). Investment with a conscience: Examining the impact of pro-social attitudes and perceived financial performance on socially responsible investment behaviour. *Journal of Business Ethics, 83*(2), 307–325.

Nolan, R. (2006). The continuing evolution of shareholder governance. *Cambridge Law Journal, 65*, 92–127.

O'Barr, W. M., & Conley, J. M. (1992). *Fortune and folly: The wealth and power of institutional investing*. Homewood, IL: Business One Irwin.

O'Fairchellaigh, C., & Corbett, T. (2004). Indigenous participation in environmental management of mining projects: The role of negotiated agreements. *Environmental Politics, 14*, 629–647.

Ontario Law Reform Commission. (1984). *Report on the law of trusts*. Toronto, ON: Ministry of the Attorney General.

Ontario Teachers' Pension Plan Board (OTPPB). (2005). *Report of the ad hoc committee on socially responsible investment*. Toronto: OTPPB.

Organisation for Economic Cooperation and Development (OECD). (2004). *Recommendation on core principles of occupational pension regulation*. Paris: OECD.

Organization for Eceonomic Cooperation and Development (OECD). (2002). *Small business, job creation and growth: Facts, obstacles and best practices*. A paper prepared by the OECD. Retrieved September 30, 2011 from http://www.oecd.org/dataoecd/10/59/2090740.pdf

O'Rourke, A. (2003). The message and methods of ethical investment. *Journal of Cleaner Production, 11*(6), 683–693.

Palmiter, A. R. (2002). Mutual fund voting of portfolio shares: Why not disclose? *Cardozo Law Review, 23*(4), 1419–1491.

Partnoy, F. (2004). *Infectious greed*. London: Profile Books.

Pateman, C. (1970). *Participation and democratic theory*. Cambridge: Cambridge University Press.

Pava, M., & Kruasz, J. (1997). Criteria for evaluating the legitimacy of corporate social responsibility. *Journal of Business Ethics, 16*, 337–347.

Peloza, J., & Papania, L. (2008). The missing link between corporate social responsibility and financial performance: Stakeholder salience and identification. *Corporate Reputation Review, 11*, 169–181.

Peng, L., & Röell, A. (2008a, January). Executive pay and shareholder litigation. *Review of Finance, 12*(1), 141–184.

Peng, L., & Röell, A. (2008b, May). Manipulation and equity-based compensation. *American Economic Review, 98*(2), 285–290.

Perez, C. (2002). *Technological revolutions and financial capital: The dynamics of bubbles and golden ages*. Cheltenham: Edward Elgar Publishers.

Peritore, P. (1999). *Third world environmentalism: Case studies from the global south*. Gainesville, FL: University of Florida Press.

Phillips, R. A., Freeman, E., & Wicks, A. C. (2003). What stakeholder theory is not. *Business Ethics Quarterly, 13*(1), 479–502.

Piller, C. (2007). Berkshire wealth conflicts with Gates mission in Sudan. *Los Angeles Times*, May 4.

Popper, K. (1963). *Conjectures and refutations: The growth of scientific knowledge*. London: Routledge & Kegan Paul.

Porter, M., & Kramer, M. (2002). The competitive advantage of corporate philanthropy. *Harvard Business Review, 80*(12), 56–68.

Porter, M. E., & Kramer, M. R. (2006). Strategy and society: The link between competitive advantage and corporate social responsibility. *Harvard Business Review, 84*(12), 78–92.

Porter, M, & van der Linde, C. (1995). Green and competitive – Ending the stalemate. *Harvard Business Review, 73*(5), 120–134.

Posner, E. A. (2000). *Law and social norms*. Cambridge, MA, London: Harvard University Press.

Posner, R. A. (2008). *How judges think*. Cambridge, MA: Harvard University Press.

Post, J., & Andrews, P. (1982). Case research in corporation and society studies. *Research in Corporate Social Performance and Policy, 4*, 1–33.

Povel, P., Singh, R., & Winton, A. (2007, July). Booms, busts, and fraud. *Review of Financial Studies, 20*(4), 1219–1254.

PRI Initiative. (2007). *PRI report on progress 2007*. Report, Principles for Responsible Investment Initiative, New York.

PRI Initiative. (2008). *PRI report on progress 2008*. Report, Principles for Responsible Investment Initiative, New York.

PRI Initiative. (2009). *PRI report on progress 2009*. Report, Principles for Responsible Investment Initiative, New York. Retrieved June 1, 2010, from http://www.unpri.org/files/PRI%20Report%20on%20Progress%2009.pdf

Province of Ontario. (1967). *Interim report of the select committee on company law*. Toronto: Province of Ontario Legislative Assembly.

Quarter, J., & Carmichael, I. (2001). Social investment by union-based pension funds and labour-sponsored investment funds in Canada. *Industrial Relations, 56*(1), 92–115.

Ratner, B. D. (2004). "Sustainability" as a dialogue of values: Challenges to the sociology of development. *Sociological Inquiry, 74*(1), 50–69.

Rauh, J. D., & Sufi, A. (2009). Capital structure and debt structure. *Review of Financial Studies, 23*(12), 4242–4280.

Reinhardt, F. L., Stavins, R. N., & Vietor, R. H. K. (2008). Corporate social responsibility through an economic lens. *Review of Environmental Economics and Policy, 2*(2), 219–239.

Richardson, B. J. (2007a). Do the fiduciary duties of pension funds hinder socially responsible investment? *Banking and Finance Law Review, 22*(2), 145–201.

Richardson, B. J. (2007b). Protecting indigenous peoples through socially responsible investment. *Indigenous Law Journal, 6*(1), 206–234.

Richardson, B. J. (2008). *Socially responsible investment law: Regulating the unseen polluters*. New York: Oxford University Press.

Richardson, B. J. (2009). Keeping ethical investment ethical: Regulatory issues for investing for sustainability. *Journal of Business Ethics, 87*(4), 555–572.

Richardson, B. J., & Razzaque, J. (2006). Public participation in environmental decision-making. In B. J. Richardson & S. Wood (Eds.), *Environmental law for sustainability* (pp. 165–194). Oxford, UK: Hart Publishing.

Ritter, J. R., & Welch, I. (2002, August). A review of IPO activity, pricing, and allocations. *Journal of Finance, 57*(4), 1795–1828.

Roe, M. (1994). *Strong managers, weak owners: The political roots of American corporcte finance*. Princeton: Princeton University Press.

Romano, R. (1991, Spring). The shareholder suit: Litigation without foundation? *Journal of Law, Economics, and Organization, 7*(1), 55–87.

Romano, R. (2001). Less is more: Making institutional investor activism a valuable mechanism of corporate governance. *Yale Journal on Regulation, 18*, 174–252.

Rosen, B., Sandler, D., & Shani, D. (1991). Social issues and socially responsible investment behavior: A preliminary empirical investigation. *Journal of Consumer Affairs, 25*, 221–234.

Ryan, L. V., & Schneider, M. (2003). Institutional investor power and heterogeneity. *Business and Society, 42*(4), 398–429.

SAM. (2009). *Alpha from sustainability*. Report, Sustainable Asset Management, Zurich, Switzerland.

Samuelson, P. (1965). Proof that properly anticipated prices fluctuate randomly. *Industrial Management Review, 6*, 41–49.

Sandberg, J. (2010). *Socially responsible investment and fiduciary duty: Putting the freshfields report into perspective*. Sustainable Investment and Corporate Governance Working Papers, Foundation for Strategic Environmental Research, Umea, 2010/3.

Sandberg, J., & Juravle, C. (2009). The heterogeneity of socially responsible investment. *Journal of Business Ethics, 87*(4), 519–533.

Scholtens, B. (2010, April). Sovereign bonds and socially responsible investment. *Journal of Business Ethics, 92*(1), 117–130.

Schueth, S. (2003). Socially responsible investing in the United States. *Journal of Business Ethics, 43*(3), 189.

Scott, J. C. (1998). *Seeing like a state*. New Haven, CT: Yale University Press.

Scott, R. (2001). *Institutions and organizations* (2nd ed.). London: Sage Publishing.

Senior, C. (2009). Green is good. *Professional Pensions, 15*.

Serota, S., & Brodie, F. (1995). *ERISA fiduciary law*. Arlington: BNA Books.

Sethi, S. P. (2005). Investing in socially responsible companies is a must for public pension funds: Because there is no better alternative. *Journal of Business Ethics, 56*(2), 99–129.

Shaw, B., & Hagigi, M. (1988). Investment prudence and fiduciary responsibility in managing defined benefit pension funds under ERISA. *Suffolk University Law Review, 22*(1), 83–102.

Shiller, R. (2000). *Irrational exuberance*. Princeton, NJ: Princeton University Press.

Shiller, R. J. (2005). *The new financial order*. Princeton, NJ: Princeton University Press.

Shleifer, A. (2000). *Inefficient markets: An introduction to behavioral finance*. Oxford, UK: Oxford University Press.

Shleifer, A., & Vishny, R. W. (1996). A survey of corporate governance. *Journal of Finance*, *52*(2), 737–783.

Shleifer, A., & Vishny, R. (1997, June). A survey of corporate governance. *Journal of Finance, 52*(2), 737–783.

Singer, A. (2009, November/December). General electric strives for greater frankness in its citizenship reports. *Ethikos and Corporate Conduct Quarterly, 23*(3).

Skankman, N. A. (1999). Reframing the Debate between agency and stakeholder theories of the firm. *Journal of Business Ethics, 19*(4), 319–334.

Skidelsky, R. (2004). *Keynes: The economist as savior*. London: Allen Lane

Skypala, P. (2009). Clear investment beliefs are crucial. *Financial Times*, p. 6.

Smith, M. P. (1996). Shareholder activism by institutional investors: Evidence from CalPERS. *Journal of Finance, 51*(1), 227–252.

Social Investment Forum (SIF). (1995). *After South Africa: The state of socially responsible investing in the United States*. Report, Retrieved June 1, 2010, from http://www.socialinvest.org/pdf/research/Trends/1995%20Trends%20Report%20-%20After%20South%20Africa%20Report.pdf

Social Investment Organization (SIO). (2008). Social investment organization annual report 2008. Retrieved June 1, 2010, from http://www.socialinvestment.ca/documents/AnnualReport2008_finalpostedversion_English.pdf

Sparkes, R. (2002). *Socially responsible investment: A global revolution*. Chichester: Wiley.

Sparkes, R., & Cowton, C. J. (2004). The maturing of socially responsible investment: A review of the developing link with corporate social responsibility. *Journal of Business Ethics, 52*(1), 45–57.

Spyke, N. (1999). Public participation in environmental decision-making at the new millennium: Structuring new spheres of public influence. *Boston College Environmental Affairs Law Review, 26*, 263–313.

Stern, L. N. (2006). *Stern review on the economics of climate change*. Report, London.

Stewart, F., & Yermo, J. (2008). *Pension fund governance: Challenges and potential solutions*. Working Papers on Insurance and Private Pensions No. 18, OECD, Paris.

Stiglitz, J. E. (1976). Equilibrium in competitive insurance markets: An essay on the economics of imperfect information. *Quarterly Journal of Economics, 90*, 629–650.

Stiglitz, J. E. (2004). Capital-market liberalization, globalization, and the IMF. *Oxford Review of Economic Policy, 20*(1), 57.

Suchman, M. C. (1995). Managing legitimacy: Strategic and institutional approaches. *Academy of Management Review, 20*(3), 571–610.

Sustainable Asset Management (SAM). (2010). *The sustainability yearbook 2010*. Retrieved June 1, 2010, from http://www.sam-group.com/htmle/yearbook/downloads/The_Sustainability_Yearbook_2010_FINAL.pdf

Sunstein, C. R. (1990, Spring). Paradoxes of the regulatory state. *University of Chicago Law Review, 57*(2), 407–441.

Sunstein, C. R. (1995, May). Incompletely theorized agreements. *Harvard University Law Review, 108*(7), 1733–1772.

Taleb, N. (2009). *The black swan*. New York: Random House.

Taylor, S. (1986). *Public employee retirement systems: The structure and politics of teacher pensions*. Ithaca: Cornell University Press.

Tett, G. (2009a). *Fool's gold*. London: Little Brown.

Tett, G. (2009b). Credit crunch causes analysts to rethink rational market theory. *Financial Times*, June 16.

Teubner, G. (1997). Global Bukowina: Legal pluralism in the world society. In G. Teubner (Ed.), *Global law without a state* (pp. 3–28). Brookfield: Dartmouth Press.

Thaler, R. H. (2008). *Nudge: Improving decisions about health, wealth, and happiness*. New Haven, CT: London: Yale University Press.

Thaler, R. H. (2009). The price is not always right and markets can be wrong. *Financial Times*, August 5.

Thamotheram, R., & Wildsmith, H. (2007, May). Increasing long-term market returns: Realizing the power of collective pension fund action. *Corporate Governance: An International Review, 15*(3), 438–454.

The World Conservation Unit (IUCN). (2006). *The future of sustainability: Re-thinking environment and development in the twenty-first century*. Report of the IUCN Renowned Thinkers Meeting, January 29–31.

Thornton, R. (2008). Ethical investments: A case of disjointed thinking. *Cambridge Law Journal, 67*(2), 396–422.

Torrance, M. I. (2007). The power of governance in financial relationships: Governing tensions in exotic infrastructure territory. *Journal Growth & Change, 38*(4), 671–695. Kentucky: Gatton College of Business and Economics, University of Kentucky.

Tuckett, D. (2009). *Addressing the psychology of financial markets*. Report, IPPR, London.

Turner, A. (2009). *Failed markets, irrational markets and environmental policy*, UCL.

UNEP FI. (2005). *A legal framework for the integration of environmental, social and governance issues into institutional investment*. Report, United Nations Environment Program Finance Initiative, Geneva.

UNEP FI. (2007). *Responsible investment in focus: How leading public pension funds are meeting the challenge*. Report, United Nations Environment Program Finance Initiative (UNEP FI) Asset Management Working Group (AMWG) and the United Kingdom Social Investment Forum (UKSIF) Sustainable Pensions Project, London and Geneva.

UNEP FI. (2008). *Demystifying responsible investment performance*. Report, United Nations Environment Program Finance Initiative, Asset Management Working Group. Retrieved June 1, 2010, from http://www.unepfi.org/fileadmin/documents/Demystifying_Responsible_Investment_Performance_01.pdf

UNEP FI. (2009). *Fiduciary responsibility: Legal and practical aspects of integrating environmental, social and governance issues into institutional investment*. Report, United Nations Environment Program Finance Initiative, Geneva.

US Gov. Senate. (2010). *TARP-Restoring America financial stability act*. May 20.

Useem, M. (1996). *Investor capitalism, how money managers are changing the face of corporate America*. New York, NY: Basic Books.

Van Marrewijk, M. (2003). Concepts and definitions of CSR and corporate sustainability: Between agency and communion. *Journal of Business Ethics, 44*(2), 95–105.

Van Wyk, D. (2007). *The policy gap: A review of the corporate social responsibility programmes of the platinum mining industry in the North West province*. Report, Marshalltown, South Africa: Bench Marks Foundation.

Viederman, S. (2004). Addressing obstacles to social investing. *Journal of Practical Estates Planning, 6*(2), 48–49.

Viederman, S. (2008). Fiduciary duty. In C. Krosinsky & N. Robins (Eds.), *Sustainable investing: The art of long term performance* (pp. 189–200). London: Earthscan.

Vos, R. O. (2007). Defining sustainability: A conceptual orientation. *Journal of Chemical Technology & Biotechnology, 82*(4), 334–339.

Waddock, S. A., & Graves, S. B. (1997). The corporate social performance-financial performance link. *Strategic Management Journal, 18*, 303–320.

Waddock, S. A., & Smith, N. (2000). Corporate responsibility audits: Doing well by doing good. *Sloan Management Review, 41*, 75–83.

Waitzer, E. J. (2009). Defeating short-termism: Why pension funds must lead. *Rotman International Journal of Pension Management, 2*(2), 4–8.

Wall, E. (2010). Mining foundations, trusts and funds, a sourcebook. In W. B. Gampdcot (Ed.), *Oil*. Geneva: The World Bank.

Walsh, M. W. (2010). Public pension funds are adding risk to raise returns. *New York Times*, March 9.

Watt, G. (2006). *Trusts and equity* (2nd ed.). Oxford: Oxford University Press.

Waygood, S. (2006). *Capital market campaigning: The impact of NGOs on companies, shareholder value and reputational risk*. London: Risk Books.

Weinrib, E. J. (1975). The fiduciary obligation. *University of Toronto Law Journal, 25*(1), 1–22.

Weiss, E. B. (1984). *The planetary trust: Conservation and intergenerational equity, working paper*. Georgetown University Law Center. Retrieved August 19, 2011, from http://scholarship.law.georgetown.edu/cgi/viewcontent.cgi?article=1335&context=facpub

Weststar, J., & Verma, A. (2007). What makes for effective labor representation on pension boards? Labor Studies Journal, 32*(4)*, 382–410.

Wheelan, H. (2008). Integrating ESG into mainstream portfolios. *Responsible Investor, 1*(1).

Whitehouse, L. (2006). Corporate social responsibility: Views from the frontline. *Journal of Business Ethics, 63*, 279–296.

Williams, C. A., & Conley, J. (2005, Fall). Corporate social responsibility in the international context: Is there an emerging fiduciary duty to consider human rights? *University of Cincinnati Law Review, 74*, 75–104.

Williams, C. A., & Conley, J. (2007). Triumph or tragedy: The curious path of corporate disclosure reform in the UK. *William and Mary Environmental Law and Policy Review, 31*(2), 317–361.

Williams, G. (2007). Some determinants of the socially responsible investment decision: A cross-country study. *Journal of Behavioral Finance, 8*(1), 43–57.

Williams, L. S. (2008). The mission statement. *Journal of Business Communication, 45*(2), 94–119.

Wolf, M. (2001). Will the nation-state survive globalization? *Foreign Affairs, 80*, 178.

Wood, D. (2009a). *What do we do with the business case for responsible investment*? PRI Academic Network Conference Paper, Ottawa, Canada, October 1–3, 2009.

Wood, D., & Jones, R. (1995). Stakeholder mismatching: A theoretical problem in empirical research on corporate social performance. *International Journal of Organizational Analysis, 3*, 229–267.

Wood, D. J. (1991). Corporate social performance revisited. *Academy of Management Review, 16*(4), 691–718.

Woods, C. (2009b). *Funding climate change: How pension fund fiduciary duty masks a collective (in) action problem*. Working paper, School of Geography and the Environment, Oxford University, Oxford.

Woods, C. (forthcoming, 2011). Funding climate change: How pension fund fiduciary duty masks trustee inertia and short-termism. In J. Hawley, S. Kamath, & A. T. Williams (Eds.), *Institutional investors, risk/return tradeoffs, and corporate governance failures*. Philadelphia: University of Pennsylvania Press.

World Commission on Environment and Development. (1987). *Our common future*. Report. New York.

Wright, P., & Ferris, S. (1997). Agency conflict and corporate strategy: The effect of divestment on corporate value. *Strategic Management Journal, 18*, 77–83.

Yegnasubramanian, A. (2008). Environmental, social and governance: Moving to mainstream investing? *Business for Social Responsibility*, June 25.

Yin, R. K. (2009). *Case study research: Design and methods* (4th ed). Thousand Oaks, CA: Sage.

Zanglein, J. (2001). Overcoming institutional barriers on the economically-targeted investment highway. In A. Fung, T. Hebb, & J. Rogers (Eds.), *Working capital: The power of labor's pensions*. Ithaca, NY: Cornell University Press.

Zimmerman, M. (1994). *Contesting Earth's future: Radical ecology and postmodernity*. Berkeley, CA: University of California Press.

Index

CPSIA information can be obtained at www.ICGtesting.com
Printed in the USA
LVOW072240120613

338347LV00006B/77/P

9 789400 723474